Campus Confidential

Date: 11/28/11

Campus Confidential

THE COMPLETE GUIDE TO THE COLLEGE
EXPERIENCE BY STUDENTS FOR STUDENTS

Robert H. Miller

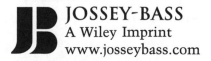
JOSSEY-BASS
A Wiley Imprint
www.josseybass.com

Published by Jossey-Bass
A Wiley Imprint
989 Market Street, San Francisco, CA 94103–1741   www.josseybass.com

Readers should be aware that Internet Web sites offered as citations and/or sources for further information may have changed or disappeared between the time this was written and when it is read.

Jossey-Bass books and products are available through most bookstores. To contact Jossey-Bass directly call our Customer Care Department within the U.S. at 800-956-7739, outside the U.S. at 317-572-3986, or fax 317-572-4002.

Jossey-Bass also publishes its books in a variety of electronic formats. Some content that appears in print may not be available in electronic books.

Library of Congress Cataloging-in-Publication Data
Miller, Robert H. (Robert Harrax)
  Campus confidential : the complete guide to the college experience by students for students / Robert H. Miller.
       p.   cm.
  "A Wiley Imprint."
  Includes bibliographical references and index.
  ISBN-13: 978-0-7879-7855-6 (pbk.)
  ISBN-10: 0-7879-7855-8 (pbk.)
  1. College student orientation—United States—Handbooks, manuals, etc. 2. College students—United States—Handbooks, manuals, etc. I. Title.
  LB2343.32.M55 2006
  378.1'98—dc22   2006012332

Printed in the United States of America
FIRST EDITION
PB Printing 10 9 8 7 6 5 4 3 2 1

CONTENTS

As always, and more than ever,
to my wife, Carolyn, whose love,
support, and understanding have
made all of this possible.

"Here comes the sun."

—GEORGE HARRISON

AUTHOR'S NOTE

This book is, in all likelihood, the last in the *Confidential* series. As you may or may not know, I have authored or coauthored the three other books in the series: *Law School Confidential, Business School Confidential,* and *Med School Confidential,* each of which features the same basic chronological format and honest, blow-by-blow treatment of the respective experience. Each of the books features an incredible team of mentors who add their thoughts and wisdom to its pages, and whose contributions make each book come alive, providing a breadth and scope that no single author could hope to offer.

The goal of the series has always been to provide the generations of students that come after us with a road map to the college and graduate school experience—to leave behind a trail of wisdom that says to those who come after us, "Here's what we did that worked and that you might want to emulate; here are the mistakes, missteps, and otherwise inane things we did that you should try to avoid if you can help it; and here's what we learned from it all that will help you enjoy the experience more and get even more from it than we did." That is the mission of the *Confidential* series in a nutshell, and it is my hope that the series as a whole, and this book in particular, will guide you well through this very important time in your life.

In some ways, the book you hold in your hand is the one I most wanted to write, because as the adage goes, to get the whole story, you have to start at the beginning—and on the critically important stretch of road that separates where you are from where I am now, this is the beginning.

For me, and for many of the mentors, college is where we built the foundations for our futures. Certainly there was drift and uncertainty and wholesale abandonment of majors, career paths, friends, hobbies, significant others, and long-held dreams and beliefs. There were a lot of mistakes and missteps, and Lord knows, if we had the chance to go back and do it all again, we would do a lot of things differently. But there are many *more* things we would do exactly the same way. And even though the college experience is different for nearly every student who sets foot on a college campus, there are a lot of common lessons to be learned, and there is a hell of a lot of really good, broadly applicable advice that will help you get more out of the college experience, enjoy it more, and help you keep your eye on the big picture.

And that's what this book aspires to be: a collection of that wisdom and advice to help you weather the little earthquakes and understand what really matters about the college experience.

Many claimed that approaching a project of this breadth and magnitude could not be done. Others insisted that college is a time of experimentation and that no one would want to read a book about how to "do" college. My own experience, conversations with the mentors, and subsequent reflection told me different, and I both hope and suspect that this book will reach those of you out there who, like us, would want to know how to milk every last drop out of the college experience—both the intellectual part and the social part—without having to waste several semesters figuring out how to do that on your own.

Time will tell whether we have been successful in our effort. But we truly hope that you will find this book useful, that you will find the parts of it that speak to your experience, and that it will help you focus on the things you want most out of college and help you get them.

If there are things you love or things you hate or things that you feel we have left out of the book that should absolutely be included, I hope you will e-mail me at rmiller@sheehan.com and share your thoughts so that we can make the next edition even better. Putting this book together was an enormous task, and there are undoubtedly things that we've given short shrift or left out that you think should be addressed. It is our goal to leave behind something of value that others can use for their benefit—and if you can contribute to that effort through your suggestions, I'd love to hear from you.

Most of all, though, I wish for you the kind of college experience that I had— one that is filled with adventure, discovery, personal growth, the development of real and enduring friendships, and one that is complete with a happy ending with great memories and few regrets.

ACKNOWLEDGMENTS

I would be remiss if I did not thank the many people who made this book possible. First and foremost, to my literary agent Jake Elwell, for never letting the naysayers get the best of me, for believing in the merits of this book, and for the many years of sound professional guidance. Although the trail from here is less certain, here's hoping that the boomalackas never end.

To my editors at Jossey-Bass, Alan Rinzler and Seth Schwartz, for believing in the project and for your patience and editorial guidance during a very difficult time in my life. To Michele Jones, my exceptional copyeditor at Jossey-Bass, for excellent editorial suggestions too numerous to recount that have made this a much stronger book. To Carol Hartland and Sophia Ho, production editors at Jossey-Bass, for their guidance and expertise. And to Anthony Robbins, whose *Personal Power* series and various other writings on the science of personal achievement have guided me for years and have, in part, inspired the freshman- , sophomore- , junior- , and senior-year goal-setting chapters in this book.

And finally, to the truly remarkable team of mentors who have joined me on this project: Dan, Jim, Tiffany, Tom, Amanda, Lyndsee, Kevin, Erica, Dave, Chase, Carolyn, Erik, Aaron, and Zoe for finding the time in your busy lives to look back over your college years with a critical eye to provide your advice and wisdom throughout the book. It is truly an honor to be joined together with all of you for posterity in the pages that follow.

July 2006

Robert H. Miller
Hopkinton, New Hampshire

PROLOGUE

If you have come to this book and are reading these opening words in the days or weeks before you head off to college for the first time, we have four well-worn words of advice to sum up what lies immediately ahead of you:

Fasten your seat belts.

The road through college is full of adventure—of new experiences, personal growth, and permanent expansion of your ideas, your views, and your perspective. It is also fraught with challenges—to your intellect, to your beliefs, and to your character. What becomes of you during the next four years will be influenced by a multitude of factors—including your roommates, your friends, the classes you take, the major you choose, the professors who move you, the people who pass through your bed, your decisions about boundaries with drugs and alcohol, and many, many other things. Ultimately, though, what becomes of you during the next four years—whether your trip on the wild and crazy road through college is an unforgettable success, a dismal failure, a wasted opportunity, or a mixed bag—depends on one person.

You.

Until now, what ultimately happened to people on the road through college was largely determined by the quality of the scattered bits of advice they managed to cobble together from older siblings and friends, freshman advisers, roommates, and classmates, and by how quickly they managed to "get it" and stitch together this advice and their own experiences into some sort of "big picture" approach to the whole thing. For many of us, the light didn't come on until very late in the game, after a large part of our college years had already been spent without the benefit of a game plan.

For you, reading these words with this book in hand, the waste of that precious, irreplaceable time need not happen.

For the first time ever, you have assembled before you the collective advice of a blue-ribbon panel of fourteen students who have recently traveled the road you are about to set out on and who have lived through the experiences you are about to encounter. Seven of us have just graduated from different colleges and universities across the country and, having done so, will counsel you on anything and everything you need to know about the college experience as it is today. There is very little, if anything, that you will encounter during college that one or more of us hasn't seen or dealt with before—and in the pages that follow, we will endeavor to share as much of that advice as we can with you. The other eight of us (myself included) are now a few years removed from our college experiences and in some cases, graduate programs, and are now out trying to make our way in the world. The eight of us have the unique advantage of being able to offer a longer view of the college experience and to lend our advice from that perspective—about the lasting effects that some of the day-to-day decisions you'll make during college will have on the life you'll lead after college. Our job is to help you put everything in perspective and to help you separate the things that *really* matter from the things that only *seem* to matter when you're in the moment.

It is our hope that armed with this collective knowledge and experience, you will be able to make better-informed decisions in your college life and to travel the road with greater confidence and with even greater success than we did.

As you browse the Contents pages of the book or start to make your way through the early chapters, it might seem that the approach we advocate in *Campus Confidential* is a little "intense."

Fear not.

In some places, when we're walking you through goal-setting activities at the beginning of an academic year, working through designing a major, or talking about how to set up your senior thesis, we *do* dial up the intensity a bit—because those are critical, foundational moments that require your stepped-up attention, focus, and clarity. In other areas, though, when we counsel you on choosing classes and extracurricular activities, planning out your semesters, and preparing for finals—we advocate a more mellow, drawn-out approach that allows you to relax, enjoy the experience, and have *plenty* of time to hang out with your friends and enjoy the social aspects of college that are so very important to the overall experience.

There is certainly an innate attractiveness in going into college with a blank slate and no defined direction and letting the tide carry you on an exploratory journey for a while. At the same time, though, there is value in taking stock of where you are at certain places along the journey through college, checking your location and direction against your values and dreams, and adjusting your path accordingly. Those two approaches are not contradictory, and in fact, the approach to college that we advocate in *Campus Confidential* harmonizes those two approaches in a way that will maximize the value of your college experience.

Most people enter college either with no plan at all about how to approach the experience or with only a hazy idea of what they hope to get out of the four years. Trust us when we tell you that your four years of college *will* be among the most memorable experiences you'll have in your lifetime and that the years will fly by faster than you can possibly imagine. Allowing us to be your guides on your road through college will require you to have enough faith in the value of our advice and experience to apply the approaches we advocate in the pages that follow and to trust that we won't steer you wrong. If you agree to do so, we can promise you that you'll work hard (but smart), that you'll experience life as you've never experienced it before, that you'll successfully keep work and play sorted out and in proper balance, and, accordingly, that you'll come out the other end of your college experience four years from now happy, well positioned to do what you want to do with the rest of your life, and armed with great memories and few regrets.

We hope you'll join us.

INTRODUCTION: HOW TO USE THIS BOOK

Is there anyone so wise as to learn by the experience of others?

Voltaire

By picking up and opening this book, you have just taken the first significant step toward building a productive, successful, and pleasurable college experience.

Though you may not fully grasp this truth yet, college can be an intimidating, foreign, and isolating place. Sure—at many colleges and universities, you may be assigned a freshman counselor or "RA" (resident adviser), and if he or she isn't too busy, you might glean a few nuggets of wisdom from that relationship. Your school may also offer a dean of student affairs, a dean of residential life, a team of orientation counselors, and a lecture to help you transition from your life in high school or boarding school, and essentially your childhood, into the wholly new experience that will be your life in college.

At the end of the day, though, whether you succeed or fail in that transition, whether you find your way in college, and whether you have a memorable, successful, and enjoyable experience is really going to be up to you.

And that's where this book comes in.

We can help, because we've all just been there. We've felt that anxiety about going to a new place, making new friends, carving out a new identity, and making a place for ourselves in the world. Collectively, we've made all the mistakes there are to make in college. We've taken too many classes, fallen way behind in our reading loads, pulled all-nighters, botched exams, and received a terrible grade or two. We've chosen the wrong schools, the wrong majors, the wrong friends, and the wrong career paths. We've thought about dropping out; thought about transferring; papered our walls with rejection letters from employers; fought with our parents, our siblings, and our boyfriends and girlfriends; and anguished over just about everything you can possibly imagine.

Yet somehow, despite all of that, we also all graduated, got the jobs we wanted (or at least *thought* we wanted), and have in fact begun to make a place for ourselves in the world.

We're not professors or people decades removed from the college experience, clueless about the realities and demands of college life today and waxing nostalgic about how wonderful the experience was when we were there. We were students, just like you; and just a few years ago (for most of us), we were right where you are now.

We're here to give you the inside scoop about the college experience and how to make the most of it—all the stuff that the books and tapes by professors will never tell you about. If you want the truth about college—what it's going to take to get in, get what you want out of it both academically and socially, and position yourself for the future—while at the same time leaving room for all of the fun and debauchery that makes college what it is, this is the book you want. We'll tell you what's important and what isn't, dispel the myths, cut through the bull, and help you find the right balance to ensure that you will look back on your college years as we do—with fond memories.

Possessing this book and applying its teachings will make you more comfortable about nearly every aspect of the college experience and give you the peace of mind to know that you won't be making the same mistakes we made during the many months of fun, hard work, and personal growth that lie ahead.

In a moment, I'll be introducing you to your mentoring team—the group of former students recently graduated from colleges around the country who will guide you through the next four years with their collective wisdom, advice, anecdotes, and personal experiences. You'll also meet a second team of "über-mentors"—a group of young people about ten years removed from the college experience, who, with the additional wisdom gained by the passage of time, will add their thoughts about the college experience and what *did* and did *not* end up being truly important in their lives after all.

GETTING THE MOST OUT OF THIS BOOK

First, though, a bit advice about how to get the most out of this book. Whether you are an underclassman in high school or boarding school just starting to think about college; a junior beginning the process of preparing for the SAT and about to embark on the application process; a high school or boarding school student already admitted to college reading this during the summer before college because you are nervous or anxious about the road that lies ahead; a student already in college; or the parent, relative, sibling, friend, or significant other of a college student or college student to be, this book has something to offer you.

Just determine which of the following sections is most applicable to you and read accordingly.

I Am a Student Just Starting to Think About College

If you are a high school underclassman picking up this book to help you understand the many choices you'll face, first in selecting, and later in attending college, you have in your hands a wealth of information and resources that will make the next six years of your life easier, less stressful and, we hope, more successful. We suggest that you read this book cover to cover before you begin the application process to get a better understanding and overview of the college experience, which should help inform your choice of schools. Once you've read the material and familiarized yourself with the process, and have a basic understanding of how the college experience will proceed, you should then go back and read each of the individual chapters, consult the recommended reading sources, and do the exercises and worksheets as they become applicable to your personal experience.

I Am a Student About to Begin the Application Process

You've come upon this book at the perfect time.

Take some time to read this book cover to cover before you commence the application process. The overview of college that this reading will give you should help you determine what factors are important to you in choosing a school and thus help you decide where to apply. The details about the experiences that await you in college may also help trigger ideas for the essays or short-answer questions that you'll find on your college applications. Additionally, the Relevance Calculus exercise and wisdom contributed by the mentors should help you determine how ultimately to choose a school from the ones that accept you.

Obviously, Part One of the book will be most salient to you now, so take the time to study it carefully. You can then go back and read each of the individual chapters, consult the recommended reading sources, and do the exercises and worksheets as they become applicable to your personal experience.

I Am a Student Who Has Already Been Admitted to College, and I'm Nervous About It

Join the crowd!

Almost everyone entering college is at least a little bit nervous about it. The transition from high school to college is, for most people, also the transition from childhood to adulthood and from dependence to independence. These are important times in your life! It is completely normal to experience some anxiety about going to a new place, making new friends, carving out a new identity, and beginning to think about what you are going to do with your life.

It is also one of the most exhilarating, liberating, and exciting times of your life—so it is important not to let the anxiety detract from your experience. Again, that's where we come in.

Unlike many of your classmates, who will stumble nervously through at least the first semester of college not knowing exactly how to proceed, you will be escorted around the traps and pitfalls of freshman year (and the college experience in general) with a step-by-step, proven plan drawn from the experiences of the mentors you are about to meet.

Take the time between now and the beginning of orientation to read this book cover to cover. Don't worry about completing the exercises or worksheets now. Just take a voyage of discovery and read for a basic understanding. Then, when college begins, keep *Campus Confidential* within arm's reach and let it be your guide through each semester, taking you safely and successfully through the experience. Use it to measure your progress and to keep track of where you are and where you are going.

This is a book of collected wisdom. Be sure to put it to work for you.

I'm Already in College—I Wish I Had Found This Sooner!

Yeah, we feel the same way! That's why we decided to write it!

The difference between you and us, though, is that at least you can still benefit from the book, whereas we had to learn all this stuff the hard way—through trial and error!

If you're already in college, take a look through the Contents and figure out where you are in the experience. We still recommend skimming the earlier chapters, as there may be some strategies, suggestions, activities, or exercises in those earlier chapters that you can apply to your experience. Take special note of the goal-setting workshops and be sure to complete the one for the year you are currently in. Once you do that, open the book to where you are in your experience, and begin in earnest. Read forward to the end of the book to get a feel for what's to come, then concentrate on specific chapters as they become applicable to your experience.

I'm the Parent, Relative, Sibling, or Friend of Someone Going to College

Want to give your friend or loved one a road map to ensure that he or she gets off to the right start in life away from home?

You're holding it in your hands.

Before you wrap it up, though, you may want to skim it yourself. If you went to college some time ago, you may want to take the trip for nostalgia's sake. Take special note of how the experience has changed and how much more directed the experience has become!

Remember too that for every college student, these four years are a time of intense personal growth and discovery—and that your job is to be as understanding as possible, to make room for that growth and discovery, and to tolerate reasonable experimentation in physical appearance, dress, music, career, choice of boyfriends and girlfriends, and many other things. The more you embrace your college student as she spreads her wings, the more likely it is that your input and advice will still be sought when she is making some of the many important decisions that arise during college.

The college years necessarily change the dynamics of family relationships. If you are the parent of a soon-to-be college student, a spin through the pages of this book might be helpful to you—especially for the thoughts of the mentors about how their parents helped or hindered their college experiences.

A WORD ABOUT THE EXERCISES AND WORKSHEETS

In different places throughout the book, you will encounter exercises that ask you to brainstorm ideas or answer certain questions.

Don't just skip over these exercises. Do them!

We suggest that you dedicate a ring binder, spiral notebook, a journal, or some other system to collect your responses to these exercises. As you'll see, you will be asked to refer back to your goals or other responses to activity questions from year to year, and as such, you'll want to make sure you can actually *find* them when you need them.

At other places in the book, you will find worksheets printed right into the book. Write all over these or photocopy them to make them bigger and three-hole punch them right into your notebook for easy access.

Remember that the more you actively engage the content of this book, the more you'll get out of it.

Okay! Enough with the preliminaries.

LET'S GET STARTED!

It is now time to meet the mentors who will guide you through the next four years of your life in college. Each mentor has a bio page to introduce them to you and to help you understand where they came from, what their interests were, and what their interests are now. Try to find one or two mentors with whom you identify. As you progress through the book, you'll be able to follow their experiences, recognize and learn from their mistakes, and replay their college experiences before your eyes. You can, and should, model some of their actions, choices, strategies, and experiences.

The one thing that all of us—the mentors, the über-mentors, and I have in common is that all of us believe that if we could go back to college right now and start over, knowing what we know now, we'd *all* do things differently. For some of us, the changes would be minor. For others of us, the changes would be as significant as choosing a different school, a different major, and a different career path.

Naturally, those discoveries are part of the experience of college, part of the learning process, and part of growing up—and we encourage you to embrace those uncertainties and the discoveries that come from working through them. But there is no reason why you can't think about the issues you'll face in college ahead of time and try to be proactive, rather than reactive, in your choices.

THE *CAMPUS CONFIDENTIAL* MENTORS

Your *Campus Confidential* mentors break out into two groups. The first group of mentors, whom we will call "über-mentors," is a diverse and exciting group of people approximately ten years removed from college. As you will see, this is an amazing group of achievers from all walks of life, who have gone on to do some really interesting things with their lives. These people are here to offer you *perspective* about what continues to be important about the college experience ten years after, helping you focus on the *major* things about your college experience that remain important many years after the books are put away. These are the people to count on for the "big picture" stuff.

The second group is composed of recent graduates of colleges and universities around the country, who will comment directly, throughout the pages of this book, on their just-concluded experiences. Fresh out of college, they will offer you wisdom, advice, and suggestions on specific subjects throughout the chapters that follow about what college was like, what they did right, what they wish they had done—and what you can do to avoid making the same mistakes they made. These are the people to count on for the nuts and bolts stuff.

Together, these two groups of people form an in-depth team that is unique in all of the literature on college success and survival.

You can count on them to steer you right.

So let's get to know the mentors!

THE *CAMPUS CONFIDENTIAL* ÜBER-MENTORS

DAN BISSELL
Portland, Oregon

B.A. Middlebury College, *cum laude,* 1993
   Major: geology

Middlebury Volunteer Ambulance Association—EMT, first
responder
Middlebury Used Bookstore—partner

M.D. University of Colorado School of Medicine, *Adler Scholar,* 2002

Emergency Medicine Student Interest Group
Volunteer in various medical clinics for the homeless
Research in medical informatics

Interests: sailing, flying, fishing, climbing, travel, reading
What I'm doing now: doctor

College offers you the promise of freedom—freedom from home and parents, yes, but more important, freedom from the curricular constraints of high school—the promise of self-directed learning, and limitless horizons to pursue. Don't be intimidated by the experience. Wade in, ask questions, and find ways to get involved outside of class. Unless you're invested enough in the experience to seek unique opportunities and ask questions, the most erudite education money can buy will be a wasted experience.

Balance is the key to success. With your first taste of true independence comes the temptation of extremes—work, parties, relationships, you name it. Finding a balance that is effective, fun, and wholesome becomes a major milestone that will set the tone for much of your life to come. These are some of the fundamental lessons that may not be in the course catalogue, but will do more to shape your life than any class in Elizabethan literature.

Knowing what I know now, I would work less and play and explore more. I was a bit too focused and directed during my time as an undergrad. Looking back, I should have sweated some of the details less and had a bit freer sense of boundaries and goals. I got a lot accomplished and had some extraordinary experiences, but I probably should have had more fun along the way.

The hardest thing in life is figuring out what you want to do—not actually doing it. College is the ideal crucible in which to test your interests and abilities and to try new things that you never imagined. Yes, you need to be pragmatic enough to make it all fit into some sort of degree and course of study, but within those broad confines lies a wide world to explore. Don't waste the opportunity of a true education on the pursuit of "career training." Train for your career in graduate school. College is for getting an education.

JIM BRIGHT
Winston-Salem, North Carolina

B.A. Duke University, *magna cum laude, Phi Beta Kappa,* 1997
    Major: history

Trip leader, Project W.I.L.D. ("Wilderness Initiatives for Learning at Duke")
Through-hiked Appalachian Trail (3/27/99–9/15/99)

Interests: hiking, mountain biking, skiing
What I'm doing now: teaching in the Winston-Salem public school system

I was excited to live in a new part of the country and to enjoy the freedom that came from making my own choices. I hoped to be challenged academically while having a lot of fun at a place where people were interested in doing both. I worried that the academics would be a letdown after the small classes I had experienced at Phillips Exeter, where there was a lot more individual attention and a seminar structure.

I learned that you can take on a huge variety of challenges simultaneously if you are doing things you love and managing your time effectively. I also learned that you need to listen to your inner voice when something does not feel right. There are many opportunities socially and academically at most colleges and universities, and if you remain open-minded throughout your four years, you'll probably end up developing interests and moving in directions you never would have expected. Finally, I learned that by working to develop personal relationships with faculty members, I became much more engaged by their teaching and subject matter in general.

TOM TEH CHIU
Brooklyn, New York

B.A. Yale University, 1993
 Major: double major in chemistry and music

M.M. Juilliard School, 1995
D.M.A. Juilliard School, 2001

Interests: fishing, baseball, cooking, billiards
What I'm doing now: professional concert violinist and leader of the internationally acclaimed new-music ensemble the FLUX Quartet

The time you spend with people in college will be far more important to you than the time you spend with books. College is a time when lifelong friendships are made. Many years down the line, that's what will enhance your life.

As someone who currently has a very rewarding career in experimental music, who fifteen years ago, started college as a chemistry major, it might be easy for me to wonder, "Were the four years I spent at Yale a total waste?" That thought, however, could not be further from the truth—because college is not just about the courses you take, the major you choose, and the grades you get. Yes, those things are important, but there is so much more! In terms of education, what Yale gave me was the ability to think critically—a far more important skill than the ability to think correctly. My college experience contributed most to my growth as a person, not just to my intellectual growth—and that provided me with a good foundation to address, confront, and resolve the different complexities of life, both professionally and personally.

One very nice thing about getting a degree from Yale is the security that there is always something to fall back on if your alternative career doesn't work out. My other possible career routes would have been graduate school in chemistry, or medical school. But I realized that I had to pursue my love of music before falling back on a more "traditional" career path. I always thought that someday I might have to go and have a "real life," but now, more than a dozen years after graduating from college, my alternative life *is* my real life!

AMANDA CRAMER
Paso Robles, California

B.A. Cornell University, *Phi Beta Kappa,* 1993
Major: mathematics

Resident adviser, 1993

Graduate study in food science–enology, University of California at Davis, 1997–2000.

DEVO ("Davis Enology and Viticulture Organization"), president, 1998–99

Interests: reading, watching movies, walking, hiking, wine tasting, travel
What I'm doing now: Winemaker at Niner Wine Estates

I was excited to meet new people and to go to a bigger school farther away from home than my high school. I am not the type of person to worry too much in advance, but once I got there, all the same things I was excited about were also the things that scared me.

In college, I learned to think for myself, to do my homework, to be prepared, and then to dare. You get a lot more out of college if you have a sense of what you want to get out of it before you go, and reassess as you go along. I also learned to show tolerance toward people who I considered to be intolerant themselves. I am pretty liberal, and I once had the head of one of the most conservative newspapers on campus tell me that I was intolerant when we were both participating in an open forum and I was scoffing at what he had to say. That really made me think.

CAROLYN KOEGLER
Hopkinton, New Hampshire

B.A. Tufts University, *cum laude,* 1993
Double major: History and Spanish

Varsity Swimming (1989–91)
Junior Varsity Field Hockey (1989–91)
Member: EPIIC (Education for Public Inquiry and International Citizenship) International Symposium: Confronting Political and Social Evil: Complicity, Resistance, Human Rights and U.S. Foreign Policy (1990–91)
Year Abroad: Madrid, Spain (1991–92)
Designed and cotaught class: "From Franco's Spain to Democracy" to first-year students
Teach for America (Bronx, NY, 1993–95)

Interests: hiking, skiing, swimming, reading, ballroom dance
What I'm doing now: on sabbatical from my position as law clerk at the New Hampshire Supreme Court to be a full-time mom to our two children

I came from a family of high achievers, and I was concerned that I would not measure up by getting into a "top" school as my parents and siblings did. Fortunately, I was accepted to Tufts, which turned out to be a *great* fit for me. I learned a great deal and had a terrific time.

During my years at Tufts, I learned to take charge of my nonacademic life and future. Before college, I had lived a very sheltered life, growing up in a small village outside of New York City and then attending a small boarding school in Connecticut. I was shepherded along and didn't have to make too many decisions about what to study—I just worked hard and earned decent grades because that's what was expected of me. In college I got to make my own choices about what to study and how hard to work.

If I had it to do all over again, I would be sure that I took advantage of every minute. I used my first year at Tufts as an opportunity to relax and celebrate, and found myself drifting. I had a great time, but at the end of the first year, felt that I had not accomplished much. I would get involved in more extracurricular activities right away and push harder to try new things. One of the great things about college is that while the academics can be challenging, there is a *ton* of free time to get involved in sports, volunteer activities, and anything else that might interest you. The key is to use that time wisely.

ERIK NORTON
Boston, Massachusetts

B.A. Massachusetts Institute of Technology, 1993
    Major: mathematics

Member of infamous M.I.T. "Blackjack Team," 1992–96
M.I.T. men's golf team, 1989–93 (captain, 1993)
M.I.T. men's hockey team, 1989–93

Interests: family time, card games, sports handicapping
What I'm doing now: hedge fund trader

Going into college, I had no idea what to expect. I hoped that I would continue to excel in the classroom as I had done all through middle school and high school in Maine, but feared that I might not, given the pending stiff competition I would encounter at M.I.T.

I learned several important things at M.I.T. First, given all of my extracurricular activities, finding the appropriate amount and quality of time to devote to everything that I was trying to accomplish was paramount. Choosing a completely filled schedule forces you to prioritize effectively. Second, I learned that you need to decide what drives you, and recognize what works for you, and live your life accordingly. Trying to emulate someone else's work schedule, work ethic, or study habits because it seems logical to you will not help you unlock your full potential, nor will it make you happy.

ZOE ROBBINS
Gouldsboro, Maine

B.A.(1) Wellesley College, *magna cum laude, Phi Beta Kappa,* 1997
Major: economics

Shakespeare Society, president
Manager, Café Hoop (student-owned cooperative)
Wellesley Women for Choice, treasurer
Child Study Center, classroom assistant

B.A.(2) University of Pennsylvania, 2000
Major: nursing

Cherry Hill Women's Center
Free Community Clinic
Research assistant at the Center for Clinical Epidemiology and Biostatistics
Registered nurse, Hospital of the University of Pennsylvania

M.S.N. University of Pennsylvania, 2001

Interests: being a mom, sailing, snowshoeing, knitting, reading, organic flower and vegetable gardening on our small Maine farm, where we also raise chickens and turkeys and make maple syrup
What I'm doing now: working as a registered nurse and being a mom

Going into college, like most people, I was worried about being as successful and happy as I felt I had been in high school.

In college, I learned the importance of doing things that really challenge or even intimidate you. Don't be afraid to change and discover yourself. Take advantage of the diversity within the college community to broaden your perspectives and your realm of experiences.

THE *CAMPUS CONFIDENTIAL* MENTORS

TIFFANY CHAN
Morris Plains, New Jersey

B.S. New York University, 2005
     Major: Communication Science

Alpha Phi Zeta Sorority—president and social chair
Judicial Board Representative
Secretary, Music Undergraduate Student Government

Interests: music, hiking, running, tennis
What I'm doing now: Working as a research assistant for the National Committee on American Foreign Policy

I was excited and ready for the challenge of college. New York City seemed like the perfect place to discover more about myself, meet new people, and to be exposed to different ideas and intellectual theories.

The most important thing I learned in college is to allow yourself the time and freedom to pursue a variety of interests. This requires diligence though. If I could go back and do it all over again, I would have pursued my studies during my freshman year with greater diligence. With New York City's vibrant atmosphere and with the relative freedom from my strict parents, I was easily distracted from my studies!

LYNDSEE DICKISON
Concord, New Hampshire

B.A. New York University, *cum laude*, 2004
     Major: East Asian studies (concentration in Japanese)
     Minor: French

Alpha Phi Zeta Sorority—secretary and philanthropy chair

Interests: writing, traveling, skiing, going to the beach
What I'm doing now: attending law school at Franklin Pierce Law Center

Like most people, I was very nervous about leaving my friends and family when it came time to head off to college. I knew I would have to grow up a lot when I moved to New York City, and I would have to start taking care of things myself. I was nervous about being in New York City, having to find my way around, and trying to stay safe. I was afraid that college-level academics would be really hard, and I wouldn't be able to keep up with everyone. I was afraid of deciding on a major and feeling like I had to decide right then what I wanted to do with the rest of my life.

I hoped to make some really close friends that I would keep in touch with forever. I was really open to establishing new relationships when I went off to college. I hoped that I would love New York City and take advantage of the many exciting activities and opportunities that it would present.

The most important thing I learned in college was to make decisions based on what was good for *me.* I figured out that in college, the only person taking care of me was *me.* It was up to *me* to balance studying, sleeping, eating, exercising, and having fun—because there was no one else there to make me study, get enough sleep, eat breakfast, or take care of my health. I had to learn how to make decisions, live with them, and find my own happiness. I also had to learn how to make financial decisions for myself, based on what was realistic for me, rather than based on what my friends were doing. A lot of my friends at NYU came from families with a lot of money, and their spending habits were much different than what I could manage. So it was important for me to learn how to spend wisely, to live within my means, and to make financial decisions based on my own personal situation.

KEVIN DONOVAN

Somerville, Massachusetts

B.A. Boston College, *honors in the major,* 2004
    Major: English
    Minor: creative writing

Interests: running marathons, writing, reading, biking, skiing, and eating at every Indian buffet I can find

What I'm doing now. journalism

Entering college, I was afraid that I would be at the bottom of the social barrel all over again, that I'd be living in close quarters with a bunch of guys and would have to be constantly proving my machismo or how fun I could be. I was a camp counselor the summer going into college, and I knew how young guys acted when they were strangers trying to show off or establish themselves in a social order. Of course, there, I was in charge. In college, I would simply be in the mix, and I was worried that I might not find the right group of friends.

I was also concerned about classes. By the end of my senior year in high school, I knew exactly what I wanted to study and exactly what I didn't care for. I liked economics, history, literature, journalism, and politics. There were plenty of other subjects I liked well enough, but dreaded having to take a class on them. The thought of having to write philosophy papers or take language or math classes again made me anxious. I knew it would be at least two years before I worked through the core curriculum and got to taking the classes I really wanted to take. That bugged me. My hopes were to really dive into a great intellectual experience. I really liked the idea of learning for the sake of learning. But, to be fair, going to college was really just "the next thing." I was one of the kids who went and didn't give it much thought except that it was something new and different.

Know that college will either give you connections for a job or an opportunity for a second degree. Realize as soon as you can which one you want: dental school or a Capitol Hill internship. I know plenty of people who were getting good grades when they should have been making contacts, and people who have all the friends in the world but can't get into law school.

I wish I had gone into school knowing that I wanted to be a journalist. All I knew was that I liked books and to write, but I didn't have an idea of what I wanted to do as a career. I wish I had had a sit-down with a mentor to discuss what I *really* wanted to get out of this experience. It may sound cheesy, but I feel like it would have been very helpful. If someone were there, checking in with me that my goals were on target, I might have thought of college more as preparation for the future rather than just a four-year holding pattern.

ERICA EUBANKS
Memphis, Tennessee

B.A. Tennessee State University, *National Dean's List,* 2003
        Major: criminal justice

Phi Alpha Delta prelaw fraternity—founding member (TSU chapter)
Alpha Kappa Alpha sorority
Tennessee State University Show Stoppers (show choir)
Step team captain

Interests: reading mystery novels, knitting, watching *Law and Order* reruns
What I'm doing now: law school

I just couldn't wait to get away from home. I have always been the kind of person to make a decision to do something and then do it. I rarely consider how or when until the time comes. Sometimes that works out well for me, and sometimes it doesn't. I applied to all the Tennessee state schools and some private ones and got in to all of them. I also applied to a few in D.C. and got in to those also. Then I did an eenie, meenie, miney, moe and ended up at TSU. In retrospect, I wish I would have had more anxieties, fears, and hopes for my future, because I definitely would have chosen Vanderbilt or American University, but TSU offered me a full scholarship. The others only offered a partial, so that also had a lot to do with it.

The most important thing I learned in college is to try to know what you want to do when you graduate from undergrad by the end of your freshmen year in college so that you can work toward that dream for the remainder of your college experience. Don't wait until you graduate to consider what the necessary requirements for your future job or postgraduate schooling are. By then it is usually too late to do anything about it. If you want to apply to a certain school, you definitely need to know their requirements. Some schools won't even permit you to apply to their postgraduate program without a certain GPA or unless you have taken certain classes. If you don't know that until your last year in undergrad or until after you graduate, you're making life a lot harder for yourself.

I always knew I wanted to go to law school, but I did not attempt to prepare for law school until my final year in undergrad. That was a big mistake. I was rushed to complete applications and study for the LSAT, and I did not have the time to fully research the schools I was applying to.

The last year of college is very hectic, and the last thing a student needs to be bothered with is researching law schools at the last minute while trying to study for tests and finals. Similarly, if you want to work at a certain place following graduation, you need to determine what their grade requirements are and whether they require you to participate in certain types of internships before they'll hire you.

DAVE IRWIN

Carlisle, Massachusetts

B.A. Middlebury College, *departmental honors,* 2004
     Major: American civilization
     Minor: education

Varsity baseball
Rugby club
Men's basketball announcer

Interests: playing drums in my band
What I'm doing now: teaching

For most of my senior year in high school, I had one foot out the door, and was only thinking about what was coming next instead of taking the time to enjoy the present. It was my hope that college would bring a much needed change of pace and more autonomy in my life. I was eager for independence.

College taught me how to budget my time. I have always had the tendency to try to fit too much on my plate, and in order to balance my academic and extracurricular activities, I quickly learned that I would need to be more diligent in my planning and scheduling.

I wish I had taken more time to think about my academic interests before I got to college. I assumed that I would figure it out as I went along, which I did end up doing. But my grades suffered a bit because I ended up taking classes that I was simply not interested in during my freshman year. Looking back on it, this stage of trial and error would have been avoidable if I had taken the time to sit down and sketch out some possible academic paths prior to registration.

Take advantage of everything that your school has to offer. My friends and I would always talk about how cool it would be to do certain things that we never got around to doing, and in that regard, I have some regrets. Being proactive can easily get impeded by laziness and a certain comfort with your own routine. The four years go by fast. Make the most of every opportunity you have.

CHASE JOHNSON
London, England

B.A. Duke University, *with Pi Alpha Theta distinction in history,* 2005
    Major: history

Speak of the Devil (male a cappella singing group), president, 2003–05
Duke student government, vice president for academic affairs, 2004–04
Duke University board of trustees, undergraduate representative, 2004–05
Academic Integrity Council, 2003–05

Interests: running, singing, playing guitar, traveling, English pubs
What I'm doing now: Colet Fellowship in London (teaching history)

I took a "gap year" between high school and college, which significantly reduced my social fears about starting at Duke, but may have increased my anxiety about finding the right activities and subjects of study. Many of the interactions I had with friends who were attending college revolved around the daunting amount of opportunity that college offered, while a significant number of conversations I had with college graduates dealt with their regrets about things they *didn't* do while in school. The combination of the two left me extremely apprehensive about what I was going to do at Duke, and whether I would make the right choices.

I learned a couple of important lessons at Duke. First, the way you work is more important than intelligence. Duke was full of overachievers and underachievers, and their accomplishments happened almost irrespective of any natural ability they seemed to possess. My freshman roommate was a math genius who struggled to graduate, while some of the most revered academics in my graduating class readily admitted that their successes were directly related to the amount they read, studied, or conversed about their subjects. It wasn't intelligence that improved my grades over the years, but the fact that I learned to work harder (and smarter).

Second, the people around you during college are *vital*—they define you during your four years as a student and have a significant impact on the nature of your postcollege plans. The single factor that most encouraged me to study more and try certain extracurricular activities, that prompted me to apply for the fellowship I now have or the law school I will be going to, was my group of friends. My friends encouraged me because they were people who expected lofty results from themselves, and their example was a driving force encouraging me to do the same. I can also vividly recall other groups of friends who were mutually destructive, encouraging each other to devalue their academic and extracurricular experiences.

AARON PASKALIS

Magnolia, Massachusetts

West Point Military Academy, then transferred to UMass Amherst

B.A. University of Massachusetts at Amherst, 2005
  Major: legal studies

Division I varsity lacrosse

Interests: lacrosse, weightlifting, woodworking, vehicle restoration, anything active and outdoors
What I'm doing now: training to be a firefighter

When I went to West Point, I was most worried about leaving my family, meeting all new people, and finding my place in a well-established lacrosse program. I was really unsure about what I was in for once I got there, but I knew that I would have no free time, and that worried me as well. When I transferred to UMass Amherst, I had a lot of the same fears about being accepted into a team that was already formed and had already been playing together for several years. It was extremely hard to leave my team at West Point, and I was worried that I would not be as close to my UMass team because I was a transfer student.

The most important thing I learned in college is that if you are unhappy where you are and with what you're doing, you should give it some time and a fair chance to work out, but after that, if you know you have to make a change, you shouldn't prolong your misery. You need to do what's right for you, even when people try to convince you otherwise.

Campus Confidential

PART ONE

Getting In

Approaching the College Search

Know thyself.

Socrates

Chances are, you've been thinking about it, at least in the abstract, for years.

Initially it might have started as a fascination with a particular college or university, based on the success of one of its sports teams or stimulated because a parent, older sibling, or other relative went there, or because the coolest teacher, youth group leader, or camp counselor you ever had was going there.

So maybe you ordered a sweatshirt or car window decal online, checked out the school's Web site, or maybe even visited the campus.

From there, as the PSATs rolled around (if not sooner), you might have started to think more seriously about the subject—about where you might want to go and, more important, where you might actually be able to *get in.*

And that's where we're going to pick up the story: sometime in the beginning or middle of your junior year of high school (or sixth form, if you're in prep school)—the time when, to maximize your chances of success in the upcoming admissions process, you should really start thinking seriously about college.

But where in the world do you start?

The world of college admissions seems so large, and the task so enormous, that it often feels easier to procrastinate and push things off for another day.

Don't.

Start now.

DEVISING A STRATEGY

The first thing you're going to need is a strategy—a way to approach the admissions process and to narrow down, based on certain characteristics that you determine are important to you, the field of hundreds upon hundreds of possible choices. Perhaps you already have a school or two that sticks out in your mind as a favorite, but even if you do, engage in the following exercise to test *why* that school is a favorite and whether or not the things that make it a favorite are more broadly applicable. If you are starting from a blank slate, do not despair. This exercise will help you narrow the field of possibilities to a manageable number for further review and study.

First, let's take a look at what some of your mentors considered in making this all-important decision.

"My first criterion was academic reputation," Zoe recalls. "I only applied to schools that I saw as being excellent liberal arts institutions. Being from a small town and very attached to New England, I also chose schools within an easy one-day drive from home. I was also attracted to beautiful, classic campuses, an ambiance that I perceived as liberal or progressive, and an ethnically, racially, and socioeconomically diverse student body."

"I looked at academic reputation, size, location, the social scene, and the opportunity to learn in small-class environments," Jim advises. "If you know, or at least have a pretty good idea of what you want to study, the strength of a university's department in that subject should also guide your decision."

"I considered only those schools with a good music program," Tiffany agreed. "But I also looked for schools that paired that music program with a strong liberal arts curriculum to supplement my musical aspirations.

"Even though I had no idea then that I would be embarking on a music career—being a musician—I did care about the music programs at the various schools I was looking at, as well as the extent of musical endeavors in the undergraduate culture," Tom added.

Other mentors were guided by their interest in high-level athletic competition.

"I applied to five schools and the factors I relied on in choosing schools were limited to the lacrosse record and what kind of lacrosse program I'd be joining if I went there," Aaron said. "I knew I was going to play college lacrosse, so that was the main focus for me in choosing where to go to school."

"I knew that I wanted to attend a liberal arts college in New England where I could play baseball," Dave agreed. "I had decent grades and my college adviser recommended that I look at some of the NESCAC schools like Williams, Amherst, Middlebury, Bates, Tufts, Colby, Trinity, and Bowdoin. All of these schools offered the combination of challenging academics and a level of baseball I knew I could compete at. The Middlebury coach showed the most interest in me, and after my visit, I fell in love with the campus and met some very friendly people. I committed to apply early to Middlebury and got in ED1, so it ended up being the only school I applied to. I lucked out big time!"

"Highly qualified students should also seriously consider the availability of scholarships or honors programs, as many colleges and universities will offer them free or reduced tuition. No loans to pay back means more freedom after college is done," Jim counsels.

Many of the mentors also stressed the importance of an intangible "gut feeling" they got while touring a particular campus.

"I went to each campus at least twice, and as I visited campuses, the main thing I focused on was a feeling of 'the right fit.' I asked myself whether I could envision myself living here happily for four years," Zoe noted.

Others similarly stressed the importance of the "gut feeling" you get during a campus visit.

"I selected Duke because there was something about it that just felt right," Chase recalls. "It was an intangible attribute that I felt when I went there on a tour. I drove away from Duke knowing that no other school made me feel that way, and I was sold."

"The feeling or 'vibe' you get from a college visit is definitely something you should trust," Tom agreed.

So now it's your turn to figure out what matters most to you. Take yourself somewhere where you can be undisturbed for the next half hour or so. And, as mentioned in the Introduction, get yourself a journal, spiral notebook, or three-ring binder that you intend to dedicate to the purpose of collecting your responses to these exercises. You'll need to access your responses again as you go through college and will want to be able to find them easily. For ease of reference, we'll refer to this as your *workbook* from now on.

Okay, now turn off your cell phone and prepare to think critically about what really matters to you.

FACTORS TO CONSIDER IN CHOOSING A COLLEGE OR UNIVERSITY—AN EXERCISE IN DEFINING YOUR INTERESTS

Think about each of the following twelve factors and how each one might help you identify things you would like (or dislike) in a college or university. After reading the description of each one, determine whether the factor is unimportant to you (0), somewhat important to you (1), or very important to you (2), and circle the appropriate number next to each factor.

Size of School   0   1   2

Do you want to be part of a small, intimate community with perhaps only a few hundred students in your college class and perhaps only a handful of students in each of your academic classes, or would you prefer to be part of a huge campus where you can study in relative anonymity, and where at least the introductory classes can contain several hundred students each? Is it important for you to know most of the people in your class, or are you happy enough simply to know a few people within the larger community? How much does the physical size of a school matter to your decision? Write down a few thoughts in your workbook.

Urban or Rural Setting   0   1   2

The next question to ask yourself is *where* you would like to be situated during college. Do you want to study in a large city or urban center, where the city's bustling cultural offerings (concerts, sports teams, restaurants, and nightlife), as well as its downsides (crime, expense, and congestion), become part of your educational experience, or would you prefer an idyllic country setting where there is less distraction and where you can keep a pet, take a run almost anywhere, and otherwise stay on campus and concentrate on your studies? There are benefits and drawbacks to each option, and the decision as to which is "better" is a purely personal one. Take a few moments to think about your preferences. Are there any cities in particular that you would especially like to consider? Are there any regions of the country that you find particularly enticing? Record your thoughts in your workbook.

Proximity to Home   0   1   2

Would you like to stay close to your family, or are you interested in getting as far away from them as humanly possible during the years you are in college? Before you make a hasty decision about this, though, consider the implications. Even if you have a rocky relationship with your family right now, that may change; and even if it doesn't, you're still probably going to have to make the pilgrimage home for at least Thanksgiving and winter break. If you're not excited to get home to begin with, it will be even more of a pain in the ass, and an expense, to have to take a five-hour flight to get home.

So how important to you is proximity to home? Record your thoughts in your workbook.

Climate   0   1   2

Simply put, how significant an impact on you will the climate have? Are you prepared to completely exclude any school that is under a blanket of snow for four months out of the year, or would climate be a factor only in choosing between two otherwise similar schools?

Unless you suffer from seasonal affective disorder or some other physical or psychological condition that is exacerbated by the weather, we strongly discourage making decisions about schools solely on the basis of their climate, but hey— we're not the ones who are going to live in Nome for the next four years either.

So how important is climate going to be to you? Write down your thoughts.

Cost /Financial Aid   0   1   2

How much school can you and/or your family afford? Alternatively, are you prepared to take on whatever student loans are necessary to bridge the gap between what a school costs and what you can afford? If you are not at all familiar with your financial aid options, it might help you to read Chapter 4 before you answer this question.

So how important is a school's price tag to you?

Academic Schedule   0   1   2

Another significant differentiator between colleges is the academic schedule they feature. The majority of colleges employ the traditional semester system, whereby the academic year is divided into two fifteen- or sixteen-week semesters, with the fall semester beginning in late August and ending before a "winter break," and the spring semester beginning in mid-January, divided by a spring break in March, and ending in mid-May. In most schools based on the semester system, students complete their final exams and semester papers prior to leaving for winter break, and again by the end of the term in mid-May, which leaves them open to begin summer jobs or other experiences from late May through mid-August.

Other colleges and universities employ the full-year, trimester system, whereby each academic year typically comprises three fifteen-week sessions. At many of these schools, students are required to attend at least one third-trimester summer term, which can disrupt recurring summer plans, such as working as a camp counselor, but may also allow students to graduate in less than four years if they elect to attend more than one of these summer terms.

Still other colleges and universities are structured on the quarter system, whereby the academic year is typically divided into four ten-week terms, each separated by a period of time off. At these schools, most students elect to study in the fall, winter, and spring quarters, leaving summers free for work or other activities. The advantages of this curricular structure include the ability to take a greater number of courses or course credits each year. The disadvantages are that with each course typically covered in ten weeks rather than fifteen or sixteen, reading loads can be heavier and there is less time to cover course material in class.

Many schools feature hybrids of these curricular structures. One popular hybrid includes a "Jan-term" intersession, during which students study only one course intensively for the month, travel, or engage in other nonacademic activities of interest.

Obviously, the curricular structure adopted by a particular school has a very significant impact on your life as a student. Is there a particular structure that strikes you as more or less attractive? Write down some thoughts about your preferences.

Curricular and Grading Philosophy   0   1   2

What about a school's emphasis on a "core" curriculum? You might be forced to take, for example, four classes in each of a designated set of curricular areas, such as the "hard" sciences (math, chemistry, physics); the "soft" sciences (economics, psychology, political science); history; and language, literature, and the arts. What about a school's insistence that you become proficient in a foreign language? Or that you spend time abroad?

What about a school's philosophy with regard to grades? Would you favor a school that lets you take a certain number of your courses pass-fail rather than for a grade, or do you want all your courses graded on a hard curve? What about schools that don't give letter grades at all?

How important is a school's curricular and grading philosophy to you? Don't worry if you don't know which schools do what. That's for your independent research, which comes later. For now, we just want you to write down your thoughts on this subject.

Curricular Strength in Subjects of Greatest Interest   0   1   2

Do you have a subject that you already know you want to study in college? Perhaps you know you want to be premed or to study economics, marine biology, American literature, or psychology. How much is a school's strength in that area going to matter to you? Is it an overriding factor or just one consideration among many? This may depend on the strength of your commitment to the area you think you want to study.

Write down your thoughts.

Fit with Special Talents, Skills, or Interests   0   1   2

Do you have a special talent, skill, or interest that you hope to continue to develop or explore in college? Perhaps you play an instrument and are especially interested in having soundproof practice rooms available twenty-four hours a day. Maybe you are an artist and need access to certain facilities outside the academic setting. If you are an athlete, will the training facilities at a school matter a lot to you?

Would you be interested in cross-registering in graduate school classes to pursue a cocurricular or extracurricular talent? Do you need access to a particular sort of library or laboratory to further an interest or conduct research in a particular area? How important would these sorts of considerations be to you in identifying places to apply? Write down your thoughts.

Housing Arrangement   0   1   2

What kind of housing arrangement would you prefer during your college years? Do you want to live on a campus dominated by the Greek system, where housing on campus is primarily centered around fraternity and sorority houses? Are you looking for theme-based dorms? Cooperatives? Do you want a single, or would you prefer to have one or more roommates? Do you even want to live on campus? How important are housing considerations to you? Write down your thoughts.

Racial, Ethnic, Religious, Cultural, and Stylistic Diversity   0   1   2

How important to you is the racial, ethnic, religious, cultural, and stylistic diversity on campus? Is this something that you want to pay special attention to? Think about the importance that campus diversity plays in your decision and write down some thoughts on the subject.

Sports and Sports-Related Scholarships   0   1   2

If you are a high school athlete, how seriously are you thinking about continuing your sport in college? How important to you are the division you will play in; the strength of the program, the coach, and the other players on the team; the training facilities; whether you are actively recruited, and the scholarship package? Do you want to zero in on specific schools based on these considerations? Write down your thoughts.

WHAT TO DO WITH WHAT YOU'VE LEARNED

Okay, let's consolidate what you've just learned. Enter your ratings (0, 1, or 2) for each of the factors on the following list:

Size of school	_____
Urban or rural setting	_____
Proximity to home	_____
Climate	_____
Cost/financial aid	_____

Academic schedule _____

Curricular and grading philosophy _____

Curricular strength in subjects of greatest interest _____

Fit with special talents, skills, or interests _____

Housing arrangement _____

Racial, ethnic, religious, cultural, and stylistic diversity _____

Sports and sports-related scholarships _____

Now take all the factors you scored as 2s and thus considered to be very important, and rank them in the order they matter *most* to you. Then do the same with the factors that you scored as 1s and thus considered to be important. Let the zeros drop off the list; if they are unimportant to you, you won't need to be further distracted by them. Assemble your rank-ordered list of factors in your workbook. This rank-ordered list of factors should now steer your search for schools. Now, it's time to dive headlong into the search itself and to figure out where to apply.

MAKING YOUR LIST

Now that you know what's most important to you, you should be able to winnow down the list of hundreds and hundreds of schools. Chances are, though, you will still feel confused about how to proceed.

Stay with us.

Get a new three-ring binder (separate from your *Campus Confidential* workbook) where you can start to capture information about your college search, and fill it with paper and dividers so you have a separate section for each school. From now on, every time you go online or go to your local bookstore to research schools, you'll bring this ring binder with you. It will be the *only* place you record information about your college search. This way, you'll always know where your information is, and you'll never lose anything. From now on, any time you print something off from the Internet, get something in the mail from a school, or take notes on a particular school, put it behind the relevant tab or divider in this notebook.

Now, on with the search.

The first schools that go in your notebook are those that you have previously identified as "favorites" for whatever reason. Start a tab for each one.

Next add the schools that each of your parents went to if they went to college, and the schools where any of your siblings went or are going. Make a tab for each one.

No, we don't care right now whether you like those schools or not. We don't care whether you know *anything* about those schools right now. What we do know is that because your parents or siblings went to a particular school, you will likely get a thumb on the admissions scale as a "legacy." At some schools, this will matter a lot. At others, it won't matter as much . . . but the fact remains, it is at least *considered* at nearly every school, so you would be remiss to ignore this immediate advantage.

The next school that goes in your binder is your state college or university. There are at least two good reasons for this. First, because you are an in-state student, you will get a *significant* tuition break over what out-of-state students will pay for the same education. Second, because you are an in-state applicant, you will have an advantage in the admissions process. We don't care whether you are a National Merit Scholar or a C student. Your state college or university should be included in your admissions plan.

NOW WHAT?

Okay, so you now have at least one and perhaps several schools in your admissions binder. Now it's time to hit the books and the Internet and do some research. There are a whole host of reference materials available to assist you in your college search. The best of these guides include *The Insider's Guide to Colleges,* compiled each year by the staff of the *Yale Daily News;* Barron's *Profiles of American Colleges,* which comes complete with an interactive CD-ROM that lets you search for colleges by particular factors; *The* Princeton Review's *Complete Book of Colleges,* featuring a similar and useful "Counselor-o-Matic" college selection tool; and the *U.S. News and World Report Ultimate College Guide.*

You can, of course, drive yourself crazy with the amount of information available to you. We suggest that you spend an afternoon at your local bookstore, consult these various sources, choose the *one* that resonates best with you, and go from there.

Once you have your chosen reference in hand, strike off on your search based on the factors you identified as important to you. It may be helpful to start your search based on the size of the schools you want to consider, whether you want to be in an urban or rural setting, and the geographic region(s) you'd most like to be in. This should help limit your search to a more reasonable size. From there, the resources in the books we mentioned in the previous paragraph will help you work with the factors you identified in the exercise in this chapter to further narrow your search of the remaining schools. Next, look for schools that excel on all or most of the factors you deemed to be very important. Visit the schools' Web sites, take virtual tours, and continue to narrow the list.

WHAT ABOUT A SCHOOL'S REPUTATIONAL "RANK" AND ITS ADMISSIONS CRITERIA?

So far, we've been talking only about what schools are best for you, and now, at last, we come to the place where the rubber meets the road.

Yup, you guessed it.

The school's reputational "rank" in *U.S. News and World Report* and its admissions criteria—those dreaded ranges of GPAs and SAT scores that appear in the description of every school in the books. How should these considerations guide your selection of schools?

"I don't want to admit it, but the reputation of your college or university matters," Dan says. "Like it or not, much of the world places stock in reputation and excellence by association. When you start hunting for a job, the reputation of the institution you are coming out of carries weight. It had some impact on my success in applying to medical school."

"Yale's reputation has definitely impacted my career development very positively," Tom agreed. "I've frequently observed that when I'm involved in discussions of projects, that affiliation with Yale gives me an instant stamp of credibility and legitimacy."

So what do you do? Junk all the work you just did trying to figure out what was important to you and just apply to the highest-ranked school you get into?

No, no, no . . .

First of all, you need to remember that the *U.S. News and World Report* rankings are driven by a number of factors, including things like student selectivity and graduation rates that might not matter a whit to you. The rankings likely also completely ignore many factors, like a school's social atmosphere, course or major offerings, or geographic location—things that may be extremely important to you.

So do you junk the rankings then?

Not exactly. But the reason we didn't put "reputation" into the factors for consideration is that we wanted you to decide the factors that mattered to you on your own. Once you've done that, you can consider the reputation of schools that offer all or most of the things that are important to you and let it guide you in making close calls.

"I think that schools' reputations fall into broad categories, like 'great,' 'good,' 'fair,' and 'never heard of it,'" Zoe says. "Wellesley's reputation certainly had a positive impact for me in grad school and beyond, but I don't think the distinctions are that meaningful outside of these bands."

And what of the admissions criteria, then?

When you apply for admission to college, a school will examine an entire con-
stellation of factors in considering your candidacy. The first factor can be broadly
referred to as your high school academic record, comprised of your high school
(or prep school) GPA, your weighted and unweighted rank in class, the range and
difficulty of courses you have taken, and the grades you earned in those courses.
The second factor is your standardized test scores, including your SAT and the
scores you've earned on any SAT II exams. The third factor, referred to generally
as "extracurricular activities," includes the in-school and community activities
you participated in and the degree of commitment and leadership you displayed
in each, any interesting things you did with your summers, and any special
talents or skills you possess. The fourth factor is the strength of your letters of
recommendation—whether these letters shed any real light on you as a person
and single you out from the crowd. The fifth factor is how you performed on your
application essays—whether you were able to make a compelling case for
your candidacy and whether your writing style in these essays seems to match up
with the writing sample you provided on the SAT. The sixth factor is the on-campus or alumni interview. Other factors that may also be considered include your
ethnicity, your major or expressed area of curricular interest, and whether your
family has an alumni relationship with the college or larger university.

Looking at this list of factors, you can see that your high school grades and
your test scores are going to play a crucial role in where you will be accepted. So
within reason, you need to be realistic about the schools you apply to.

"You *do* have to be realistic about your chances," Kevin noted. "Although you
never know what ultimately makes the difference up or down to an admissions
committee, you'll know if you've got a good shot at the premier schools or not. If
you don't, no amount of legerdemain will deceive them into thinking that a guy
with a 3.0 GPA and no sports skills belongs at Princeton."

"But don't be afraid to apply to reach schools," Lyndsee challenged. "You never
really know what they're looking for to fill out the class, and you might be the one
who has it!"

As you consider schools, you should place them into one of three categories:
(1) "likely" schools—places where your credentials generally exceed the published
averages for that school and where your admission is likely; (2) "coin toss"
schools—schools where your credentials generally fall in the middle of published
averages and where, therefore, many students with credentials similar to yours will
be accepted *and* rejected; and (3) "reach" schools—schools where something *else*
in your admissions package: a knockout essay; a killer interview; consistent, stel-
lar recommendations; an exceptional talent in a particular area; or an obvious "fit"
with the school in some other way—is going to have to carry you.

As you do this, do not disqualify any school simply because it is a reach for you. The best colleges and universities in the United States are reach schools for nearly all their applicants. No one is a surefire admit to Yale, Williams, Juilliard, or the like. Just be honest about the way you categorize your schools so that you don't end up with too many reach schools and not enough coin tosses.

How many, you ask?

Ultimately, the number of schools that you take to the next stage of the process is up to you. At a minimum, though, we suggest that you apply to no fewer than two fit schools, six to eight coin toss schools, and two to four reach schools. We've known good students who have applied to as many as twenty-five schools; and, of course, if you are one of the lucky people who get admitted by early action or early decision to their top-choice school, you'll only apply to one. For most people, though, the final number tends to range between eight and fourteen schools.

Your list will be a work in progress for some time. Get comfortable with that reality and don't try to hurry yourself down to a final list. Part of the decision-making process requires some time for you to process and reflect on all the information and impressions you are gathering. As your friends go through the same effort, they may identify schools that deserve a look from you, and vice versa. Be sure that you never apply to a college just because your friends do—but if their research turns up a school that fits your profile, by all means add it to your list.

Oh, and there's one more really important thing.

You need to make yourself and us a promise. Repeat after us:

"I will not apply to any school that I would not attend if it was the only place I got in."

In addition to pure common sense, this is also a matter of economics and time management. You will already be applying to a pretty large number of schools. That will be both expensive and time-consuming to do well. There is simply no point in going through this process with a school if you know you wouldn't actually *go* there if you got in.

A WORD ABOUT GUIDANCE AND COLLEGE COUNSELORS

Finally, a word about how best to use your high school guidance or college counselor. Unless you attend a well-heeled prep school (where there will be plenty of individualized attention, though the application rules may be more restrictive), you will likely find your high school's guidance office to be overwhelmed. The combination of too many students and insufficient manpower can lead even the most well-meaning counselors to give you short shrift or to suggest schools to you based on an incomplete understanding of your needs and interests.

This situation can be immensely frustrating, and, if you don't take control of the process, can end up pigeonholing you into a category you might not want to be in. Fortunately, there are ways to ensure that you get the attention you need from your overburdened guidance office or college counselor.

First of all, *always* be polite and respectful to these people. For one thing, they are ridiculously overworked and underappreciated. For another, in many cases they wield a lot of power. Many high school guidance counselors, particularly senior ones who have been around awhile and have come to know many college admissions officers personally, can significantly affect your chances of admission positively or negatively with a well-placed word or two about you when these admissions officers come to your school, or with a good suggestion about what to emphasize on your application to a particular school. These people decide how to prioritize the dozens and dozens of recommendation letters they have to write each season. They hold a wealth of historical knowledge about which candidates from your high school were successful in gaining admission to a particular school, what their credentials were, and what, if anything, might be transferable to your application. Finally, they also know a lot about trends in the admissions game and how your high school is presently viewed by different colleges and universities.

It is important to get on the "good side" of the high school guidance counselor assigned to you—and there are very specific and effective ways to do this. First, if you haven't done so already, stop by during a free period or before or after school and introduce yourself. Shake hands and make eye contact. In the spring of your junior year, before SAT season but after the crush of the college admissions process has subsided, schedule an appointment with your counselor and bring along a copy of your updated résumé to help the counselor quickly get better acquainted with who you are and what you are all about. If you are reading this at the beginning of your senior year, do this *right away*. Have a frank conversation about your grades and where you hope to attend college. Seek the counselor's advice, but don't be afraid to push back if he or she suggests schools that you don't like or that you feel are not good fits for you. If you know what your top-choice school or two is already, make that known. Finally, as the meeting ends, thank the person for his or her time, promise to keep him or her up-to-date about your scores and accomplishments, and pledge to show up for your next meeting with a well-researched list of schools to discuss.

There is nothing a high school guidance counselor appreciates more than a polite, respectful, and well-prepared student. Guidance counselors are in place to help you—but you first need to be able to help yourself.

ADDITIONAL RESOURCES

The Insider's Guide to Colleges

Barron's *Profiles of American Colleges*

The Princeton Review's *Complete Book of Colleges*

U.S. News and World Report Ultimate College Guide

www.collegeboard.com (database on colleges, scholarships, financial aid, and majors; online registration for SATs; downloadable applications)

www.usnews.com/usnews/edu (college profiles)

www.collegebound.net (advice and resources for college search)

www.nytimes.com/college (searchable directory of articles on majors or fields of study)

www.collegenews.com (college newspapers)

www.campustours.com (links to virtual campus tours, maps, and pictures)

www.collegiatechoice.com (handheld college walking tour videos—for sale)

Beating the New SAT

Training is everything.

Mark Twain

There is simply no getting around it: the SAT is a critical component of your college application. Get a bad score on the SAT, and, practically speaking, you completely take yourself out of the running at the most competitive schools, and you probably put yourself behind the eight ball even at schools where you expected to be competitive.

Like it or not, the SAT is used as the "great equalizer," the one standard measuring tool that almost every student takes, whether he or she goes to the top-ranked boarding school in the country or the poorest public high school with the fewest available resources. And like it or not, the data continue to confirm that performance on the SAT does, in fact, predict future performance in college better than any other factor used in the admissions process.

That's the bad news.

The good news is that the test is not *that* difficult—and it can be prepared for and "gamed" for maximum performance.

YOU MUST PREPARE FOR THE SAT

The first question most students ask when confronted with the specter of the SAT is, "What is the best way to prepare for the exam?" And in response, many people will tell you that if you're a good student and you've studied hard throughout junior high and high school, you should just get a good night's sleep and treat the exam like any other exam you've taken up to this point.

Those people are dead wrong. *Don't* listen to them.

"You *must* study for the SAT. Don't believe the people who tell you that you will do well because you are naturally 'bright,'" Carolyn warns. "This is absolutely a test that you can and should prepare for, and very often, that preparation will make a big difference."

"Given that comfort and confidence are, in my opinion, the hallmarks of a successful test taker, taking practice tests and learning from them is the most effective preparation," Chase advises. "Practice tests give the test taker confidence about timing and working through difficult problem types. By the date of the test, I knew that nothing strange or unexpected was going to leap out at me. I was comfortable that I could answer the questions in the time allowed, and I had developed a methodology for solving the problems that used to stump me."

Studying and preparing for the SAT means you should either take a review course—which will force you to learn the exam, the different question types featured on the exam, and the different strategies for handling these questions, and will also force you to drill with the questions until you master them—or at a minimum, buy an SAT strategy course in book form and drill with that.

This exam is not like any other exam you've taken to this point. Sure, you've taken standardized tests before, and you may have taken the PSAT, and you may have even done really well on them. That's all well and good.

This test is different. It counts. A lot. In fact, it counts so much that if you shank it, it can ruin three years of great work in high school, and if you really ace it, it can make up for some subpar performances in high school.

"Okay, okay," you say. "I get it. The exam is important. I have to study for it. So what the hell am I supposed to do to get ready for it? And how far ahead should I start preparing for it? And what's on it, anyway?"

Glad you asked. We'll start with the format.

THE FORMAT OF THE NEW SAT

The format of the SAT changed in March 2005, thus garnering the moniker the "New" SAT. And this new arrival is not your big brother's SAT. The analogies from the Verbal section are gone, as are the quantitative comparison questions from the Math section. In fact, the whole Verbal section has been reconfigured and renamed the Critical Reading section. Oh, and there is a whole new Writing section too.

Length and Scoring

The New SAT is 3 hours and 45 minutes in length—45 minutes longer than the old exam—primarily due to the addition of the new Writing section. The scoring range (200–800) is the same, but you will now receive *three* scores (Math, Critical Reading, and Writing); thus a top score on the SAT is now 2400, rather than 1600. The average New SAT score is about 1500, or 500 per section. In addition to this score, you will receive a percentile rank for each section, which will tell you how you scored relative to the other students who took that administration of the exam. So, for example, if you got a 780 on the Math section and scored in the 98th percentile, that means you scored better than 98 percent of the other students on that section of the exam.

The Math Section

The Math section of the exam is 70 total minutes in length and is broken down into three sections typically comprising twenty multiple-choice questions (25 minutes); eighteen questions, including ten free-response questions (25 minutes); and sixteen multiple-choice questions (20 minutes). Topics covered in the Math section of the New SAT include number series and operations, Algebra I, Algebra II, functions, geometry, statistics, probability, and data analysis. These subject areas break down further into the following general categories of questions: fractions, even-odd relationships, factors, exponents, percentages, equations, angles, parallel lines, triangle geometry, circle geometry, geometry of other shapes and figures, number lines, coordinates, inequalities, and averages.

The Critical Reading Section

The Critical Reading section of the exam, also 70 minutes in length, tests skills through sixty-seven questions, all of which are multiple choice. Topics covered on the Critical Reading section include sentence completion and short and long reading comprehension passages. The sentence completion questions require you to "fill in the blanks" in a sentence from a list of choices provided, testing your mastery of vocabulary, usage, and context. The reading comprehension questions come in six flavors: (1) short passages of 60–120 words followed by two questions; (2) paired short passages followed by four questions asking you to compare and contrast the arguments contained therein; (3) long passages of 400–550 words followed by five to seven questions; (4) longer passages of 550–700 words followed by eight to ten questions; (5) a "mega" passage of 650–850 words followed by thirteen questions; and (6) paired long passages followed by thirteen questions asking you to compare and contrast the arguments contained therein.

The Writing Section

The new Writing section of the exam, which is 60 minutes in length, features forty-nine multiple-choice questions and one essay broken down into three sections. The first section, which runs 25 minutes in length, requires you to construct an essay and measures your ability to define, support, and effectively communicate a position. According to the New SAT's own scoring guide, the best of these essays (the ones that achieve the highest score) will (1) "effectively and insightfully develop a point of view on the issue and demonstrate outstanding critical thinking, using clearly appropriate examples, reasons, and other evidence to support its position"; (2) "be well organized and clearly focused, demonstrating clear coherence and smooth progression of ideas"; (3) "exhibit skillful use of language, using a varied, accurate and apt vocabulary"; (4) "demonstrate meaningful variety in sentence structure"; and (5) be "free of most errors in grammar, usage and mechanics."

The second section, which runs 25 minutes in length, will require you to identify grammatical errors and improve grammatical structure in sentences and passages by selecting the appropriate correction from a multiple-choice list provided. The third section, which runs 10 minutes in length, will again ask you to improve grammatical sentence structure.

The essay is assigned a subscore between 2 and 12; the multiple-choice questions are assigned a score between 20 and 80; and the entire section is scaled to the familiar 200–800 range.

The Experimental Section

As before, there is also an experimental section on the exam, which can be in any of the three sections (Writing, Critical Reading, or Math). The experimental section is designed to road-test questions before they are actually used on future exam administrations, and as such, does not count toward your score. Although you will be able to determine, based on the appearance of an extra set of questions, which section (Writing, Critical Reading, or Math) contained your experimental questions, there is no good way to determine which of the two sets of questions in that section was the experimental set—nor should you try to do so. Simply do the best you can on every section of the exam and let the chips fall where they may.

Format Overview and Example

The SAT has many different formats, even in the same test room during the same administration (where the sections contain the same questions but are ordered differently in different test booklets to discourage cheating), so the order of sections can vary from person to person. The only thing you can reliably count on is that the New SAT will always comprise ten sections, the 25-minute essay section will always be the first section on the exam, and the 10-minute multiple-choice writing section will always be last. Other than that, the sections can come in any order, and the experimental section can be slipped in anywhere on the exam.

To help you better understand how the exam is organized, here is a sample format from a recent administration of the New SAT:

Section	Time	Number of Questions
1. Writing (essay)	25 minutes	One essay topic
2. Math	25 minutes	20 total
		20 multiple choice
3. Critical Reading	25 minutes	24 total
		8 sentence completion
		2 based on short passage
		2 based on short passage
		12 based on "mega" passage
4. Math	25 minutes	20 total
		20 multiple choice
5. Writing	25 minutes	35 total
		11 sentence improvement
		18 grammar/usage errors
		6 passage revision
6. Math	25 minutes	18 total
		8 multiple choice
		10 student produced
7. Critical Reading	25 minutes	24 total
		4 based on paired short passages
		6 based on long passage
		5 based on long passage
		9 based on longer passage
8. Math	20 minutes	16 total
		16 multiple choice
9. Critical Reading	20 minutes	19 total
		6 sentence completion
		13 based on paired long passages
10. Writing	10 minutes	14 total
		14 sentence improvement

Given what you know about the basic format of the New SAT, you can deduce that one of the twenty-question multiple-choice math sections (either section 2 or section 4) was the experimental section on this exam, but of course, you have no way of knowing which one it was.

FAQs ABOUT THE NEW SAT

As we've already forcefully suggested, you must not take the SAT cold. Yeah, sure, we've heard the stories of the wunderkinds who walked into the exam hung over and pulled a 2400 out of their hats. Someone wins the lottery every week, too. We're not interested in the exceptions here. We're trying to give you the very best shot you have at acing this exam, . . . and like most things, that requires dedication and preparation.

Which Administration Should I Take, and When Should I Start Studying?

So how far out should you start?

Well, the first thing you need to know is *when* you intend to take the exam. The SAT is offered on Saturday mornings seven times a year: in October, November, December, January, April, May, and June. On those magic Saturdays, the test is offered at various test centers nationwide—most commonly in high schools. The test is also offered on Sundays for individuals whose religious practices preclude testing on Saturday.

We strongly suggest taking the exam at the April, May, or June administration in your junior year. There are a few good reasons for this recommendation. First, most students cover all the math concepts tested on the SAT by their sophomore year, or by their junior year at the latest. The longer you wait after that, the more you'll forget and have to relearn. Second, most students cover grammar and usage during their freshman or sophomore year English classes—so the same argument holds there. Third, if you think you might be applying to one or more schools for early action or early decision, you'll need to have an SAT score on file very early in your senior year. Fourth, you want to give yourself some leeway in case something goes wrong. You could get sick unexpectedly, there could be an illness or a death in the family, or something could go wrong in the test center, requiring you to cancel your score. *Do not wait until the last possible administration to take the SAT!!*

So let's assume you've decided to take the SAT for the first time at the May administration at the end of your junior year of high school (a wise choice, in our view). That means you should begin your preparations shortly after Christmas of your junior year, if not sooner. Yes, that's right—four to six months before the actual test administration. Of course, the more time you allow yourself to prepare, the more prepared you will be, and the more relaxed and enjoyable your preparation can be (another worthy consideration!).

Remember, the SAT is a critical component of your college application. A very high score can propel you to success in the admissions game. A tough day on the SAT can be catastrophic. And the truth is, there is no reason to have a catastrophic day on the SAT. If you train well, train long enough, and train thoughtfully—which means examining your mistakes, recognizing your weaknesses and the types of questions that trip you up, and drilling with them—by the time you get to the SAT, the experience should be as routine as a day at school.

Do I Really Need to Take an SAT-Prep Course? They're Expensive!!

Yes they are. They're also well worth the expense if you take them seriously.

Whether you actually need to take a prep course from one of the national test preparation centers like the Princeton Review or Kaplan depends a lot on your personal style. Are you self-motivated, or do you need the discipline of a classroom environment and a regular course schedule to keep your preparation on track? Are you disciplined enough to read an SAT-prep book thoroughly, to take sample tests under real-time conditions, and to force yourself to go back and examine the answers you got wrong and to learn the tricks that tripped you up? Or would you rather have the test administered to you, your test computer-analyzed, and a series of questions created for you based on your weaknesses?

"I took the Princeton Review class. It was very expensive, but it worked wonders," Kevin advises. "Beating the SAT requires a strong vocabulary, familiarity with a few dozen types of mathematical puzzles, and lots and lots of practice. People say that the SAT tests nothing more than how skilled you are at taking the SAT. This is absolutely true, which is why learning *how* to take the test is so important."

"Beating the SAT is all about learning how the test works," Dave agreed. "Figuring out how the test is trying to trick you or manipulate your thinking is the key to cracking the test."

You can certainly prepare well for the SAT using a book you pick up for $20 at your local bookstore. If you're worried at all about being disciplined enough to follow through on a self-study program, though, pony up the money for a course. It's a small price to pay for the significant increases in scores that these courses produce for people.

How Should I Practice?

Whichever approach you decide to adopt, allot a certain amount of time to SAT preparation every day. Treat it like one of your courses. Learn the types of questions, the tricks, and the traps—there are only so many types of questions on the SAT, and a finite number of ways they can be asked. Don't just drill with questions—analyze your mistakes so you learn from them. Learn to pace yourself so that as you practice, you work up your speed in handling the questions. The biggest reason for disappointing SAT scores is a failure of pacing—and having to guess blindly on a number of unanswered questions at the end of a section.

As you get closer to the actual exam, take two or three practice tests in real time and at the same time the actual exam will be administered. You need to become comfortable with the idea of getting up early and answering questions at eight in the morning. Remember, you want *everything* about the actual test to feel old hat to you by the time the real thing comes around.

How Do I Register for the Exam?

Hop online, go to www.collegeboard.com, and follow the relevant links. There you will find a list of dates and locations for all administrations of the SAT, all the information and materials you need to register, and even a couple sample exams. Just don't read their propaganda about how the exam cannot be studied for. You know that's wrong. While you're there, sign up for a free account, which will allow you to get your scores online a couple of weeks earlier than everyone else gets theirs by mail.

How Do I Know When I'm Ready?

What you're shooting for is comfort with the exam and familiarity with its directions, its format, its question types, and all the tricks and strategies that you'll learn from your prep course or prep book. If you find yourself smiling during a sample test—recognizing and stepping around trap after trap and employing strategy after strategy to plow through the questions—you know you're there.

If you're taking sample exams under real conditions (that is to say, 3 hours and 45 minutes straight, timing the sections properly and not resting between sections or otherwise getting interrupted) and your scaled scores are in the range of where you need to be for the schools you want to attend, you're ready.

Beating the SAT is not an impossible task. All it takes is the discipline to prepare. Anyone who tells you this exam cannot be studied for, learned, gamed, and beaten is just wrong.

It's really as simple as that.

What Do I Do the Night Before the Exam?

Gather your sharpened number 2 pencils, erasers, calculator, ID, and test pass, and some easy-to-conceal energy-producing food items (Lifesavers, an energy bar, a can of RedBull, whatever) and put everything in a place where you can find it easily. Yeah, yeah . . . we know they say that bringing food into the test center is verboten. We also know that we all did it, and we don't know *anyone* who has *ever* been thrown out of an SAT administration for sneaking in some Lifesavers. Just be discrete about it. Jam the can of RedBull during the bathroom break between sections. Stash the Lifesavers unwrapped in a plastic bag in a sweatshirt pocket, and keep a steady stream of sugar going.

Have a favorite meal for dinner, review general strategies one more time, and then relax. Get a good night's sleep, be sure to set an alarm clock and a backup, and be sure to wake up early enough on the morning of the test so that you won't feel rushed.

Have a good breakfast, get to the test site a little bit early, and stay loose. If you've followed our advice, you will be one of the best-prepared people in the room and poised to have a winning day.

I Bombed It, I Know It—Should I Cancel My Score?

Okay, listen closely.

No one feels really great about the SAT when he or she leaves. Taking the test is an exhausting experience, and no matter how well prepared you are, you can't help but feel a little nervous about it, given the importance of the exam. The real thing *isn't* going to feel like a practice test. So don't panic.

Having said that, there are a few good reasons to cancel your score.

If you *know* you misbubbled on a section and as a result probably got a large number of questions wrong, that's a good reason to cancel.

If you got sick in the exam room and missed time during the exam, that's a good reason to cancel.

If you were sick going into the exam, had a brutal night's sleep before the exam, were hung over coming into the exam, or otherwise know you were *way* off your game, that might be a good reason to cancel.

If any of these scenarios applies to you, you can either fill out a Test Cancellation Form before you leave the testing room or notify ETS within three business days (by Wednesday) after the administration.

If you just feel nervous about your performance, though, that's not good enough. I left the test center feeling concerned about my performance on the SAT and ended up doing very well. My experience seems to be common. Trust yourself. Unless you can point to a specific reason why you *know* your performance wasn't up to snuff, leave it alone.

If you intend to cancel your score, call your top-choice college admissions offices and find out how they react to cancelled scores. If you had a good reason to cancel (such as illness or a death in the family), ask the admissions offices if they would accept documentation of the problem for your file so that your file doesn't receive a negative inference as a result of the cancellation. Many schools will accept such documentation if your reasons for canceling were valid. On the other hand, admissions officers are on to the trick of taking a dry run at the SAT to get the experience, canceling the score, and then doing it for real at the next administration—and they don't look favorably on it.

When Will I Receive My Score?

It will take approximately six weeks to get the results. Your scores will be automatically sent to you and up to four colleges you identified on your registration form. You have to send score reports to every college you apply to anyway, so you might as well take advantage of this free service. You can request score reports for additional colleges on the Internet by going to www.collegeboard.com and following the relevant links. At press time, these reports cost $6.50 each. At the busiest times of the year, it can take up to a month for the College Board to mail out these reports after you request them, so be sure to plan ahead—particularly if you are applying early action or early decision and have a deadline looming.

Yes, if you screw up, you can pay your way out. Call the College Board at (800) 728-7267 with credit card in hand, pay them the $23.00 penalty plus $6.50 per report, and they'll mail out reports to anyone you want within two business days.

If the thought of waiting six weeks for your score makes you sick, you have two other options. Approximately two weeks before your scores reach you by snail mail, they are available to you on the Internet. Point your browser to www.collegeboard.com, and if you registered for the account we told you about earlier in the chapter, you will see a box that says "View Scores," which will give you access to your scores. If you blew us off and didn't register for the account, ETS won't let you do it after the fact. So you either have to wait for the mailman or pay the $8.00 "I blew off good advice" penalty by calling (800) SAT-SCORE; give them a credit card number, your Social Security number, birth date, and test date, and you can get your score from your friendly automated operator.

I Performed Below My Expectations—Should I Take the Test Again?

It depends on what you're talking about.

If you were expecting a 2100 and ended up with a 2080, no, you should not take the exam again—unless of course, you commit to another program of study that gives you reason to feel that you'll raise your score by 50 points or more. If, in contrast, you were expecting something around a 2100 based on your sample tests and you ended up with a 1950, now maybe you have reason to revisit the exam.

First, call two or three of your top-choice schools and find out what they do with multiple SAT scores. Will they just look at the highest one, or will they average your scores? If they average the scores, you'd have to do substantially better the second time around in order for an averaged score to make a meaningful impact on your application.

If you do decide to take the exam again, don't just reload and fire away at the next possible administration (unless, of course, you have no other options). If the administration you took is one of the ones where answers and reasons are provided, ask for that feedback and *study* where you went wrong. Learn from those mistakes and figure out how to recognize and correct them. Then go back, drill with those kinds of questions, take more sample tests, and *then* take another shot.

REVIEW: THE TEN THINGS TO REMEMBER ABOUT THE SAT

1. In the fall of your junior year, go to the College Board's Web site (www.collegeboard.com), research the schedule of spring SATs, and figure out which one you are going to take.

2. Begin preparing for the exam four to six months before your chosen date.

3. Register for an SAT-prep course or use a prep book, but in either case, study actively; learn the question types and strategies for each of them; and track, catalogue, study, and learn from your mistakes.

4. About a week before the exam, start getting up early and doing banks of SAT questions to get yourself in the habit.

5. On the day before the exam, stop studying and try to relax. There is nothing you can do to "cram" for the SAT, and if you've been studying diligently all along, there is nothing that you should need to do on the last day.

6. On the night before the exam, gather together your number 2 pencils, eraser, calculator, ID, test pass, and secret stash of energy food, and put it all together in one place so that you can simply grab it on your way out in the morning.

7. Have a good dinner and get a good night's sleep.

8. Have a good breakfast and arrive at the test center early. If you have the option to choose a seat, choose one in the back corner of the room away from the windows.

9. Force yourself to stay on schedule. The biggest mistake students make on the SAT is spending too much time on a stumper and then running out of time.

10. Don't cancel your score unless you got sick during the exam, know you mis-bubbled, or know for certain that you had to guess on an inordinate number of questions due to timing problems.

ADDITIONAL RESOURCES

Kaplan SAT Review Course (offered in cities worldwide)

The Princeton Review SAT Course (offered in cities worldwide)

Gruber, Gary R. *Gruber's Complete Preparation for the New SAT.* New York: HarperResource (annually)

KAPLAN, SAT Premier Program, Kaplan, Inc. (annually)

Princeton Review. *Cracking the New SAT.* New York: Random House (annually)

Acing the Application Process

Some people dream of success, while
others wake up and work hard at it.
Henry Hartman

So you've been through the exercise in Chapter 1, figured out what general factors matter to you in the college or university you seek, and narrowed down your list to an appropriate number of likely admit schools, coin toss schools, and reach schools. And if you've followed our advice, you've completed all this research by no later than the early spring of your junior year in high school. Now, whether you know it or not, your college admissions process is about to begin.

THE IMPORTANCE OF THE INFORMATIONAL CAMPUS VISIT

There is only so much you can tell about a school from what you read in books and college promotional materials. Although the advent of the Internet has made it possible to take "virtual" tours of college campuses and to view streaming video of interviews with current students, there simply is no substitute for the real thing. To make the best-informed decision between and among the schools on your list, you must walk their campuses, visit their dining halls, attend their classes, talk to their students yourself, and get a real feel for each campus's students and its architecture, atmosphere, and "vibe." By visiting a campus, walking around, observing life on campus, and watching the way the students interact with each other (and with you), you should be able to get a feel for what it would be like to go to school there—and for how well you would fit in to the lifestyle you observe.

Some of this is quantifiable and to that end, we have compiled a state-of-the-art methodology we call the Relevance Calculus for deciding between and among schools. You will find an explanation of the calculus, and individual worksheets to photocopy and use for each school, in Chapter 5.

Despite this, however, we are all human, and the preference for a particular college, like the preference for a particular kind of music, art, or literature, is still the product of a certain zeitgeist that a person must feel and personally observe to understand.

The upshot of this is that no matter what the cost in dollars or in time away from other things, you really *must* make the time to visit as many schools as your schedule and your financial means make humanly possible.

This does not mean that you need to fly from one city to the next and stay in hotels everywhere you visit. If you can't afford to do that, plan out your itinerary on MapQuest and call the admissions office of each campus ahead of time so that they can make arrangements to have you housed with a current student, on campus, at virtually no cost to you. Many schools will also provide you with dining hall vouchers such that even your meals will be paid for.

Maybe you won't be able to see schools on both coasts this way, . . . but you should at least be able to see most of the schools on your list. It is critical that you at least make time to see your top-choice schools.

WHEN TO GO

Try to schedule your initial campus visits at a time when students are on campus and classes are in session, so that you can get a realistic sense of what a typical day on campus feels like. To accomplish this, you will need to avoid midterm week (usually the last week in February or the first week in March), the two weeks in March when students are typically on spring break, and any time after the third week in April, as that is often when "reading period" begins and students hole up to begin preparation for spring-term exams. You're also going to want to visit at least your top-choice schools during the school week so that you can sit in on classes.

We say "initial" campus visits, because for most of the schools on your list, if you follow our advice, you'll actually be making *two* visits to campus. The first of these visits will be for information gathering and to test the list of schools you've researched and tentatively chosen for "fit." Your second round of visits will be for on-campus interviews. We'll get to those later in the chapter.

Prepare to Go Twice

Yeah, we know that traveling around the country not once but twice and stepping around all these scheduling landmines is going to put a huge burden on you and your family. We know it is going to be hard for you to find the time during school, during your sports season, and in the middle of your various other commitments, not to mention those of your parents and your siblings, to make this happen. We know it is going to be expensive and that you'll have to put hundreds, if not thousands, of miles on your car. And we know about all the other excuses you can come up with.

But you know what?

Every year, thousands and thousands of students make it happen—and the ones who do get a serious leg up, both in terms of the knowledge they gather and in terms of access in the admissions game. Maybe you'll have to pick a few days of high school that you can afford to miss. Maybe you'll have to dedicate some or all of your February break or your spring break to visiting colleges. Whatever it takes, though, make this happen at as many schools as you can possibly work in.

Call the Admissions Office to Pick Dates and Schedule Meetings

As you are planning your itinerary of campus informational visits, give each admissions office a call to ensure that classes are in session and that you are not planning to visit in the middle of exams or at another inopportune time. While you have the admissions receptionist on the phone, ask him or her whether the admissions office will be giving informational sessions on the day you are planning to visit and at what time they will be occurring. Ask the same question about campus tours.

If you would like to speak to a particular faculty member in an area of academic interest, you can typically schedule these appointments through the admissions office. The same is true if you would like to meet with a particular coach of a sport for which you hope to be recruited.

Finally, ask the person what the first date is that the school begins accepting appointments for on-campus interviews. Record all this information on some blank sheets in the section of your three-ring binder dedicated to this school.

When you've done this for every school on your list, compile the kickoff dates that each of your schools begins accepting appointments for on-campus interviews— as well as the phone number of the admissions office of the school—and get these dates and phone numbers into the relevant sections of your binder. This will help you keep track of the dates when you need to call each school to schedule your on-campus interview.

Think of this the same way that you think about ordering tickets for a concert. If tickets go on sale at 10 A.M., you are on the Internet or on the phone at 10 A.M., or you won't get tickets. On-campus interview slots are almost as much in demand these days as tickets to the hottest band, so plan accordingly.

To *interview* on campus at each of the schools on your list, or at least at your top-choice schools, you will need to work out a second travel itinerary. Try to block out ten days early in the summer when you can complete this important task— and then call each school *on the first day* that interviews are being scheduled, to fit the school into a slot that works for you.

Get On-Campus Admissions Interviews Wherever You Can

"My advice is to do everything you can to get an on-campus interview," Aaron suggests. "Doing so helps the admissions people get to know you as a living, breathing individual rather than just another paper application."

When scheduling interview times, try to pick either the last slot on the schedule before lunch or the last interview of the day. Try to put your top-choice schools somewhere in the middle of the process so that you'll have an opportunity to get a couple of interviews under your belt before the high-pressure ones hit, but not so late in the process that you'll be too exhausted or such that your answers will seem too rehearsed or "canned." Scheduling interviews in early summer puts you on campus at a time when the admissions staff will be fresh.

The rationale for choosing the slot immediately before lunch or the last slot of the day should be obvious. If the interview is going well, you won't be artificially constrained by a time limit imposed because the next applicant is waiting behind you; and the more time you have to talk to an admissions officer, the more time you will have to burn an impression in her or her head.

Why are these interviews so important?

First of all, at many schools, admissions officers conduct the on-campus interviews, and at many of those schools, the admissions officer who interviews you will be the person who presents you "in committee" if your candidacy makes it that far. In a highly competitive game where candidates present with incredibly similar credentials, every little edge you can get matters a whole hell of a lot. If you can make a strong impression on an admissions officer, you can pull yourself out of the stack of people with identical credentials and make that officer want to "pull" for you a little harder because he or she met you and can speak for you personally, in three dimensions, beyond what appears on the printed page. The other similarly credentialed candidates who didn't take this additional step remain in two dimensions.

Will some of them get in anyway?

Sure they will.

But in the close cases, the three-dimensional candidate—the candidate who has left a strong positive impression with an admissions officer—will get the little nudge that can make the difference in the horse race.

We'll get to the nuts and bolts of the interview in a little while. At this stage, all you need to know is that you should do everything in your power to get one.

WHAT TO DO WHEN YOU GET TO CAMPUS (INFORMATIONAL VISIT)

Head for the Admissions Office

Your first stop, when you get to campus, should be at the admissions office. When you get there, introduce yourself *politely* to the receptionist, explain that you are in town for an informational visit to campus, and ask if it would be possible to introduce yourself to the admissions officer in charge of your high school, state, or area of the country. This will be hit or miss, because admissions officers are frequently out on the road giving presentations, or, if you arrive prior to April 15, they may be at home reading files or on campus but sitting in committee. It never hurts to ask, though, and an opportunity to say a *brief* hello and to make polite contact is always worthwhile.

While you are in the admissions office, pick up a copy of the current year's application. They don't change much from year to year, and, if the college does not use the Common Application or requires additional essays, this will give you the entire spring and summer to brainstorm essay topics. You should also ask for a copy of the current year's program of study or course catalogue; any and all promotional materials, CD-ROMs, DVDs, or informational binders that the office has on hand; and a copy of that day's campus newspaper. Finally, ask if the office happens to give out dining hall vouchers so you can take a meal in one of the dining halls. Not all schools do this, so don't be put off if a particular school doesn't offer this perk, but as with most things, it never hurts to ask—and because you're on a budget, every little bit helps.

Put all these materials into a big manila folder with the college's name on it so that you'll keep all your materials straight and have them available for further study.

Attend an Information Session

If you noted earlier on that there would be an information session run by the admissions office, be sure to attend it. These sessions, which are typically run either by admissions officers or current students, provide the latest information about the college, trends in admission, and plans for improvements during the years you would be on campus. There is almost always an opportunity to ask questions at the end of the session, so if you have any specific questions at that point, there will be an opportunity to have them answered.

Take an Official Campus Tour

Next, see what your notes say about a campus tour. Chances are, there will be one leaving from the admissions office or, at the very least, the admissions office will direct you to the place where the next tour will be departing. Take this tour first, use it to get your bearings and a sense of the campus, but don't let it be the only tour you take of the campus. Campus tours will *always* highlight the parts of the campus that a college is most proud of. They will take you through the new library, the new gym, the newest dorm, the most progressive dining hall, and the most aesthetically pleasing parts of the campus.

Be sure, though, that that's not all you see.

After you take the tour, which will almost always be given by a particularly enthusiastic current student who will be putting the best possible "spin" on everything about the college, break away.

Check Out a Dining Hall

If it is around lunchtime by this point, take a meal in a dining hall rather than at a fast-food joint or local restaurant. Remember, you are on an information-gathering mission here. You already know what McDonald's is like. What you want to know is whether the food on campus is edible, what the options are like, and how flexible the dining plans are. Nearly all college dining halls are more than happy to sell you a meal (or give you one for free if you picked up a voucher in the admissions office). Are there enough options? Is there a fresh-looking salad bar? A pasta bar and sandwich bar? Is there an express option if you are running between classes or a lab? Is your dining hall card transferable, such that you can eat anywhere on campus, including in the grad school dining halls, or are you limited to certain places? Make some notes on a blank sheet and file these thoughts in the relevant section of your binder.

Talk to Students

Make your next stop the campus bookstore, wherever it is. As you wander around trying to find it, stop a few students, tell them you are a high school student visiting the campus, and ask them the following questions:

- Why did you decide to come here?
- What is the best thing about being here? What is the thing that you would most like to change?
- What was your other top-choice school that you were considering?
- If you had the choice to make over again, would you still pick this school?

As soon as you have finished talking to someone, record your thoughts and file them in the section of your binder for this school so you won't forget who told you what about which school. In this midst of a whirlwind tour of campuses, you'll be amazed at how quickly information starts to blur together.

Visit the Campus Bookstore

When you get to the bookstore, ask for a copy of the school's student-authored course review guide. Again, not every school will have one of these, but many do, and the insights and the distinctions between schools that you can glean from reading them are well worth the cost of picking one up at every stop.

Meet with Faculty and Coaches and Visit Departmental Offices

If you scheduled a meeting with a faculty member or a coach, you'll need to fit that in wherever the person's schedule allowed. If you didn't, but you have some sense of a subject or two in which you might want to major, make a stop in the departmental office of that major and take a look around. How does it feel? Introduce yourself to the receptionist or to a secretary in the office. Perhaps there is a professor around the office with whom you could speak for a few minutes. Again, you are on an information-gathering mission. Take advantage of any and every opportunity you get to test your impressions.

Get out the Map and Wander Around

Finally, wander the campus some more. Have a cup of coffee in the local campus coffee place. Let the vibe of the campus pour over you, and take some time to record your "gut feelings" about the place, independent of any objective criteria. Do the students seem happy? Does the place just "feel right" to you, or does it feel uncomfortably large, small, cold, or distant? Don't let the weather (good or bad) on the day of your campus visit unduly influence your reaction to the campus. Similarly, don't let a single bad interaction with someone infect your entire impression of the place. Go for an overall, general impression and write down some thoughts about it.

Sample the Nightlife

If you are staying on campus overnight, try to have dinner in a different dining hall and try to sit with a group of current students and engage them in a discussion about the school during dinner. In the evening, don't even *think* of going back to the hotel and ordering up the in-room movie. Go to an event or activity on campus. If you need to figure out what's going on the night you are there, stop by the campus post office or student union, read the postings on the walls or kiosks, or read the table tents in the dining halls. If there is a campus speaker, a play, a musical performance, or anything else of interest, take it in.

Review Your Materials

When you finally retire to your hotel or to the room where you are staying for the night, go through the notes you've made, and make sure you have gathered up all the necessary information and filed it in the proper section of your binder. Then get a good night's sleep, because tomorrow you are likely to be traveling to your next stop.

Resist the Urge to Jump to Conclusions

One final thought.

Be careful about cutting your trip short if you think you have found your "dream" school early, or even in the middle of the process. Remember that the college admissions game is fraught with uncertainty. This exercise is not just about identifying your top-choice school. It is about gathering information about *all* the schools on your list, such that, informed by your own research and your own impressions, you can put them into a rank order and eliminate any schools that clearly don't mesh with you.

The importance of campus visits and information-gathering to the process really cannot be overstated. Once you've finished this stage of the process, you're ready to move on to the execution stage.

HOW TO HANDLE ON-CAMPUS INTERVIEWS

If you followed our advice, you should have a full slate of on-campus interviews scheduled for sometime early in the summer and either just before lunch or in the last slot of the day. You should have a likely admit school scheduled first and a couple of coin flips scheduled ahead of the reach schools on your list that matter most to you. Once you've done that, you're ready to begin.

So what are the nuts and bolts of the on-campus interview?

Review the Notes from Your Campus Visit and Subsequent Research

On the evening before your interview, pull out the notes from your campus visit and your subsequent research, and refresh your memory about the school. What were your likes and dislikes the last time you were there? Whom did you talk to, and what did they have to say? Was there anything remarkable about the tour or your subsequent wanderings around campus? Was there anything noteworthy about your visits to the departmental offices of your potential majors, the classes you saw, or the professors or coaches you spoke with? By conducting this review, you're looking to arm yourself with topics for conversation tomorrow.

Review Your Résumé and Decide What Three Things About Yourself You Want to Accentuate

Remember, chances are that at the time you interview, you will not yet have applied for admission, so the admissions officer or student representative you speak with will not know anything substantive about you. He or she won't know your test scores, your grades, your activities, or the things that "make you tick." In other words, you're facing thirty or forty-five minutes of tabula rasa.

What an opportunity to make an impression!

As you prepare for the experience, though, recognize just how fleeting the opportunity is. This is your thirty or forty-five minutes to sell your candidacy to the school. It is time to put your best foot forward and leave a lasting memory of yourself in the mind of your interviewer.

In other words, this is not a time to talk for long about grades or test scores. Those things are largely colorless and can be easily gleaned from the admissions officer's later review of your transcript. Think of the interview as a conversation about who you are and what really makes you tick.

So?

Who are you?

What were the one or two defining experiences in your life? Your biggest victory? Your most crushing defeat? Your most memorable moment? Your most critical learning experience?

What is your most important extracurricular activity? Why is that so? What has it taught you about life and about yourself?

Who is your hero? (And don't just pick your mom or dad unless you can articulate a *really* good reason for it.) Whom do you most respect? If you could have dinner with any one person from any point in history, whom might you pick?

What is your favorite book? What are you currently reading?

And why, oh why, would you rather go to this school than any other school in the country? What about it distinguishes it in your mind?

We hope these questions will trigger some reflection and help you define who you are. They are among the most common college interview questions.

Decide on the three most defining things about you that you want to get across during the interview and then make sure you communicate them convincingly in the time you have.

Wear Appropriate Clothing

For the men, at *least* a jacket, tie, pressed pants, and dress shoes. A suit is fine too. It depends on the image you're going for and what you're comfortable with. Never jeans, never sneakers, and never anything other than an oxford-style shirt. For the women, a business suit, pants and a blouse, or a skirt and a blouse. Avoid flip-flops, sandals, or anything similarly casual.

Don't come in chewing gum or smelling like cigarette smoke. Doing so is disrespectful and will turn people off.

Finally, if your green hair, multiple facial piercings, or obvious tattoos define who you are, that's okay—but recognize that if your interviewer that day is the sixty-three-year-old director of admissions, he may not "get" it. If he doesn't, maybe this isn't the school for you anyway, but just realize that the more "controversial" you are, the greater the risk.

Arrive on Campus Early and Do Some Due Diligence

On the morning of your interview, get to campus at least a couple of hours ahead of time, get a cup of coffee and a copy of the campus paper, and read. What are the burning issues or controversies of the day on campus? Who is coming or has just been to campus to speak? How are the teams doing?

What you're looking for are a couple of issues to *casually* work into your interview that will let the admissions officer know that you're interested in the school and what's happening on campus. Don't just awkwardly jam them in there, though. Wait for your spot or a lull in the conversation. You always want to have something in your back pocket in case you hit a dead spot or in case the admissions officer asks you if you have any questions for him or her. This is your ace in the hole for those moments.

Once you've armed yourself with this information, take a walk around campus and refamiliarize yourself with what's going on. If you've noticed some new construction around campus, or anything else that catches your eye, make a mental note of it and either mention it or ask a question about it during your interview. Talk to whomever might be walking around on campus. Look to engage at least one person in a substantive conversation about the school. Again, if you meet Professor Wildman from the Department of Anthropology standing in line for coffee at the Daily Grind and have a good conversation with him about life at the school while waiting for your triple grande breve latte, it might provide you with a subject for substantive conversation in the interview.

Show Up at the Admissions Office Fifteen Minutes Early

Arrive for your interview fifteen minutes early, no matter what. If your interviewer is available, you might get to start five minutes early. In any case, it is a simple matter of courtesy to be prompt.

When you arrive, shake hands firmly with the receptionist, make eye contact, introduce yourself, and let him or her know what time your interview is scheduled to begin.

Make a Good First Impression

When your admissions officer appears, smile, make eye contact, rise to meet him or her, and shake hands firmly and confidently. Follow the admissions officer wherever he or she takes you and wait to be offered a seat.

Once seated in the office, don't slouch. Sit up straight, but comfortably. Make frequent eye contact with the admissions officer, laugh easily, smile often, speak confidently, and tell your story.

And make your three points.

If you can't sell you, nobody can.

Take a Student Interviewer in Stride

At some schools, current students conduct interviews for the admissions office. Typically, there is no difference in the weight accorded to the interview, whether it is conducted by a student or by the director of admissions. Your interview will still be written up on the same forms and given an ultimate score (usually on a 1–9 scale) that will end up in the same place on your admissions "scorecard" if and when your file makes it into committee.

There is one important difference, of course, and that is in the psychological benefit of having the person who interviewed you in the committee room pushing for you. It is clearly preferable to be interviewed by someone who will actually be sitting in the committee room and can advocate for you if you made a good impression. Admissions officers sit in committee. Students don't.

Unfortunately, there is nothing you can do to "request" a particular interviewer or to request that you see a member of the admissions staff as opposed to a student. You get who you get, and you simply need to make the best of it.

Remember that student interviewers' scores *do* count just as much as admissions officers' scores. Don't let down your guard or exhibit disappointment if you get a student interviewer. Doing so can deal a deathblow to your candidacy.

Exit with Style

When the interview is over (take your cues from your interviewer—don't *ever* look at your watch), stand up, smile, and thank him or her for spending time with you. If—and only if—the school is your certain first choice, you can mention that point firmly and without hesitation as the interview is concluding. A simple remark like, "Ms. Burnham, I've really done my research on this, and Yale is absolutely my first choice. I intend to apply early decision. For whatever it's worth, I just want you to know that," is all you need to say. If the school is not your first choice or if you don't have a clear first choice yet, just skip this part. Do not, under any circumstances, try to fake it or tell more than one school that it is your first choice. The admissions community is *very* small. Admissions officers from different schools often end up touring together and attending the same circuit of events during the summer, and they *do* talk.

Once you've made this point, immediately ask your admissions officer for a business card, shake hands firmly again, and wait for him or her to lead you back downstairs. Don't ever ask your interviewer "how you did," or worse yet, "What are my chances?" Simply let the interview speak for itself.

Follow Up

The day after your interview, direct a *brief* handwritten thank-you note to the interviewer, mailed to the address on the business card you picked up. Try to mention a single subjective point of the interview that you particularly enjoyed—which will also trigger a corresponding (and, we hope, positive) memory in the mind of the admissions officer when he or she reads your note.

Once you've done that, you're finished until you file your application.

DECIDING TO APPLY EARLY ACTION OR EARLY DECISION

Applying "early action" allows a student to apply to a school by November 1 and have a *nonbinding* answer back from the admissions office on or about December 15. Fewer and fewer colleges and universities are offering early action programs, primarily due to the difficulties that these nonbinding decisions pose to committees trying to accurately calculate admissions *yields* (the percentage of students offered admission who actually matriculate).

For this reason, most schools now offer early decision programs instead, which allow students to apply "ED-1" by November 1 for a decision by December 15 or "ED-2" by December 1 for a decision by January 15. These decisions, however, are *binding* upon a student offered admission—and a successful early decision candidate must withdraw all of his or her other applications for admission and agree to matriculate in the college or university offering admission.

The ED-1 and ED-2 programs allow a student to apply early to his or her top-choice school ED-1 and then, if that application results in a deferral or a rejection, to apply to his or her second-choice school ED-2.

So how do you decide whether you want to participate in early decision? And are your chances of admission better or worse in the early decision pool than they are in the regular admission pool?

The answers to these questions are largely dependent on the individual applicant and the individual school, but there are a few truisms across schools.

Generally speaking, the percentage of candidates gaining admission to a particular school is *higher* in the early decision pool than it is in the regular admissions pool. This, of course, is largely due to the fact that ED candidates typically present with higher average GPAs and SAT scores than candidates in the regular pool. But it is also because the class is completely empty at the time of ED decision making, meaning that there are more seats to fill than there are when the regular admissions process takes place and because any upward trend in number of applications or average scores has not yet manifested itself. As the result of all of these factors, admissions officers tend to be a bit "looser" in choosing candidates during the ED process.

So what does this mean for you?

If you have a clear first-choice school, your credentials put you in the ballpark for admission to that school, and you do not expect anything about your candidacy to notably improve between the ED1, ED2, and regular admissions deadlines, we recommend applying early decision to your top choice school. In addition to signaling your preference, doing so will place you in the most favorable position available for gaining admission. And hey—if you get in, you're done!

However, if your grades are below the mean for that school, but are trending upward such that another set of grades might materially improve your GPA, you might want to wait to apply until those grades can be considered as part of your application. Similarly, if your SAT score was below expectations and you have decided to take it again, waiting to apply until that score can be considered may be your best bet.

This discussion again highlights the importance of performing diligently throughout your high school years, and then getting a jump on your application process by completing your college research and your test administrations early. In this case, the early (and qualified) birds often get the worm.

THE APPLICATION

The Common Application

An increasing number of colleges and universities are using the Common Application—a standardized, "one size fits all" online college application form. Some schools use the Common Application exclusively. Some schools use the Common Application, but supplement its requirements with one or more additional, college-specific essays. Some schools inexplicably give you the choice of completing the Common Application *or* using a school-specific application available from the admissions office. Finally, other schools refuse to use the Common Application in any capacity. You can find the Common Application, information about how it is used, and which schools use it in which way at www.common app.org.

Although other resources and sometimes the admissions offices themselves will tell you that it makes no difference which application you use, we disagree. It is our position that if a school accepts both the Common Application *and* its own individual application, using the school's individual application at least subconsciously suggests that the school was important enough to you for you to actually get its specific application form.

The Personal Information Section

The personal information section, as you might suspect, gathers your personal information, such as your name, your contact information, and the name and address of your high school or boarding school. It also typically requests, but makes optional, such information as your racial or ethnic background and your intended major.

With respect to your intended major, many colleges and universities are pressing to matriculate a greater number of science, math, and engineering majors—and particularly women who are interested in these subjects. If you fit the bill and your high school record and teacher recommendations will support it, you should identify your major. If, however, you intend to matriculate as one of the hundreds of English, history, political science, or economics majors, you're probably better off calling yourself "undecided," unless you are very strongly favoring a major and are using it as a selling point in your application.

The Activities List

Whether you are using the Common Application or an individual school's application form, you will be asked to provide a list of your activities and employment during your high school or prep school years. And whether you are using the Common Application or an individual school's application form, you will no doubt discover that the form documents leave nowhere near enough room to type in anything meaningful about your activities.

Not to worry. Unless the application form you are using specifically prohibits you from attaching additional sheets, you can, and should, create your own.

"These lists of your activities and employment history are going to be templates that you will use on multiple applications, so start early, and complete your compilations and editing of this basic information as soon as possible," Chase advises. "The worst feeling when applying to colleges comes when things are rushed and you worry that you might have missed something or made a mistake."

Set up a landscape-formatted table with the following columns: Activity, Years, Position Held, Hours per Week, and Description. Then, using a clean, crisp font, appropriate spacing, and active verbs, concisely provide the content for each of your activities.

Set up a similar landscape-formatted table for any relevant employment history, with these columns: Company, Years, Position Held, Hours per Week, and Description. Again, using a clean, crisp font, appropriate spacing, and active verbs, concisely provide the content for each of the jobs you've held. Make some judgment calls here. If you babysat the neighbor's kid for the past three years, that's probably not something worth listing here. On the other hand, if you worked at a summer camp, as a lifeguard, founded your own company, or simply explored career options by working at a company or a professional office, you should, by all means, include that information.

The Short-Response Questions

Students sometimes wonder just how important these short responses are.

The answer to that question is simple.

Every word you submit to an admissions committee is important, because every word influences the reader one way or the other. You want, of course, to do something to positively distinguish your file from the dozens of others your reader will be reviewing that day. That can happen with a show-stopping short response just as easily as it can happen with anything else in your application.

Take these questions seriously. Each one is an opportunity, and you *are* playing a zero-sum game: if you don't help yourself with every word you write, then you've missed an opportunity you'll never get back.

The Long Essay Question

Most schools use an open-ended question, similar to any of the interview questions we highlighted earlier, to stimulate your long-essay response. Your response will be "graded" on substance, construction, and delivery—and each of these is equally important.

We encouraged you to collect copies of college applications during your informational visits because the long essay questions are often the same from year to year, and the sooner you have a working list of what the topics are, the more time you and your subconscious mind will have to think about them. Choosing a subject to write about can be the hardest part of your task. Once you know what you're going to write about, succeeding at the rest comes down to time, hard work, and revision. Deciding on something to write about can take a moment, or several months—but you'll "know" when you have it because the essay will come pouring out and almost seem to start writing itself.

"An eighth-grade English teacher of mine, Mrs. Maguire, always told us to write about two things: what we knew, and what we cared about," Dave recalls. "I applied that advice to my college admissions essay. I found that writing about something that I cared about and that I knew well was the best way that I could let the admissions office know who I was and what was important to me."

"If you have had any unique life experiences, tell one of those stories in the essay," Tiffany advises.

"It's also really important not to try to be someone you're not," Lyndsee cautions. "When I read a bunch of sample essays before I applied to college, they were always extraordinarily creative ones, and that really freaked me out. Later, I realized that you can grab the reader's attention just by being yourself. Think about what makes you different from everyone else and try to play off that theme in your essay. Everyone has something unique to say, and if you present it effectively, it will stand out, because it will feel authentic."

"If you experienced a special situation or circumstance that truly affected you, those types of essays work best," Erika suggested.

Kevin added a word about style.

"Your admissions essay is your sales pitch, and it should, as we say in journalism, be 'sexy.' That does not mean that you have to be avant-garde, to experiment with the essay form, or to be postmodernist about the whole application process, though. Just write from the heart about your world."

A word of caution about all of this, though . . .

Be certain that you actually answer the question.

If you can use an essay for more than one college because the subject matter you addressed is clearly responsive to both questions, that's great. But don't try to "adapt" an old essay written for some other college if it isn't clearly responsive to the question asked on your application. Admissions readers can spot this tactic from a mile away, and what it says to them is exactly what you would think: that you didn't care enough about your application to *this* school to write a new essay.

And that can be fatal to your application.

Finally, a word about authorship and how to pull your long essays together.

It goes without saying that you *must,* without exception, write your essays yourself. Hiring someone to write your essay for you, downloading an essay from one of the various essay services on the Internet, or "borrowing" one from a friend or older sibling is dishonest—and if you get caught, you can be certain that your application to any school that catches you or learns about this by word of mouth will be rejected outright.

Colleges employ "spot-checkers" to hop on the Internet and verify that the essays you submit are your original work. It's not hard to spot a fraud—all they need to do is compare the writing style and sophistication of a submitted essay with the style and sophistication of your SAT writing sample.

Forgot about that on-the-spot SAT writing sample, didn't you?

All it takes is a few days on the job for an admissions reader to become proficient at rooting out cheaters—who are more common than you'd imagine.

Write your own essays.

Which brings us to our next point: editing your essays. Who should do this, how, and when?

Obviously, the definition of cheating isn't always as black and white as downloading a complete essay off the Internet, . . . and sometimes the line between doing your own work and having others do it for you can become blurry.

The same spot-checkers who verify the originality of your work also know about all of the "essay advisory" services out there that will "advise" you about your essays for an exorbitant hourly fee. And they know that this advising often means editing the hell out of your essays such that very little of your original work product remains.

And guess what?

When the "voice" of your essays doesn't match the "voice" of your SAT writing sample or your answers to the short-response questions, alarm bells go off in the admissions reader's mind.

Although you're unlikely to get tossed for cheating in such circumstances, you won't get a top score on your essay, either.

It all comes down to the one word that admissions directors use to describe what they're looking for.

Authenticity.

Your essay must be authentically you.

What does that mean?

It means that you, and only you, must come up with the idea and the substance for your essays and that they should be informed by the experiences of your own life. It means writing your first and second drafts *on your own*, without editing from your parents, siblings, friends, or teachers. It means unhurriedly polishing the thing over time, in draft after draft, until you think it is absolutely your best work.

Then, and only then, do you pick two or three people to show it to.

If you follow this advice, anything those editors do to your essay should be well to the safe side of the line. Moving paragraphs around, breaking a paragraph into two, or choosing an opportune spot for a one-word or one-sentence paragraph by breaking something off from somewhere else is legitimate. Changing a word or a sentence here and there in response to an editor's suggestion is fine.

The voice of the essay will still be authentically your own.

Be forever vigilant about crossing this line.

Writing your long essays should be, by far, the most time-consuming aspect of your college admissions process. If you have decided to apply early, be sure you get cracking on those essays first. Good writing takes time—and there is simply no substitute for it.

"I always imagined an admissions officer sitting at his or her desk buried in applications, having already read several hundred that day," Chase notes. "The clock reads 7:30 P.M. on a Friday. The phone rings and the admissions officer answers. A friend is on the line and wants to know if their 8:00 P.M. dinner is still on. The admissions officer has my essay open on the desk. What can I possibly write that will make my essay worth reading, following on the heels of the hundreds that preceded it, when all this admissions officer wants to do is leave for the weekend? That's how I chose my topic. You must always remember that someone with a sense of humor, a heart, and a life is reading your essay. Your job is to reach out from the page and grab that reader somehow."

The Optional Essay

This is truly a misnomer. There is no such thing as an optional essay. An optional essay is only optional for people who don't care about getting in. See our discussion two sections earlier about opportunity and opportunities lost.

Teacher Recommendations

The most common question here, of course, is whom to ask. Do you simply default to the teachers who gave you the best grades in the toughest courses you took, or do you pick the teachers who know you best?

The answer depends on your individual circumstances. If you are applying to a top school as a prospective economics major and the teacher who knows you best is your gym teacher who is also your neighbor, you're obviously going to want to keep looking. On the other hand, you don't want to just pick teachers from tough courses who gave you good grades if they don't know you well.

In choosing a recommender, you're looking for someone to paint a picture of who you are—someone whose comments about you will ring true in light of the rest of the materials you submit. You're looking for the people who can comment credibly on your academic horsepower but also talk about your work ethic; your reputation with your peers, faculty, and administration; your contributions to school and community; and what kind of person you are.

"The best advice I can give you is to choose someone who knows you well enough to write an insightful recommendation," Erika says. "If you choose a teacher solely because of the grade you got in his class, you have asked the wrong person to write your recommendation, and wasted a huge opportunity. You must connect on more than a classroom level with the people you ask to write your recommendations."

Chase and Lyndsee agreed.

"Pick someone who can say something unique about you," Chase implored. "There is no new information conveyed in the statement 'John is a good student and got As in my class.' Such a statement is painfully bland and will make no impact. I would want to find the teacher who could write, 'I recommend John for admission not because he received an A in my course, but because his dedication and integrity would be the traits I valued most.' The second statement actually says something about *you*."

"Choose teachers who can say things about you that the admissions office won't get anywhere else in your application," Lyndsee echoed. "Things like drive, enthusiasm, work ethic, and heart. Anecdotes and concrete examples of these things will bolster your application and make the admissions people remember you."

"My best recommendation actually came from a teacher who gave me my lowest grade," Aaron recalls. "But that teacher was someone who understood me, despite the grades I got in his class, and had a lot of positive things to say about me. I'm glad I didn't just rule him out because I wasn't at the top of his class. His letter showed the admissions committee *why* I would be successful *there*, which I think was the most important part."

Most students have at least one easy call. It is usually the second recommender that poses the harder choice.

In deciding whom to choose, look for the person who will add some breadth to your application—who can say things about you that your other recommender can't or won't.

When I was choosing my two teacher recommendations, I asked my junior year American literature teacher, who I knew could speak to my academic capabilities, my writing ability, and my participation in life outside the classroom. For my second recommendation, I went to my sophomore year biology teacher, who was also my senior year AP Bio II (anatomy and physiology) teacher—the person who taught what was widely perceived to be the most difficult science course offered at my high school. I chose him because I was going to be premed, and having chosen an English teacher for my first recommendation, I wanted to highlight a different side of my academic capabilities. I knew that the voice and style of their recommendations would be very different, and I thought that would be valuable.

Although I was the editor in chief of my high school newspaper, which had for years won national awards from the Columbia Scholastic Press Association, I did not choose to get a recommendation from the adviser of the newspaper, because I had not had her as a teacher. I'm sure she would have written me a great recommendation, but when your prospective colleges ask for *academic* recommendations, they mean recommendations from teachers that address your academic credentials first and foremost. Anything your recommenders can then say about your extracurricular involvement is great—but they must first touch all the academic bases for you.

When asking for recommendations, after you've chosen your first-choice targets, approach your teachers *in early September of your senior year,* after school or during a free period. Tell them which colleges are on your application list and ask them, politely, whether they feel that they can write you a *strong* recommendation to those schools.

"When you ask a teacher to write a recommendation, don't just ask if they can write a recommendation on your behalf," Chase adds. "Ask them if they feel comfortable writing an *exceptional* letter about you. If they can't, just thank them and move on until you find someone who can. You need your letters to differentiate you from other applicants and you cannot waste even a single one of these opportunities."

If your chosen recommenders agree to write enthusiastic letters, immediately schedule a second appointment with each of them. Bring along a copy of your updated résumé and your transcript, and discuss your course load and the specifics of your extracurricular involvement to allow your teachers to get a real sense of who you are and what you do outside their classroom. When the meeting is over, leave copies of your résumé and your transcript with your teachers so that they can refer to them when it comes time to write your recommendations. Doing this is likely to give your recommendations more flavor and more weightiness compared to those from students who don't take this affirmative step.

Remember, it's all about the little things. The points of distinction in the admissions game are so narrow these days, you must do *everything* you can to make your application a little bit sharper and more in focus than everyone else's.

Provide your recommenders with a copy of each of your recommendation forms, with a stamped, addressed envelope clipped to each one. On the inside flap of each envelope, write your last name, the name of the school, and the date the recommendation should be mailed in order to get it to the school in plenty of time for your early action, early decision, or regular decision application deadlines. This little hint will help ward off the inadvertent mailing of the wrong form to the wrong school or the wrong student's recommendation to the right school, or having a teacher forget that you were applying early.

Finally, as your application deadlines approach, politely remind your teachers about when your recommendations are due. When the forms have been mailed and received by your colleges, be sure to write a little thank-you note to your recommending teachers. Contrary to what many students seem to think, writing college recommendations is not part of the teacher's job description. It is an extra effort and a favor that is deserving of your recognition and thanks.

The Guidance Counselor or College Counselor Recommendation

Nearly every college or university requires a guidance counselor or college counselor recommendation. This form asks the counselor to speak to the comparative difficulty of your course load relative to those of the other students in your class, to speak to the substance behind your GPA, to provide your unweighted and weighted class rank, to describe any trends on your transcript and possible reasons for those trends, and, finally, to provide a statement comparing you to your high school classmates.

The guidance counselor or college counselor recommendation provides another golden opportunity for you to distinguish yourself from your fellow applicants. Many students don't know their counselors well and won't make the time to get to know them. These students' recommendations will be "flat" assessments of their high school record, without any illumination of their other activities and contributions or who they are as people.

In other words, they are an opportunity lost.

For you, this will be a chance to get another leg up on the competition.

If you've followed our suggestions earlier in the book, you will have already met with your college counselor twice: once last spring as a junior—to introduce yourself, get to know the counselor and help him or her get to know you, and share preliminary thoughts about where you intended to apply to college—and again first thing in the fall of your senior year to firm up your application list. This time, though, you will be scheduling a substantive "get to know you" appointment, and this appointment will take the same form as the one we encouraged you to have with the teachers you are asking to write recommendations. Bring a copy of your résumé and your transcript, and "teach" your counselor about who you are and where you are going. Breathe some life into your numbers and scores. Help your counselor give you a three-dimensional recommendation. Be respectful; display passion and enthusiasm for who you are, what you are doing, and where you hope to be going; and *make* the counselor want to help you on your path.

At the end of the appointment, provide your counselor with the counselor recommendation forms for each of your colleges, with a stamped, addressed envelope clipped to each one. On the inside flap of each envelope, write your last name, the name of the school, and the date the recommendation should be mailed in order to get it to the school in plenty of time for your early action, early decision, or regular decision application deadlines.

Finally, be sure to thank the counselor for his or her time and help.

The "Extra" Recommendation

Most colleges and universities either ask you specifically or allow you, at your option, to submit an additional recommendation. Usually the college will suggest that this recommendation be from a coach, an employer, or the head of an extracurricular activity in which you are heavily involved. As you have probably guessed, there is no such thing as an optional recommendation. If the school allows you to submit one, take advantage of the opportunity.

In looking for the right person to submit this recommendation on your behalf, take stock of whom you have already chosen to recommend you and what they are likely to address. If you have two heavily academic recommendations but have worked for years as a counselor at a summer camp, a recommendation from the director of the camp about your creativity, your personality, and your ability to interact with peers, children, and parents might be just the trick to illuminate other aspects of who you are. If you have written an essay about a particularly meaningful experience, perhaps there is a tie-in to be found in a recommendation from someone who witnessed or participated in the experience or who works for the organization or group in which the experience took place.

Remember, you are looking for ways to make your application "hang together" in a meaningful, cohesive way. You want the story of who you are to be an all-encompassing, illuminating, inspiring, and consistent one. You should therefore look for ways to tie things together and, to the extent you can, have something in your application that can speak to all the meaningful experiences you've had.

If you've volunteered for years at a homeless shelter, worked construction on the same crew for a couple of summers, tutored or mentored younger kids in an after-school program, or led your varsity team out of the doldrums to a season worthy of Hollywood, look to someone involved with those experiences for your additional recommender. Remember—you're seeking to light up some new squares and add breadth with this one.

Submitting Additional Materials

Here, however, is where you draw the line.

Although we have implored you, at every step of the process, to submit every "optional" piece of information colleges and universities will accept—what we have not done, and will *not* do, is encourage you to submit *anything* that your prospective colleges and universities have *not* asked you to submit.

Unless your college states otherwise, this means that the DVD of your dance recital, the book you had published as a high school freshman, the CD of your rock band (even if you have a record deal and opened for the Stones), or the most recent copy of the literary magazine for which you are the editor in chief are *out*.

It means that the additional academic recommendation you want to submit because you "just can't decide" which of your three favorite teachers to choose to recommend you for your top-choice schools is *out*.

It means that the videotape of you bicycle-kicking the winning goal into the top corner of the net to win the state soccer championship and of your follow-up interview on ESPN is *out*.

Most important of all, and please hear us clearly about this, it means any gimmickry, whether humorous, serious, or ridiculous, is *out*. Rest assured, it has all been tried before. Admissions officer after admissions officer tells us with rolling eyes and exasperated groans that the videotape of your senator standing with you and endorsing your candidacy for admission to college, your application arriving in the admissions office accompanied by a mariachi band or a town crier, or your application arriving in the admissions office rolled up in a shoe with a reference to your now having your "foot in the door" won't do a thing to help you. It will not make your application stand out. Even if it is funny (and remember, this is always a subjective assessment), it will almost always suggest to the admissions office that you don't think your application can stand on its own merits.

Don't do it.

The chances of your making an ass of yourself and damaging your chances of admission are much higher than the chances of your coming up with the first-ever gimmick that helped an applicant get in.

Does this mean that you should *never* submit any unsolicited materials as part of your application?

No, it doesn't. What it means is that you need to be extraordinarily careful about submitting anything extra.

If, for example, your grades in sophomore year tanked because your father was dying of cancer and you opted to spend most of your time with him rather than studying trigonometry, that might warrant a *brief* additional explanatory statement. So too if you were expelled from school or subjected to disciplinary sanctions—and wish to explain the circumstances.

Other than that, though, we recommend sending nothing additional to the admissions committee.

If you are torn by this advice and really feel that something compact that could easily fit into your file, such as your award-winning photograph, your short story that got published in the *New Yorker,* or a print of a painting of yours that is hanging in the Met warrants inclusion, we advise you to *call* the admissions office, get an admissions officer on the phone, and ask her whether she would like you to send it along. If your additional material is special enough, a school or two may invite you to send it in. The vast majority, however, will politely decline a copy of your school newspaper with your feature story in it, the video of your solo from the school Christmas concert, or a sample of the artistic Tibetan wool hats you knit.

These people have to read thousands of files every year, and nearly every applicant has something he or she could send along.

Have some mercy.

WHEN EVERYTHING IS READY TO GO

When your application materials are complete, error free, and as polished as you can make them, put your name and Social Security number in the upper right-hand corner of every page of your application materials to ensure that if the pages of your materials ever become separated, they can be easily reunited. If you are using the Common Application and intend to apply online, be sure you have saved all your materials under a file name that clearly identifies them as the final version, and upload your materials pursuant to the online directions.

If you are applying on paper, send your materials by some mechanism that allows you to track their receipt (registered or certified mail or next-day services all do this). Once you've been notified that your materials have been received, wait a few days and then call the admissions office to ensure that it considers your application materials, including all recommendations and financial aid documents, to be complete.

When you get the all-clear on this, rest easy.
Now the waiting begins.

An Investment in Your Future

Funding Your Undergraduate Education Through Loans, Grants, and Scholarships

*If you would know the value of money,
go and try to borrow some.*

Benjamin Franklin

In 2006, the *average* annual cost of attending a four-year private college or university (tuition plus room and board) was approximately $24,000 per year, or just shy of $100,000 for the complete four-year experience. Of course, that's just the average. The annual cost at some of the most selective schools in the country is nearing $50,000 per year. The news is somewhat better at the average four-year public university, whose annual cost tops out at around $12,000 per year.

Because you probably don't ordinarily go out and blow a hundred grand on a whim, you are going to need to take some time to figure out how exactly it is that you plan to pay for college. A proper treatment of this subject could consume an entire book by itself (and there are many good ones available to you), so we won't try to reinvent the wheel here. What we're going to do in the next few pages is simply give you a view of the financial aid landscape, explain in clear language the different sources of financial aid to you, and then direct you and your parents to the necessary resources to take care of the financial aid component of your application in a timely and effective fashion.

Sound good?

Let's begin.

SOURCES OF FUNDING

The good news is that there are a number of sources of funds available for college students. Absent a personal fortune or a benevolent relative, your funds for tuition and expenses will likely come in the form of a combination of loans, grants, and scholarships. In 2006, well more than half of all students applying to college received some form of financial assistance, with the average student saving as much as 40 percent on tuition and fees. The average aid award given by each college and university is typically available for review on the college's Web site or in their application materials. As you compile the list of schools to which you intend to apply, you should gather this data for your parents so they will have some idea of what the cost burden of attending each school is likely to be.

In general, financial aid can be divided into three categories: (1) gift aid; (2) student loans; and (3) work-study programs. Gift aid, such as grants and scholarships, is clearly the best type of financial aid to receive, for as the name suggests, it is a "gift" from the source, which does not require you to pay it back. Student loans, which come in several forms, *do* require you to pay the money back, but can generally be deferred until you complete your education and actually start earning money, offer favorable interest rates, and are widely available such that almost anyone with a decent credit rating can qualify to borrow money under these programs. Finally, work-study programs provide you with jobs on campus (such as washing dishes in a dining hall or manning the help desk at the library) for an average of ten to fifteen hours per week. Depending on the school, the income the student earns from the work-study job is either directly credited against the student's tuition bill or simply given to the student in the form of a paycheck. (The student is expected to use the funds to pay for college-related expenses.)

The best specific sources of information about securing funds for college are the financial aid offices of the individual schools to which you are applying. Each school will have a different relationship with the federal government loan programs; they also have different scholarship capacities depending on the size of their endowment and how they choose to allocate funds from it. Contact the financial aid office of each school as soon as you have decided to apply. Most schools will require you to complete their own financial aid data forms as well as the boilerplate federal forms. The earlier your financial aid file at a school is complete, the earlier the school can act on your application and the more money the school will have remaining available in scholarships and grants.

Do not procrastinate!! In this case especially, time is money.

Before we look at the different sources of financial aid in greater detail, we need to talk about some of the forms you'll have to complete.

FAFSA, THE CSS PROFILE, AND OTHER FORMS

The U.S. Department of Education has created the Free Application for Federal Student Aid (FAFSA) to determine individuals' eligibility for the various federal student assistance programs. Each year, the FAFSA form is made publicly available in November or December. You can obtain a paper version of the FAFSA application from school financial aid offices, or you can download it from the government Web site (www.fafsa.ed.gov). FAFSA Express software, which allows you to transmit the application electronically, is also available. The FAFSA can be submitted any time after January 1 of the year that you intend to begin school. Send it in as soon as possible for priority consideration.

Many private colleges and universities will also require you to complete the "CSS Profile," a form from the College Scholarship Service, an offshoot of the College Board, the nice folks who bring you the SATs. This form, which you can access online at http://profileonline.collegeboard.com, provides schools additional information not available on the FAFSA; these colleges use the CSS Profile to make decisions about the award of aid from their own funds. If your parents own a business or a farm, they may have to complete a business/farm supplement, and if your parents are divorced or separated, your noncustodial parent will also be required to fill out a Divorced/Separated Parents Form as a supplement to your CSS Profile.

In addition to all *those* forms, some colleges and universities will then require you to fill out yet another application specific to that institution. Usually your filing a FAFSA or a CSS Profile with a school will trigger them to send you this form, but in the bureaucratic crush of admissions season, oversights can and do occur, so it is advisable to phone the financial aid office of each college to which you are applying to ensure that you have all the necessary paperwork to complete your financial aid application.

Plan to file your personal income tax return early in the year you apply to schools in order to make filling out your FAFSA easier, as you will need your total income figures to calculate your Expected Family Contribution (EFC) on the FAFSA form. The EFC is the amount of money an individual and his or her family are "expected" to be able to contribute to the individual's education in a given year. This figure is calculated even if your parents have no intention of contributing *anything* to your tuition. Schools typically expect a contribution of 35 percent of a student's assets toward tuition and room and board, but only an average of around 6 percent of parents' total assets. Accordingly, as you approach college age, it is generally to your benefit to minimize the assets held in your name, because doing so will reduce your EFC and could increase the amount of financial aid for which you will qualify. Your parents should schedule a meeting with their accountant to determine the best strategy to employ to maximize your chances of receiving financial aid.

Most state schools use the "federal methodology" in determining an individual's eligibility for financial aid. This method bases its estimate of your EFC, and ultimately the amount of reduced-interest aid you qualify for, on your statement of personal income, assets, and financial liabilities. Private universities, by contrast, also use the "institutional methodology" to evaluate financial aid eligibility for funds under the school's direct control (unsubsidized loans, grants, and scholarships). Be prepared to complete additional profile forms if you are applying to private colleges and universities.

Many students mistakenly assume that if their parents are not going to be contributing to their tuition, they do not need to fill out these additional profile forms. This is incorrect! Failing to complete *all* financial aid forms sent to you will result in your financial aid application's remaining incomplete and your being disqualified from receiving any aid award.

FEDERAL PROGRAMS: GRANTS

Grants are renewable, need-based awards provided by the federal government that do not need to be paid back. The most well known federal grants are the Pell Grant and the Federal Supplemental Educational Opportunity Grant (FSEOG). Let's take a look at these.

Pell Grant

The Pell Grant is the primary source of need-based financial aid from the federal government and is awarded only to undergraduate students. The maximum annual Pell Grant award for full-time undergraduate students in 2005 was $4,050. Distribution of Pell Grant funding is made directly to colleges, which then inform students how much money each of them will be receiving in his or her financial aid package. The grants are made annually and are renewable each year, based on need. Because these grants do not need to be paid back, they are highly desirable and can dramatically reduce your debt load.

Federal Supplemental Educational Opportunity Grant (FSEOG)

Funding for FSEOGs also comes from the federal government, but is more limited, and is therefore distributed to participating colleges and universities based on school-specific formulas. Participating schools then distribute FSEOG funds to their students in annual grants of up to $4,000. As with Pell Grants, these grants are made annually, are renewable each year based on need, and do not need to be repaid.

FEDERAL PROGRAMS: LOANS

There are a number of federal loan programs that merit your attention, including Stafford Loans and Federal Direct Student Loans, Perkins Loans, and PLUS Loans. We address each of these loan programs below.

Stafford Loans and Federal Direct Student Loans

There are two types of Stafford Loans: subsidized (need based) and unsubsidized (not need based). For subsidized loans, you are charged no interest until you begin repayment after graduation and any deferment periods. In other words, the federal government "subsidizes" your loan during this period. For unsubsidized loans, you are charged interest from the moment the loan is disbursed until the time it is paid in full. If you allow interest to accrue while you are in school, any unpaid interest gets capitalized (rolled in) to the principal amount of your loan. The amounts you can borrow depend on what year of college you are in, and whether you are a "dependent" or an "independent" undergraduate student, as shown in the following list.

	Dependent Undergraduates	Independent Undergraduates
Maximum amount you can borrow:		
Freshman year	$2,625	$6,625, no more than $2,625 subsidized
Sophomore year	$3,500	$7,500, no more than $3,500 subsidized
Junior year and Senior year	$5,500	$10,500, no more than $5,500 subsidized
Maximum Stafford Loan total (subsidized and unsubsidized)	$23,000	$46,000, no more than $23,000 subsidized

The Federal Direct Student Loan program mirrors the Stafford Loan program. The difference between the two is that funding for Federal Direct Student Loans is provided directly by the federal government, whereas Stafford Loans are administered by private lenders. Most colleges and universities use one or the other.

Perkins Loans

The Perkins Loan is offered by participating colleges and universities and, like the subsidized Stafford Loan, is based on need. School financial aid offices use the FAFSA to evaluate student eligibility for the Perkins Loan. Currently the interest rate on the Perkins Loan is 5 percent, and all interest is paid by the government during the period of your education. Repayment obligations begin nine months after graduation and are typically spread out over ten years.

The maximum annual distribution for undergraduates under a Perkins Loan is $4,000, and the maximum aggregate distribution is $20,000. When repayment obligations begin, students are responsible for paying the school back, as it is the school that is acting as the lender (with funds contributed by the U.S. government).

PLUS Loans

PLUS Loans are unsubsidized loans made to your parents to help them pay the costs of dependent undergraduates. Parents typically apply for PLUS loans after your financial aid package is in place so as to allow time to determine whether the loan is necessary, and if so, in what amount. Qualification for PLUS loans requires a creditworthy borrower, and the maximum amount of the loan is determined by the costs of all dependents in college minus any financial aid awards received. Interest rates on PLUS loans are adjusted annually, but are capped at 9 percent. Applications for PLUS loans are available from your college or university's financial aid office or from private lenders.

To learn more about federal loan programs and for the most up-to-date information on rates and program changes, research these programs on the Web at www.studentaid.ed.gov, or call the Federal Student Aid Information Center toll free at (800) 4-FED-AID (1-800-433-3243). You can also use this number to check on whether your FAFSA has been received and processed by the federal government.

THE FEDERAL WORK-STUDY PROGRAM

The Federal Work-Study Program arranges employment for students who need additional funding to bridge gaps in financing their education. Awards are granted based on need, and the total amount of an award is determined by several factors, including (1) when a student applies for the program, (2) the student's level of need, and (3) the funding provided by the student's school.

Once an award is made, a work schedule is determined based on each individual student's total financial aid package, class schedule, and academic progress, and students are guaranteed at least minimum wage and often higher, depending on their skill sets and experience. Schools pay the student directly and must do so at least once a month, or, if authorized to do so by the student, can credit a bank loan or any institutional charges, such as tuition, room and board, and other fees.

STATE PROGRAMS: GRANTS AND LOANS

Every state administers a grant and loan program. To be eligible for these grants and loans, a student must typically be a resident of the state, and is often also required to attend an in-state school. Although most state grants are need based, some are merit based. The types of state loans available to help you fund your education vary from state to state. To research the grants and loans available in your state, check out your state's higher education Web site. You can find your state office's URL and phone number in the table here.

State	Department of Education Web Site	Telephone
Alabama	www.ache.state.al.us	(334) 242-1998
Alaska	www.state.ak.us/acpe	(907) 465-2962
Arizona	www.acpe.asu.edu	(602) 229-2435
Arkansas	www.arkansashighered.com	(501) 371-2050
California	www.csac.ca.gov	(888) CA-GRANT
Colorado	www.cslp.org	(303) 305-3000
Connecticut	www.ctdhe.org	(860) 947-1800
Delaware	www.doe.state.de.us/high-ed/scholarships.htm	(302) 577-3240
District of Columbia	http://seo.dcgov	(202) 727-6436
Florida	www.fldoe.org	(800) 366-3475
Georgia	www.gsfc.org	(770) 724-9000
Hawaii	http://doe.k12.hi.us	(808) 956-8213
Idaho	www.idahoboardofed.org/scholarships.asp	(208) 334-2270
Illinois	www.isac-online.org	(847) 948-8500
Indiana	www.in.gov/ssacli	(317) 232-2350
Iowa	www.iowacollegeaid.org	(515) 242-3344
Kansas	www.kansasboardofregents.org	(785) 296-3518
Kentucky	www.kheaa.com	(502) 696-7393
Louisiana	www.osfa.state.la.us	(225) 922-1012
Maine	www.famemaine.com	(207) 626-3263
Maryland	www.mhec.state.md.us	(410) 260-4565

State	Department of Education Web Site	Telephone
Massachusetts	www.osfa.mass.edu	(617) 727-9420
Michigan	www.michigan.gov/mistudentaid	(517) 373-3394
Minnesota	www.mheso.state.mn.us	(651) 642-0567
Mississippi	www.ihl.state.ms.us/financialaid/default.asp	(601) 432-6997
Missouri	www.mocbhe.gov	(573) 751-2361
Montana	www.mgslp.state.mt.us	(800) 537-7508
Nebraska	www.ccpe.state.ne.us	(402) 471-2847
Nevada	www.nde.state.nv.us	(775) 687-9200
New Hampshire	www.state.nh.us/postsecondary/fin.html	(603) 271-2555
New Jersey	www.hesaa.org	(800) 792-8670
New Mexico	www.nmche.org/collegefinance/stateaid.html	(505) 476-6500
New York	www.hesc.com	(518) 473-1574
North Carolina	www.ncseaa.edu	(919) 549-8614
North Dakota	www.ndus.education/student_info/financial_aid/default.asp	(701) 328-2960
Ohio	www.regents.state.oh.us/sgs	(614) 466-7420
Oklahoma	www.okhighered.org	(405) 524-9100
Oregon	www.osac.state.or.us	(541) 687-7400
Pennsylvania	www.pheaa.org	(800) 692-7392
Rhode Island	www.riheaa.org	(401) 736-1100
South Carolina	www.che400.state.sc.us	(803) 737-2260
South Dakota	www.ris.sdbor.edu	(605) 773-3455
Tennessee	www.state.tn.us/tsac	(615) 741-1346
Texas	www.thecb.state.tx.us	(512) 427-6340
Utah	www.utahsbr.edu	(801) 321-7101
Vermont	www.vsac.org	(802) 655-9602
Virginia	www.schev.edu	(804) 225-2600
Washington	www.hecb.wa.gov	(360) 753-7800
West Virginia	www.hepc.wvnet.edu	(304) 558-2101
Wisconsin	http://heab.state.wi.us	(608) 267-2206
Wyoming	www.k12.wy.us	(307) 777-7763

LOAN FORGIVENESS PROGRAMS

There are a limited number of opportunities for you to have some or all of your government loans "forgiven" after you graduate. To qualify, you must typically spend at least a year working for a qualifying organization and meet all of the criteria specified by the program. For example, students who enter the military, the Peace Corps, or Americorps; students who become full-time teachers in traditionally underserved areas; or students who become nurses may be eligible for various loan forgiveness arrangements.

Although the benefits provided by these programs are significant, they also require a significant commitment of your time. Because your interests can change so radically during your college years, enrolling in one of these programs offering loan forgiveness after you graduate should not become part of your precollege financial aid strategy. Instead, you should view any loan forgiveness program as a "bonus" should you still desire to participate in an experience after college that offers one.

"For my second undergrad degree and grad school at Penn, I received a National Health Services Corps Scholarship," Zoe explains. "They paid for a lot of school while I was there and in return I owed them two years of work as a primary care provider in an underserved area of the United States after graduation. This was a risky proposition because the NHSC can send you anywhere, but it worked out well for me and I landed a great job in exactly the corner of the country where my husband and I wanted to be."

For more information on loan forgiveness programs, check out www.studentaid. ed.gov.

GRANTS AND SCHOLARSHIPS

Private grants and scholarships, whether need based or merit based, are also offered by a host of institutions, organizations, corporations, and private foundations. Spend some time in your high school guidance or college counseling office and be sure to apply for as many scholarships as you can. When you have exhausted the local offerings, surf the Web or research in your school or local library to identify additional sources.

"My strategy was to apply for everything possible," Zoe recalls. "I received a National Merit Scholarship and a few thousand dollars in local scholarships. Although many of these were only for a few hundred dollars each, most were also renewable year-to-year. I also received a grant to cover a summertime volunteer internship through the Sevringhaus Foundation and a Barnett-Miller research grant that paid for my three-week thesis research trip to Cuba."

"During my freshman year, I saw a flier advertising a 'balanced man' scholarship paid for by a campus fraternity," Chase added. "The application consisted of a set of essays and a couple of interviews, all of which were very low stress. I received $1,500 in financial aid from this after spending only a handful of hours filling in the application. Obviously, that was time well spent, as every dollar counts when it comes to reducing debt. There are lots of opportunities around—the key is being active in seeking them!"

Treat this search like a part-time job, because you'll be literally *amazed* at how many scholarships there are available to you and how many of them *don't get awarded because there were no applicants!* One free source of such information, which claims to have a database of more than ten thousand grants and scholarships in all areas of academia, is on the Web at www.absolutelyscholarships.com.

PRIVATE LOANS

Private loans are personal loans from a bank or private lending institution. Of all the ways to finance your college education, private loans are the most expensive, as they generally carry much higher interest rates and will come with a number of extra charges and insurance fees. Just as with unsubsidized federal loans, interest on private loans accrues during school.

If you must take out a private loan to bridge a financial gap between your expenses and your aid package, do everything you can to reduce the overall cost of these loans by shopping around extensively to find and secure the lowest possible interest rate. Having a cosigner on the loan or securing the loan with personal assets will reduce the bank's risk and may persuade a bank to lower its interest rate for you. If your family maintains a special relationship with a particular bank, that bank may be willing to give you a special rate. You will have to, and should, negotiate these points with a bank to determine the degree of flexibility they have with their rates. The overall cost to you of even a quarter of a point on an interest rate can be extremely significant over time, so make the effort to shop around and bargain hard for the best deal you can find.

When you begin your negotiation with a bank regarding a personal loan, there are a number of variables to consider, all or many of which can be bargaining chips in that negotiation. In addition, information or concessions you receive at one bank can and should be used to negotiate with the others. Be sure to determine and negotiate the following:

- The interest rate and how it is determined
- Whether the interest rate is variable or fixed, and whether the rate is capped
- Whether the loan can be paid off early without penalty
- What the term of the loan is (how long you have to pay it off)
- Whether the loan has origination fees, and whether these can be waived
- Whether the bank requires a cosigner and whether having one can reduce your interest rate due to the decreased risk to the bank
- Whether the loan needs to be secured with collateral and whether doing so would reduce your interest rate
- Whether interest on the loan is tax deductible

Once again, making an appointment with a tax planner or a financial adviser can bring benefits here. There may be tax advantages to structuring loans in certain ways or to taking certain types of loans, depending on your personal circumstances. Taking advantage of these tax breaks can bring significant savings over time, so don't blow this off.

"GAMING" YOUR AID PACKAGES

In the crush of the admissions season, financial aid offices are literally inundated with paper, and despite everyone's best efforts, things do occasionally get lost or misfiled. Even if you think you have filed all the necessary paperwork with the schools on your list, it is always a good idea to call each school's financial aid office and confirm that it considers your financial aid application complete.

Once you have done this, you must simply sit back and wait for the news to arrive.

When you begin to hear back from schools, do not be surprised if you receive a wide array of disparate aid packages. Each school has different methods of determining eligibility and different grant and scholarship capacities. Use the best of the financial aid packages you received as leverage with the schools that have given you less desirable packages. Don't be obnoxious, but do call the financial aid office and speak to the financial aid officer in charge of your file, or have your parents make the call for you. Explain your situation, express your preference to attend that school over the school that offered you the better aid package, and *politely* ask if there is any way for the office to "reconsider" your aid award. The use of the word "reconsider" is actually important here, because some schools will cite to you a "policy" not to "negotiate" aid awards. Although really nothing more than an issue of semantics, using the proper terminology and offering to fax in competing aid awards or additional information to "help" the financial aid office reevaluate your aid award can, and often does, bring dividends.

The earlier you make this call, the better your chances of convincing a financial aid officer to sweeten your till.

TUITION PAYMENT PLANS

There are nearly as many tuition payment plans as there are colleges that offer them. Some allow you to pay off your tuition in a steady stream of monthly payments, rather than in one or two lump-sum payments. Others allow you to prepay tuition for the year, or even for your entire education, and offer you pricing options, such as locking in the tuition rate at the freshman year price for all four years. How attractive these various options are will depend on the state of the economy at the time you apply to college. As usual, you should gather as much information as you can and then schedule an appointment with your family's accountant, tax adviser, or financial planner to determine which option is best for you.

PAYING IT OFF

Although this chapter is about finding and arranging the funding for your undergraduate education, it is never too early to consider how you plan to pay off your debts after graduation. Outstanding loans can easily begin to influence career decisions. Nobody likes the feeling of lugging around a huge debt burden, and the temptation to pay it off as soon as possible may cause you to change or adjust your career goals.

"I knew that college was extremely important," Erik recalls. "I also knew that my parents didn't have the money to send me to an expensive four-year private college. I decided that, whatever the cost, and however long I was destined to be in debt to repay the cost of attending a top institution, that it was a sound investment in my future and that I was willing to undertake that daunting commitment."

"I had no strategy whatsoever, and that came back to bite me," Amanda added. "I thought my parents would be able to pay for the whole four years, but that didn't work out. I took the fall semester of my sophomore year off and got financial aid the rest of my time in college—mostly loans and work-study, very little in the way of grants. I did not look very hard for additional funds, which was a mistake, but I got a job as a Resident Adviser my senior year, which was a great job with very good benefits."

Once you are in the middle of the experience, you may find yourself drifting away from your original career goals and being drawn toward more high paying jobs. These feelings may be related to a genuine change in career objectives, but many times, the change is actually motivated by money and a desire to pay off your debt burden as fast as possible in order to "get on with life."

Although debt is uncomfortable, it is preferable to selling yourself out and settling for a life other than the one you designed for yourself. Determine whether a temporary detour for a several-year tour of duty at a high-paying job in a consulting firm or an investment bank in the name of debt relief will still allow you to find your way back to your chosen career path. If you conclude that it will, set some clear financial goals, force yourself to save money and reduce your debt, and plan your exit strategy and route back to your goal. Many, many graduates find themselves seduced by high dollar offers, get hooked on the lifestyle associated with these high-stress, high-paying jobs, and never actually make it back to the original plan they had for their lives. These are the people who then end up on the therapist's couch suffering from a midlife crisis.

Sure, some people find satisfaction and happiness in this change of plans. Many others, however, simply become victims of inertia and don't recognize the abandonment of their professional goals and dreams until everything comes apart in midlife. Don't let a temporary debt burden frighten you into making bad decisions that will have a long-term negative impact on your life.

"I owed a lot of money when I graduated," Erik said. "And I didn't find a real job for more than a year after I graduated. But given how most student loans are structured with low rates and deferment options, I was mentally prepared that I was going to be spending the next four to eight years paying off these loans, and that is ultimately what happened. My debts did not have any impact on my life or what career I was choosing given the prospect of spreading out payments over a very long period of time."

Tom agreed.

"I don't think you should let the prospect of debt influence your career and life choices. Find your passion. When you do that, you'll always be able to find a way to make a living."

Jim, though, had a different take.

"Having no debt meant that I could work and travel without financial concerns. This has allowed me to teach high school, which is something I really wanted to do. Had I had loans to pay back, I probably would have had to stay with a job I did not like for far longer."

ADDITIONAL RESOURCES

Web Sites

www.ed.gov (information on Stafford Loans, PLUS Loans, and FSEOGs)

www.pellgrantsonline.ed.gov (information on Pell Grants)

www.studentaid.ed.gov (information on Perkins Loans and Federal Direct Student Loan programs)

www.finaid.com (financial aid calculators)

www.collegeboard.com (home page of the College Board; provides overview of financial aid, cost calculators, search engine for loan programs and scholarships, and CSS Profile forms)

www.absolutelyscholarships.com (offers a searchable database of ten thousand scholarships)

www.collegescholarships.com (scholarship search engine)

www.fastweb.com (scholarship search engine)

www.scholarships.com (scholarship search engine)

www.wiredscholar.com (comprehensive financial aid Web site)

Books

Greene, Howard R., and Matthew W. Greene. *Paying for College.* New York: St. Martin's Griffin, 2004 (provides a good overview of the financial aid process)

Anderson, Trent, and Seppi Basili. *Straight Talk on Paying for College.* Chicago: Kaplan, 2003 (provides a good overview of the financial aid process)

Kaplan, Ben. *How to Go to College Almost for Free.* New York: HarperResource, 2002 (a must-read for scholarship searchers)

Tanabe, Gen, and Kelly Tanabe. *1001 Ways to Pay for College.* Los Altos, Calif.: SuperCollege LLC, 2005 (contains an excellent compilation of loan forgiveness programs, organized by state)

Using the "Relevance Calculus" to Choose Your School

*It is in your moments of decision
that your destiny is shaped.*

Anthony Robbins

If all goes well, by the close of application season, you will have secured admission to college. We hope that you'll have several offers to choose from. So it's time for the big question: How do you decide which college or university to attend?

Yeah, yeah . . . we know you have a gut feeling. There was a place you loved the best, where the sun was shining and everyone was smiling, and you just felt like you had arrived—like you were in the "right" place for you.

But then there are the other factors. Such as the fact that other schools offered you more money. Or the fact that the school you felt best about is ranked much lower on the *U.S. News and World Report* rankings list than other schools you got into—and you don't know whether that should be important to you or not. Or the fact that you got into your father's or mother's or uncle's or grandmother's alma mater, and you're worried about offending him or her if you are the first person in four generations not to go to there.

Look—we're big on gut feelings, instincts, and general impressions, as you've probably discerned already. But this is a *huge* decision. *Huge.*

As you've already heard from a number of the mentors, it is not overstating things to point out that where you go to college can play an important role in your life for the rest of your life. The reputation of your college or university will directly affect your chances of getting into graduate school. That reputation, along with the strength of your college or university's alumni network, will also directly affect your ability to open doors and get attention during any job search you undertake, both during the summers while you are in college and especially during the job search you undertake in the years after college. So it is not a decision to be made lightly.

"Okay," you say. "I get it. It's an important decision. So what am I supposed to consider in helping me make the decision?"

Glad you asked.

Obviously, if you've read this far, you've done your homework. You've done your research in Barron's *Profiles of American Colleges,* The Princeton Review's *Complete Book of Colleges,* or the *U.S. News Ultimate College Guide,* as we suggested in Chapter 1. You've visited the campuses and talked to students currently enrolled at the school and asked them the questions we suggested that you ask. You've done your on-campus and alumni interviews, talked to your guidance office, and talked to your friends to get their impressions. In the end, though, you probably find yourself wishing for some objective tool you could use to compare the schools, one against the other, on the factors that matter most to you.

Well guess what? We wished for the same thing.

So now there is one.

CHOOSING A COLLEGE USING THE RELEVANCE CALCULUS

A little later in the chapter, you will find the list of 119 defined factors that make up the Relevance Calculus to help you decide which college to attend. If you've done your homework, collected the necessary materials from each school, and asked the right questions, you should have all the information you need to determine where each school stands with respect to each of these factors. Following the list of factors is the Relevance Calculus chart, which will help you really think about each of the factors and its importance to you and to your decision.

Here's how it works.

First, because there are so many different factors that go into choosing a college or university, we have broken the Relevance Calculus down into six primary categories: (1) Academics, (2) Students, (3) Campus Life, (4) Campus Facilities and Infrastructure, (5) Geography, and (6) Financial Aid. Read the descriptions of these six primary categories in the box that follows, and assign each of these categories a "Category Importance Score" from 0 to 2 in the space provided. Give the category a 0 if it is of little or no importance to you, a 1 if it is somewhat important to you, and a 2 if it is very important to you. Be sure that once you assign a category a Category Importance Score, you use the same score for that category across all colleges and universities that you are considering and comparing.

DESCRIPTIONS OF THE PRIMARY CATEGORIES

Academics

The Academics category includes such factors as the quality and scope of your college or university's course catalogue offerings, the reputation and quality of the professors who teach there, and the flexibility with which the various departments allow students to pursue their interests.

    Category Importance Score assigned: ____

Students

The Students category aims at examining and measuring your reaction to the people with whom you would be sharing the college experience over the next four years at a given school. Covered in this category are such factors as your perceptions about the level of students' academic curiosity, your perceptions about what aspects of the college experience are most heavily emphasized by these students, and your perceived "fit" with the people you met.

    Category Importance Score assigned: ____

Campus Life

The Campus Life category measures the quality of life on the college's campus, the variety of the social and extracurricular offerings, and the approach that students at the school take to college life.

    Category Importance Score assigned: ____

Campus Facilities and Infrastructure

The Campus Facilities and Infrastructure category examines the bricks-and-mortar facilities that the college offers, including housing and dining options, exercise facilities, health clinics, and security.

    Category Importance Score assigned: ____

(continued)

Geography

The Geography category examines the campus's relationship to the world—what city or community it is located in, what the climate is like, the availability and proximity of natural and manmade attractions, and the ease of travel to and from campus.

Category Importance Score assigned: ____

Financial Aid

Simply put, how generous is the school with its financial aid program? What percentage of last year's incoming class received some form of financial aid, and what was the average and median award of aid per student?

Category Importance Score assigned: ____

Now that you've scored the meta-categories, its time to delve into the factors within each one. But before we do that, let's look at how you're going to use this information, so that you'll have some advance notice about how to organize this activity in your own mind.

First, read the descriptions of the various factors listed in the pages that follow, and assign each of them a Factor Importance Score, just as you did with the primary categories. As before, give a factor a score of 0 if it is of little or no importance to you, a 1 if it is somewhat important to you, and a 2 if it is very important to you.

Also as before, be sure that once you have assigned a factor a Factor Importance Score, you give it the same score across all the schools you are considering.

Note that we have left several blank spaces in the chart under each meta-category in case you want to write in extra factors that matter to you.

From there, you will assign each of the colleges you are considering a score from 1 to 5 for each of the factors discussed. For example, for the "housing options" factor under the Campus Facilities and Infrastructure category, give a school a factor score of 1 if its housing options are truly lousy, a 2 if they are below average compared to what you have seen, a 3 if they are average, a 4 if they are above average, and a 5 if they are outstanding.

Once you have completed this evaluation for all the factors in all six of the categories, you will need to do some basic math to get the scores for each school. Don't worry—this isn't rocket science. Follow along with this example.

Assume that you have deemed the meta-category Campus Facilities and Infrastructure to be very important to you. You have therefore assigned that entire category a 2, meaning that every factor within that category will eventually be multiplied by 2. Now assume that within that category, you are considering "housing options," and because the quality of on-campus accommodations is also very important to you, you have assigned that particular factor a Factor Importance Score of 2. Now assume you are comparing two different colleges, UCLA and UC Berkeley, on this very important factor within this very important meta-category. Let's say that you found the housing options at UCLA to be average and the housing options at Berkeley to be above average. You would thus assign UCLA a housing options factor score of 3 and Berkeley a housing options factor score of 4.

Now, pulling it all together, you would multiply your Campus Facilities and Infrastructure Category Importance Score of 2 by your housing options Factor Importance Score of 2 by the scores that you gave each school on that factor. So, continuing with the example, you would have the following result:

Berkeley: 2 x 2 x 4 = 16

UCLA: 2 x 2 x 3 = 12

Thus Berkeley would score 16 points for housing options, and UCLA would score 12 points. Do this for all the factors within each category, and you'll have a handy way to compare one school against the other in terms of the individual factors.

To compare one school against another by total scores, you'll need to do one more step.

Because each meta-category has a different number of factors within it, you need to take the average of the school scores on all the factors within a meta-category so that you won't be giving undue weight to meta-categories with more factors in them.

If your eyes just glazed over, read that paragraph one more time. You just need to get an "Average Factor Score" for each meta-category. Once you have the chart filled out, add up all the numbers in the School Score on Factor column within each meta-category, and divide by the number of factors within that category. Voila! You now have the Average Factor Score for each meta-category.

Add up all six of these, and you have a Final School Score that you can use to rank the various colleges you are considering.

Remember, though, not to let the process trump the substance. It can be very interesting to rank the schools you are considering according to this method. Once you do so, though, dig deeper. Rank the schools again on the individual primary category scores and see how *those* shake out. Looking at different snapshots of this data can really be eye opening and can certainly help break the logjam and assist you in making a decision.

Okay, enough math. On to the description of the various factors in each of the six categories of the Relevance Calculus. Remember to assign each factor a score of "0" (not important), "1" (somewhat important), or "2" (very important).

DESCRIPTION OF FACTORS IN THE RELEVANCE CALCULUS

Meta-Category: Academics

Course Offerings   Number, scope, and variety of courses offered to undergraduates. Opportunity to cross-register for classes in other areas of the university should also be considered. For specifics, consult the school's course selection guide, available online, by mail, or in all admissions offices.

Course Selection Process   How do students choose courses? Is there a lottery? Are classes frequently capped? Do underclassmen have access to upper-level seminars? Is preference for popular courses given to students in the major? Again, consult the school's course selection guide or talk to current students for details on these issues.

Academic Reputation of Faculty   What is the academic reputation of the faculty members at the school you are considering? Consult the most recent *U.S. News and World Report* Annual Rankings of Colleges and Universities for a ranking of the faculty of every American college and university.

Teaching Reputation of Faculty   Regardless of their fame, can the faculty at the schools you are considering actually *teach?* You'll need to dig a little deeper for the answer to this question. Again, talk to current students and pick up a copy of the school's underground guide to professors and courses when you visit the campus—if such a guide is available—to get the skinny on what students at that campus think of their professors. If such a guide is available at a particular school, you'll find it at the campus bookstore.

Political Orientation of Faculty   College professors tend to be fairly liberal as a lot. If you're liberal too, that probably won't be an issue for you. If you are conservative or *really* conservative, however, this can sometimes become a problem if one or more of your professors become hostile to you. Is the faculty at this school known to be especially political?

Workload   What is the minimum and maximum credit load permitted each semester? How many credits does the average student take each semester? Again, each school's course selection guide will answer these questions for you.

Faculty-to-Student Ratio   Simply put, how many full-time faculty members are there compared to the number of students? Be wary of just accepting these numbers at face value, though. Some schools slip adjunct faculty or faculty who are based in the graduate schools into their numbers. What you want is the number of full-time faculty based at the undergraduate college or university, compared to the number of students.

Average Class Size   This is an important derivative of the faculty-to-student ratio. Needless to say, the lower this number is, the better.

Median Class Size   Because averages can be thrown off dramatically by huge survey courses like Psych 101 and Intro Bio, which often have hundreds of students in them, the better number to use is the median class size. To arrive at this figure, the school ranks all the classes offered from smallest to largest and tells you the size of the class in the exact middle of that list.

Availability of Famous Faculty to Undergraduates   Even if a school has celebrities on its faculty, that won't matter much to you unless those famous faculty members actually teach undergraduates. Ask around, or check the school's course selection guide to find out.

Opportunities for Professor Contact   Do professors routinely have coffee, lunch, or dinner with students before or after class? How easy is it to meet and talk with a professor outside of class? Ask current students to find out.

Opportunities for Independent Research   Suppose you find an area of academic interest that really fascinates you, but there isn't a course offered on it. Will the school permit you to register for an independent study with a professor, for credit, to explore it? Is there a cap on how many times you can do this?

Opportunities to Go Abroad   Does the school offer semester or year abroad programs? Are they limited to the junior year, or can you go abroad during other years or during the summers? How varied are the programs? Where are they?

Impression of Classes Visited   If you visited classes on campus, what were your impressions? Were the professors interesting and animated or flat and boring? Did the students seem engaged in the material or bored and asleep? Was this a class that you'd want to attend three times a week?

Number of Majors   What number and variety of majors does the school offer? Read through the course selection guides and compare what is offered at different schools. Just about every school offers a major in economics or political science. It is the rest of what is available that makes for the distinctions here.

Ability to Design Your Own Major   What if you want to double or triple up or, better yet, pick and choose to design your own major? Will your school allow you to do it, with the guidance of a faculty adviser?

Strength of Department in Your Likely Major(s)   Every school is known for strengths in some areas and weaknesses in others. Think about what you are most likely to study. Is the school strong or weak in those areas?

Academic Schedule   Do classes begin in mid-August and end in early May, or begin in mid-September and end in mid-June? Is the school on the semester, trimester, or quarter system, or something even funkier than that?

Mean Grade/Grade Inflation   What is the mean grade at the school? Is there one, or does it vary by majors and departments? Are courses graded on a strict curve imposed by the college or university, or can professors depart from such a recommendation? How prevalent is grade inflation? Remember, this can work for you or against you. If your school has an abnormally tough curve, your grades will appear lower to graduate schools and employers who are not accustomed to seeing candidates from your school. This can work against your interest. You may not be any better served, though, if your school doesn't use grades, uses only written summaries instead of grades, grades every course pass-fail, or is known for rampant grade inflation. Most colleges and universities post a B/B- mean across programs and majors.

Thesis or Senior Project Required?   Other than the twelve to fifteen classes you'll need to take to fulfill your major, what else will you need to do? Is there a senior thesis that you'll need to write? Is there a senior project that you'll need to complete? Is this something you'll look forward to—or dread? Rate accordingly.

Presence of Women and Minorities on Tenured Faculty   Does diversity on the faculty matter to you? If it does, consult the school's Web site, course selection guide, and marketing materials, or call the admissions office to find out the percentage of women and minorities on the faculty. Then ask for the percentage who have *tenure*—as those are the only professors who are virtually certain to be there when you arrive.

Postcollege Placement of Undergraduate Students   Where does most of a school's senior class go after graduation? What percentage go off to law school, med school, and Wall Street? What percentage are employed six months after graduation? What happens to everyone else? Call the college's career planning and placement office to get these figures.

Meta-Category: Students

Collegiality   Simply put, did the students you met seem friendly and collegial with you and each other, or were they cold and aloof? Did you observe a lot of socializing and camaraderie on campus, with students congregated in pairs or groups, or were students generally off on their own?

Personality   Did the students you met and observed seem to be interesting and to have personality, or were they boring, colorless, and lifeless?

Intellectual Excitement   Did the students you met seem intellectually exciting? Did the prospect of spending time around people like this excite you?

Interest and Involvement in Their Studies   Did the people you met seem engaged, involved, and interested in their studies, or were they bored and directionless?

Interest and Involvement in Campus Life   Were the people you met involved in the various goings-on around campus? Were they involved in student government, singing groups, intramural sports, or campus groups? Was there a palpable "buzz" of life on the campus, or did things seem dead?

The Driving Force   What force drives the campus? Is it the intellectualism? The sports teams? The parties? Are students more interested in hooking up or dating than studying? Does the Saturday afternoon football game trump all? Where are people on Sunday afternoons? In the library studying, or in the dorms trying to sleep off their hangovers?

Balance Between Work and Play   What was your sense about the balance of the place? Was the combination of academics, extracurricular involvement, sports, and social activity in proper balance—or was it all out of whack?

Classroom Culture   Were the students in the classes you observed actively engaging the professors, or were the classes you saw note-taking snoozefests?

Prevalence of Drug Culture on Campus   How prevalent is marijuana use in the dorms, in the fraternity and sorority houses, and at parties? What about harder drugs like mushrooms, LSD, crystal meth, Ecstasy, and cocaine? Is there peer pressure to use? Current students are the best resource to ask about this—but if you want an honest answer, you'd better ask the question out of earshot of parents, admissions staff, and other adults.

Prevalence and Importance of Alcohol   What is the campus reality when it comes to alcohol and underage drinking? Yeah, yeah . . . we know what the law is, so that is probably the expressed campus *policy* too. But policy and reality are two different things. What you want to know about is the reality. Has campus policy forced drinking underground such that alcohol drives the entire social scene on campus, forcing freshman to travel like herds of elk in search of it, or is it available enough to just be a normal part of the social scene? Again, consult current students (out of earshot of parents, admissions staff, and other adults) to get the straight dope about this.

Campus Dating Scene   Do students just randomly hook up with each other, is there a serious dating scene on campus, or is the hookup and dating scene driven by the downtown bar scene?

Importance of Fraternities and Sororities to Social Scene   Does the campus Greek system drive campus social life, or is it just one component of it? This is a very important question—especially if you are not into the frat scene—so ask some current students for their views about this.

Importance of Varsity Sports to Campus Social Scene   Does athletics drive the social life on campus, or is it just a component of it? If you are not an athlete and not into sports, will you be comfortable on this campus when the remaining 110,000 undergraduates are packed into the football stadium?

Geographic Diversity   Where is everybody from? Talk to the admissions office to get precise information about this. If you're looking to escape the culture you experienced in high school, don't go somewhere where 90 percent of the student body comes from the same state where you went to high school.

Racial and Ethnic Diversity   Simply put, how diverse is the student body? Remember, some of the most valuable teaching and learning that goes on in college is that which takes place between students. If you're looking for diversity in culture, background, and experience, look for schools with a diverse student body. Again, the admissions office can provide you with this kind of information.

Religious Diversity   Are you looking for a school where religion is a singular and important influence on campus life; where a variety of religions are practiced, and religious groups flourish and welcome those who are searching; or where the influence and impact of religion are largely absent? Current students are your source for information about the influence of religion on campus.

Socioeconomic Diversity   Do you care whether the student body includes individuals from a variety of socioeconomic backgrounds? Unless you want to find yourself in a real-life remake of *Heathers*, check in with the admissions office to find out what percentage of the incoming class qualifies for financial aid and what percentage of the class is on some form of work-study.

Stylistic Diversity   Is the campus stylistically diverse, or does everyone look like they just stepped out of the latest J Crew catalogue? Do you care?

Hours per Week Spent Studying   Talk to a few students (try to get a sample). From those conversations, determine the schedule of the typical undergrad on campus.

Competition for Grades   Are undergraduate courses graded on a strict curve, are professors on their own to determine how to grade their students, or does it vary from department to department and major to major? If you are interested in being premed, pay particular attention to this one, as schools featuring a strict curve in premed classes are likely to harbor some nasty competitive behavior among students in those classes.

Pressure for Postcollege Placement Opportunities   Same deal here. Do premed and prelaw advisers at the school prescreen candidates, discourage underqualified students from applying to med school or law school, or refuse to provide necessary recommendations for students they deem to be underqualified? This is another dirty little secret that some schools don't want you to know about—so ask in advance. Current students and the school's dean's office or career planning and placement office are your sources on this question.

Perceived Social Aptitude of Students (the "Dork Factor")   Do most students seem social and comfortable in a social setting, or did you see a lot of introverts wearing short-sleeved oxfords with pocket protectors? In other words, how high was the "Dork Factor"?

Overall "Fit"   This is your overall gut feeling about how well you would fit in with the student body at this school. First impressions are usually right here.

Meta-Category: Campus Life

Academic Pressure and Workload   What are your perceptions of the negative influence of things like academic pressure, workload, and competition for jobs and graduate school slots on the day-to-day life at the school?

Emphasis on Learning   Did people seem more concerned about learning for learning's sake—or more stressed out about grades and less focused on learning?

Emphasis on Grades   Are grades posted publicly by name? (Yes, believe it or not, some schools actually do this.) Is there a strict curve in all classes or in some departments and majors, or are professors left to their own devices when it comes to grading?

Emphasis on Social Life   Do students tend to congregate after class in the student union, in the quad, on the green, or whatever the gathering place is at the school you are considering? What happens on campus from Thursday night to noon on Sunday? Is there a proper emphasis on social life? Talk to current students or observe for yourself during your campus visit.

Intellectual Excitement   What is the feeling like on campus? Who is coming to speak at the political union or in the campus lecture series in upcoming weeks? What are students talking about as they walk to class with friends—something academic, something going on in the world, or last night's must-see TV? What is your sense about the level of intellectual stimulation on the campus?

Primary Weekend Activities   What generally happens socially on campus on the weekend? Is it the understanding that parties are generally "open"—meaning that they can be attended by any students who happen by—or are parties "by invite only"? Is the Greek system the focus of the social world on the weekends? Is there an on-campus movie series? What about plays, music, or performances by campus singing or comedy groups? How much does this school's social setup on weekends suit you? Talk to current students to find out what really goes on and whether the atmosphere is a welcoming one or not.

Commuting Out on Weekends   Do a lot of students leave campus for the weekend, or is campus the focus of attention? This is another question for current students.

Major Campus Social Events   What are the really big campus social events every year? Is there a homecoming, Parents' Weekend, or Octoberfest celebration? A winter formal or winter carnival? A campus casino night or other themed campuswide party? What is this school known for in terms of its big social events?

Influence of Fraternity and Sorority Life   How major a role does Greek life play in the social fabric of the campus? Do you have to be a member of the Greek system to have a meaningful social life? The best way to get a good answer to this question is to find a couple of students who are *not* in a fraternity or sorority and ask them how happy they are with their social lives and what they do on the weekends. If you get anything other than a really happy response, beware.

Percentage of Student Body That Is "Greek"   This is a simple question for the admissions office. A high percentage here should influence your thinking about the previous question—even if you got a satisfactory answer.

Main Activities of the Fraternities and Sororities   What are the major activities of the fraternities and sororities on this campus? Do they do any community service work? Do they tutor high school kids, work with after-school athletic programs in area schools, act as big brothers and big sisters to local kids—or is Greek life really just about finding a niche socially, getting hammered, and hooking up?

Campus Rules on Pledging, Rushing, Hazing, and Initiation   What's the story on this? Have there been any major negative examples of hazing on campus in the past few years? Are there any clear rules governing rush week and pledge period? Are any fraternities or sororities on probation? Are there any that have been kicked off campus or had their charters suspended or revoked? Why? If you're going to be part of this experience, it pays to know what you're getting yourself into.

Pressures to Drink   How serious is the peer pressure to get hammered every weekend? What else do students on campus do for fun?

Pressures to Experiment with Drugs   Same question with drugs. Is there a serious drug culture on campus? Is there peer pressure to participate?

Campus Policy on Alcohol and Underage Drinking   What is the official campus policy on alcohol and underage drinking? What is the *real* campus policy on alcohol and underage drinking? How does this suit your desires and expectations?

Safety   How safe is the campus? What about the town or city that surrounds it? The admissions office maintains the campus crime report, so ask them to let you see a copy. Has there been any violent crime in the past couple of years? What are the most commonly reported crimes on campus, and how prevalent are they? How common is date rape and the use of date-rape drugs on campus? The campus women's center typically maintains those statistics, so check in there as well. How safe do you feel walking around?

Clubs for Special Interests and Hobbies   Ask the admissions office for a list of officially registered clubs and activities. Is everything you are looking for on it?

Intramural Sports Scene   How active and how competitive is the school's intramural sports program? Is the level of play so competitive that not everyone who wants to play "just for fun" will be welcomed, or is the intramural sports scene more social than athletically competitive?

Residential College System   Is the school set up into a residential college system or residential house system to ease the formation of social groups? You should know all about this from the college's marketing materials.

Special-Interest Housing or Dining Halls   Does the school offer special-interest housing or dining options, such as foreign language houses, substance-free houses, foreign language dining halls or eating clubs, co-ops, kosher kitchens, and the like?

Student Government   How active and influential is the student government? What are the last three important things student government accomplished for the student body? This is a question for the dean's office, the admissions office staff, or a savvy upperclassman.

Campus Political Scene   What is the campus's political orientation like—and how good a fit is that for you? Are the political unions especially active?

Campus Movie Series   Is there an on-campus movie series, or at least an on-campus or nearby movie theater to give you some alternative social options?

Campus Plays   Is there a theater or drama school affiliated with your university? What about plays put on by the campus thespian group? How often do they put on plays? Are auditions open to everyone or restricted to theater majors?

Campus Speaker Series   How frequently do outside speakers come to campus? Is there a speaker series sponsored by the political unions or by certain departments of the college or university?

Music Scene   Is there a club on campus that features live music on a regular basis? Do you have to be twenty-one to get in, or just twenty-one to drink? Where are the nearby arenas or amphitheaters that bring in the major touring rock stars? Can you get to them easily?

Relationship and Liaison Among Students, Faculty, and Administration   What is the relationship like among the students and the faculty, the students and the administration, and the faculty and the administration? Have there been strikes, walkouts, or work-to-rule periods in recent years?

Overall Vitality of Campus   Did you feel a palpable energy or "buzz" when you visited the campus? Was there a sense of excitement? Or did the place feel dead and drained of energy?

Meta-Category:
Campus Facilities and Infrastructure

Sufficient On-Campus Housing All Four Years   Simply put, is there enough housing for all undergraduate students who want to stay on campus—or are some upperclassmen forced off-campus against their will because of a shortage of housing? It is best to ask an upperclassman or two about this, as you may get "spin" from the admissions office.

Overcrowding   This is a corollary to the previous question. Are students living in overcrowded conditions in the dorms? In other words, has the university made quads out of rooms that were built to be doubles, or added beds to rooms that were built to be common spaces in a suite in order to accommodate everyone on campus? Again, it is best to ask an upperclassman or two about this.

Individual Internet Access   Do the dorm rooms offer Internet portals to every student—even if the dorms are overcrowded?

Size and Variety of Rooms, Suites, and Living Options   What are the different housing options and the configurations of the various rooms available on campus? Do the available options suit you?

Furnishings, Décor, and Utilities   How are the various rooms furnished? Are there built-in bookcases and desks, hardwood floors, or working fireplaces? Are there individual beds or bunks? How big are the windows? Is there air conditioning? Is the heating system controllable?

Laundry Facilities   How are the laundry facilities that you will be using? Are there enough machines to keep up with demand, or are there typically long lines in the laundry rooms? Are the machines broken all the time, or does the campus repair service do a good job keeping up? Talk to current students about this.

Campus Dining   What are the various dining plans available on campus? How affordable are they compared to other schools? How good is the food, and what are the daily offerings? Is there a salad bar and a pasta bar offered at every lunch and dinner in case you are looking for a light meal or don't like the entrees? Are you required to eat in the same dining hall for every meal, or is your dining card transferable? Where else can you use your dining card besides the dining halls? Are there pubs, local sub shops, ice cream shops, or coffeehouses that take it?

Quality, Size, and Variety of Classroom Facilities   Are the classrooms old and broken down, or newly refurbished? How are the seats and desks? How are the acoustics? Take a tour of the campus and get a look at some of the lecture and seminar facilities, and ask students for their impressions.

Quality, Size, and Variety of On-Campus Meeting Spaces for Students   Do the dorms have lounges or conference rooms? Can you book meeting rooms at the library if you have a group project and need a place to meet? What about if your fantasy baseball or football league needs a place to hold its draft or if you want to hold auditions for a campus group?

Quality, Number, and Availability of Music Practice Rooms and Pianos   Do you want a place to play piano, to rehearse with your instrument, or to practice with your rock band? How many soundproof music practice rooms does the campus offer? Are they reservable, or are they available only on a first-come, first-served basis? What about pianos? You can't take yours with you to campus—does the school have pianos available for you to practice or play on?

Intra- and Intercampus Transportation   If the campus is spread out—and particularly if you need to use public transportation to get between classes—how is the campus transportation? Are the stops well marked and well spaced? Is the service timely and reliable? Talk to current students.

Student Union or Student Center   Does the school have a student union or a student center? What amenities does it offer?

Gym/Fitness Center Facilities   How new is the gym, and what does it offer in terms of equipment? What are its hours? Are there enough treadmills, stationary bikes, elliptical machines, and rowers to keep up with demand? What about a Nautilus circuit and free weights? Do the varsity teams get priority use of the equipment? If so, does that leave any time for you if you're not a varsity athlete?

Indoor/Outdoor Track, Pools, Tennis Courts   Does this school have an indoor or outdoor track, pool, and tennis courts? How available are they to students? What about racquetball and squash courts? What else does the school offer for athletic amenities?

Undergraduate Health Services   What impression do current students have of the school's undergraduate health services? What are its strengths and weaknesses? Ask around and rate accordingly.

Counseling Services   One of the things to ask about specifically is the availability of counseling sessions and services—particularly for depression and stress. Are these services available? How easy is it to book an appointment to see someone? Again, ask around.

Career Planning and Placement Office   Take a look at it—is it spacious, modern, well appointed, and computerized, or is it cramped, disorganized, and still largely or completely paper based? Is there a sizeable full-time staff? Does the office put on seminars or talks for students about the job market and prospective careers? Does the office sponsor a campus job fair alone or in conjunction with other area colleges and universities? Talk to a senior about how effective the office is in helping students find summer and permanent employment.

Alumni Services Office   Do you know if the school even has one? Talk to the admissions office and upperclassmen about this—they will certainly know. In short, the alumni services offices keeps track of alumni all over the world, usually organized by the fields they work in. It is a great place to begin your networking effort to find a summer or permanent job.

Campus Police Presence   Does the school have its own police force? What is its relationship with students? Is it collegial or adversarial? Does the campus police see its role as protecting students from violent crime and theft or as a vice squad out to bust you for underage drinking? The answers to these questions can have a serious effect on the atmosphere of the campus—so find out.

Lighting Is the campus well lit so that students feel safe walking at night?

Security Phones   Does the campus have enough emergency/security phones, and are they convenient and well marked?

Dorm Security   Are the dorms secure? Do they use keycard or barcode passcodes, which can easily be disabled if your card is lost or stolen, or do they still use keys? Are there security guards or RAs with whom visitors must check in, or can people just walk right in? Talk to students and look around.

Escort Service for Late-Night Travel   Does the school provide a late-night escort service if you must walk home late from the lab or the library by yourself? Is the service reliable?

Computer Centers and Printing Access   What's the word on the campus computer centers and access to printers if you don't have your own computing equipment? Are there enough networks around to meet demand? Is the equipment reliably functional, or are the computers and printers broken or offline all the time? Do the various centers take reservations for computer time?

Library Infrastructure   How good is the campus library system? Are the libraries likely to have everything you might need? Is there a good interlibrary loan program in place in case you need to get a book or copies of a journal your school's system doesn't carry?

Library Hours   Are the library hours generous—accommodating your study schedule instead of requiring you to accommodate the library hours? Is there at least one library that stays open twenty-four hours a day? There should be.

Availability of Study Carrels, Seating, and Quiet Areas   Does the library have sufficient seating and tables to meet the demand? Are there good places to nestle in comfortably with your evening's reading? Does the library have a quiet area that is strictly enforced?

Library Copy Machines   Particularly in your upperclass years, you will frequently need to make photocopies at the library. Is there a sufficient number of photocopy machines at the library, and are these machines in good working order?

Campus Bookstore or Co-op   How extensive is the campus bookstore or co-op?

Proximity to Bus, Train, or Airport   How convenient is the campus to bus, train, or air transportation home or to different cities?

Meta-Category: Geography

Relationship of Campus to Community   Does the school have a good relationship with its surrounding community? Do students typically mingle harmoniously and volunteer in that community, or is there a palpable "us versus them" mentality?

Safety of Surrounding Community   How safe is the area around the campus?

Offerings of Surrounding Community   What does the town or city where the school is located have to offer? Are there professional sports teams? Is there a good concert venue where major acts come and play? Are there good rock or jazz clubs, good bars, good restaurants, and a variety of movie theaters? What about art galleries, bookstores, health food and grocery stores, farmers' markets, and good places to shop for clothes? Is there a mall convenient to the campus for your big-ticket shopping needs? What about open spaces, parks, rivers, lakes, beaches, or mountains?

Opportunities for Volunteerism in the Community   Are there widespread opportunities to volunteer in the surrounding community?

Off-Campus Housing   If you want to move off-campus, how nice, safe, and reasonably priced are the nearby alternatives?

Proximity to Family   This rating depends on how you feel about your family. Whichever emotional direction you may veer, how do you feel about how far away you would be from them if you went here?

Proximity to Friends   Of course, you'll be meeting a whole new network of friends in college, but it is still comforting to have an old friend or two nearby to call on if times get tough. How far away would your best friends be if you went this school?

Proximity to High School Significant Other   Some people insist on trying to make the long-distance relationship thing work for a while. One or two of them even manage to thread the needle and end up getting married. You probably won't be one of them, so we don't recommend giving this factor a lot of weight—but hey, it's here if you're hopelessly in love.

Proximity to Favorite Outdoor Activities   How far to the beach, the lake, or the mountains? How close is the nearest mountain biking trail or the nearest place you could go for a run without getting mugged or run over by a bus?

Overall Appeal of Surrounding Community   How appealing is the town or city where the school is located? Is it a place where you are likely to want to spend time, or are you likely to be restricting your activity to the campus? What is your overall impression?

Meta-Category: Financial Aid

Percentage of Class Receiving Aid   What was the percentage of last year's incoming class that received some form of financial aid?

Average Aid Award   What was the average aid award given out last year?

Median Aid Award   What was the median aid award given out last year? The median may be the more informative number, because the average can be skewed by students who received full scholarships.

Variety of Aid Sources Available   Does the school offer inventive financial aid programs, such as loan repayment programs for volunteer commitment after graduation, alumni scholarships, or other school- or major-specific opportunities?

Aid Award—Grants and Scholarships   How much aid did the school give you that will not need to be repaid?

Aid Award—Loans   How much did the school attribute to loans that will need to be repaid?

> **Aid Award—Work-Study** How much did the school attribute to work-study programs that you'll need to satisfy during your undergraduate years?

Okay, now remember how this works. First, you give each factor a score of 0, 1, or 2 based on how important you think the factor is to you. Then, after you've given each of these 119 defined factors a score, make sure that you have enough information to give each school you are considering an honest grade on each factor. If you need more information, it's time to hop on the Internet or to make some phone calls. Once you have all the information you need, turn to the Relevance Calculus chart on the next pages and fill in the Category Importance Score at the top right of each page and in all the cells in the Category Importance Score columns; also fill in all the Factor Importance Scores for each meta-category. That way, when you photocopy these pages, they will include the same importance ratings across all the schools you will be comparing. Make several photocopies of the Relevance Calculus chart, and then fill one out completely for every school you are seriously considering, giving the school a score of 1 to 5 on each of the 119 factors in the calculus. Then join us in the pages after the chart to find out what to do next!

The Relevance Calculus

School: _____

FINAL SCHOOL SCORE (sum of the six meta-category Average Factor Scores): _____

META-CATEGORY: ACADEMICS

Importance Score: _____
(0 = not important; 1 = important; 2 = very important)

Average Factor Score: _____
(derived from chart below)

Factor Description	Category Importance Score	Factor Importance Score	School Score on Factor	Total
Course offerings				
Course selection process				
Academic reputation of faculty				
Teaching reputation of faculty				
Political orientation of faculty				
Workload				
Faculty-to-student ratio				
Average class size				
Median class size				
Availability of famous faculty to undergraduates				
Opportunities for professor contact				
Opportunities for independent research				
Opportunities to go abroad				
Impression of classes visited				
Number of majors				
Ability to design your own major				
Strength of department in your likely major(s)				
Academic schedule				
Mean grade/grade inflation				
Thesis or senior project required?				
Presence of women and minorities on tenured faculty				
Postcollege placement of undergraduate students				
Other:				
Other:				
Other:				
			Total =	

Total of School Score on Factor column divided by the number of factors = Average Factor Score (write this in the space provided at the top of the chart)

META-CATEGORY: STUDENTS

Importance Score: _____
(0 = not important; 1 = important; 2 = very important)

Average Factor Score: _____
(derived from chart below)

Factor Description	Category Importance Score	Factor Importance Score	School Score on Factor	Total
Collegiality				
Personality				
Intellectual excitement				
Interest and involvement in their studies				
Interest and involvement in campus life				
The driving force				
Balance between work and play				
Classroom culture				
Prevalence of drug culture on campus				
Prevalence and importance of alcohol				
Campus dating scene				
Importance of fraternities and sororities to social scene				
Importance of varsity sports to campus social scene				
Geographic diversity				
Racial and ethnic diversity				
Religious diversity				
Socioeconomic diversity				
Stylistic diversity				
Hours per week spent studying				
Competition for grades				
Pressure for postcollege placement opportunities				
Perceived social aptitude of students (the "Dork Factor")				
Overall "fit"				
Other:				
Other:				
Other:				
			Total =	

Total of School Score on Factor column divided by the number of factors = Average Factor Score (write this in the space provided at the top of the chart)

META-CATEGORY: CAMPUS LIFE

Importance Score: _____
(0 = not important; 1 = important; 2 = very important)

Average Factor Score: _____
(derived from chart below)

Factor Description	Category Importance Score	Factor Importance Score	School Score on Factor	Total
Academic pressure and workload				
Emphasis on learning				
Emphasis on grades				
Emphasis on social life				
Intellectual excitement				
Primary weekend activities				
Commuting out on weekends				
Major campus social events				
Influence of fraternity and sorority life				
Percentage of student body that is "Greek"				
Main activities of the fraternities and sororities				
Campus rules on pledging, rushing, hazing, and initiation				
Pressures to drink				
Pressures to experiment with drugs				
Campus policy on alcohol and underage drinking				
Safety				
Clubs for special interests and hobbies				
Intramural sports scene				
Residential college system				
Special-interest housing or dining halls				
Student government				
Campus political scene				
Campus movie series				
Campus plays				
Campus speaker series				
Music scene				
Relationship and liaison between students, faculty, and administration				
Overall vitality of campus				
Other:				
			Total =	

Total of School Score on Factor column divided by the number of factors = Average Factor Score (write this in the space provided at the top of the chart)

META-CATEGORY: FACILITIES AND INFRASTRUCTURE

Importance Score: _____
(0 = not important; 1 = important; 2 = very important)

Average Factor Score: _____
(derived from chart below)

Factor Description	Category Importance Score	Factor Importance Score	School Score on Factor	Total
Sufficient on-campus housing all four years				
Overcrowding				
Individual Internet access				
Size and variety of rooms, suites, and living options				
Furnishings, décor, and utilities				
Laundry facilities				
Campus dining				
Quality, size, and variety of classroom facilities				
Quality, size, and variety of on-campus meeting spaces for students				
Quality, number, and availability of music practice rooms and pianos				
Intra- and intercampus transportation				
Student union or student center				
Gym/fitness center facilities				
Indoor/outdoor track, pools, tennis courts				
Undergraduate health services				
Counseling services				
Career planning and placement office				
Alumni services office				
Campus police presence				
Lighting				
Security phones				
Dorm security				
Escort service for late-night travel				
Computer centers and printing access				
Library infrastructure				
Library hours				
Availability of study carrels, seating, and quiet areas				
Library copy machines				
Campus bookstore or co-op				
Proximity to bus, train, or airport				
Other:				
			Total =	

Total of School Score on Factor column divided by the number of factors = Average Factor Score
(write this in the space provided at the top of the chart)

META-CATEGORY: GEOGRAPHY

Importance Score: _____
(0 = not important; 1 = important; 2 = very important)

Average Factor Score: _____
(derived from chart below)

Factor Description	Category Importance Score	Factor Importance Score	School Score on Factor	Total
Relationship of campus to community				
Safety of surrounding community				
Offerings of surrounding community				
Opportunities for volunteerism in the community				
Off-campus housing				
Proximity to family				
Proximity to friends				
Proximity to high school significant other				
Proximity to favorite outdoor activities				
Overall appeal of surrounding community				
Other:				
Other:				
Other:				
			Total =	

Total of School Score on Factor column divided by the number of factors = Average Factor Score (write this in the space provided at the top of the chart)

META-CATEGORY: FINANCIAL AID

Importance Score: _____
(0 = not important; 1 = important; 2 = very important)

Average Factor Score: _____
(derived from chart below)

Factor Description	Category Importance Score	Factor Importance Score	School Score on Factor	Total
Percentage of class receiving aid				
Average aid award				
Median aid award				
Variety of aid sources available				
Aid award—grants and scholarships				
Aid award—loans				
Aid award—work-study				
			Total =	

Total of School Score on Factor column divided by the number of factors = Average Factor Score (write this in the space provided at the top of the chart)

Note that the Financial Aid meta-category is split into two sections—one for students who do not yet have a financial aid award—and one for those who do. If you already have a financial aid award from the school, skip the first four factors (after all, once you know what *your* award is, the average aid award is irrelevant!) and complete only the last three. If you do not yet have an aid award, do the first four and skip the last three—but come back and revisit this section of the calculus after all your aid packages have come in.

PLAYING WITH THE DATA

You're almost done!

To make sure you get the most out of this exercise, though, let's look at how you might play with the Average Factor Score data. Let's say that you're seriously considering five different colleges and are having a hard time deciding between them. How can you use the Relevance Calculus to help you?

First, you will examine the five different schools in terms of their Final School Scores. To do that, refer to your Relevance Calculus charts for these schools to find each school's Final School Score; make a table listing the schools and their scores in rank order (see the following table).

Name of School	Final School Score (the six Average Factor Scores added together)
University of Earth	26.1
University of Sun	25.8
University of Moon	25.6
University of Mars	22.4
University of Saturn	22.2

This table tells you that your top three choices scored really close to one another—which might explain why you are having such a difficult time distinguishing between them. What should you do now?

The thing to do is look at the three closest-ranked schools in terms of their raw and average scores in the meta-categories that you thought were most important. So let's do that.

Remember that at the beginning of this exercise, you gave each of the meta-categories a Category Importance Score? It's time to bring those scores together in yet another table; list them in rank order (see the following table).

Meta-Category	Category Importance Score
Academics	2
Students	2
Campus Life	2
Facilities and Infrastructure	1
Geography	1
Financial Aid	0

Now go back to the Relevance Calculus charts and get the scores you gave to each school—both the totals (the sum of the ratings in the School Score on Factor column) and the averages (the Average Factor Score)—and create a list like the one here.

Academics	Students	Campus Life
Moon 101 (4.8)	Earth 109 (4.8)	Earth 131 (4.7)
Sun 94 (4.5)	Sun 106 (4.7)	Sun 127 (4.6)
Earth 91 (4.4)	Moon 99 (4.4)	Moon 122 (4.4)

So what does *this* tell you?

Of your three schools that ranked the highest and most closely together, University of Moon ranked significantly higher on academics than the other two schools, but ranked significantly lower on students and campus life than the other two. So that should help your thinking at least somewhat, right? Even though you initially said that the Academics, Students, and Campus Life meta-categories were all very important (thus earning 2s on the score chart), if you can now say that academics is the *most* important thing to you, you'd probably choose to go to the University of Moon.

On the other hand, if you are willing to sacrifice a little bit in the academics department in order to get a slightly more desirable campus life and student body, then maybe you'd choose University of Earth.

Or if you want to take the middle ground across the board, you might take University of Sun.

Play with the data like this and see if it doesn't help clear your thinking somewhat. Remember that you can always go back to your scoring on the most important individual factors within a meta-category too, such as choice of majors or availability of a year abroad, to tease out differences between your top-choice schools.

How you use the data is up to you. We trust you'll find, however, that having this kind of information in front of you makes the decision-making process a lot more comfortable. Instead of relying exclusively on a "gut feeling," you can now figure out specifically what it is that's driving that gut feeling.

"If I could have chosen differently, I would have taken a harder look at the make-up of the student body," Kevin admitted. "My school had a fairly homogeneous population, not in race, but in their character. The student body at BC was primarily composed of well-dressed, well-funded, nonintellectual Catholic school kids from the tri-state area. The world view of the campus was narrow.

You should also be certain that the school you're looking at has strength in the programs that interest you. Don't compromise your interests to get a 'big name' school. I work in radio now and would have been better served at Emerson College in Boston where there is a world-class broadcast journalism program, rather than at BC, where the communications program was the modern-day 'rocks for jocks' major."

"I made the same mistake that a lot of high school students make," Aaron admits. "I was too busy to really visit and evaluate a large variety of schools, so I picked my school based on prestige, and the quality of the lacrosse program. I ended up paying for this mistake later by transferring to another school."

"The information you get from direct visits is paramount," Tom explains. "That would be my strongest recommendation to any prospective college student. After going through the print materials and Web sites and doing your initial due diligence, make a short list of the colleges that really interest you and visit them."

"I think you have to imagine yourself at all of the schools you are considering and figure out where you will be the happiest," Chase advises. "The beauty of picking a school based on how you project yourself there is that it partially overcomes the whole ranking debate. So many people simply attend the highest ranked school that accepts them. But who leaves college on a better track—the student who chose an ill-fitting school based on its rank and suffered to be happy or the student who found a place that suited his personality and therefore enabled him to thrive?"

PART TWO

Considerations
for Freshman Year

The Ten Things to Do Before You Arrive on Campus

In life as in chess, forethought wins.

Henry Buxton

The summer between high school and college is inevitably a time of transition—a bridge between what is past and what lies ahead.

For many of us, it was a bittersweet time . . . a last summer spent with childhood friends in old, familiar haunts. For many of us, it was also a time to say good-bye—good-bye to the town where we grew up; good-bye to the friends we grew up with, knew, and trusted; and good-bye to the comfortable, familiar life we had known for so long. There were difficult conversations with boyfriends and girlfriends who would soon become casualties. The severing of ties is never easy, but the process is an important part of moving on. At times, it will feel liberating. At others, it will feel heartbreaking. Take solace in the process. We've all been through it, and trust us . . . the excitement of the life that lies ahead is well worth the discomfort of breaking some of the ties that bind you to your childhood.

"If I could do one thing differently, I would have ended my high school relationship more delicately," one mentor explained. "We went through a lot together— both good times and bad times—and had a lot of 'firsts' together too. With the passage of time, and after dating a lot of other people, I realize that I loved and respected her even more than I thought . . . but because we were going to different schools that were far away from each other, we had this abrupt, kind-of nasty breakup that really didn't make much sense at all. I think we were both trying to keep from feeling the pain, you know—of getting hurt."

For many of us, the month before college was also a time of high anxiety—flooded with concerns about what to buy, what to bring, what our roommate(s) would be like, and how to manage all the changes associated with moving to a new city or town, moving away from home (perhaps for the first time), and adapting to a new environment.

Well, rest easy.

Your mentors have assembled the following list of the top ten things you actually *need* to worry about doing before you head off to campus for freshman year. Make sure you do each of these things—they will ease your transition, enhance your experience, and generally make your life easier. Everything else can wait.

RETRIEVE YOUR ACADEMIC HISTORY FROM YOUR HIGH SCHOOL

Before you leave home, stop in at your high school's guidance office and request a copy of your academic file. If your city or town is like most places, this file has followed you around from kindergarten through graduation from high school—and should have all sorts of valuable historical information in it, including all your standardized test scores, report cards, transcripts, inoculation records, and countless other things associated with your academic history. You are entitled to a copy of everything in it, but in most cases, this file is kept for only three years (or less) before it is either archived in a warehouse somewhere out of reach, or destroyed.

Although this record may not seem important to you now, it is a part of your history that you may someday need, or wish you had kept.

You may need copies of your SAT II scores to place out of introductory college courses or foreign language requirements, copies of your high school transcript for summer job searches or applications to summer programs, and copies of your SAT scores for application to certain graduate school programs. You may need to prove to your college or university that your inoculations are up-to-date—either before you matriculate or as soon as the first measles outbreak starts burning through the campus. Finally, you may just want to have these things for old time's sake—to show your own children someday or to remember your childhood by.

Get the original of this file or a copy of everything in it, then throw the contents into a clearly labeled, brightly colored folder so that you can locate it easily and won't misplace it. If your inoculation record was included, pull it out and put it in its own folder.

It's a quick trip, and it's worth it. Make the time.

CONFIRM THAT YOUR ACADEMIC FILE HAS YOUR INOCULATION RECORD IN IT, AND IF IT DOESN'T, GET A COPY FROM YOUR LOCAL DOCTOR

If your academic file does not contain your full inoculation record, stop in at your doctor's office and get a copy of it. Most colleges and universities require you to provide them with a copy of this before they allow you to register for classes. If your school hasn't asked for it yet, it probably will, so get ahead of the game by getting your hands on a copy. Keep this in another brightly colored and clearly labeled folder so you won't lose it. You'll be going back to this folder for reference again and again—in college, before graduate school, for summer programs, and the first time you step on a rusty nail at a frat party and wonder whether your tetanus booster is up-to-date.

SIGN UP FOR AND ATTEND YOUR SCHOOL'S FRESHMAN ORIENTATION PROGRAM

These days, most colleges and universities have a whole series of elaborate orientation programs—from multiday backcountry camping trips, rafting or kayaking trips, and canoe expeditions to freshman-only campus concerts, carnivals, and trips to amusement parks or other attractions. In many cases, your school will offer you a choice of several of these programs.

Find something that sounds fun—and go.

Yeah, yeah . . . we know you have to stay home to work and make an extra few days' worth of money. Or it's your girlfriend's birthday. Or you have a family reunion. There are a million excuses you can come up with for not going to one of these events.

They may call these things "orientation" trips, but they are really "bonding" trips. Your college or university has probably spent a lot of time and effort figuring out how to make these events fun and effective ways for nervous freshmen to mix and get to know one another. And guess what? They usually work.

"Attending orientation was extremely beneficial for me," Lyndsee recalls. "I ended up meeting some people that I stayed in touch with all through college. It was nice because when college started, I already had a few friends to visit, check out their rooms, and meet their roommates. That really gave me a jumpstart on getting to know people. The first person I met at NYU orientation is still my best friend today!"

People who go on these trips *do* bond, . . . at least for the first few weeks of school. This gives them an initial "critical mass" of new friends to go out with at night, eat meals with, and network with. Each of those people will have roommates and friends whom you'll meet through him or her, and soon you'll be on your way to building a new peer group in college. What you need is an easy way to start—and that's what these orientation groups and trips give you.

If you're not a hiker, go canoeing. If you're afraid of the water, sign up for the ropes course challenge or the day at Six Flags. But do *something* to give you an easy way to meet new friends. The first few days of college are a critical time when new peer groups form out of the ether, and because of the newness of the experience and everyone's collective anxiety, new bonds are easier to form.

"Everyone at Middlebury goes to orientation," Dave said, "and if there is an option at other schools, I would say you would be a fool not to go. At orientation, everyone is in the same boat that you are in, and it is a great chance to meet people and get acquainted with the campus. Middlebury offered an outdoor trip, which I went on, and I met one of my best friends on that trip. We went on the mountain biking trip and quickly learned that we would be the ones lagging behind for the next three days. I had a hunch that we would be spending time together when I realized that we had the most rickety-looking bikes out there. We were laughed at because we didn't have any kind of suspension on our ten-speeds."

"My experience at orientation, and my conversations with friends at other schools about their orientations, lead me to recommend going to any orientation program your school may offer," Chase advises. "Even if the program is mediocre (which mine was), you can bond with your new classmates over the mediocrity of the orientation. Interacting with other students is far more important than actually digesting the information given to you at the orientation.

I attended a lot of the information sessions during the three days before school started. I was inundated with information about classes, buses, nightlife, advisers, drugs, and extracurricular activities. What I remember most vividly, though, was sitting on the quad with three new friends and having a conversation about what we thought college would be like. That's orientation."

Don't be too cool for school and blow off orientation. You'll only find yourself on the outside looking in.

STUDY YOUR SCHOOL'S COURSE SELECTION GUIDE AND ACADEMIC HANDBOOK

By late in the summer before your freshman year, your college will mail you a copy of its course selection guide and academic handbook. If you will be attending a large college or university, cracking the course selection guide, which can be several inches thick, can be very intimidating. Because of this, a lot of students make the mistake of *never reading* through the guide, and they end up choosing their courses on the basis of what their friends and roommates are taking.

This is a huge mistake.

Invest the time to work your way through the guide. Read the introductory sections, which will probably explain your college's credit and course requirements and how the guide is organized. Most colleges and universities require their students to complete some sort of "core" curriculum—that is, you have to earn a certain number of credits in various core disciplines—in order to be allowed to graduate. In Chapter 11 we'll get into these requirements and some strategies for completing them. For now, just locate them in your course selection guide, read them, and try to understand how your school breaks courses down into core disciplines. Then take the guide a little bit at a time. Spend the first couple of visits with it just browsing through it with a highlighter, stopping to mark anything that sounds interesting to you. Start thinking about what discipline(s) you might conceivably want to major in, and look over the course offerings.

Familiarize yourself with how courses are described in the guide and what all the abbreviations, symbols, numbers, and letters mean.

Once you've done this, you've done enough for now. We'll come back to a complete discussion of these issues in Chapter 11.

Finally, find the copy of your school's academic handbook and read through it as well. In it you will find things like your school's code of conduct and a description of your school's disciplinary procedures for underage drinking, drugs, date rape, cheating, and plagiarism. Although many of these things may appear self-evident to you, pay particular attention to your school's rules on plagiarism and source attribution. Chances are that in high school you may have written only one or two papers requiring you to cite secondary sources. In college, however, such papers will be the norm—and professors tend to be deadly serious about source attribution. Read these rules carefully and learn them. Remember that plagiarism is not just cribbing a complete paper from an Internet research paper site and representing it as your own work. Plagiarism can also include taking even a single idea or sentence from another person's work without providing attribution for it. We've known more than a few students who have been suspended or even permanently expelled from college for failing to give proper credit for such ideas in their written work.

So read the code of conduct and figure out what it requires of you.

TALK TO YOUR FRESHMAN COUNSELOR, RA, OR AN UPPER-CLASSMAN ABOUT YOUR SCHOOL, AND GET THAT PERSON TO ANSWER "THE THREE QUESTIONS"

Somewhere in your preregistration materials, you will have received the name of your freshman counselor, academic adviser, or resident adviser (RA). If for some reason your school did not provide you with the name and contact information for this person, perhaps you know an upperclassman at the school you will be attending. Just find someone at the school whose judgment you can trust. Call this person before you set out for campus and get him or her to answer the following Three Questions. When you get answers to these questions, write them down in the space provided immediately below so you'll have them here as a record. Although these questions may seem simple, you'll be amazed at the nuggets of wisdom you'll pick up and the trouble you'll save yourself by simply asking these questions and heeding the responses you get.

Okay, okay, so what are the questions?

Here they are, with space to write in responses:

Question 1: What were the three biggest mistakes you made during your freshman year, how could you have avoided them, and what did you learn from them?

1. _____

2. _____

3. _____

Question 2: What were the three best decisions or choices you made during your freshman year, and why do you consider them good decisions?

1. _____

2. _____

3. _____

Question 3: What are the three most important things you learned during your freshman year?

1. _____

2. _____

3. _____

This is simple but important wisdom. Learn from the people who went before you. Ask the questions!

CALL YOUR ROOMMATE(S) AND BEGIN A CONVERSATION ABOUT YOUR LIVES TOGETHER

Sometime in mid- to late summer, you'll receive a piece of mail with the name and contact information of your roommate(s) in it. If you've grown up in rural America somewhere, it can be nerve wracking to learn that you'll be rooming with someone from New York City, or vice versa. Remember, though, that this is part of the learning experience at college. Most of us came to the end of our college experience and felt that the most memorable moments, and even the most significant intellectual moments, happened in conversations with roommates and friends *outside* the classroom. The bottom line is, someone needs to break the ice. Don't wait for one of your other roommates to do it. Make the calls yourself.

Once you get past the introductory stuff—you know, the "How's it going," "How have you spent your summer," "Are you nervous about starting school" talk—you'll need to engage in at least some minimal shoptalk to ensure that you don't end up with two televisions and no stereo. Find out who has the extra TV, stereo, couch, easy chairs, rugs, coffee table, and lamps to bring along; or, if you are all traveling to college from nondriving distances, come to some general agreements about what you'll want to buy for your room or common space. You can get everything when you get to campus, as there will be sales of every used item under the sun once you get there.

Exchange e-mail addresses and shoot a few e-mails back and forth to help develop a rapport between you that you can call on during the inevitable rough patches that commonly characterize the first few days of school. It is a lot easier to resolve disagreements with someone with whom you've already conversed and e-mailed than with someone with whom you've had almost no contact.

READ AND SAVE EVERYTHING YOUR SCHOOL SENDS YOU, BUT RESIST THE URGE TO BUY ANYTHING (EXCEPT POSSIBLY A COMPUTER)

By midsummer, the postman who delivers the mail to your house will start groaning under the weight of all the junk mail, correspondence from various student groups, and daily "one time only" offers. These will be promising to teach you to speed-read or to enhance your memory, urging you to preregister for graduate school admissions tests, offering to have your laundry taken out and delivered or your linens and towels changed . . . and just about anything else you can possibly imagine. It will seem as though everyone is trying to sell you something—and guess what?

They are.

So how do you cut through all the crap and figure out what you really need?

Well, here's a little secret. Those supposedly "one-time-only" offers usually have a way of reappearing as a "this-weekend-only" or "last-chance" opportunity once you get to campus, so there really is no reason or pressure to buy much of anything until you've arrived on campus and settled in a bit. Then you'll know how much space you have, and you'll have the added advantage of seeing what other students, particularly upperclassmen, have done to outfit their living spaces. Considering that there is no penalty for waiting, you should generally hold off on doing any major purchasing of goods and services until you get to campus.

There are a couple of notable exceptions, though.

First, if you don't have a reasonably new IBM-compatible laptop computer, look for the offer from your campus computer services department and take advantage of their "bundle" deals. Companies like Dell offer deep discounts to universities, which buy in bulk, and the deals to be had on computers, monitors, printers, scanners, WI-FI gear, and other technology can't be beat. These computers usually *do* need to be preordered by the deadline stated in the literature your school will send to you—and these deals are usually *not* offered again until the following year, so if you need new computer equipment, you *should* act on the offer that comes to you during the summer.

You'll also need to come to some sort of consensus with your roommates about whether or not you want to subscribe to the university telephone service, or whether each of you will subsist with your cell phones. Our advice is to kick in the additional scratch and get the telephone service. For one thing, if you don't, you won't get listed in the campus directory—which can make it difficult for classmates, friends, and even date-seekers to contact you. Second, professors will occasionally need a way to contact you, and they use the campus directory to find their students.

If your school requires you to pay to activate your high-speed in-room Internet access, you'll obviously want to do that, and the same goes for establishing a campus e-mail account. When the paperwork for those services comes in, turn it around right away so that your room will be wired, connected, and ready to go when you arrive.

Cable television access is another option offered by many schools. If you're a television viewer, you'll probably want to have that hooked up so that you don't have to wait several days once you get to campus.

The last thing you need to figure out is what to do about your meal plan. Every school is different in this regard, so the best advice we can give you is to find out what the majority of students at your school do, and sign up for that. Unless you are living off-campus and plan to cook for yourself, spend a fortune on takeout, or subsist on Ramen noodles, you'll probably want some semblance of a meal plan, at least at first. Freshman fall is enough of a whirlwind without having to worry about grocery shopping or where you'll take your next meal. Yes, the food is radically overpriced and often of forgettable quality. But many schools have added salad and pasta bars to indulge finicky students, and you simply can't beat the convenience of popping into the dining hall after practice and grabbing a quick dinner on the run before your evening study session.

So: computer, telephone, Internet, cable television, and a meal plan—that's what you need to cull out of the piles of junk mail. Everything else can wait.

USE THE SUMMER BEFORE SCHOOL BEGINS TO GET IN SHAPE

You've heard of the Freshman 15, right? The fifteen pounds of pizza and beer that many freshmen add around their waistline by the time the first year is over? It's no myth. College life moves fast. You'll work hard and play hard, and many times you'll be grabbing meals on the run. The dining hall offers "all-you-can-eat" food at every meal and there is always ice-cream and dessert available there, too. Then, when the weekend approaches, there is the beer and pizza.

A lot of it.

And you don't need the ghost of Dr. Atkins to tell you what that will do to you.

Accordingly, whether you are an athlete or not, we encourage you to start a workout routine this summer and to try to stick with it. Find something you like—whether it is running, biking, swimming, blading, lifting, or whatever—and develop a routine around it. Do it at a particular time every day, and build some endurance. This will energize you, build your immune system, and give you both confidence about your physical appearance and a great outlet to relieve stress and blow off steam.

Chances are, you'll be amazed at the fitness facilities available to you when you get to college—but there will be a much greater chance of your using them and building exercise into your everyday life if you start now.

Before college.

Before the hectic pace of life sets in.

Before other things become "more important."

Make exercise a priority now, and you'll make it a priority for your whole life. And that's a good thing.

APPLY FOR *ONE* GENERAL-PURPOSE CREDIT CARD

By the middle of your summer before college, the credit card applications will start streaming in, and as long as you maintain reasonably good credit, they'll keep streaming in, sometimes two or three a day, for the rest of your life.

The first time you get one, though, will be one of the most exciting days of your life.

Be careful, though. Note that we said to apply for *one* credit card.

One. Not several.

Credit is something that the bounds of this book will not allow us to explore in depth, but suffice it to say that many, *many* college students get themselves into very serious trouble with credit cards. Many of them incur such staggering debt that they actually have to declare *bankruptcy* to get out from under.

Trust us—that's not the way you want to start your life. Try buying an apartment or a house or applying for a loan to pay for graduate school after you've filed for bankruptcy.

Find *one* credit card that offers you attractive perks, whether it be cash back, discounts on air travel, or whatever, and get that one card. If you know that you have a tendency to outspend your ability to pay, you might be better off with a debit card to keep things from running away from you. Whatever the case, apply for *one* card so that you can pay for major expenses like books, supplies, and day-to-day living essentials without having to haul large sums of cash around with you on campus.

Having a credit card on campus provides much-needed flexibility, and limits your need to carry cash. But it is also a huge responsibility.

Treat it accordingly.

DECIDE IF YOU INTEND TO TEST OUT OF ANY ENTRY-LEVEL CLASSES OR YOUR SCHOOL'S LANGUAGE REQUIREMENT

If you took any of the SAT IIs or Achievement Tests, you'll want to determine whether you earned scores sufficient to test out of the introductory classes in those subjects at your school. Look in your course selection guide or academic handbook to determine how your particular school handles these issues, and be sure you have the proper documentation with you to substantiate your scores.

Testing out of introductory classes gives you some increased flexibility in choosing a schedule—particularly in fitting in upper-level electives in a particular subject. But it is not always the best approach.

Remember that college is *not* high school. In college, you will necessarily explore subjects in much greater depth that you were able to do in high school. You'll often be taught by professors who are on the cutting edge in their respective fields of study, who publish in that discipline, and who (we hope) care intensely about the subject and know how to teach it. In the case of the sciences, you'll have accompanying laboratory sections that will drive home important concepts through hands-on experience and the completion of lab reports.

So how do you decide whether you need to take Intro Bio again or whether you can skip it and move right along into biochemistry and genetics with sophomores and juniors?

We recommend getting a copy of the syllabus for the introductory course in any subject you are considering waiving out of, and reading it. How much of the subject matter did you actually cover in your high school class? Do you have a general familiarity with the subject matter, or does half the syllabus read like Greek to you?

Finally, how relevant will the class be to other classes you may want to take?

If you are premed and intend to be a biology major, but half the Bio 110 syllabus looks unfamiliar to you, you might want to retake the introductory-level course and establish a good base of knowledge on which you can build in your upperclass years. On the other hand, introductory classes tend to be large and impersonal, with sections and laboratories often taught by, and exams graded by, graduate student teaching assistants. These introductory classes are also most often graded on strict curves, making it harder to do well in them.

There are plenty of pros and cons to testing out of these classes. Think through your options, and get the "local spin" on the issue by discussing your choices with your RA or freshman counselor as soon as you get to campus.

What You Need and What You Don't Need to Take to College

One needs only two tools in life: WD-40 to make things go, and duct tape to make them stop.

G. M. Weilacher

The weeks leading up to your departure for college are inevitably filled with excitement, anticipation, nervousness, and, chances are, an insatiable urge to start buying things.

But what do you *really* need to buy before you get to campus—things that would save you money by buying them at home and cramming into the car—and what can you safely wait to purchase once you and your roommates get to campus? And how can you figure out how your room on campus is configured and how much space you'll actually have for all the "stuff" you are thinking about taking with you?

Relax. We've got you covered.

WHAT YOU *DO* NEED TO BRING TO CAMPUS

Room assignments for freshman are generally made by the college registrar's office or the college's undergraduate dean's office in midsummer. Chances are that by the end of July you will have received a letter from your college with your room-mate(s)' name(s) and contact information, and also the address of your campus residence for the upcoming year. If for some reason you *don't* get that information by the beginning of August, you should place a call to your college registrar's office and make an inquiry, as it may have been lost in the mail.

Once you get the name of the dorm and your room number, it's time to spring into action. First, and most obviously, if you live close enough to campus to pay a visit, you might simply choose to take a leisurely drive over on some weekday afternoon with a tape measure and your digital camera and see if the dorms are open. College dorms are often used during the summer for high school programs, athletic training camps, music camps, and the like. You may be able to gain access (with permission of the current resident, of course) to the very room you'll be staying in, and be able to take some pictures and get a rough idea of the dimensions so that you'll know whether your favorite couch or easy chair will actually fit anywhere. If you get this chance, be sure to take some digital pictures to e-mail around, and write the dimensions down so that you can share them with your roommates.

In the event that your dorm is locked, closed for renovations, or otherwise inaccessible, don't give up! Because you're on campus anyway, pay a visit to the custodial services department or, if you can't find that, to the nearest campus police substation. Tell them that you've driven all this way and were hoping to get a quick peek into your dorm room to determine what furniture would fit into it. If things are quiet and you are polite and persistent, you may well find yourself on the receiving end of a quick private tour of your room to be.

If you are refused, make a trip to the registrar's office, introduce yourself, and ask politely for a photocopy of your dorm-room layout with dimensions. Someone should be able to help you or point you directly to someone who can. Somewhere on campus, there is a record of the dimensions and contents of every dorm room. That's what you're looking for.

If you can't make the trip to campus, and one of your roommates can't tackle this task on your behalf, it's no big deal. Simply call the registrar's office and put the request directly to someone there. Remember, you are asking them for the dimensions and contents of your room. They may connect you to the custodial services department or to a central office in your dormitory building. Someone should be able either to tell you directly or to fax you a layout of the room.

Your Own Bed or Futon, or Help for Theirs

Perhaps the most important question to ask, whether in person or over the phone, is whether the college allows you to opt out of using its furnishings—and if it does, whether the college will store its furniture for you. You will encounter this issue most commonly with beds.

It's highly likely that your college will provide you with a nasty iron cot and an uncomfortable, scratchy mattress not fit for a homeless dog to sleep on. Or worse yet, bunk beds comprising two of these units stacked on top of each other. You'd certainly love to be able to take your own bed or a futon with you instead, but the question is, will the custodial services people agree to remove the iron beds and mattresses and store them if you bring your own, or at least provide you a place to store them? You *need* to get the answer to this question before you make the decision to haul a bed to campus. We know many, many students who arrived with beds in tow, only to discover that the custodial services department refused to provide storage for the college-issued units. This resulted in students' either throwing the college-issued units away and paying a hefty fine at the end of the year to replace them, selling their own beds to upperclassmen because they had no place to put them, or using one or the other of the beds as a makeshift couch.

None of these options is advisable. Get the information you need in advance, and you won't end up in this predicament.

If it turns out that you have to sleep on the college-issued bed, there are still some tricks you can use to make it more comfortable. First, consider bringing a piece of twin mattress–size plywood with you to provide more back support for the mattress. You may also want to bring along one of those space-age foam mattress pads that go on top of the mattress and mold to your body, which will make any bed more comfortable. Alternatively, you might want to purchase an egg-crate mattress cover. Whatever your preference, you'll probably want to get *something* to make that bed more comfortable. Add a couple of sets of your own sheets (properly sized for the bed, of course) and a couple of pillows, and you're all set.

If bringing your own bed is permissible, we'll leave it to you to decide how to get it to campus. If your preference is to purchase a futon, though, you might want to hold off on buying one until you get to campus, as local retailers and entrepreneurs typically sell inexpensive, durable models on or near campus at the start of every school year, and you may do better there than you would buying it at home and hauling it to campus.

Whatever your decision, remember that you need to get your bed up to your room, which may be on an upper floor of a dorm building—and that not all dorms have elevators.

"The most useful thing I brought to campus from home was comfortable bedding," Lyndsee noted. "In the beginning, night time was when I missed my house and my family the most. Having a comfortable, cozy bed to sleep in made things a hundred times better."

Desk

The college will usually provide you with a desk as well, and if you would rather bring or buy your own desk, you'd be well advised to make the same inquiries you did for your bed so that you don't end up with two desks and no space. Once again, a little advance reconnaissance is very helpful here. Chances are, the college-issue desk will be either a bad, rickety one with drawers that stick and that is too small to have much utility, or a built-in one with shelves that will suit your purposes perfectly. Knowing which one you'll end up with should make your decision as to whether buying a desk is necessary.

If you choose to buy a desk, you might want to visit your local office supply superstore before setting off for campus; there you can purchase an inexpensive, modular unit that is boxed up and ready to be assembled in your room. Remember that your room may be on an upper floor and that you might be hauling your belongings up the stairs. Desks and stairwells don't get along.

"I also brought along a nice chair for my desk," Dave noted.

"And bring a lot of things like tapestries, posters, and photographs to hang on the walls," Carolyn added. "Dorm room walls are notoriously bare, depressing, and in need of cover up. They are often also made of concrete or cinderblock, meaning that you'll need stick-on hooks or other hardware to allow you to hang things on those walls!"

Small Toolbox

You'll thank us out loud for this one.

Before you set out for campus, grab a hammer, a regular and Phillips screwdriver, a small cordless drill with drill bits and screwdriver attachments, some screws and nails, tacks, a couple of packages of drywall and plaster mounting supports, a pair of needle-nose pliers, a small can of drywall patch, and a putty knife, and throw them into a toolbox or small duffel bag. This way, when it comes time to assemble your new desk, mount your new stereo speakers, hang pictures on a plaster wall, or fix screw holes in drywall so you won't get fined, you'll have everything you need in one place.

Sure, campus maintenance people are around. Wanna try calling them and asking to borrow a screwdriver?

"My starter tool kit was the most useful thing I brought to college hands-down," Kevin agreed. "Mine had a big hammer, Phillips and flat-head screwdrivers, hexagon keys, and a ratchet wrench. You bring this along, and everyone will want to use it."

Computer, Monitor, and Printer

You'd assume this would go without saying, yet every year, thousands of students arrive at college without a computer—condemning themselves to the whims of the campus computer laboratories or computer clusters in the basements of dorms when it comes time to write papers.

Don't do this to yourself.

If your budget allows (and even if it doesn't), watch the summer mail for the incredible computer bargains you'll be offered through your campus computer center. Because these centers buy in bulk, they can offer steep discounts—far better than anything you'll find on the street, in magazines, or on the Internet. Remember that no matter *what* you'll be majoring in, you'll occasionally have to write papers—and most professors these days insist that papers be word-processed and cleanly printed.

Computers are cheaper than they've *ever* been. Remember that you don't need the most modern, up-to-date model to run a word processor. You don't need to break the bank for a computer that can run fancy graphics packages or the most memory-intensive interactive games. A basic model that can handle word processing and can interface with your campus's Internet and e-mail server is all you really need.

We recommend getting a laptop as opposed to a desktop model because of the added advantages a laptop provides. A laptop is portable and can be carried with you to classes and back home on breaks. Once you learn how to outline in the built-in word-processing program, taking notes in class is a breeze—and because most of us can type faster than we can write, taking notes has never been easier. You can also edit your notes and add, delete, and move text around. Try doing that in a spiral notebook!

So what about a printer? Sure, you can blow a ton of money on a high-powered laser printer that can print twenty pages per minute or more . . . but why? Most of your college papers will be twenty pages or less. A simple laser or inkjet printer, available for less than two hundred dollars, will suffice.

If you don't buy technology you don't need, you should be able to pick up a laptop computer and basic printer bundle for less than a grand. Trust us—compared to long nights writing papers in a stuffy computer lab, it may be the best thousand dollars you ever spend.

"My laptop and printer were definitely the most useful things I brought from home," Tiffany agreed.

Stereo, Television, DVD Player, and Video Games

Otherwise known as procrastination aids.

Obviously you have to have these, but talk with your roommates to make sure you don't end up with four televisions and no DVD player. Try to work things out so that everyone brings something. You'll also want to watch your mail for the offer from the cable company if your dorm has cable television access. Ordering in advance means that your room will be hooked up when you arrive. Failing to do so means waiting two or three weeks for an appointment after you arrive on campus.

Clock Radio or Alarm

Even if you're an early riser now, you might need a little help rousing yourself for your nine o'clock class on Friday morning.

Trust us.

Coffeemaker

On some mornings, you'll need more than your alarm clock to rouse yourself for your nine o'clock class.

Nearly every campus is littered with terrific coffee shops, and if Starbucks hasn't run yours out of town yet, you'll come to appreciate just how valuable a place it is. They are great places for taking a casual date, posting campus news, hanging out with friends, and meeting with your study group. You'll also come to appreciate just how much money you'll blow in a semester paying $3 (or more) for a latte every morning before class.

If you are on a budget, bring a coffeemaker to campus. You'll save a bundle brewing your own—and you won't have to roll out of bed ten minutes earlier to account for your wait in line at the Daily Grind.

What? You say you don't like coffee?

Just wait. You'll like coffee soon enough.

Small Microwave

Again, you need only one of these, so talk to your roommates about who has one and who will bring it to campus. You're not going to be cooking Thanksgiving dinner in it, so you don't need a new convection model or anything fancy. Something that can handle a bag of microwave popcorn, warm up a cup of soup, or reheat a mug of coffee is about all you need.

WHAT YOU *DON'T* NEED TO BRING TO CAMPUS

We live in a capitalist society—and opportunistic merchants everywhere know that teenagers, particularly college-age teenagers, are among the most prolific spenders in our society. To that end, when college opens for the year, people come from miles away to hawk their wares on campus—everything from used furniture, carpeting, and rugs to posters, music, and incense. In those first few days, you may feel more like you're at a bazaar than on a college campus.

When you get to school, you'll see what we mean.

The point, though, is that competition is fierce, and prices for everything are therefore very competitive. In some cases, things are downright cheap.

So before you go strapping Dad's old easy chair or that nasty plaid basement rug to the roof of the car, think about whether you and your roommates might be better off shopping for these things at the campus bazaar. You can enhance camaraderie and reduce early disagreements and roommate squabbles if you go on a joint shopping trip once you all arrive on campus, rather than forcing your roommates to live with your grandmother's camphor-scented and completely uncomfortable Victorian-era couch.

You also won't need to bring rugs or carpets. You'll find plenty of those, in the right sizes to fit your dorm-room dimensions, at the bazaar.

The same goes for anything you might want to decorate with. Remember that students have been living in these dorm rooms for generations—and businesspeople, accounting for that, will be happy to sell you everything you might possibly need or want.

"I would recommend that you not bring a lot of stuff with you from home," Aaron noted. "Get to campus, get settled, and then figure out what else you'd like to have from home. At first, just bring the basics."

I can remember searching two or three bathroom stores back home for a convenient basket-type carrier I could use to haul shampoo and shaving gear back and forth from the communal bathroom. I probably spent three hours shopping around, eventually settling for something that wasn't even close to what I was looking for. When I got to school, though, the campus cooperative had about six different varieties of the exact item.

So when you're packing for campus, remember this: bring clothes, music, and other belongings that are distinctly "you," such as pictures, sports equipment, and whatever. But don't go shopping for college at home. Shop for college at the college bazaar. You'll save a lot of time and money.

The Eleven Things to Do Right After You Arrive on Campus

Doing the right thing at this moment puts you in the best place for the next moment.

Oprah Winfrey

Once you have dealt with the humiliation and embarrassment of having your parents and relatives meet your roommates, showing them around campus, and taking the required trip to the campus bookstore to get the sweatshirts, foam fingers, and car window decals, it's time to lay the groundwork for a great freshman year.

To that end, there are eleven important things you need to do within the next couple of days to ensure that your college experience gets off to a comfortable and positive start.

Add these eleven items to your to-do list. You'll be glad you did.

GET YOUR COLLEGE PHOTO IDENTIFICATION CARD

The college registration process begins with the issuance of your college photo ID card. At most colleges and universities today, given the increased emphasis on security, you need this ID card to get just about anything or anywhere on campus. Because of this, the freshman ID issuance process causes one of the biggest bottlenecks of the opening days of school, and the lines can often be very long.

Review your orientation materials, be sure you bring whatever proof of identification your college requires (often a driver's license or state-issued ID and one other item, such as your Social Security card), and make this your first stop in the morning.

Oh, and remember: this card will follow you around for four years, and you usually don't get to reshoot the picture, . . . so if you're concerned about that, grab a shower before you go.

INTRODUCE YOURSELF TO YOUR RESIDENT ADVISERS OR FRESHMAN COUNSELORS

Most colleges and universities place several resident advisers (RAs) or freshman counselors in every dormitory. Part older brother or sister, part mediator, part cop during the course of your first year, these experienced hands can be an invaluable source of information and advice during your first days on campus.

Introduce yourself!

Usually you'll have a few to choose from, so meet them all and then find the one you are most comfortable with. Once you've identified that person, ask him or her the same Three Questions you asked your other contact at the school over the summer (Chapter 6). Remember, what you're looking for at this stage of the game is information: knowledge of where the pitfalls are and how to avoid them; ideas about what worked for others and how to implement those strategies in your own experience.

"Talk to your adviser or RA," Chase notes. "Ask what common problems he or she sees in freshmen at your school, so you can be alert to them. Find out about the reputation of different courses and professors so you don't get bad courses during the first term. Advisers can also help you think about majors, or if you think you know your path already, what courses you have to take and how to best spread them out across your time. College is confusing. Ask questions!"

"Be reflective," Amanda adds. "In other words, think about stuff! Give some serious thought to your academic, social, athletic, and musical interests and how to get the most out of your college experience. Plan, prepare, and dare!"

Here are the questions again, with space to write in the responses:

Question 1: What were the three biggest mistakes you made during your freshman year, how could you have avoided them, and what did you learn from them?

1. _____

2. _____

3. _____

Question 2: What were the three best decisions or choices you made during your freshman year, and why do you consider them good decisions?

1. _____

2. _____

3. _____

Question 3: What are the three most important things you learned during your freshman year?

1. _____

2. _____

3. _____

GET YOUR COMPUTER, INTERNET, E-MAIL, AND TELEPHONE SERVICES ESTABLISHED

Two or three days after students start arriving on campus, the people who administer your college's e-mail, Internet, computer, and telephone services and systems are going to be inundated with service calls. A lot of people will need new versions of operating software, new drivers for printers or modems, new Ethernet or wireless cards. Other, less technology-savvy students will be completely lost and in need of significant hand-holding. Lines at your campus computer center can be hours long at the beginning of a new year.

Don't get caught in that nightmare.

As soon as you get to campus—before you unpack, go furniture shopping with your roommates, start partying with your new friends, or do anything else—get wired. Make sure you have the right operating system and all the software and hardware you need to fully integrate yourself into your campus's computer system. Double-check to make sure everything works. If it doesn't, get right on the phone with a technician, before things get out of hand. Doing this will ensure that while others are wasting aggravating hours standing in long lines at the computer center, you can be doing something more useful with your time.

GET THE KEY TO YOUR CAMPUS MAILBOX

If you're one of the lucky ones, your college will deliver your mail directly to your dorm, in which case you can just pick up your mail key from your RA or residence hall postmaster and skip this section.

For the rest of you, though, the next place you'll want to go is to your campus post office—the other madhouse on campus at the beginning of any semester. To save yourself some grief here, best make this trip first thing in the morning too, as soon as possible after the post office opens. And don't forget your driver's license and college ID card.

CHOOSE A LOCAL BANK AND SET UP A LOCAL CHECKING ACCOUNT

The other places where lines get ridiculously and frustratingly long at the beginning of the school year are at the local banks. Virtually every student will need to set up a local bank account, and as you may already know from experience, that involves another set of tiresome, time-consuming paperwork.

Accordingly, the next order of business is choosing a bank and getting an account set up before everyone else starts doing it.

In our view, there are three principal considerations in choosing the bank you'll use during your college years. First, choose the bank with the most convenient ATM machines. When you're running out to party on Thursday night, you're not going to want to have to cross town to your bank—and why pay $2.00 per transaction when you could be getting cash for free? Second, pick a bank that doesn't require you to maintain a minimum balance in your account. With the intense competition for business on a college campus, you should be able to find a bank that requires no minimum balance, or at least a negligibly small one ($250 or less). Finally, choose a bank that lets you do your banking online.

SPEND AN AFTERNOON ORIENTING YOURSELF ON CAMPUS

Break out a campus map and spend a leisurely afternoon just walking around.

Figure out which buildings are which, where the dining halls are, where the libraries are, and where the gym is. Figure out where the different fraternities and sororities are. Look for the best place to get coffee in the morning. If you're a runner or a blader, take note of good running routes around campus. If you like to study outside, look for some nice courtyards, gardens, cafés, or other places that might be suitable. Notice where the campus police substations are and what the campus security phones look like and where they are.

There is no real agenda here. Just allow yourself to wander, taking in the layout of your surroundings. You're looking for a sense of comfort—of belonging—that comes with familiarity. The sooner you get that, the easier your adjustment will be.

FIND A QUIET, OUT-OF-THE-WAY PLACE TO STUDY

As you will soon discover, college life is rife with distractions. Between campus events, roommates tempting you to take a study break, television, the Internet, your cell phone, and the general bustle of your dorm, it can be hard to buckle down and actually concentrate on studying!

Hence task number 7: find one or two campus "hideouts" where you can concentrate and study without distraction.

Remember, these are places to *study*—not places to go to be seen or to scope people out. Look for places that are quiet and off the beaten path. Avoid places that give you a view of the whole room or of doorways, where you will be likely to watch the comings and goings of others. Don't pick a place near your roommates or friends, and don't pick a place like a coffee shop, café, or bar, where noise may prevent you from concentrating. You're looking for a place where you can be alone with yourself and focus on your studies.

I had two such places. One was a comfortable leather chair in an alcove in the reading room of the main campus library, with a reading lamp and a window that I could open for fresh air. I used that spot to do all my nightly reading assignments for the four years I was at Yale. I also had a hidden carrel high in the library "stacks," again next to a window, where I did all my more intense studying and exam preparation. The reading spot, warm and cozy, fostered that activity. The studying spot was less comfortable and much more remote—ensuring that I wouldn't get distracted by anyone or anything and that I would focus *only* on the matter at hand.

With all the temptations associated with life on campus and especially life in the dorm, it can be really easy to blow off studying for a night in favor of partying with friends, going to a movie, or just hanging out and socializing. But soon, one night becomes two, then a week, and before you know it, you're way behind in your classes.

There is a certain momentum that comes from getting up and getting away. For one thing, you remove yourself from many of the tempting sources of distraction. Further, if you pick a good place for your hideout, it can actually be fun to go there to "get away" from everyone and be alone with your studies. After a few productive evenings in your campus hideout, you begin to associate positive vibes with it, and the place itself can become a motivator for you. After a while, this routine becomes almost automatic.

Try it. You'll see.

CHECK IN WITH THE REGISTRAR

In a few days, classes will begin, and with that the process of registering for those classes. Before you can register for any classes, however, your tuition bill must be paid in full, your inoculation record must be up-to-date, and all your personal information must be updated and on file.

With the enormous volume of paperwork that the good people in your school's registrar's office have to deal with, mistakes do happen. Checks get misplaced, and paperwork gets misfiled. Data entry errors occur. Sometimes you even forget to send in something they need.

Before the semester begins, drop by the registrar's office. Say hello and ask someone there to check and make sure you are registered in good standing for the semester. That way, if something is missing or if an error has been made, there will be sufficient time to remedy the problem before it begins to affect your ability to register for classes.

And remember, even if you find that someone has made an error, always treat the people in the registrar's office with respect and courtesy. They wield significant power, and they can at least temporarily remedy just about any problem you may have if you show them the proper courtesy.

MAKE YOUR ROOM A HOME AND GET ORGANIZED!

For most of us, going away to college was the first significant time we spent away from home. You're in a new place, with new people and new surroundings. The experience can be somewhat disconcerting for even the most confident among us. So once you have the groundwork taken care of, spend some time setting up your living space—and make it your own.

First and foremost, make it comfortable. Spend a few dollars for a good pillow, good sheets, and a comforter that will allow you both to sleep well and to make your bed with a minimum of fuss. Hang some posters. Put out some framed pictures of family and friends to remind you of your connections to others in these exciting (and sometimes scary) days of disconnection in your new place. Create the vibe you want.

Tinker with your room until you get the right feel from it. Remember—this is your home.

Set up a simple filing system for important documents so that you can find things easily, and set up the workspace around your computer to allow sufficient room to spread out. Leave a spot somewhere to shelve your class textbooks and notebooks or binders so that you can find them easily when you need them. Get a laundry basket to catch your laundry so that it doesn't end up strewn all over the place. Get some hangers for your closet and some stackable milk crates or cubes to hold shoes, sweaters, and whatever else.

Remember that keeping your area clean and organized will reduce your own stress and also reduce problems with your roommates.

BE SOCIAL

Be as social as you can during these first few days. Sure it feels awkward.

It feels awkward to everyone. There are hundreds or even thousands of new people to meet. There will be people from all over the country and all over the world, people from backgrounds similar to yours, and others who are completely unlike you.

Some you will like. Others you won't.

Resist the urge to stereotype people, to just cling to your roommates or to your friends from high school or boarding school, or to gravitate to the people most like you. Resist the urge to be shy.

Branch out.

Explore!

Dare.

The first days of college are unlike any other time you will ever experience again. Drink deeply of the experience and live in the moment.

"Try to meet a lot of people and to stay open-minded," Lyndsee advises. "You have to remember that in these first days, people are nervous and very self-conscious, and how they appear when you first meet them might be a product of those emotions rather than a true reflection of their personality. Give them a chance."

"I made a conscious decision to surround myself with all different groups of people," Erik recalls. "I think, generally speaking, the more you can surround yourself with quality people whom you respect and admire and who are from different cultures, backgrounds, and areas of interest, the more fulfilling and rewarding your life will be for having them be part of it."

"Freshman year is like the opening scene in *Animal House* before Flounder and Pinto meet Bluto," Kevin said. "You know, that scene where they're awkwardly hanging around the WASPy frat. It's a big, uncomfortable series of meetings, goings-out, and phone number collecting. I really believe you have to settle yourself socially before you can really begin concentrating on schoolwork."

"But don't necessarily just settle for the people who happen to be on your hallway or in your dorm," Jim added. "There's a whole, big campus out there. Deeply assess the character of the people with whom you are spending time. If you really value who they are, you are lucky. If not, keep searching, because there are undoubtedly people at your school whose friendships you will enjoy deeply. It's okay if you don't meet them right away."

HAVE A ROOMMATE OR SUITE MEETING TO SET THE GROUND RULES

The importance of getting off on the right foot with your roommates and suitemates cannot be overstated. As soon as all your roommates or suitemates have arrived on campus and all parents and relatives have departed, gather everyone together and review the subject matter we discuss in Chapter 9.

Keeping the Peace with Your Roommates and Suitemates

An inexhaustible good nature is one of the most precious gifts of Heaven.

Washington Irving

One of the most important determinants of whether your college experience gets off on the right foot is how well you get along with your roommate and your suitemates if you have them.

Fortunately, no matter which college or university you attend, you have a great deal of control over how well this process goes for you—and taking ownership of the process is one of the most important things you can do to get your college career off to the right start.

THE ROOMMATE QUESTIONNAIRE

Sometime during summer, after you've made a decision about which college you will be attending, your college will send you a "roommate questionnaire." Some of these questionnaires are more involved than others; some are online, others on paper. Some ask for written responses; others are multiple choice. Much has been written about these questionnaires and how best to approach them. We are of one voice on this subject, and we feel strongly that there is only one correct way to answer these questionnaires.

Honestly.

Period.

Do not try to "game" the roommate selection process at your school by making yourself appear to be as antisocial as possible in the hopes of getting a single. Do not try to make yourself sound like a churchmouse so that you end up with a churchmouse for a roommate, with the idea that you'll be able to dominate or to boss that individual around. For every urban legend floating around about the person who made himself sound like Charles Manson and was successfully awarded a single, there are ten stories about people who did this and ended up with a totally incompatible roommate.

Listen to us.

When you get the roommate questionnaire, you'll see that it asks you about your personal habits—things like whether you are an early riser or a night owl, whether you sleep with the windows open or closed, whether you are a smoker or not, and whether you prefer to study with music or in silence. Answer the questions honestly. Believe it or not, colleges and universities actually spend some time devising these questionnaires and the matrixes that are used to analyze the responses and match up compatible students. If you take the questionnaire seriously, answer it honestly, and send it back prior to the deadline, you dramatically increase your chances of, amazingly, ending up in a compatible housing arrangement that will serve you well and support you in your freshman year.

If you screw around trying to "game" the questionnaire or, worse yet, simply fail to send it back at all, you get what you deserve—which, oftentimes, ends up being a room with Samhain, the Devil incarnate. And then you have to fight your RA and the college housing policy to get a room change, which in many cases can be about as easy as going to a bank and asking for free money.

We trust we've made our point.

ALLOW YOURSELF THE CHANCE TO BE PART OF YOUR SCHOOL'S ROOMMATE MATCH PROCESS

So what about rooming with a friend or friends from high school, a sibling attending the same university, or simply avoiding the whole mess by living off-campus right away? Wouldn't that take all of the uncertainty out of the equation and ensure that at least your housing arrangement is the way you want it at the beginning of college?

The answer is that we strongly discourage all three of these approaches as you enter college. Here's why.

Part of the reason you go to college is to grow and change as an individual. If you room with the same people you hung out with in high school, you are likely to fall into the same patterns you did when you were *in* high school. You're likely to socialize with the same people, go to the same places, do the same things, and have the same conversations. College will end up being an extension of high school.

That's not what you're paying for.

Give yourself a chance to grow. Push yourself. Take the risk of living with some people you've never met before; exposing yourself to different ideas, different cultures, different ways of thinking; and being forced to "work things out" with people. More often than not, these situations either work out well or at least lead you to a new social network of college friends that will expand your base. You can still hang out with your high school friends if you want, and you can even merge the two groups if you feel like it. But give yourself a chance to spread your wings and meet some new people. Only then will you be allowing yourself the full range of possible experiences in college. The same holds true for rooming with siblings—only in that case, the opportunities for volatility are even more dramatic. Unless you have an unusually perfect relationship with your sibling, you probably don't want every little thing you do in college to be observed by a family member, do you? Like whether you're studying hard enough to justify your parents' contribution to your tuition? Or how obliterated you got at the homecoming dance? Or how you hooked up with two different people that weekend?

These are not the subjects any of us would want coming out in a fight over Thanksgiving break.

Finally, there is the whole off-campus question. It is our collective view that one of the great benefits of the college experience is the camaraderie that comes from living in close quarters with other freshman. Yes, we know that dorm prices can be a total rip-off compared to what is available off-campus. Yes, we know that dorms can be really old and ridiculously cramped. As a freshman at Yale, I lived in a room that formerly served as the "servants quarters" for students' personal attendants. Back then, two servants lived in this room; . . . but when I lived there, they jammed four of us into it. In fact, my three roommates and I had the "distinction" of living in the very smallest quad on the Yale campus, because the roofline of the dorm cut off a large chunk of our living space. We couldn't control the heat—which often meant having the windows open in the dead of winter. Don't talk to me about lousy accommodations, because I had the absolute worst accommodations known to mankind during my freshman year. And you know what? I'd go back there in an instant and live through it all again if it meant I could spend another year as a student in New Haven.

In other words, none of that stuff mattered a whit to us. What did matter was the spontaneous late-night poker games that would break out in our suite. The full-contact hallway soccer games that would start up when we all returned from the library. The nights of *Monday Night Football,* good conversation, political debate, deep philosophical discussions about everything under the sun, exposure to new music, new ways of thinking, and countless laughs that would all have been abandoned in the name of nicer accommodations.

You make the call. To us, the choice is pretty clear. Study in the library, but live in the freshman dorms. It is an absolutely essential part of what college is all about—and you will miss that quintessential experience if you opt out.

"Realize that it's going to be hard at first," Lyndsee suggests. "Think about it. You're moving into a room with someone you've never met before in your life, all of your stuff is thrown in there with the other person's stuff, and then you have to figure out how to live together and make it work. But that's the whole point.

If you're lucky, your roommate will turn out to be a great friend, almost as close to you as a sibling. If not, though, it doesn't mean that your relationship can't still be successful. You don't have to be best friends or even to hang out together to live together happily as roommates. I had a lot of friends who were the complete opposites of their roommates, but that's why they *liked* living with them. They had their own lives, but then they got to go home to these people with totally different lives who did different things all day.

You can really learn a lot from a roommate who is not exactly like you. Even if you don't become best friends, you at least get to experience how different people can be, and discover the importance of tolerating and trying to understand those differences."

"My advice would also be to not put too much weight on first impressions," Aaron counsels. "However good or bad you think your roommate is, your opinion will change over time. Give things a little time to settle out. Remember that you're coming from different places and experiences and will have different outlooks on things. Be open-minded to perspectives other than your own, and you'll probably find some common ground on which to build a friendship."

"Theoretically, they use some algorithm to match freshman roommates, but neither my freshman roommate nor I could ever figure out how we got put together," Dan recalls. "He was a nice guy, and we were certainly friendly, but we were very opposite. He was pretty much into getting baked day in and day out and that really wasn't my thing. Then again, I did manage to get nicknamed McGuyver after I fashioned an emergency screen and bowl for his bong out of a coke can and part of a window screen late one night, which illustrates that it is possible to find common ground."

ONCE YOU'RE AT SCHOOL: THE FIRST-NIGHT TALK

So what happens when you get to campus?

First of all, if you end up in a double with bunk beds, do *not* pick a bed until you've had an opportunity to discuss preferences with your roommate. Maybe your roommate wants the top bunk, and you want the bottom—in which case, everything will work out fine. If you both want the same bed, compromise. Rotate by semesters or by months. Try your best to make every initial decision as fair and democratic as humanly possible. Avoid using coin flips and other methods that, although inherently fair, can still engender bitterness in the loser.

Once all your roommates are present and moved in, we strongly recommend having a suite meeting—or what we refer to as the first-night talk. The importance of having this talk and of having everyone present and participating in the talk cannot possibly be overstated. This is the talk where ground rules get established and the rules of the road get written. Schedule the meeting at a time that works for everyone. Block out a couple of hours and make sure that everyone is present and that everyone takes it seriously.

"My freshman roommate and I had a good relationship during the beginning of the term because we built up a mutual group of friends," Chase notes. "However, the situation became difficult later when he elected to start staying out later and adopted a different set of acquaintances. At that point, I asked him if we could lay out some guidelines about not having people in the room late on weekday nights and about how the room should be kept. He agreed in principle to a set of standards, but the unfortunate reality was that there was no mechanism for enforcement. If he broke our agreement and brought friends to the room at 3 A.M. on a Monday, I had little rational recourse.

"In retrospect, we should have set standards from the very beginning, even when there was no apparent need. This would have created a set of expectations and habits, as well as avoiding the appearance that I was creating and trying to impose rules on him."

To this point, we recommend actually setting an informal agenda for this meeting so that everything that needs to be covered actually *gets* covered and discussed up front, before there is any time for disagreements to arise. At a minimum, the following topics should be included on this agenda. We discuss each in depth to give you some ideas.

Personal Property

You need to reach agreement about how to handle issues of personal property. If someone has donated his or her television or stereo to the common space, does everyone have equal rights to it? We recommend that anything "donated" to the common space become the shared property of all roommates for the duration of the school year—meaning that if your stereo goes out there, you should expect to come back from class greeted by your roommate's rap music and have nothing to say about it.

Anyone donating televisions, stereos, and the like to the common space should have an understanding with roommates or suitemates about what will happen if the equipment is broken during the year. How will you be compensated for your loss? Do you care? Will you share in repair or replacement costs equally? If so, will the new equipment become the property of everyone in the suite? If you are not comfortable with the arrangements being discussed, do not put your equipment in the common area.

There should also be some discussion about other personal property, such as clothes, Walkmen, iPods, CDs and tapes, DVDs, and video games. Everyone need to have a clear understanding of what can be borrowed and what cannot. Establish whether or not you want people to ask permission to borrow things first, and what to do if you're not around to be asked. Is it enough to leave a note, or would you rather be asked in person?

Get clear on everyone's preferences.

One of the most sensitive subjects in this regard is the use of computers. Because of the variety of ways that disagreements can arise and trouble can occur involving computers, we recommend that roommates and suitemates *not* share computers. You should password-protect your computer to prevent unauthorized access to it, and not leave your Internet connection on or open while you are away from your room. For a more complete discussion of this subject, check out the chapter on legal issues for college students (Chapter 21).

Joint Costs

What, if anything, do you want to buy collectively for the suite? Perhaps everyone will want to chip in to buy a rug or couch for the common area. Maybe you've agreed that it is the best policy to buy a stereo and a television collectively so that everyone will be collectively on the hook if it is broken or stolen during the year. What about cable television? Linen or laundry service? A refrigerator—and how to stock it? Do you want to agree on a weekly "shopping list" of community items for the fridge, and have a schedule of who is responsible for stocking it? Do you want everyone to buy his or her own stuff and establish a rule that if it isn't yours, you shouldn't touch it? Or do you want to just collect receipts in a single place, agree that everything is communal, and handle reimbursements at a suite meeting once a month? There is no one right way to handle these issues. The only important thing is to discuss them up front and to reach consensus.

Try to be sensitive to the fact that each person in your suite is coming to school with different (sometimes wildly different) financial concerns. Do not assume that because you can afford it, everyone will be okay paying ten bucks a month for satellite television or that everyone will want laundry or linen service in the room. On the other hand, it is not fair for a roommate to cry poverty in order to avoid paying for cable and then mooch cable television for the entire year. These are the issues you need to talk out in your suite meeting—and each one will be different depending on the individuals and their circumstances.

Again, it is not the method or the specific decisions that matter. What *does* matter is coming to an understanding and a consensus that everyone can live with. That way, no one can complain later about being held to that bargain.

Cleanliness and What That Means

Everyone has a different idea of what it means to keep a room or a common area neat and clean. Are you a neat freak who irons and folds all your clothes and requires weekly dusting? If you are, you may find that you need to step back and accept something less than your concept of "clean." On the other hand, you should not have to wade through boxes of moldy half-eaten pizza and your roommate's dirty underwear, either. Once again, communication, flexibility, and compromise are the keys to success here.

Some basics to cover are who takes out the trash and how often, where laundry needs to go to get stored out of the way, who (if anyone) needs to clean the bathroom, and what everyone's pet peeves are—so that you can avoid pushing someone's buttons accidentally. Some people *hate* having damp towels draped over doors and furniture. Others can't handle food items getting left out. For others, it is generic clutter like books, papers, and backpacks in common spaces that drives them crazy.

Whatever your issues are, express them so that all of you can establish a general baseline for cleanliness. Make sure everyone is on board. Then, as soon as the situation starts to slip below that baseline, you can politely bring up the topic with the offending roommate—so that good behaviors get established early on.

Ground Rules for Suite Hours and Use of Common Space

Another important thing to establish in the suite meeting is a set of general ground rules governing conduct in the suite and use of your suite's common space. Do you want to establish some rules about when the suite can be open to others for social time and when it should be closed to outsiders for quiet time? You should discuss with your roommate and all members of your suite what their habits are likely to be. Do they plan to study at the library or in some other remote location? When they are writing papers, will they be doing so in the suite or out? Are they likely to be getting up early or working until the wee hours of the morning? If schedules appear to be incompatible, you'll need to work out a system so that one person's sleep is not routinely interrupted by another person's study habits.

What are the rules going to be about playing music in the suite during the evenings? What about television? Do you want to play it as you go, or do you want to set some general rules about this up front so that everyone knows what the expectations are?

Talk these things out. Again, flexibility and compromise are the keys to success in all these areas.

Overnight Guests

Perhaps the biggest source of frustration and discontent in roommate situations occurs when rules about overnight guests are not clearly established. This may be the most important set of rules to work out—and, not surprisingly, it can also be the most contentious.

The first thing to decide is whether, as a group, you are going to allow overnight guests at all. Assuming that you are, do you want to draw a distinction between, on the one hand, friends coming over and crashing in common areas and, on the other, boyfriends, girlfriends, or "random hookups" coming over and displacing a roommate from his or her bed for a night (or longer). Or, perhaps, do you want to ban overnight guests only during midterm and exam weeks, or during weeks when any of the roommates has a significant paper or project due?

Assuming that you go the permissive route here, the next thing you'll need is a schedule of each of the roommates' midterms, finals, and major papers and projects so that everyone is clear on when the suite needs to be closed to outside visitors. Respecting these "stressful periods" will be paramount to gaining consensus for an otherwise permissive system to prevail—so it is important that these periods be respected without exception.

You'll need a method of alerting other roommates that the room is occupied by an overnight guest. A simple and discreet system, such as hanging something nondescript on the door handle, will do the trick. Typically, this will relegate the other roommate or roommates to "couch duty" for the evening. Proper etiquette in these situations requires that pillows and blankets get moved to the common area for the displaced roommate. Forgetting to do this really puts your displaced roommate in a very uncomfortable situation and is a majorly selfish blunder—so don't forget to do this.

You'll also need to work out some other basic rules with respect to overnight guests of the opposite sex, such as how many times per semester you can relegate your roommate(s) to couch duty, how to guarantee the safety of your roommates and their belongings if you bring home a "random hookup," and what rules will prevail if your random hookup ends up stealing or breaking your roommates' or suitemates' belongings.

Believe us, stranger things have happened—and the safety issue here is one that is truly worth discussing.

Finally, you may want to work out a system for how to manage "high traffic" times—homecoming weekend, winter formal, spring formal, and the like—when multiple roommates may be looking for private time. Are you going to make it first come, first served? If roommates have significant others from out of town, will the roommate whose significant other has not yet visited be given priority? Again, remember that to the extent possible, you should try to set up a system that allows fundamental fairness to prevail. If a roommate's boyfriend or girlfriend is visiting for the first time for the winter formal, a coin flip should not allow another roommate's on-campus boyfriend or girlfriend to stay over for the sixth time. Such a system *will* engender conflict.

"My roommate and I shared a tiny room, but didn't initially have any trouble getting along," Zoe notes. "We had a lot in common, were both relatively low-maintenance people who kept similar hours, and even took some classes together.

The main friction was related to boyfriends spending the night. It was a drag for each of us to regularly get kicked out of our respective bunks on Saturdays, depending on whose boyfriend was visiting. It really helps to set some ground rules about this that you both can agree to at the beginning of the year."

Telephone Messages

Although much of the telephonic communication on campus is now done by cell phone, most students still choose to have a land line in their college dorm as well. Even if your college telecommunications system allows for student-specific voice-mail (most now do), there are still those times when you will answer the phone and have to take a message for one of your absent roommates.

It is easy to avoid conflict in this area: have a central place (a message board, a corkboard, or something similar) where everyone agrees and understands that messages will be left. If you take a call for a roommate, be sure to take down the correct information and then immediately post the message in the agreed-on place.

Nothing frustrates roommates and can cause ill will or misunderstanding more quickly than undelivered or forgotten messages.

You should also come to an understanding early on about whether or not you will be willing to "cover" for a roommate when his or her parents or significant other calls. For example, if your roommate's parents call on a Thursday night and ask you where your roommate is, and you know he or she is at a frat party or, worse yet, is passed out on the floor in front of you, are you going to be willing to cover for your roommate by saying "I don't know"? If your roommate's boyfriend calls, and you know your roommate is presently in your room hooking up with someone else, how are you going to handle that call?

For some people, the concept of covering for your roommate comes easy, and is seen as a question of loyalty and necessity. For others, it is seen as lying—especially if you also have a relationship of any kind with your roommate's parents or significant other and feel put in the middle. For still others, it becomes a question of scope, frequency, and specific facts.

Whatever your take on this issue, be sure to communicate it clearly to your roommates at the beginning of the year so that expectations are clearly established up front. This is another one of the major sources of strife in roommate relations.

Smoking and Drinking in the Room

If one or more of your roommates are occasional or regular smokers, the ground rules about smoking will need to be worked out up front as well. Most of these issues are teased out by the roommate questionnaire, as colleges almost never put a smoker in the same room as a nonsmoker. Nevertheless, not everyone answers roommate questionnaires, and even if they do, not everyone answers them honestly. Habits also change, particularly for students who are away from home for the first time.

Because this is as much an issue of health as it is of choice, the general default rule should bar smoking in bedrooms or common spaces unless *all* roommates agree to the contrary. Try to avoid being judgmental or strident in establishing these ground rules, though. In most cases, a calmly expressed preference for the room and common areas to remain smoke free is all you will need to do to get the cooperation of your smoking roommate(s).

In most states, underage drinking and the personal use of marijuana and other recreational drugs are illegal by law. It is also a well-known fact that these activities are commonplace on nearly every college campus in America. Obviously, each student's use of these substances is a matter of habit and personal choice that you are unlikely to be able to change by having a conversation about it. When bottles of booze or a bag of pot (or worse) is left in plain view in common areas or in a shared room, however, issues of possession can become blurred and can potentially have a legal or disciplinary impact on nonusing roommates.

It is important for each roommate to express his or her views on these subjects in your initial roommate meeting, and for you all to try to establish some compromises that will allow everyone to live in peace and harmony. If issues of possession concern you, ask your roommates to keep their alcohol and other illegal substances in areas that are unambiguously their own, or ask your college housing authority to move you into a different living arrangement.

"If you have a real problem, get help from your resident adviser," Amanda notes. "As an RA for forty students at Cornell, I never had an advisee with a problem of this magnitude."

Parties or "Partying" in Your Room or in Common Areas

On a related subject, you should also discuss the use of your rooms or common spaces for campus parties where drinking and other legally questionable activities might occur. Look to a couple of trusted upperclassmen for guidance on the issue of how your campus police or administration polices such activity. In many cases, you will discover that your campus police and college administration tend to "look the other way" when there are in-room parties or larger, dormwide parties, opting instead to concentrate on such issues as the prevention of theft and violent crime on campus. Knowing this may help calm roommates concerned about possible legal or disciplinary ramifications. If you discover, however, that your college closely enforces rules about underage drinking and the like, then respecting the concerns of your roommates is of paramount importance. Take your lead from responsible upperclassmen at your college or university on these issues.

In any event, in-room cocktail parties or the use of your living space for a larger dorm party should always be the product of a unanimous decision by all affected roommates, discussed and reached in advance of the event. Your failure to do this can result in ill feeling or, worse, a disaffected roommate's reporting the party to the police or the administration.

Decoration of Personal and Common Areas

Obviously, if you share sleeping space with one or more roommates, any common areas of that space must be decorated by the agreement of all. It is not appropriate for anyone to take unilateral action to co-opt common space by, for example, moving a desk into a common room or common area without the agreement of everyone else. You may also want to establish some ground rules about whether the door to your suite, the walls of your common areas, the exterior of your windows, or any other common spaces can be used for political expression.

As I've already explained, I spent the majority of my years at Yale living with seven roommates who became some of my closest friends in the world. We also have some very divergent political viewpoints. We spent our senior year living through the hotly contested election of 1992, which pitted President George Bush (the elder), the embattled incumbent, against Bill Clinton and Ross Perot. Our suite divided bitterly in that election, and there was nary a televised debate that occurred that year that didn't prompt angry debate bordering on ill will—and that was among fast friends.

We opted to handle that issue by agreeing to make our suite a public forum. Each individual suitemate's personal areas, including doors and windows, were open to political expression, but common areas remained off-limits to signage and the like. Having some set ground rules definitely helped ease tensions.

Although it is impossible to imagine every possible scenario that might arise in the decoration of personal or common spaces, it is best always to ask the following question and seriously reflect on your response before taking any action in your room or common area: *Would this be irritating to me if one of my roommates did this without asking me first?*

If you even hesitate in answering that question, ask first.

Respecting Differences

College is all about discovering, learning about, and embracing or at least respecting diversity. To get along in the dorm, in the classroom, and in the world, we all need to learn this lesson early.

You should not assume that you and your roommates are going to agree on the color of your couch, the justifications (or lack thereof) for the war in Iraq, the efficiency of capitalist markets, or the existence of God. You will be up late at night debating Tarantino's new movie, biblical allusions in *Moby-Dick,* the merit of the war on drugs, why marijuana is illegal when alcohol isn't, and the meaning of life.

If you talk more than you listen, and fail to at least seriously consider the merits in other points of view, you cheat yourself out of one of the most important learning experiences that college has to offer: the opportunity to have your thoughts, views, positions, and ideas challenged, tested, and either confirmed or altered by those of your roommates and classmates.

No matter how dogmatic your views on a subject, approach any interaction of a substantive nature with your roommates or classmates respectfully, allowing for differences of opinion and listening to ideas and opinions that contradict your own. Whether your opinion ultimately changes or not, you'll be surprised at how much you learn.

During your first night talk, get this subject of mutual respect for your differences on the table for discussion.

Handling Disagreements

Rest assured that no matter *how* good your relationship is with your roommates, and no matter how clearly your expectations are laid out, disagreements will still arise. It may be about something as simple as an undelivered phone message from a significant other that causes an unnecessary misunderstanding for one of your roommates, or it may be about something as serious as a breach of trust.

Whatever the specific facts, you should establish some ground rules up front about how to handle these disputes when they arise.

If you share your sleeping space with one or more people as part of a larger suite, your first line of communication should be with those individuals. Make sure it is clear to everyone that problems and disagreements should be brought out into the open and not allowed to fester or take on a life of their own. Disputes should be talked out and should be handled by looking for compromises rather than by taking votes, flipping coins, or using other decision-making mechanisms that produce winners and losers.

The same should be true of decisions involving all your suitemates. Be sure that everyone has a chance to express his or her opinion and to have that position or opinion heard and respected by the others. Sometimes, simply having the chance to air grievances or to be "heard" by the others is all that people need to feel better about a situation.

Respecting Reciprocal Privacy and Privilege

For good or for ill, the roommate relationship is an intensely personal one. You will learn more about your college roommate(s) than you know about most people—including intimate details of their personal lives, finances, family, and the like. Discussions with your roommate(s) about any of these things are intended to be private, and should not be gossiped about or discussed openly with others, either in or out of the presence of the person who shared the information with you.

You may find that learning about your roommates' personal lives is an enriching experience that teaches you valuable lessons and draws you closer together. Or you may find, particularly when your roommate attempts to draw you into his or her intense family or severe personal or emotional problems, that it is too much for you to handle.

There are a few subject areas that typically surface in these intensely personal roommate discussions that can provoke discomfort. These subjects include revelations about sexual identity, depression, suicidal thoughts, or addiction. If one of your roommates reaches out and trusts you with personal information on any of these subjects, first and foremost, listen carefully. It is critically important to respect your roommate's privacy with regard to these subjects. However, if a discussion with a roommate becomes uncomfortable, communicates a sense of urgency, or leaves you with the impression that your roommate may harm himself or herself or others, you should immediately call your campus's anonymous hotline on the subject matter at issue, or consult a campus professional for further assistance. It is best to take that approach rather than to communicate your concerns directly to your roommate's parent or parents. Relationships today are complicated, and you may end up doing more harm than good.

Issues about family and personal relationships, questions about sexual identity, and concerns about life direction can usually be contained and discussed privately. When the conversation wanders into such areas as depression, addiction, eating disorders, suicidal thoughts, or other potentially life-threatening scenarios, you should never hesitate to reach out to a confidential helpline for further advice about how to manage the specific situation.

The worst thing you can do in one of these situations is to keep the confidence and do nothing.

The "Most Important" Question to Ask Your Roommates

So at last we come to the most important question you can possibly ask your roommate(s), the question that more than any other will help ensure that you get along.

Ready?

Here it is:

"What is the most important thing I need to know and respect about you or your things that will help us get along this year?"

This question will inevitably prompt a response and follow-up questions. You will be amazed at how easily it gets you into the areas you most need to discuss, and at how much you will learn about your roommate(s) by listening to the response you get.

Try it during your first-night talk.

SOME OTHER THOUGHTS AND SUGGESTIONS

Living with others in close proximity, particularly when you are doing so for the first time, requires patience, understanding, a willingness to communicate, and an ability to compromise. Before you go nuclear on a roommate, take a step back and review the situation. Were you as respectful as you could or should have been? Could the issue be the product of a misunderstanding? Might you let this one go, and chalk it up to someone's being a little self-absorbed or having a bad day? Pick your battles. Someone's eating your last package of Ramen noodles is not as important as your roommate's putting you on couch duty on the eve of an important exam.

If you do choose to engage a roommate on a subject, be assertive rather than aggressive. Ask a lot of questions, and don't interrupt your roommate when he or she is responding. Try to be creative and collaborative, rather than combative, in searching for a solution that works for everyone. In any roommate situation, you have an inalienable right to your own safety and bodily integrity and to have your personal property respected. Everything else is the product of compromise and negotiation.

"It can be hard to share a bedroom with a complete stranger," Zoe counsels, "but being quiet, kind, and respectful goes a long way. Try to deal with issues directly and as soon as they come up. Even a heated argument, when face to face, is much less damaging to a relationship than getting caught whining about a problem behind your roommate's back."

"The best strategy for good roommate relationships is to always be respectful, flexible, and willing to listen, compromise, and work things out," Tom added.

"Kill 'em with kindness," Chase adds. "Everyone has their idiosyncrasies and annoying habits. Win your roommate over by embracing all of their good features and acquiescing to some of their desires so that when they are doing something that bothers you, they will be more likely to try to please you, too."

"Avoid being hostile or accusatory. Find somewhere to study outside of your room. Ask your roommate to use headphones if music is an issue. Establish rules for sleep that you can both buy into. And be prepared to be forgiving, as drunken mistakes are pretty common during freshman year," Jim counsels.

"Get to know each others' schedules and routines so that you can anticipate situations and respect them," Lyndsee added.

"The ideal freshman roommate is a partner in crime," Kevin concludes. "You work together in harmony to make a squadron of new friends, watch each others' backs, offer counsel, share frustrations, and are open with each other.

"Although it doesn't always work out that way, passive aggression will only make you both angry, so don't take that approach. If Scott keeps throwing his wet towel on your bed after taking a shower, don't ball up the towel and throw it into the hall—talk to Scott about it! Recognize that emotions can run pretty high in such close quarters, particularly with everyone adjusting to a new environment. Getting along is really all about cutting the other person slack."

"Communicate!" Dan agrees. "Recognize that everyone is adjusting to a new environment and new stressors. Try to be clear about your needs and at the same time, to be respectful of theirs."

IF YOUR ROOMMATE SITUATION SUCKS . . .

So let's say you've tried all our suggestions, and your roommate situation still really sucks. Maybe your roommates have similar views on life that diverge radically from your own, such that compromise is virtually impossible. Maybe you are the "odd man out," or your roommates have turned on you, and despite your best efforts to find common ground, there isn't much ground to be found. Maybe your roommate is an addict, a racist, a bigot, or just an incomparable asshole.

What then?

First, try to take some pressure off your living arrangement by focusing your life outside the dorm. Get involved in extracurricular activities, Greek life, or social service activities, and find friends in other dorms to hang out with. Being away from your room a lot and looking outward rather than inward for your social network may make the year tolerable.

But what if your situation is *truly* intolerable?

If your roommate situation involves a real threat to your personal safety, if your roommates are engaged in illegal activity, if you have been physically harmed, or if your personal belongings and privacy are being invaded, it may be time to solicit the involvement of others. Before you cry wolf, though, be sure you have taken every step and tried all of the approaches we've discussed. Document on paper the efforts you have made to handle things privately.

Once you've done this, if your situation has not improved, make an appointment to see your freshman adviser, resident adviser, hall director, or residential college dean. Explain your situation calmly, without becoming emotional or otherwise overstating or overreacting to the situation. Be assertive in asking for solutions and don't allow yourself to be brushed off. If this approach does not work, take your complaint up the chain of authority until you get satisfaction.

"One friend of mine had a freshman roommate who refused to bathe or to ever change her bedsheets," Kevin noted. "She would also whisper under her breath every night as the two of them were lying in their beds. That is a rough roommate."

Staying Safe on Campus

Safety is something that happens between your ears.

Jeff Cooper

Whether you are attending college in a large urban center, a small town, or in the middle of nowhere, your campus will be an attraction for criminal activity. A high concentration of young people with cash, computers, and lots of the latest hot electronic gadgetry, coupled with the frequently lax security of propped doors and open windows, creates a prime target for criminals. According to recent surveys, one in three college students will be a victim of criminal activity before he or she graduates. So how can you protect yourself?

At the beginning of your freshman year, your college will conduct an on-campus security briefing. Many of your classmates will scoff at attending this event, claiming to be too worldly and sophisticated to need a briefing to learn how to protect themselves. You may feel that way too, but go to it anyway. These briefings are typically run by the heads of your campus police or security detail and include extremely valuable information, such as trends in crime on your campus, the most frequent crimes at your particular school and how best to prevent them, information about particular campus security devices and how to use them, and news from your local police precinct about any particularly dangerous neighborhoods or other areas that border your campus.

The security briefing will probably last only an hour. Spend the time. Beyond that, here are the most important things to consider.

THE TEN MOST CRITICAL CAMPUS SAFETY TIPS

Safeguard Your Keys, Security Access Card, and College ID Card

It may seem so obvious as to not even need mentioning, but you'd be shocked to learn how many people lose their keys, access card, or ID and then go days or even weeks without reporting it. Remember, this is more than an issue of your own convenience. A key, access card, or college ID with a barcode on it gets a thief past most levels of campus security and into the gym, the libraries, classroom buildings, and the dorms. Remember that possession of one or more of these items can also give a criminal the appearance of legitimacy in the eyes of campus security officials or another student. Don't wait: report the loss of any such item immediately so that it can be disabled, and then obtain a replacement.

And although it is a popular thing to do, you should *never* attach your college ID card to your key chain. A lost set of keys, by itself, still poses a challenge to a would-be thief. A lost set of keys with your ID card attached to it draws a map to your doorway.

Maintain the Perimeter Security of Your Dorm

Many college dorms and residence halls have an outer perimeter of locked gates that enclose courtyards, recreation areas, dining halls, performance spaces, and classrooms in addition to the dorms themselves. These gates are typically controlled either by a separate key, an electronic access card, or the magnetic stripe on your college ID card. These perimeter security features only work, however, if they are allowed to function as intended—as a barrier to entry to those without the proper means of access. Be vigilant about whom you allow to breach this perimeter. This means not holding the gate open for complete strangers following you into your campus courtyard (and thus giving them access) without asking them for identification. It means reporting any suspicious person in or around your dorm to campus security immediately—even if you're not certain that the person doesn't belong. It means not propping open gates to dormitory courtyards to run things in from your car, or disabling automatic locks on dormitory access doors so that friends from other dorms can get up to your room without a key. Remember, gates and locks work only if you use them.

"Don't loan anyone your keys and don't hold the dorm door or the main door open for *anyone,*" Amanda agreed. "This means you have to get comfortable with shutting the door in someone's face, which some people might find rude."

Prevent Access to Your Dorm Room Itself

This means closing the windows to your dorm room when you leave for class in the morning or when you go out at night. It means not sleeping with all the windows to your room wide open unless you live on a high floor. And yes, it means locking the door to your dorm even when all you are doing is going down the dorm hall to take a shower or go to the bathroom.

Ridiculous, you say? Consider this.

Thieves who steal on college campuses are typically not the sort of folks who just happen to be passing by and decide to try to gain access to a dorm just for the hell of it. They can be fellow students, members of the maintenance staff, or "townies"—but the one characteristic they all share is that they know what they're doing. They are keen observers; they spend lots of time watching and waiting, looking for opportunities. And chances are, they've been in your dorm before and know how to prey on good-natured students to get in again. They *will* be waiting at the gate to your dormitory courtyard, loaded down with bags so it appears that they can't easily access a key card. Or claiming to be there for an activity meeting and running late. Or there from out of town to visit a friend who is not answering the phone. Or there to fix a problem in the dorm, with a nonfunctioning access card. They know all the tricks to get good-natured college students to help them breach security, and they'll use any or all of them to gain access to your dorm. You can be as apologetic as you want, but if you don't recognize the person as a classmate or a resident of your dorm, you *cannot* let the person get in. Offer to call the campus police to help the person out. But don't think you're being "nice" by letting an unknown person into your dorm. You're not. You're putting all the residents of your dorm, including yourself, at risk.

Once he's in, it takes only a second for someone to watch you leave your room; slip in behind you; grab your laptop, your wallet, or your iPod; and slip away and be gone long before you've even put the toothpaste on your toothbrush. And of course, if you are reckless enough to allow someone to get into your dorm room, you are putting your faith in the belief that all he wants is your laptop.

Do you really want to take that chance?

Be "Street Smart"

Know your campus well enough to know which streets and campus walkways are the most well lit and well traveled at night. When walking at night, try to walk in pairs or more, or use campus security escort services or your college shuttle service to get around. Memorize the phone number for these services so you will be able to easily access them when you need them. If you must walk alone, avoid dark corners, entrances to alleyways, or deserted areas, such as empty lots, parking garages, parks, playgrounds, or cemeteries. When walking, stay off your cell phone so you can be aware of your surroundings. Be alert to who may be waiting ahead of you or following behind you, and don't approach strangers or let them get close to you. If someone appears to be following you, or if you spot someone waiting on a bench or sidewalk ahead of you, cross the street, reverse your direction, or head for the nearest open business establishment. Walk briskly and with confidence—thieves look for meek and easy targets.

"Don't wear a Walkman or an iPod or whatever when you're walking alone at night," Amanda cautions. "You are allowing people to approach you without your being aware of them. And don't walk alone at night. Most campuses have escorts you can call or free buses you can take at night. This sounds simple, but it means you need to think about how and when you'll be getting home before you leave home."

"Stay in a group as much as possible," Lyndsee adds. "When you're in a group, you are much less likely to be the target of crime."

Trust your instincts. If a developing situation feels uncomfortable to you, remove yourself from it or call the police from your cell phone or the nearest campus security phone. It is better to call your campus police on a false alarm than it is to wait for a criminal act to fully develop.

"Your instincts will often be right, so if something or someone seems 'off' to you, do what you need to do to get away or get help," Lyndsee added. "I went to school in New York City for four years and was never a victim of any crime because I followed and applied these simple suggestions."

If you must wait for public transportation after dark, do so at the busiest and most well lit stop, even if that means you need to walk a little bit farther to get to it. When walking to this stop, travel well-lit streets.

Do not run at night without a companion. If you need to blow off steam at night, go to the gym or run your dormitory stairs. Lone joggers are among the most frequent victims of campus crime after dark.

Finally, be especially careful when returning home after a night in the bars or at frat parties. If you are impaired, you are likely to be less vigilant, making it all the more important to travel in groups, or at least on the buddy system.

Understand How to Use Your College's Emergency Phones

Learn the locations of your college's "blue light" emergency phones on your most frequently traveled routes, particularly routes that you take at night—for example, from your dorm to the library or your favorite study spot and from the bars and fraternities to your dorm. In most cases, these phones simply require you to press a button to activate an emergency response to the location of the phone, and don't require you to dial or explain your situation. Learn how to use this equipment in advance so that you'll know how to use it in an emergency.

Be Especially Vigilant Around ATM Machines

ATM machines, particularly those in remote locations, in unlocked buildings, or open to the street make attractive and easy targets for criminals. When withdrawing money from an ATM, choose one inside a bank or in an active, central area. Avoid withdrawing money at night—even in a place where a door locks behind you, as thieves often watch these locations and can be waiting for you when you emerge from the enclosure, often disguised as another person waiting to use the machine.

What to Do If You Are Confronted by a Thief

If, despite your best efforts, you are confronted by a mugger at close range, *cooperate*. Activate a personal alarm or campus security phone only if you can do so without being detected; otherwise, *do not resist or try to be a hero.* Do not wait to be shown a weapon. Try to stay calm and speak in a soft, measured voice. Give the person your wallet, keys, jewelry, or whatever other possessions the person asks for. Do not lie about or try to hide something the mugger wants. Remember that your life is more valuable than any of your possessions. Don't make any sudden moves that might startle the mugger into violence. When reaching for your wallet or jewelry that has been requested, let the person know what you are going to do so that he doesn't mistake your movement as an effort to reach for a weapon.

In most cases, a mugging lasts only a matter of seconds: the mugger grabs your purse or wallet and departs. When the mugging is over, note the general direction in which the mugger departed and notify campus police as soon as you can after reaching a place of safety.

In the rarest of cases where an unknown assailant tries to force you into a car, an abandoned building, or to another remote spot, you should resist. Offer the mugger any of your belongings that he might want. If he is not satisfied and insists that you get into a car or follow him into a building or an alley, you'll have to make a break for it. When doing so, drop anything you are carrying and run in a zigzag pattern to make it harder for the mugger to shoot you. Run toward the nearest well-lit, well-traveled place, staying near the middle of any street or road, and notify the police as soon as you have reached a place of safety.

Always Lock Your Bike and Don't Leave Personal Items Unattended

The most common crimes on college campuses are petty thefts, and the items stolen most often are bikes, backpacks, and laptop computers. Register your bike with the city or campus police; get a sturdy combination lock and lock your bike *every* time you leave it somewhere—even on a quick stop at the campus bookstore or to drop off a paper for a professor. It takes only a moment for a waiting thief to snatch an unattended bike and ride away.

Likewise, do not leave your backpack, purse, or laptop unattended in a classroom, public space, or the library. If you must leave to go to the bathroom, take a call, or retrieve something, ask someone nearby whom you know and trust to watch your belongings. If there is no one around whom you know, take your things with you. A stolen backpack is an inconvenience. A stolen laptop with a semester's class notes and papers on it is an unmitigated disaster.

"The only crime I ran into at college stemmed first from the mistakes of students, not the ingenuity of criminals," Chase noted. "Most crime was small-scale theft of items that were left where anyone could grab them. So don't go to the bathroom and leave your laptop on the table in the coffee shop, don't leave your purse in the computer lab, and don't go jogging by yourself at 3 A.M. with your bright white iPod because you are feeling stressed."

"It is also prudent to keep your wise comments to yourself if someone has something to say to you that is disrespectful," Erika added. "These days, you need to watch what you say and choose your battles wisely."

Be Sure Your Dorm-Room Smoke Detector Is Operational and Know Your Escape Route in the Event of a Dormitory Fire

Dormitory fires are rare, but they do happen, and when they do, they can be deadly. Be sure your dorm-room smoke detector is operational and that you replace the battery at the start of every new term. Even more important, determine a couple of escape routes in the event that you awaken to find your dorm on fire—remembering that in a worst-case scenario, the nearest stairwell may be involved in the fire. Finally, choose a central meeting location somewhere outside your dorm in the event of an emergency so that you can quickly account for the whereabouts of all of your roommates.

Exchange Emergency Information with Your Roommates and Keep a Call List in the Room

At the beginning of the year, obtain a list of the names and contact information for each of your roommates' parents and siblings and keep that list near the phone in your common room. That way, in the event of a sudden illness or emergency involving one of your roommates, you can easily make contact with the necessary people.

SOME ADVICE ABOUT DATE RAPE

Date rape, or acquaintance rape, is an increasingly common problem on college campuses all over the country, and involves people of both sexes. Rape is defined by most state criminal codes as unwanted sexual penetration—and the proof problems inherent in that definition are cause enough to spend a moment acquainting yourself with this issue and how to protect yourself from becoming involved in a date-rape situation.

First of all, go into any situation—be it a date, an evening at a bar, or a party at a fraternity—with a clear sexual limit in your own mind *before* you find yourself in the situation. Know what you want, and once you've decided what that is, be sure not to let flirting cross the line into the world of mixed messages that could be misunderstood by others observing your behavior. Many date-rape cases devolve into "he said, she said" situations and thus involve testimony from witnesses at a bar or club who are asked to describe what they saw.

Don't assume that another person will know what your limits are or will respect those limits unless you have clearly and assertively articulated them. Although silence does not constitute consent, silence also does not communicate a limit. Don't assume that just because you are with a friend or someone you've dated before, you don't need to set clear limits—alcohol or drugs can impair judgment no matter who is involved.

As with all things, trust your instincts. If a situation becomes uncomfortable to you, particularly if your partner is not respecting your clearly expressed limits, is attempting to cajole you into exceeding those limits, is attempting to control you, or is becoming forceful or belligerent, remove yourself from the situation *immediately.* Understand that if a scenario has proceeded this far, you might need to be rude, scream, or even use force to remove yourself from the situation. Don't hesitate to do so, and once you've removed yourself from the situation, seek help immediately.

We also need to remind you that in recent years, the introduction of date-rape drugs into some campus cultures has produced even more frightening scenarios. Typically these situations arise when someone buys you a drink and, before handing it to you, slips a sleeping pill, antihistamine, or recreational "club drug" like ecstasy, rohypnol ("roofies," "R2-Do-U," "rope"), GHB ("Easy Lay," "Liquid Ecstasy," "Scoop"), or ketamine ("Special K," "Vitamin K," "KO") into it. Because these drugs are usually tasteless, odorless, colorless, and fast acting, they are virtually undetectable to you, but will make you act without inhibition, often in an affectionate or sexually responsive way, and may ultimately render you incapable of thinking clearly, expressing limits, or resisting advances. Consumed in sufficient quantity, these drugs can even render you unconscious. Further, because all traces of these drugs typically leave your system within seventy-two hours and are not picked up by any routine toxicology or blood screening, their presence is often difficult to detect. In most cases, their aftereffect leaves the victim with no clear memory of what happened while the drug was active in her system—making the victim a very poor witness in any attempted prosecution.

There are, of course, some simple steps you can take to protect yourself from being victimized by a classmate looking to use a date-rape drug.

Use the Buddy System

Use the buddy system when going to parties or clubs, and do not abandon your buddy unless you are *certain* that the situation is safe.

"If you are going to a party, have a plan *before* you go about who you'll be with, how much you plan to drink, and how and when you plan to get home. Then share that plan with a friend who will be there so you can mutually keep track of one another," Zoe advised.

"The buddy system was practically invented to prevent the downside that can be encountered when too much alcohol is involved," Erik noted. "I know several people who experienced date rape and it almost always happened at parties where there was alcohol readily available and one or both of the people involved became completely drunk and incapable of controlling the environment."

"A buddy system *can* be useful, but it has its drawbacks," Amanda explains. "I have way too many stories of people who promised to stick together and then didn't, resulting in someone who didn't want to be left behind getting left behind. Your buddy must be trustworthy and your agreement firm. Remember, if you are looking for romance and considering ditching your buddy, anyone who is worth kissing will still want to kiss you when you are both sober."

"Don't get drunk in places that are unfamiliar to you," Jim added. "Women need to be especially careful about this given the high incidence of date rape. Freshman women, in particular, are targeted because of their naiveté."

Take Rumors and Gossip to Heart

If you hear rumor or gossip that drinks at a certain club or fraternity party may be tainted, take these rumors seriously and either don't go to the club or party or leave immediately. Remember that these drugs are virtually undetectable, and you may not know you have been affected until it is too late.

Get Your Own Drinks

Although it may be flattering and romantic to allow others to buy drinks for you, do not accept drinks from strangers and do not assume that the bartender is beyond reproach. When getting a drink or buying a round, watch the bartender pour your drink and then control your order yourself—don't allow someone else to deliver it to you.

Don't Leave Your Drink Unattended

Don't leave your drink unattended while you dance or go to the bathroom. Doing so allows more than sufficient opportunity for someone who has been watching you to tamper with your drink while you are away and then appear later to take advantage of you. Take your drink with you or leave it with a friend you trust.

Do Not Drink from Common Sources

Pitchers, punchbowls, and Jell-O shots all provide someone with bad intentions the opportunity to slip something into a serving directed to you. Be extremely vigilant when consuming from these sources.

Consider Using Test Strips to Help Protect Yourself

Recognizing the increased prevalence of date-rape drugs in our culture, several companies are now producing technologies to help you inconspicuously and nonchalantly test a drink or a drink source for contamination by date-rape drugs. These technologies, which typically come in the form of a coaster or a test strip, change colors to alert you to the presence of one of the major date-rape drugs in your beverage. The strips, in particular, are easy to carry in a wallet or purse, and they allow you to conduct a discreet test almost anywhere and at any time. For more information, visit www.drinksafetech.com. Remember, however, that testing the occasional drink should not replace ordinary vigilance or your adherence to the other suggestions we've made here.

A Brief Overview of the Typical "Core" Curricular Requirements

It is, in fact, nothing short of a miracle that modern methods of instruction have not entirely strangled the holy curiosity of inquiry.

Albert Einstein

As students have become more and more interested in specialization, colleges and universities have struggled to come up with ways to ensure that all their students graduate with some basic experiential familiarity with each of the four core disciplines in the liberal arts—namely, humanities and the arts, social science, natural science, and quantitative reasoning—as well as proficiency in a foreign language and a demonstrable ability to write effectively.

Whether this effort is called a "core curriculum" or is couched as a series of "foundational" or "distributional" requirements, what it means to you is a series of additional curricular obligations that you need to be aware of and vigilant about satisfying.

In almost all cases, these requirements can be found in the early pages of your course catalogue, which was mailed to you during the summer. Take a close look at this now if you haven't already done so, and familiarize yourself with the particular requirements your school considers foundational to the eventual award of your degree. Next, if you haven't already done so, write these core curricular requirements into your *Campus Confidential* workbook. We'll begin to sketch out a semester-by-semester map detailing how you intend to complete them in Chapter 13.

Although every school's core curriculum or foundational requirements are somewhat different, there are some commonalities. We address each of these briefly here as a starting point to your inquiry.

THE COLLEGE WRITING REQUIREMENT

Perhaps no other requirement is becoming more widespread (and, frankly, more necessary) than the college writing requirement, as more and more college graduates have appeared in the working world and in graduate school without good writing skills. Expect to see a requirement of at least two courses that provide special attention to prose composition.

FOREIGN LANGUAGE PROFICIENCY

As our country becomes more diverse and as advances in transportation and technology make the world smaller, proficiency in more than one language is becoming increasingly important and in fact more of an expectation in the business world. In response, most colleges and universities are now requiring their students to achieve proficiency in a foreign language. Some are even going a step further and requiring students who enter college already proficient in a second language to meet the same requirements for a *third* language. Expect to see a proficiency requirement here—typically requiring three to four courses.

QUANTITATIVE REASONING

This is the fancy name for math and statistics. Expect a requirement of one or two courses in this area to impart basic mathematical skills that students will need throughout their lives. If this scares the hell out of you because you have math anxiety, look for courses that are referred to as "writing intensive," which means that the weekly problem sets count for much more, and the exams count for much less.

HUMANITIES AND THE ARTS

This field encompasses the study of cultural, literary, artistic, and philosophical questions from a historical and critical perspective. Languages, literature, religion, art, music, drama, and writing all fall into this category. Expect to have to take at least two classes in this area.

NATURAL SCIENCES

The natural sciences involve the systematic examination of the animate and inanimate world through biology, chemistry, physics, geology, astronomy, environmental studies, and the like. Most colleges and universities require you to take at least two classes in this area on the theory that studying a science requires students to think critically in different ways and to learn the methods of close analysis, deductive reasoning, observation, and experimentation that characterize the work of scientists. If the fear of this requirement keeps you awake at night, don't panic. Most school curricula feature hard-science workarounds (called "gut" courses) for fearful humanities students who would rather spend years in a Turkish prison than spend one moment in a chemistry lab.

SOCIAL SCIENCES

Like those in the natural sciences, courses in the social sciences rely heavily on the analysis of data, but they concentrate on the study of people and institutions. Most colleges offer a wide array of coursework in these areas, including history, political science, government, economics, psychology, sociology, and cultural studies. Expect a minimum of two courses in this area.

PREMED

Most medical schools require a year of biology with laboratory, a year of inorganic chemistry with laboratory, a year of organic chemistry with laboratory, a year of physics with laboratory, a full year of college-level English courses, and a semester of college-level calculus. Some of the more competitive medical schools require additional coursework in the sciences, social sciences, and writing. The Association of American Medical Colleges (AAMC) publishes a guidebook, *Medical School Admission Requirements*, affectionately referred to as the MSAR, which lists the admissions requirements of the 148 licensed medical schools in the United States. If you already have some specific medical schools in mind, you may want to consult a copy of the MSAR in your college library. For a full treatment of premed strategies and ideas about how best to schedule your premed coursework, consult our sister publication *Med School Confidential*, available at all local or online bookstores.

USING ADVANCED PLACEMENT (AP) CREDIT TO "PLACE OUT" OF CURRICULAR REQUIREMENTS

Colleges and universities recognize that students enter college with different degrees of proficiency in various subjects. Many of these colleges and universities therefore allow students to "place out" of certain introductory-level courses or other core curricular requirements. At some schools, placing out of such introductory-level courses as biology, inorganic chemistry, and physics can satisfy your premed requirements *and* your natural science requirements at the same time, offering you a tremendous advantage in flexibility in scheduling coursework in your major and other electives. Likewise, placing out of a language requirement or a writing requirement can save you four to six class slots that you can then use in other ways.

Eligibility for AP credit can be demonstrated by meeting or exceeding benchmark scores set by your college or university on individual AP or SAT II examinations, or by passing a departmental examination administered by your college or university at the beginning of the semester.

Note well, however, that not every school treats these credits the same way. Some schools will allow you to use them to circumvent core curricular requirements, providing you with an instant reward of curricular flexibility. Other schools merely let you use AP credit to "qualify" as a freshman for a more advanced class in a particular subject. Needless to say, there is a big difference between these two systems, and knowing which one your college or university employs is critical to understanding what your curricular requirements actually are. Read your course catalogue carefully and then check in with your registrar's office to confirm your understanding.

Many students chafe against the requirements of the core curriculum. With the breadth and scope of courses offered in each of the "core" areas, however, there is little cause for concern.

"I'm in favor of core curricular requirements to the extent that they prod students to explore new or foreign subjects and to expose themselves to ideas that might be in opposition to their own," Zoe says. "As adults, in both the workplace and in society in general, we're well served by people who can see problems and solutions from multiple perspectives. Higher education is certainly not the only place to acquire this perspective, but it is a rich opportunity."

"I believe in a liberal arts education," Amanda agreed, "because I think it gives you the most well-rounded education and allows you to go in many directions later on, not to mention giving you the ability to hold an intelligent conversation on a variety of topics in the years to come."

"A core curriculum is beneficial, but it certainly doesn't have to be limiting," Tom advises. "There must be hundreds if not thousands of courses that can be taken at college!"

Your Freshman Year Goal-Setting Workshop

Beginnings are always messy.

John Galsworthy

T he benefits of setting goals have long been well known in the business and professional world, but very few college students ever commit to sitting down and developing a well thought out set of goals for each year of college, for their college years as a whole, and for their lives after college.

"Wait a minute," you say. "I've always understood my college years to be a time for me to explore interests, make some mistakes, get tossed around a little bit, and, through those experiences, gain wisdom, grow as a person, and figure things out."

We don't have a problem with that. That's certainly what we did when we were in college. This goal-setting workshop doesn't foreclose *any* of that. What we're about to do, though, is get you to sit down and harness the power of goal setting by thinking about what it is that you'd *like* to explore during the next year, the next four years, and, perhaps, your life as a whole; committing those thoughts to writing; and then setting up a plan for actually pursuing those goals. That way, rather than wandering around aimlessly wasting a lot of time and coming out the other end of your college years having missed a lot of opportunities, you will actually do a lot more of the exploring you want to do and achieve a lot more of your goals than you ever thought possible.

Trust us.

Just trust us and do the exercises in this chapter. You'll be amazed at how empowered you feel when you finish and at how much you can accomplish when you create a plan and actually set it in motion.

So if you're ready to proceed, take yourself somewhere where you won't be disturbed for the next hour or so. Turn off your cell phone, get out a pen and your *Campus Confidential* workbook, and concentrate. You are about to engage in one of the most fun and most important activities of your life to date. Be sure that you actually keep your responses to this activity in your workbook because we're going to refer you back to them throughout your four years in college and you'll want to be able to access them easily. Your responses to these questions through the next four years will also be a testament to your growth during college.

We've divided the workshop into six categories: (1) academic and career goals, (2) social goals, (3) extracurricular goals, (4) physical goals, (5) financial goals, and (6) spiritual goals. Concentrating on these individual areas separately should allow you to better focus your brainstorming and come up with a more complete list of ideas.

Remember not to censor yourself. Just write down everything that comes to mind. You'll have a chance to go back through the ideas later to decide on priorities. For now you just want to dump your pent-up thoughts down on paper. Try to keep writing in each category for at least five minutes.

Ready?

Let's begin.

YOUR FRESHMAN YEAR ACADEMIC AND CAREER GOALS

What are some of the academic goals you have coming into college? What possible careers do you find turning around in your head? Are you premed? Does the idea of becoming a lawyer appeal to you? Or perhaps you are focused on a career in business or are interested in becoming an entrepreneur? What subjects would you need to take to properly explore these fields? Maybe one of your goals should be to establish a plan of action to properly explore and perhaps complete one of these programs.

What about teaching or working for a nonprofit?

Or are you interested in a career in finance?

Or something else in the health professions?

Would you need to talk to an academic adviser to help you along?

What courses did you enjoy in high school that you might want to study more intensively in college? Did you enjoy American literature? Maybe you were a history buff. Perhaps you want to try to really understand economics.

Do you want to learn to speak another language, whether just for fun, for larger career reasons, or with an eye on doing a semester or a year abroad later in college?

Are you into computers or electronics? Are there some courses or programs that you might want to take to explore those interests and to give you some hands-on experience?

Are you into art or music? Do you want to study an instrument or learn to sing, draw, paint, or sculpt? Or learn more about art and art history? You can major in art or music in college, you know—they're not just extracurricular activities!

What kinds of skills do you want to try to master during your freshman year? Do you want to learn to be a more analytical writer? A more creative writer? Do you want to become a more careful reader? Or just someone who can read more or for longer without tiring? All of these things are really about practice.

Do you want to learn to be a better note taker or develop more critical listening skills so that you can get more out of your lectures? Do you want to learn how to be better organized?

What kind of academic life do you think would give you the greatest satisfaction? Do you want to be doing a lot of pleasurable or analytical reading? A lot of writing? Are you someone who learns better by doing, such that laboratory work might be of interest to you?

What about class size? Do you want to take a lot of large introductory survey courses this year, or do you want to find one or two small seminars that will allow you to talk out ideas more in a small-group setting?

What academic things do you want to get out of this year and out of college generally? Write down everything that you'd like to try to explore this year or at some point during college.

You have five minutes. Keep your pen moving and remember to record all of your responses in your *Campus Confidential* workbook

Go!

If you've reached the end of your five minutes and you want to keep going, by all means do so. If you've written a good list of at least ten or twelve items and you've listed everything you can think of right now that qualifies as an academic goal for this year or for college generally, then go ahead and move on to the next section.

During the next day or two, more things will come to mind. As they do, be sure to add them to the list in your workbook. Don't just let them wander into and out of your consciousness. Capture your thoughts so that you can turn them into goals!

On to the next section.

YOUR FRESHMAN YEAR SOCIAL GOALS

For a great many of us, college is a time for reinvention—a chance to wipe the slate from high school or boarding school clean and to start a new life in a new place. So who is it that you'd like to become? Do you want to be more outgoing, to force yourself to get out of your comfort zone, to be more daring about asking someone out? Or were you someone who got labeled in high school as a flirt or player or phony or brownnoser, and now find yourself eager to shake that rap as you start your new life in college?

Or are you somewhere in the middle—someone who is just resolved to make a few new good friends, find someone you care about (and actually date the person, rather than just wistfully think about dating him or her), and make a good life for yourself in college?

Whether you were wildly popular, an outcast, a nerd, or anything else on the social spectrum in high school, the slate is clean again now.

What did you learn from your high school experiences? What do you hope to do differently this time, freed from the labels that you wore then? Who and what do you hope to become socially? How do you plan to get there?

Is pledging a fraternity or a sorority important to you? If so, what kind of "fit" are you looking for? Think about it now, before your feelings get clouded by what you hear from others.

Is getting out and meeting a lot of new people on campus going to be important to you? Or are you going to be satisfied to make a few really good new friends and drink deeply of those relationships?

What kinds of choices are you planning to make about drugs, alcohol, and sex?

It truly *is* possible to recast yourself in a new image in college, and as long as you are doing so for the right reasons, it can be a really liberating experience. Freed from the bonds of the perceptions everyone had of you in high school, you can really spread your wings and grow into the person you want to become.

But who is that?

Think about this—for yourself, not for what you think others will think is "cool" or what you think will be "popular." What aspects of your personality and behavior do you want to dial up in your new life, and what aspects do you want to dial down? Do you want to be a better or more thoughtful friend? Do you want to become someone who talks less and listens more? Do you want to challenge yourself by trying to become more expressive of your thoughts and feelings than you were in high school?

Are there aspects of who you are that you'd like to move front and center now? Maybe your outdoorsiness or your musical tastes or your politics or your religious beliefs or your sexual orientation needs more expression than it had in high school. Maybe you just want to try to have a little more fun or to take life a little less seriously. Or maybe you need to get more serious about life now.

Or maybe you're happy with yourself just the way you are. If you are, that's great! But most of us found that as we entered college, we were eager to do a little tweaking to our personalities and to recast ourselves in a slightly different way than we were perceived by our peers in high school.

We're talking about social goals for your freshman year—as you get the chance to try on a new skin, break out of your old mold, and become the person you've always wanted to become.

Who is that?

Write for at least five minutes, listing everything you'd like to try, everything you'd like to explore, and anything that you'd like to experience socially this year or at some point during college.

Go!

It's kind of exciting to create the blueprint for the "new you," isn't it? Again, the key here is to focus on the things you want to become, basing your thoughts on what you learned in high school or boarding school—not on what you think will be popular with your new peers. You need to be comfortable in your own skin and to be genuine.

So what did you find out?

You probably thought of a few things you'd like to tweak—a few interests or qualities you might want to accentuate, and a few that you might want to shelve in your new life. That's great. This is, after all, a brainstorming session. More on what to do with these ideas in a little while. As before, if additional thoughts hit you in the coming days, be sure to add them to your workbook.

For now, though, let's move on to extracurricular goals.

YOUR FRESHMAN YEAR EXTRACURRICULAR GOALS

As you are well aware, college is about much more than simply taking the classes you need to complete your major and graduate with your degree. Along the way, there will be countless opportunities to get involved with varsity or intramural sports and a blinding array of campus and community activities.

The sad part is, you can't even come close to sampling them all.

What you *can* do, though, is brainstorm a list of things you'd like to try during freshman year or during college generally, so that you'll have a better way to manage the barrage of opportunities as they come at you.

Were you recruited to play varsity athletics in college? Maybe you weren't recruited, but believe yourself to be good enough to "walk on" to the team. Or maybe the sport you're most interested in wasn't offered in your high school—but is offered at your college. And what about club sports or intramurals? Is there a sport you'd like to learn or get more involved with on a social level?

Have you always wanted to explore acting or singing? If so, maybe trying out for a play, a musical, a student film, or a singing group should be on your list.

What about politics or religion? Interested? If so, maybe the campus political unions or campus chapter of the Young Republicans, Young Democrats, or Green Party needs to be paid a visit. Thinking of switching religions, exploring a new religion, or simply becoming more devoted to your own? Perhaps you'd like to check out the local congregations or groups.

What about working in the community? Want to explore teaching by volunteering in an underserved school for an afternoon a week? Or explore medicine by "candy striping" at the local hospital? Or use your skills by teaching languages, sports, or other skills to area kids?

Want to write for the campus paper? Or the literary journal? Want to get involved with the campus radio station?

Want to interview prospective applicants, give campus tours, or help run your college's recruiting effort?

Is there something you're interested in doing in college that doesn't seem to have a group yet? Would you be interested in finding out how to start such a group?

The sky's the limit as to the extracurricular activities you can do in college. So dig deep inside and think about the things you might want to do. Think too about the things you did in high school and whether or not you want to continue them in college.

You have five minutes.

Go!

Okay. So now you have your list of potential extracurricular activities that are of interest to you. As before, you will no doubt be supplementing this list over the next few days and indeed throughout college. But think of this as a starting place.

Let's move on.

YOUR FRESHMAN YEAR PHYSICAL GOALS

So what are your physical goals for freshman year?

We've mentioned the Freshman 15 and you had probably already heard about it: the number of pounds the typical freshman adds due to his or her rocky transition to the beer-and-pizza diet of college. Do you have a plan to keep this from happening to you?

Maybe you've always wanted to take up running or rollerblading or mountain biking. Maybe what you want most of all is simply to stay dedicated to an exercise program. Do you want to train for a road race or even a marathon? Maybe you've always wanted to start lifting weights, but never had the facilities available to you. Check out your college gym—they're available to you now.

Maybe you've always been curious about yoga or meditation, or wanted to take up a martial art. Those are physical activities too—and yup, they're available to you in college, sometimes even for credit.

And what *about* that diet?

If you signed up for one of your college meal plans, you probably have a serious variety of options available to you—even if some of them are overcooked London broil and fluorescent-colored seafood Newburg. Do you want to set any goals about your diet this year, such as—having a salad every day, skipping dessert on certain days, or staying away from carbs at night during the week?

What about sleep? Are you worried that now that you're in college, you might sleep too little or too much? Do you want to establish some ground rules to make sure you get enough sleep but don't hibernate? Be reasonable. Don't set goals you know you can never keep, such as trying to get up every morning at 4 A.M., but think about what kind of schedule you'd like to keep. Are you a morning person or a night owl? Remember that sleep is an essential component of health and that to stay healthy and performing at your optimum level, you need to get adequate, regular sleep.

Think about all things physical and envision what you'd like to look like and feel like in May, when freshman year draws to a close. Make your list of things to pursue to ensure you arrive looking and feeling the way you want to.

You have five minutes.

Go!

Good job. Are you getting excited about all the ideas that are starting to flow? Don't worry if you are starting to feel overwhelmed by how much you've written. Later in the chapter we'll give you a way to manage all this great output. For now, just keep brainstorming.

Let's move on to financial goals.

YOUR FRESHMAN YEAR FINANCIAL GOALS

"Financial goals?" you ask incredulously. "What financial goals?"

Yeah, yeah . . . we know you're indebted up to your eyeballs in student loans. We're not talking about making your first million during your freshman year (although if you wanted to set that as a goal, we're certainly not going to dissuade you from doing so!). What we're talking about here is laying out some ground rules for managing your finances during your freshman year.

If you haven't been already, you're about to be inundated with offers for credit cards. Before long, it will seem as though every credit card company under the sun will be offering you credit.

Be careful.

If you follow our advice, you'll sign up for one credit card and use it only for emergencies, as running up credit card debt for impulse purchases is one of the quickest ways college students get into financial trouble. Remember that bad credit will typically follow you around for seven years—which can affect your ability to get loans for graduate school, start a business, and buy an apartment or a house down the road.

So what financial guidelines do you want to set for yourself?

Are you on a budget? Should you be? If so, maybe you want to draw it up so you'll know what kind of plan you need to stick to.

Are you on a work-study plan? Have you figured out how you're going to fit those hours into your week so as to minimize the disruption of your academic and social schedule?

Do you want to get a part-time job at the campus music store or bookstore or at a local bar or restaurant to make some extra cash? Maybe you could tutor someone in one of your strong subjects to make some extra cash. What are your other marketable skills?

What about scholarships? Have you spent enough time looking around campus or surfing the Web to try and find additional funding to defray college costs? It only takes a couple of small scholarships to make this time well worth spending. Is this something you want to investigate this year?

Don't be afraid to think outside the box here.

Have you closely examined your cell phone plan and other monthly expenses to make sure that you are optimizing your expense-to-use ratios?

Do you really need to have your car on campus? If so, might you want to work out some sort of car-sharing arrangement that would produce some additional income for you or at least help defray the expenses of insurance, gas, and parking fees? If you do pursue this kind of arrangement, be sure that you have proper insurance on the car and that anyone who uses your car is insured as well.

Take the next five minutes and think about the various ways you can help yourself financially this year. Remember that managing your finances requires you to play offense and defense. Think creatively and make your list.

Go!

We hope you came up with a few creative ideas to keep your finances in check or maybe to earn a few extra bucks to make your college experience a little more comfortable for you.

We have one category of goals left to brainstorm.

YOUR FRESHMAN YEAR SPIRITUAL GOALS

Now hold on. Before you go flipping past this section, stay with us a minute.

We're not necessarily talking about religion here, although if you *are* religious, exploring your beliefs or finding a congregation on or near campus can be a very reassuring and centering thing to do.

But you don't have to be religious to be spiritual.

Maybe for you, being spiritual means taking a few hours each week to practice yoga or meditation.

Maybe it means taking a long walk in the woods one morning a week to be alone with your thoughts and to reflect.

Maybe being spiritual means reading reflective works or listening to music and letting your thoughts wander away from the mundane and the everyday.

Maybe for you, being spiritual means volunteering to help the less fortunate at an area shelter or soup kitchen.

Maybe it means pondering the interconnectivity of our lives in the universe and thinking about the little "coincidences" that happen every day and shape our lives by their happenings.

Maybe it means sitting on a stoop somewhere and reading some good poetry.

Whatever spirituality means to you, do not underestimate its power to enrich your life. In your campus world, where people will often seem very id-driven or self-absorbed, maintaining some perspective can be really helpful. And whether that means you'd like to get to church or synagogue once a week or simply that you want to read *The Tao of Pooh* this semester, don't forget to pay some attention to your spiritual side. You'll be amazed at how refreshed and centered it will make you feel.

Think about a few ways to nurture your spiritual side during freshman year and write them down.

Resist the urge to just dismiss thoughts about this topic out of hand.

Think about it for five minutes now and jot down a few ideas.

Go!

NOW WHAT DO I DO WITH ALL OF THIS?

Congratulations!

If you've stuck with us this far, you should now have an abundance of good information written down to help ensure that your freshman year is as productive and satisfying as you hope it will be.

But you're not done yet.

If you've followed our directions, you should have written down a stream-of-consciousness list in each of the six areas. We hope you didn't censor your thoughts as you were writing. If you didn't, your lists may be quite long.

You now need a way to manage all those ideas and to go through them and cull the ones that are most critical to you—to choose the ones that you think will give you the most bang for your buck, so to speak.

Here's what you're going to do next.

Go back through each list and read what you've written down. Think about each item and see how it resonates with you. Some of the ideas will get you fired up as soon as you think about them. Others, upon reflection, may not seem that important or that exciting after all.

It's all good. That's part of the goal-setting process.

Go through each list and pick the three things from that area that you are absolutely committed to accomplishing during your freshman year or, if you want to think more long term, during college as a whole. Pick the three things that you feel are most critical to making your experience a success—three that would make you feel great about yourself if you were to accomplish them.

Circle those items in each list.

Feeling really ambitious? Want to pick four or five? That's fine, . . . but don't feel that you have to. You want to keep the number of goals manageable—so that you'll actually follow through and complete them. Three in each category is fine. More in some categories and less in others is fine too, but make sure you have at least one goal in each category to maintain some balance.

Remember: pick the ideas from each list that excite you the most or that, on reflection, seem to make the most sense or to be the most important.

Go ahead and make your choices now.

ONE MORE STEP . . .

Okay.

You should now have chosen somewhere around eighteen goals for your freshman year or perhaps for college in general.

But you're not done yet.

Setting goals is one thing. You've probably done it informally every year on January 1. You know—the resolutions you think about on New Year's Day, act on for a day or two, and then forget about until next New Year's Day. Following through on these goals is quite another thing. How many New Years' resolutions have you actually kept, even for a month or two?

Not many, right?

We don't want that to happen with this set of goals.

So now, for each one of these goals, we want you to articulate at least one very good reason why it is *essential* for you to follow up and to achieve that goal during your freshman year. Make sure your reason compels you—that it lights a fire under you and propels you toward meeting the goal.

Here's an example.

Suppose that you wrote down "Get in really good physical shape" as one of your physical goals. Suppose further that you are not currently dating anyone but would really like to be in a relationship with someone, and that you already know that next summer you'll be returning to your job as a counselor at an overnight summer camp.

Your rationale might read something like this: "Getting into really good physical shape will ensure that I have the boundless energy and health I need to get off to a great start in forging my new identity in college. It will also help me look and feel my best, which will give me the confidence to make new friends and approach the people I meet who I am interested in dating. Finally, it will ensure that I will look and feel better than ever next summer when I return to camp and see my old friends."

Pretty compelling, right?

Articulating a powerful rationale makes it far less likely that you will simply forget about these goals once you conclude this exercise and close this chapter. So really take the time to do this well. Amend and edit your reasons. Choose powerful language and drill down into the real motives compelling you to achieve these goals.

Create a master list of each of your goals and your rationales for achieving them, and keep it in your *Campus Confidential* workbook or somewhere else where you can refer to it often. Your setup should look something like this:

Physical Goals:	Rationale:
GET INTO SHAPE	Getting into really good physical shape will ensure that I have the boundless energy and health I need to get off to a great start in forging my new identity in college. It

will also help me look and feel my best, which will give me the confidence to make new friends and approach the people I meet who I am interested in dating. Finally, it will ensure that I will look and feel better than ever next summer when I return to camp and see my old friends.

Tape your list of goals up to the wall over your desk or on the mirror in your closet. If you don't have that kind of privacy, keep it in your desk drawer or your day planner—but refer to it *at least once a week.* Daily is even better.

Do this for your entire first semester, and you'll be hooked for life. You won't believe the progress you'll make.

Congratulations on completing the freshman year goal-setting workshop. As you'll see, we do one of these at the beginning of each academic year and check on your progress throughout the year. For now, though, celebrate the fact that you now have a concrete list of the most important things you hope to accomplish during your freshman year and, more important, the reasons why those things are important to you.

And consider where this puts you, in terms of your preparation for a terrific first year of college, relative to your uninitiated peers. If you have a good friend or two on campus already, you may want to turn him or her on to the power of goal setting as well so you can keep each other focused and motivated throughout the year. As you will see, once you start achieving results, this activity becomes addictive in a hugely positive way.

ADDITIONAL RESOURCES

Robbins, Anthony. *Awaken the Giant Within.* New York: Free Press, 1992.

Robbins, Anthony. *Personal Power* (audio series). Robbins Research International. (www.anthonyrobbins.com)

Robbins, Anthony. *RPM Planner Kit* (time management system). (www.anthonyrobbins.com)

Robbins, Anthony. *Unlimited Power: The New Science of Personal Achievement.* New York: Free Press, 1997.

Choosing Your Classes

Scheduling Secrets for the Freshman Year

*Understand that the right to choose your
own path is a sacred privilege. Use it.
Dwell in possibility!*

Oprah Winfrey

If you've been following our advice so far, you should have taken a serious voyage through your school's course catalogue (Chapter 11) and put together a chart of your core curricular requirements (and the requirements for your major or preprofessional program if you know what that is already). If you blew off our advice or didn't bother to complete that exercise, go back and do it now, because we're about to start building on what you learned from that activity. If you *did* do the exercise, flip back to the section of your *Campus Confidential* workbook where you laid out the requirements of your college or university's core curriculum and take a look at it now.

The first thing to consider is any advanced placement credits you might have earned based on your scores on your AP or SAT II Exams. If you placed out of any introductory-level classes that are relevant to your major or preprofessional program, go ahead and take them off the list—but only after you confirm with the registrar's office that you have indeed waived out of the requirement. The last thing you want to do is proceed on a mistaken assumption for four years, only to discover the problem during senior year when the registrar won't let you graduate because you're missing a core course that you thought you had satisfied with AP credits.

As the old saying goes, trust, but verify.

The next thing to consider is your school's foreign language requirement, if it has one. Pay a visit to the departmental offices of any foreign language you took in high school or have proficiency in due to your ethnic background, and attempt to pass the departmental exam to give yourself the flexibility to get out of the language requirement.

Note: this does *not* mean that we don't think studying a foreign language in college is a worthwhile use of your time—in fact, the exact opposite is true. All we're suggesting is that if you *have* achieved proficiency in a foreign language, your school should award you credit for that and give you the flexibility to enroll in more advanced courses in that language, take a third language instead, or, if your interests lie elsewhere, use your time in other ways. The purpose of the foreign language requirement at most schools is to get students to at least participate in the study of a second language other than English. If you've already done that, you've met the core requirement, and whether you want to continue or not should be up to you. So if you passed the departmental language exam or earned AP credit in a language—and your college registrar agrees with you—you can take the language requirement off your list.

Flexibility in scheduling during college is vital. All we're trying to do is maximize that flexibility for you.

"The only class I struggled to wrap up was my language requirement," Kevin recalls. "I took my beginner Latin class as a sophomore rather than as a frosh. Then I went abroad for the first semester of my junior year, and couldn't complete the whole intermediate program to fulfill the core requirement. I remember having a vivid, bone-chilling moment of realization on a boathouse in Amsterdam (I know . . . what a place for an academic epiphany) that I would be totally screwed unless I figured out how to complete this albatross of a language requirement before the end of my junior year, because there was no way I wanted to be stuck taking Intermediate Latin as a senior. So this story ended with me taking only the second semester of Intermediate Latin and squeaking by. Lesson learned, though: the choices you make freshman year are not made in a vacuum. What you don't take can come back to haunt you."

What you're left with after all these machinations is the remaining core curriculum that you're responsible for over the next four years. This will be the starting point for the creation of your course schedule each semester until there is nothing left on the list. As we'll discuss more fully in Chapter 30 ("Choosing a Major and Designing a Course of Study"), you're going to want to knock off as many of these core requirements as you can as early as you can in your college career, so that your upperclass years can be reserved for your major and for the interesting seminars and elective courses open only to upperclassmen.

SHOPPING FOR CLASSES

Now, let's have some fun. Go back through the course catalogue and start making a list of classes you want to "shop" during your class selection period (often called "add-drop period" or "shopping period"). Make a list of the days and times that each class meets, the name of the professor teaching the class, and where the class meets. Do this for each class you're interested in taking, in every subject. Don't worry that your initial list may have too many classes on it—that's okay. We can whittle things down later. For now, you're merely shopping for things that sound "interesting" to you. Keep this list in your *Campus Confidential* workbook so you'll have it available for reference and a starting point for shopping in future semesters.

"My freshman year course of study might be summed up as Tasmanian Devil," Chase explained. "I tore into the coursebook, dog earing every interesting page and then picked the courses I couldn't resist. I took some great courses, everything from math, astronomy, economics, creative writing, and the politics of music."

"Designing my curriculum went smoothly due to the large amount of guidance I got from my athletic advisers," Aaron explained. "Befriend your adviser early and meet with him or her regularly at first if you're overwhelmed."

"When you're shopping for classes, take the time to talk to upperclassmen about who the best professors are," Carolyn added. "I found that the classes I enjoyed the most and benefited the most from in college were those that were taught by well-organized professors with a passion for teaching."

Once you've compiled your list, you're ready to start thinking about your freshman year class schedule.

EASE INTO YOUR COLLEGE EXPERIENCE WITH A MANAGEABLE FIRST SEMESTER

Now listen closely.

The biggest mistake that college freshmen make when arranging their freshman fall class schedules is to commit to an overly ambitious course schedule. Their analysis usually goes something like this: "I took eight classes in high school, so what's the big deal if I take six or seven in college—I can handle it!" Or "I took seven classes in high school while playing three varsity sports, running the school newspaper, and working two jobs. I can certainly manage six classes here without any extracurriculars to bog me down."

The problem with that analysis is that it presupposes that your college courses are going to have workloads similar to those of the classes you took in high school. Let us assure you that you will *not* find that to be the case. Your college courses may start out slowly, repeating material you learned in high school or easing you in with seemingly manageable reading assignments. But by the time you hit October, things are going to shift into overdrive, and those reading assignments are going to start doubling or even tripling in volume. Then midterms will hit, and before you know it, you're going to be overwhelmed.

We've all been through it ourselves—and we've seen this "superhero syndrome" too many times to ignore it.

Remember that you've never been to college. You have no idea how much reading your professors are going to assign or how long it will actually take you to complete those reading assignments. You have no idea how easily you're going to adjust to college life and how rapidly and readily you'll be able to strike the right balance between work and play. You'll be forging new relationships, managing a new living arrangement with a roommate or roommates, and adjusting to living away from home and in a new place.

That's a lot of change, and change affects people in different ways.

Take it relatively easy during your first semester. Four classes. Five at the most. You want to give yourself a little time to adjust, to ease into the experience, and to build up some confidence that you can "hit the pitching" at the college level. You'll want to leave yourself plenty of time to develop good study habits, get into a routine, meet friends, be social, and figure things out. It is also hugely important to your psychological well-being that you do well during your first semester of college. So ease up a little and help yourself get there.

SUCCESSFULLY APPROACHING THE ADD-DROP PERIOD

Nearly every college and university has a period at the beginning of every semester during which students are free to "shop" for the courses they're going to take that semester. Typically a week or two in length, this period enables you to wander around campus, sit in on various professors, pick up syllabi, compare notes with your friends and roommates, and get a feel for your class schedule. This shopping period is extremely valuable for the orchestration of an optimal class schedule, so take it seriously and don't feel as though you need to commit to a class schedule and stick with it from day one before you've had a chance to look around. Use shopping period to evaluate your professors' teaching styles, to determine course requirements, to examine syllabi and confirm your interest in a course's subject matter and its approach to that subject matter, and to otherwise "dry run" your schedule.

DETERMINING YOUR CLASS SCHEDULE

Once you've shopped all the classes on your list, it's time to make some hard decisions. First of all, take another look at the chart of your core curricular requirements. Make it your habit to take *something* off that list during every semester—including this one. With some luck, you may even be able to kill two or even several birds with one stone, so try to be creative about your core requirements. For example, if you are thinking about being premed, you might be able to take Intro Bio and its associated laboratory and knock off several requirements at once. First, Intro Bio is one of the preprofessional curricular requirements for med school. Second, it will almost certainly satisfy your school's core curriculum requirement of at least two hard-science courses. Finally, if you also opt to major in a hard science, your Intro Bio course *may* also count toward satisfying the requirements of that major. Of course, if you took the AP or SAT II exam in biology and placed out of your Intro Bio course, you'll knock off some of these requirements without ever having to take the class at all!

Next, try to work out some balance among the disciplines in your schedule. Even if you intend to be a math major, you probably don't want to be taking three different math courses at the same time. Ditto for English classes if you are an English major. No matter how much you might like to read, too much of anything can detract from the enjoyment of the experience. If you are an English major, take a poli sci class that interests you, knock off a science requirement, and take a couple of English courses. That way, you'll keep your curricular requirements in check, make some progress toward your intended major, perhaps complete some prerequisites toward advanced courses in your major, and still have a pleasurable schedule.

"My strategy of trying to get all of my requirements out of the way as soon as possible is not one I would recommend to others," Dave advised. "By following a more normal course path, I would have eventually fulfilled all of my requirements anyway."

"I entered college thinking that I would double-major in math and women's studies," Zoe explained. "To that end, my first-year courses included Calculus II and Intro to Women's Studies in addition to a mix of other courses including philosophy,

Spanish, biology, art history, and writing—a roster representing a balanced mix of requirements and curiosities. To my surprise, I found that I really didn't like the courses on math or women's studies very much at all and totally scrapped my plans to major in either one. Despite the fact that I had never considered economics to be an area of interest, I signed up for an introductory econ class on a whim. I loved it immediately and before long had declared econ as my major. The point here is that each choice you make and each seemingly random conversation that you have has the power to turn your life in a direction you never imagined," Zoe continued. "Keeping your eyes, ears, and heart open will invariably lead you to whatever and wherever you are meant to be."

Tom echoed this sentiment.

"I think part of the charms of college, as well as life itself, is to allow yourself to be a little bit elastic with your planning and control and see where it takes you."

"I didn't know what I wanted to do going in," Jim recalls, "so I spent my freshman year taking courses, including ecology, international relations, calculus, American history, and advanced French, that fulfilled a diverse array of requirements and would prepare me for several majors I was considering, while also leaving me eligible to study abroad in a French-speaking country. From this experience, I discovered that I had the most interest in history, and the requirements for the major were light, which would allow me to complete a minor in another field."

"One of the best decisions I made during freshman year," Lyndsee said, "was to depart from the course of study I thought I wanted to pursue—biology—and try a course, Japanese, in the East Asian Studies department. I had a small introduction to Japanese in high school, but I never thought of continuing it in college until I saw that course listing and decided to give it a try. After that, I continued on with Japanese and found that I was interested in other courses in the East Asian Studies department as well and ended up switching my major—all because I decided to try that one course in my freshman year."

While you're doing all this, you'll also want to pay attention to the actual *schedule* for these classes—both in terms of when the classes meet, when each class's major requirements (midterms, papers, projects) are due, and when the final exam or final paper is due. Use shopping period to figure out whether you can actually get from one class to another comfortably in the time allotted between the class meeting times without having to run into class perspiring and out of breath. Jogging a mile from Science Hill to the English department building in the ten-minute interval between your 9:30 and 10:30 classes may not seem like a big deal now, but it might get to be a real drag when you try to do it in a foot of snow or subzero temperatures.

"Be realistic and know your habits," Dave added. "Before you sign up for an 8:00 A.M. class on Friday mornings, consider whether you will be out partying all night on Thursday."

Examine your class syllabi carefully to determine how much work each class looks like it is going to be and how that work is distributed during the course of the semester. Use pen and paper to plot the primary assignments for each class so that you can visualize what your weekly workload is going to look like, and make sure your work is spread around. You don't want to take three classes that all have a problem set due on Monday or a paper due on Friday.

Finally, pay attention to final exam schedules, times, and types *before* you commit to a course. Most colleges and universities spread out final exams over a two-week period at the end of the semester. The very last thing you want to be facing is two finals on the same day or a whole series of finals on back-to-back days. Why would you *knowingly* set yourself up for a miserable end-of-semester experience if you can easily avoid it?

Ideally, your exams will be spread at least one day apart. Better yet, shoot for a freshman fall class schedule that features a couple of final exams, a final paper, and a final project, so that you can figure out which method of review and assessment you prefer. That way, you can allow your preferences, discovered this term, to steer your course selection in future semesters.

"I had no particularly clear strategy for mapping out a course of study during freshman year," Dan explained. "As I sampled various things, I let my interests and passions guide me. One of the classes I took happened to be Introduction to Oceanography. I knew I was interested in the sciences, but knew next to nothing about marine science. I loved to sail, though, and I noticed in the course catalog that the class included a weekly lab on the school's research vessel on Lake Champlain. Sounded pretty good, so I signed up. As it turned out, I really enjoyed the class, loved being out on the boat each week, and ended up becoming good friends with the professor. One day in her office, I mentioned that I had decided that I wanted to go to sea for the experience. I had been interested in some of the small-ship semester at sea programs, but they were all pretty pricy and a little difficult to fit into my schedule. I was still researching and mulling the idea over when she pulled me into her office a few days later and told me that she had just been asked to join a consortium of small New England schools that would be doing joint polar marine research in Antarctica. She wondered if I'd like to come along and do my senior thesis project as part of the overall research on climate change. Needless to say, I jumped at the chance and ended up compressing my course load into three-and-a-half years so I could take my junior spring completely off to prepare for and go on a month-and-a-half research cruise to the Antarctic Peninsula. My work on this project turned into another research cruise the following summer, and eventually, into a job with Columbia University working on their ship throughout the world's oceans. This is a prime example of the value of asking questions and getting to know your professors. You just never know where it may lead you."

Athletics on Campus

*Those who think they have no time for exercise
will sooner or later have to find time for illness.*

Edward Stanley

When you hear the words "college athletics," chances are you conjure up an image of a hundred-thousand-seat Big-Ten football stadium packed to the gills on a beautiful Saturday afternoon in the fall, or of Cameron Indoor Stadium with a sea of Cameron Crazies blowing the roof off the place as Duke battles North Carolina in the ACC tournament. And in fact, college football and college basketball are a huge part of the campus experience at many colleges and universities. But they are only two facets of the image of "varsity sports" on these campuses . . . and the image of "college athletics" is much broader still.

Athletics on the college campus takes many forms—not just the high-visibility sports but also the lesser-known "club" sports and intramural competitions in everything from soccer to inner-tube water polo, which can be as much about the exercise and social experience as they are about the actual "competition." And of course, the broadest idea of college athletics also encompasses your hastily organized running, cycling, or rock-climbing club, daily blading trips along the river, and your Saturday morning pickup hoops game.

In short, there is a place in college athletics for *everyone* on campus, as a participant and as a spectator. Let's take a quick spin through your options to get you thinking.

VARSITY SPORTS

If you were a varsity athlete in high school, don't just blindly sign up for four more years of the same just because you think you might be able to make the team. *Consider* this choice before you make it.

What is your motivation for wanting to play a varsity sport in college?

If you are aiming to play for a Division I school with an eye on one day possibly turning pro, you have a whole different set of considerations—most of which are obviously well beyond the scope of this book. If you are fortunate enough to be in this position, though, we recommend that you pick up one of Dion Wheeler's books (see "Additional Resources" at the end of the chapter), which will take you step-by-step through the college athletic recruiting process and otherwise guide your thinking about how to maximize your chances for success.

For the rest of you, though, your participation in varsity athletics is likely to be driven by things like a love of the sport or of athletic competition in general, or a desire to blow off steam, develop close ties with teammates, and stay in shape. Though you may still be good enough to get a scholarship to play for your school, you must remember that you are in college to get an education. Remember that accepting a varsity scholarship carries with it a substantial set of obligations to your school, your team, and your teammates. This may represent a dream come true for some of you (and if it does, that's great), but for others with concurrent designs on getting into graduate school, it can become a lot to juggle.

"My athletic scholarship paid for the majority of my education," Aaron explains, "but I had to work hard athletically *and* academically to keep it, because no scholarship is guaranteed, and the coaches decide every year how much money you deserve."

Further, at *any* level, playing for a varsity team is almost certainly a year-round commitment. During the off-season, you will likely have to commit to a regular and rigorous diet and exercise program and to travel with your teammates on training trips during one or more school breaks. In season, you may be looking at lengthy "one-a-days" or even "two-a-days," road trips that can interfere with your class and exam schedules, and tournaments or scrimmages that may consume the entirety of one or more of your other school breaks.

Playing varsity is a monster commitment that will consume a good part of your college career. At the same time, the dedication, commitment, and camaraderie that varsity athletics engenders make the college athlete's college experi ence uniquely satisfying. There are many good arguments on both sides of this important decision. All we are saying here is to *consider* the decision to play varsity before you sign on.

"I am an extremely active and competitive person and my goal since I was in sixth grade was to play Division I lacrosse," Aaron said. "Nowhere else on a college campus will students find the camaraderie, pride, friendships, physical health, and academic support than that present on a varsity team. You're just not going to develop the kinds of relationships with other students hanging out in the dorms or going out to the bars that you will getting up at 5 A.M. on Saturday mornings for team runs."

"For as long as I can remember, it was always a goal of mine to play collegiate athletics," Dave explained. "The advantage of playing at Middlebury, or at any Division III school for that matter, is that your sport does not become your life. Baseball was a big part of my college experience, but by no means did it define who I was. I think that Division III athletics follows an admirable approach that academics come before athletics. My coaches were always supportive of taking care of academic issues first. We took our baseball very seriously, but within that seriousness, we all had separate lives and could pursue other academic and extracurricular interests while still being active and contributing members of the team.

Being part of the baseball program at Middlebury has been one of the most meaningful experiences in my life. I share a bond with my coaches and teammates that is very special to me, and as an alumnus of the program, I am connected to a great network across the country."

Erik agreed.

"I played varsity golf and ice hockey at M.I.T. Playing goalie for the hockey team was kind of a dream of mine growing up," Erik recalls. "I had played outside on the ponds in Maine since I was maybe ten or eleven years old, but I could never afford all the equipment, so I always had the most rag-tag collection of 'equipment' out there. I played with my baseball glove as my catching glove, I used a regular skater's glove to cover my blocker hand, and I used an old sweatshirt with a pillow sewn into it as a chest protector! Going to college at such a prestigious school that also happened to have a varsity ice hockey team was just an ideal scenario for me to realize that dream.

The advantages of being a varsity athlete are numerous and far outweigh any of the disadvantages. To name a few, being part of a team is a truly special experience. Having an outlet to blow off some steam is invaluable. And if you are competitive, then having the arena in which to compete is very fulfilling. The disadvantages, in terms of the time constraints that being on a team place on your time to study or prepare for classes will stretch you out, but the sacrifices that you find yourself making are almost always worth the rewards.

I still remain close friends with several of my teammates from both the hockey and the golf teams," Erik concluded. "As far as juggling my time among playing sports, working, and studying—I feel it served me well to help develop the necessary time management skills that I still use to this day."

If You Are Not Recruited but Still Want to Play . . .

Many high school athletes, and some very good ones, are not recruited to play at the college level, but still want to make their college team. Or perhaps you want to try out for a varsity sport that was not even offered at your high school.

During the summer before you arrive on campus, contact the head coach of the team you are interested in and let him or her know of your interest in trying out. Ask for a copy of the summer training schedule sent to the students who were recruited to play the sport. Inquire whether the team requires you to have a physical performed before you get to campus in the fall. Finally, most college teams, particularly in those sports that are not offered at all high schools, will have a period of open tryouts during which you will practice or scrimmage and be evaluated by the coaching staff. Find out when those tryouts are and whether you will be welcome to try to "walk on" to the team.

At many less competitive programs or at schools in less competitive divisions, persistence and attitude (when coupled with at least *some* talent) go a long way. If you are committed to playing a varsity sport in college as a walk-on, make your intentions known to the coaches, don't miss a practice, and practice and scrimmage your heart out. Your good attitude may take you further than you think.

CLUB SPORTS

Club sports are sports that have lost (or never had) varsity status on campus but are funded by contributions from players or alumni. Rugby, fencing, wrestling, and archery are common club sports at many schools.

Collegiate club teams compete against other club teams from around the country, and have training programs and schedules that can be as rigorous as varsity teams. These clubs may make cuts to select their teams. At other places, club sports provide more of a social outlet and opportunity to travel while bonding with teammates, competing together, and staying in shape. These clubs will typically accept anyone who wants to make the commitment to train and play—though not everyone will make the traveling squad for every game.

Your university athletic department will have a list of the club sports available on your campus. Almost all of these clubs will select members after the beginning of the school year, so either call the athletic department to find out when tryouts or initial practices are being held, or watch your campus signs and table tents for information.

"I was an EMT (emergency medical technician) for the Women's Rugby Team," Dan quipped. "Ahh . . . the stories I could tell . . ."

INTRAMURAL SPORTS

Chances are, your college or university also features an intramural athletic league comprising randomly selected teams or teams representing dorms or residential colleges. These leagues can be more or less competitive, depending on the college and the sport, but will almost always welcome recreational players who are interested in the sport and eager for a little athletic competition.

We've seen intramural sports in everything from the old standbys, such as men's, women's, and coed soccer, softball, and touch or flag football; to more unusual offerings, such as coed inner-tube water polo, ultimate Frisbee, billiards, minigolf, and Texas Hold 'em; to the bizarre, such as competitive eating and drinking.

Intramural sports are a good way to stay in shape, a welcome break, and a great social outlet. Once you're on campus in the fall, get a list of all the intramural "sports" offered by your college or university and find something fun to participate in.

EXTRACURRICULAR CLUBS FOCUSED ON ATHLETICS

As we noted at the outset of this chapter, there is literally something for everyone in college athletics. If you have a particular athletic interest that is not represented by a varsity team, club sport, or intramural activity, chances are there will be an extracurricular club that will allow you to participate. We've seen extracurricular clubs for everything from mountaineering and ice climbing to mountain biking, kayaking, and roller-skiing. And if by some remote chance, the activity you want to do is not available on your campus, you can always start your own club!

BEING ACTIVE

Finally, there is the most basic level of college athletics: being active and getting some exercise every day. Most colleges and universities have gyms and workout facilities open to all students; many of them rank among the best in the world.

Avail yourself of the opportunity to use these facilities for regular workouts or pickup games while you're on campus.

"I worked out twice a day, in the wee early morning hours before breakfast and at the end of the day before I went to bed," Erika notes. "We had a full fitness center with trainers and everything, so it was easy to stick to."

ADDITIONAL RESOURCES

Wheeler, Dion. *A Parent's and Student-Athlete's Guide to Athletic Scholarships—Getting Money Without Being Taken for a (Full) Ride.* New York: McGraw-Hill, 2000.

Wheeler, Dion. *The Sports Scholarships Insider's Guide—Getting Money for College at Any Division.* Naperville, Ill.: Sourcebooks, 2005.

chapter 15

An Approach to Extracurricular Activities

Today is life—the only life you are sure of.
Make the most of today. Shake yourself awake
and get interested in something.

Dale Carnegie

A s you've probably discovered by now, there are more organizations, clubs, and activities on campus than you can possibly experience. At many schools, there is an on-campus organization, or at
least a presence, for every conceivable activity, hobby, and interest.

So how in the world do you decide which of these organizations to join? And
how do you determine how much time you'll have available to devote to such
activity?

Our first suggestion is to go back to your freshman year goal-setting workshop
(Chapter 12) and figure out what you determined your freshman year priorities to
be. What did you identify as the things you most wanted to experience? What things
did you want to try for the first time? What experiences or hobbies did you resolve
to continue from your life in high school? Which ones did you decide to retire?

If you haven't done so already, stop by the dean's office and ask the receptionist there for a list of all the clubs, organizations, and activities that have "registered"
on campus. The dean's office or, in some cases, some other campus office maintains this list in order to know what offerings are present on campus, but also
because most if not all of these organizations typically look to the school for some
type of funding every year. Take a look at this list and see what jumps out at you.

Some advice is warranted, though, as you look over this list.

BRANCH OUT AND TAKE SOME CHANCES

Do not simply gravitate to the things you did in high school or to the hobbies and activities that you are "good at" or "have always done," without taking some time to reflect on what you're doing. College is your chance to reinvent yourself, to explore new things, and to learn about what motivates you. If you never leave your comfort zone, you'll never get a real sense of who you are. However, if you still love a particular activity that you engaged in during high school, you will probably be able to find and to easily step into the same activity in college. Our point here is simply to encourage you to take stock and make *active* decisions about what to pursue. There is a whole world of possibility awaiting you out there on campus.

"I love singing and always have and I did show choir in high school, so my auditioning for the TSU Showstoppers was an easy decision," Erika noted. "This was an elite group, and out of fifty or more people who auditioned, I was the only one chosen. That definitely boosted my confidence! We performed all over Tennessee."

"The single decision that I made as a freshman that constantly paid dividends for me was joining Speak of the Devil, Duke's male a cappella singing group," Chase noted. "Throughout my four years at Duke, my membership in Speak of the Devil was not only the hub of my friendships, but was also the way I defined myself. I took pride in my academic work, but I derived more satisfaction from singing with Speak of the Devil. I was able to record two CDs, sing at Duke basketball games, perform for thousands of my peers, and be surrounded by eleven guys who all shared those experiences. Last, being in a group like Speak of the Devil gave me a way to leave a positive mark at Duke. Thousands go to college and end up leaving the place four years later much the same place that they found it. Speak of the Devil, though, will exist long into the future and will always be shaped by the four years during which I was a member. Joining Speak of the Devil was something I knew I wanted to do when I arrived at Duke and it may have been the smartest thing I did in the four years I was there."

"I played several intramural sports and I was also very active in my residential college life," Tom added. "My participation in many of these activities was spurred on by the fact that my friends were doing them, but that was a deliberate choice of mine, and that's okay. The big thing to keep in mind is that all extracurricular activities contribute further to the social fabric that you're creating and that will impact your life forever. Always remember that building lifelong friendships is one of the most important consequences of college."

STRIVE TO FIND A BALANCE

As we've noted a couple of times already, you are looking for *balance* in your undergraduate life. That means finding a couple of extracurricular activities that give breadth and meaning to your life in college—and allow you to grow, enjoy a variety of experiences, and explore areas outside your academic bull's-eye, to the extent that you even have one yet. When considering your choices, think about the different areas that extracurricular activities can occupy. For example, joining the cycling club will keep you exercising, joining a campus theater troupe and getting a part in the semester production will allow you a creative outlet and an opportunity to pursue a hobby, and tutoring inner-city kids or volunteering at the soup kitchen or local homeless shelter will keep you grounded and remind you of those less fortunate. A life including all three of these activities, your course work, time with your friends and roommates, and time to attend campus lectures, performances, and concerts would make for a full, satisfying, and balanced freshman year. And of course, the iterations and variations on this theme are limited only by your imagination.

TAKE YOUR TIME IN MAKING DECISIONS

Question yourself before you commit to participating in a college activity because even though you're in college and living away from home, you won't have limitless time. Your coursework in college will be harder than what you experienced in high school. Your nightly reading will be more onerous and more voluminous; your responsibilities for papers, problem sets, and exams more numerous; and the threshold for getting a "good grade" will be more competitive. As a general principle, we recommend getting involved with no more than two or three extracurricular activities during your freshman year. You want to become known as a contributor, not a joiner. In other words, you should be prepared to attend the meetings and actively participate in any organization you join. If you commit to giving swim lessons to inner-city kids on Saturday mornings, you need to make good on that commitment and *show up*. If you sign up for your campus's branch of Amnesty International, Young Republicans, or Habitat for Humanity, you need to make the meetings and be prepared to road-trip with the group on the various activities it undertakes.

Of course, you need to allow yourself some time to explore these various organizations before you make a commitment to them, and that's fine. Go to as many meetings of as many different organizations as you want during your freshman fall as you explore what you're interested in doing. Take a run with your campus running club. Go to some meetings of the thespian society, the bridge club, or the photography group. Try out for a singing group, a comedy troupe, or a part in a campus play or musical. Go to a couple of intramural soccer practices to see how high the skill level is and whether you are comfortable with the level of competition. Take your sweet time in deciding which activities you want to keep in your life. You can even wait until you are an upperclassman to get involved in something on campus.

But when you commit to something, commit.

"I joined project W.I.L.D. when I returned from France in my junior year of college," Jim noted. "The outdoors became a passion that has deeply influenced me ever since. I spent six months walking the Appalachian Trail, and routinely head to the mountains in my free time. I was also fortunate to meet my wife through this pursuit."

"I did very little extracurricularly," Amanda added. "Outside of academics, I preferred more individual pursuits rather than organized clubs. The one type of group I probably should have gotten involved with would have been an outdoor adventures type thing because it was so beautiful around Cornell and I should have explored it more. I did do some of that type of thing at Davis when I first arrived there. I learned to rock-climb, which is something I continue to enjoy."

You can attend all the meetings you want as you explore what you want to do. Doing so will help you get to know all kinds of different people with interests similar to yours. It can be a great way to make new friends, meet new people, and even spark a romantic interest. You may form some of your best and most enduring friendships with the people you meet in the extracurricular organizations to which you belong. Eventually, though, you will likely be asked to "sign up" for the organization, to take on some responsibilities, or to become a reliable member of the "team."

At that point, it's time to fish or cut bait. The one thing you absolutely, positively do *not* want to become known for on campus is joining campus groups for the résumé value, but not fulfilling your commitments to the group.

If at any point you find yourself overwhelmed, or if you discover that you've taken on more responsibility than you can carry in light of your course load or whatever else, *resign* or assume *inactive status* with any organization for which you will not be able to follow through on your commitments.

Joiners occupy the same place in the campus hierarchy as moochers—which is to say, the very bottom rung of the ladder. It's not a place you want to be, because once you earn that reputation, it can be nearly impossible to shake.

IF YOU CAN'T FIND THE ACTIVITY YOU WANT

If you find yourself on a campus that doesn't have a club, organization, or activity that you want to become involved with, start it up yourself! Talk to your dean of students and learn about your college or university's policy or process for founding a campus organization. Typically you simply need to submit a few signatures of interested students and some paperwork, and voilá—you have founded the organization.

Fraternities and Sororities

Determining Whether the Greek Life Is the Life for You

*Individual commitment to a group effort—that is what makes
a team work, a company work, a society work, a civilization work.*

Vince Lombardi

Deciding whether or not to "go Greek" will, along with your choice of major, and for better or for worse, be one of the defining moments of your college career.

There are advantages and disadvantages to being in a fraternity or sorority. The decision is an intensely personal one, and one that depends your personality, your goals, and the particular college you are attending (and its social construct).

Whatever your thoughts on the subject, there are a few universal truths to get out of the way right off the bat.

SOME BACKGROUND

First, fraternity (and sorority) life is no longer characterized by the excess for which it was known in the 1960s, 1970s, and 1980s. Influenced by a flurry of lawsuits and by the passage, clarification, and intensification of state laws governing these organizations, nearly every college and university in America has cracked down on its fraternity and sorority system and the pervasive environment of underage binge drinking and abusive hazing activities that used to characterize them (as culturally memorialized in fabled films like *Animal House*). So the world of fraternities and sororities today is just as often characterized by disputes with school administrations and national headquarters, threats of being thrown off campus and having their charters revoked, and conflicts with campus or town police as it is for wild revelry.

Second, the selection process for gaining membership to a fraternity or sorority is often hasty, brief, and arbitrary. You may well make terrific friendships and bond closely with your frat brothers or sorority sisters, but that is more the product of participating in the overall experience than it is the selection process itself. People are selected for membership in fraternities and sororities for a host of different reasons—and whether you get a bid from every house you rushed or from none, you should not view it as any objective measure of your self-worth. The rush process simply does not lend itself to a careful evaluation of a person's attributes.

Finally, most fraternities and sororities are, first and foremost, social networks organized to bring like-minded people together for the purpose of partying and meeting each other. Any commitment to community service and the like, though usually present and certainly admirable, will always be a secondary motive of most such organizations. If your primary purpose for rushing a fraternity or sorority is to make a commitment to community service, you are probably better off joining one of myriad campus organizations devoted solely to community service. If your motivation for rushing is a combination of wanting to meet new people, develop a network of friends on campus, have a turnkey social life, have a lot of fun, *and* do some occasional community service work—then you're fine going the Greek route.

HOW IT WORKS

The fraternity and sorority "admissions" process (for lack of a better term) comprises three stages: rush period, pledge period, and bid period. During the rush period, the various fraternity and sorority houses throw parties to which everyone is invited to attend and to meet the members of those houses. "Rush," as it is known, used to happen first thing in the freshman fall, but an ever increasing number of colleges and universities are pushing rush off to second semester or even limiting the fraternity and sorority rush to sophomores and up in an effort to better police the process.

Rush is also notably different for fraternities and sororities.

Sorority Rush and Pledge

The sorority rush period is typically brief and concentrated, usually spanning less than a month. Many schools, particularly those in the South, have a formal rush process in which participating women are required to visit *every* sorority house. Not all schools employ this requirement, however, allowing women to choose which houses they want to rush.

During the sorority rush, the first rush "events" (that is, parties) are brief, simply providing opportunities for women to meet, mix, and mingle with the sorority sisters in a casual environment. As the rush period wears on, the parties become longer and more directed, with sorority sisters spending more individualized time with individual candidates.

Eventually, you will likely be asked to have a brief ten- to fifteen-minute substantive interview with one or more of the sisters in the sorority. During this interview, the sisters will typically ask you questions about yourself, your general academic and nonacademic interests, and your views on certain subjects.

"Ask a lot of questions and get to know a lot of people in the house during rush," Lyndsee advised. "If you are serious about joining, make sure at least a couple of people know who you are and know something about you so they can speak up for you when the organization is deciding whom to offer bids to."

"I always had a close group of girlfriends in high school and I was looking for the same thing in college," Tiffany explained. "I found the city atmosphere harder to meet this group of close-knit friends with whom I could hang out regularly. I went to all the different sororities to meet each organization. Take the time to speak to several girls from each one. Although you may have established a bond with one particular person, it is best to get a feel for the organization as a whole by getting to know several members."

When this process is complete, rush period ends, and "bids" will be offered to a certain numbers of candidates inviting them to "pledge" the house. You can only pledge one house at a time (hence the word), so if you receive more than one bid, you will have to choose from among them.

With respect to sorority rush, the most important advice we can give, whether you are required to rush every house or not, is to *be yourself.* There will always be a temptation to try to be "cooler" or more "hip" than you actually are in real life, by dressing, talking, or acting differently in an effort to curry favor with those who would judge you.

Don't.

Pretending to be someone you're not may well fool the screening committee, but even if it does, the outcome will place you in a house full of sisters who actually do *not* share your values or outlook—and the most common result of that bad fit is dissatisfaction with the experience down the road.

Although the rush process can feel dehumanizing, remember that the purpose of it is to find a group of peers with whom you identify and want to spend time. Go with your gut feeling about which group of women "feels" like the right fit to you. Forget about which houses are perceived to be "cooler" by others on campus. Those reputations shift and change from time to time. You should also not be beholden to your mother's or older sister's sorority unless that sorority also feels like the best fit to you when you attend rush events there.

If your approach is to focus on the house or houses where you honestly feel you are a good fit, chances are that the connection will be noticed and reciprocated . . . but it does not *always* work out that way. There is a fair amount of serendipity in the process, and keeping a clear perspective is very important in case the rush process doesn't go the way you had hoped.

Remember that all a sorority does is provide a mechanism for you to meet people and establish bonds with classmates. You can do this within the Greek system or outside it. Don't allow the outcome of the process define who you are or affect your sense of self-worth.

Once you have accepted a bid to pledge a house, you are "committed" to that house and to the process. Understand that although the pledging process takes only about a month, it involves a serious commitment of time during that month that can and typically *will* draw your attention away from your studies. During the pledge process, you will typically be asked to wear a pledge pin or other symbol of your commitment to the house, to perform a series of tasks for the sisters of the house, and to attend various pledge events, which are closed to anyone not in the house or the pledge class.

If the tasks you are asked to do make you feel degraded or uncomfortable, chances are, you have crossed the line into illegal hazing. Faced with such a situation, you must make the decision whether you want to tolerate the experience, to refuse to participate on grounds that you are uncomfortable doing so, or simply to depledge the house and withdraw from the entire experience. If the hazing has *really* crossed the line, you may want to report the activity to the house's national chapter, to the university's Panhellenic organization, or to the university's disciplinary board.

When pledge period is over, the membership of the house will take a vote, according to the house charter or bylaws, to accept you as a full member of the house. Unless you have done something unusual or had previously hidden your true personality, this vote is typically a formality.

Your female mentors wholeheartedly recommend that you wait to pledge a sorority until sophomore year; waiting allows you to establish yourself academically on campus and to establish an independent identity and group of friends. This grounding will also help you approach the process in a much more relaxed way and with a much greater degree of confidence and maturity.

"I joined a sorority at TSU called Alpha Kappa Alpha—the first African American sorority, founded in 1908," Erika explained. "I joined this sorority because they were advocating the things I felt were important: sisterhood, community service, and education. I got to participate in meaningful community service outreach programs that were geared toward truly needy individuals and I have been exposed to endless opportunities and have had countless doors opened for me. The benefits of my membership have yet to end. I would *definitely* do it again."

"I kind of fell into rushing," Lyndsee said. "I met a girl in class whom I became friends with, and she happened to be in the sorority. She asked me if I wanted to come to one of their parties. When I went, I had a great time meeting everyone. I really liked the people she introduced me to and I went back a few more times and started getting to know them better. NYU is a really big place and I thought if I joined a small organization, I would get to know more people on a more personal level.

"There were a lot of positive *and* negative experiences associated with being in the sorority. I made a lot of great friends, expanded my social circle, and learned a lot from the upperclassmen—everything from which classes to take to which bars and clubs were the most fun. There were lots of people around to bounce ideas off of and to hang out with. I did lose a few friends who didn't join houses and didn't understand the time commitment required for the social and community service events. All in all, though, I would do it again because there are a few close friends I met through the sorority that I would never want to be without," Lyndsee concluded.

Fraternity Rush and Pledge

The fraternity rush period is typically more casual and spread out than sorority rush, often consuming a couple of months or more. There is no standard rush process, and unlike with the sorority rush, there are no widespread requirements for students to rush all the houses.

Fraternity rush events are usually casual house parties, sometimes with themes and almost always with free beer, offering opportunities for guys to hang out and casually meet the brothers. Unlike in the sorority rush, few fraternities have any formalized process for selecting pledges. Formal rush parties and interviews are rare.

When the fraternity rush period has concluded, bids will be offered to a certain numbers of people inviting them to pledge the house. As with sorority pledging, you can pledge only one house at a time (hence the word), so if you receive more than one bid, you will have to choose from among them. Pledging is usually a formality, meaning that unless you act like a complete ass or hit on a brother's girlfriend, if you're offered a bid, you're in. At many schools, there is both a fall and a winter pledge class, offering you more flexibility in deciding whether and when to rush.

Generally speaking, forced drinking and borderline (or *over* the line) hazing is more prevalent in fraternities, where many of the pledging rituals are kept secret from the administration. As always, common sense dictates the proper response to any situation. If you are asked (or forced) to do anything that makes you truly uncomfortable (compare, for example, being forced to refer to your fraternity brothers as "sir," to clean the frat house basement on hands and knees, or to streak through the sorority house on the next block [all typical], to being *forced* to drink, vandalize property, or answer questions while a venomous snake is draped over your neck [obviously *not* okay]), recognize that your participation in the process is *optional.* Be a good sport about some rites of initiation, but don't be afraid to draw the line. And if the brothers don't respect your boundaries after you draw the line and insist on it, then you probably don't want those cats as brothers anyway.

"Try to spend at least part of the time you are rushing sober so you can evaluate what is going on with a clear head and nonintoxicated perspective," Jim warned. "Consider what you will give up in terms of other opportunities before you decide to pledge. And seriously consider waiting until your sophomore year to make that decision. Pledging can be academically destructive.

"I joined Sigma Nu at Duke because I was having fun attending the parties and the brothers were fun and welcoming. I met a large number of people through the fraternity, particularly upperclassmen who had some good perspective on the college experience beyond freshman year. But being a brother took a lot of time away from other activities available at Duke that I would later enjoy. The scene proved to become less exciting by my sophomore year and I regretted not spending more of my time looking into other social outlets, so I left the fraternity sophomore year. I just felt like I wanted to pursue other opportunities. Thankfully, I kept looking for other outlets and I found them," Jim concluded.

"Rush is extremely hectic," Erik added. "I tried to see too many houses and met too many people to really spend enough quality time with any of them and as such, I did not receive a bid to a fraternity. At the time, I was disappointed, but in retrospect, I think it greatly worked to my advantage to live in the dorms. I had an incredibly hectic schedule with my classes and playing a varsity sport every season of the year, so I'm not sure I could even have been a fully contributing member, which would have bothered me, and certainly would have bothered the brothers.

"It turned out that I had teammates who were members of dozens of different fraternities, so I had the best of both worlds: I could spend time with them at key functions and parties and get to experience some of that, while at the same time having the freedom to come and go as I pleased."

When You're "Made"

When you are offered brotherhood or sisterhood in a house, that offer comes with some obligations you need to know about. First off, most houses charge a one-time initiation fee, which can range anywhere from a few hundred to several thousand dollars depending on what school you attend and what house you are joining. Once you pay the initiation fee, you will also be subjected to semester dues, which help underwrite the cost of the house and its activities. It is wise to check on these obligations *before* you pledge a house so that you won't be surprised after the fact.

Further, not all members actually *live* in their fraternity or sorority houses. Although every house is different, residency in the house is rarely an obligation of your membership. In fact, many houses don't have sufficient space to board all their members—resulting in uncomfortable accommodations on sleeping porches (think summer camp, with bunks, shared space, and no privacy) or residency by seniority, lottery, or ability to pay.

DECIDING WHETHER GREEK LIFE IS FOR YOU

If you followed our advice earlier in the book when you were selecting the schools you chose to apply to, and again when you chose which school to attend, you should already know whether or not Greek life dominates the social life on your campus. We hope that if you hate the idea of joining a fraternity or sorority, you did not matriculate on a campus where they dominate, because on a campus where the social life revolves around the Greek system, it is unquestionably easier to be a participant than an outsider.

Joining a fraternity or sorority gives you an easy way to bond with a group of men or women of similar age, and to meet and get to know a lot of people in a short period of time. It also gives you a turnkey social life right from the beginning of college, which can help eliminate a lot of the awkwardness and discomfort associated with being in a new place with all new people.

Remember, though, that although joining a fraternity or a sorority guarantees you a group of fellow travelers, the safety and comfort of numbers, structure and hierarchy, and a sense of identity at a time when you feel the most vulnerable and isolated—it does not guarantee that you will fit in or get along with those people. Judging that "fit" is your task during the rush period. You must resist the urge to rush or pledge a house simply because it is perceived (properly or not) to be the "coolest" or (properly or not) to have the best connections or the best accommodations. You join a house for the people and because you sense a good fit between your personality, philosophy, and goals and those of the majority of the brothers or sisters in the house.

At their best, and when properly chosen, fraternities and sororities offer you a great and tightly knit group of friends, a ready-made social life, a sense of place, and an opportunity to meet your classmates in a comfortable way and from a position of confidence and belonging. They can provide you with opportunities for leadership: in the house, as an officer, committee chair, or member of the governing board; on campus, as a member of the university council or administration; or even on the national level. They offer you opportunities for community service and outreach, which can connect you with the world and broaden your horizons. Finally, they can provide you with a host of helpful resources, including course notes, outlines and copies of old exams (with answers), and a good network of contacts to help you get jobs and other opportunities in the world after you graduate.

At their worst, fraternities and sororities can be nondiverse, isolated hives of racism, bigotry, and peer pressure, where members lose their individual identities and are dragged down to the level of the lowest common denominator. Fraternities and sororities can also be isolating, in that there is always beer to be had, a TV to be watched, and people to hang out with, making it all too easy to forget that there is a whole world of opportunity out on campus that you are missing every time you default to hanging out at the house.

WHEN TO RUSH

As we've said, in response to societal pressures against hazing and binge drinking, more and more fraternities and sororities are pushing their rush periods to second semester or foreclosing freshman participation completely. At other schools, rush period is slated as early as the week *before* classes begin. At still other schools, there are two rush periods each year, one in the fall and one in the spring. You can find out what system your college is using by reading the admissions materials you receive during the summer before you go off to college.

If you're not certain about the Greek system, it's worth participating in some rush events just to see how it feels. There are many misconceptions and misperceptions about fraternities and sororities. Whereas the popular trend a generation ago was to flock to them, many students today write the whole system off without giving it a chance. Neither approach is necessarily the best.

Having said that, adjustment to campus and college life can be difficult enough without having to respond to the peer pressure and "unnatural selection" that characterizes rush period. If the system at your school gives you the option to do so, consider waiting until second semester or even until sophomore year to rush. Allow yourself to get acclimated to campus life, meet friends outside the Greek system, and get your academic career launched. Use the time to figure out what Greek life is like and whether you feel it would add a positive dimension to your college experience. If you are leaning toward participation, use your first semester (or first year) to figure out which houses are which (and where they are), which houses are known for what, and which ones seem like the best fit for you. Forcing yourself to participate in the rush period before you know what you're doing can be stressful, can lead you to act in ways that you might later regret, and can often result in your pledging the wrong house. In other words, take your time, consider your options, and make the choice that is right for you.

NON-GREEK HOUSES OR SOCIETIES

Every campus is set up somewhat differently, and some campuses offer non-Greek houses, societies, or membership clubs either in addition to or instead of the Greek system. A treatment of all of these different organizations is beyond the scope of this book, but suffice it to say that if your college or university offers such options, you should talk to upperclassmen and check them out to see if what they offer is right for you. In many cases, these clubs make it possible to break the campus social scene down into smaller and more workable units, which can aid you in making friends and finding your niche.

"Wellesley is an example of a school that doesn't have sororities in the usual sense, but instead, has 'societies,'" Zoe explained. "These societies are similar to sororities in that they're exclusive, self-contained groups that require going through a rush process (called 'tea-ing,' as in attending a tea party). They differ from most sororities in that they are nonresidential, although most have their own houses on campus that are used for meetings, events, and parties. Each society has a theme or mission, mostly related to the arts (literature, music, theater, and the like), but most members would admit that the social function is a key facet and draw.

"I joined the Shakespeare Society sophomore year. At the core of the 'life' of the society is a student-acted and -directed Shakespearean performance each semester. I was largely drawn to the acting element of the society, but also to the idea of having a 'home' on campus, and becoming part of a group that had been in existence for about a century and that I would continue to be a part of for the rest of my life.

"In terms of your decision to join an organization like this, try to get to know what the group is all about before you consider pledging, and once you do decide, be yourself as much as possible. Do you really want to enter an intimate, exclusive group having been accepted based on a portrayal of yourself that isn't authentic?

"Being part of my society at Wellesley helped me to feel planted and at home. I don't think it is *necessary* to join a sorority or a society to have that experience, by any means, but for me, it was formative."

"I chose to join a selective house as opposed to a fraternity because I was turned off by the whole idea of pledging," Chase recalls. "I was just getting my academic confidence and didn't think that the pledging requirements of the Greek system would do much for my study habits. Having eliminated Greek life in favor of selective housing, I simply looked at which of my peers were planning on going to which houses. Joining a selective group is an experience I would certainly repeat. Living in a large group setting exposes you to many more people than you could meet under normal circumstances and also opens up opportunities that otherwise would be difficult or impossible to experience. The house offered turnkey social interaction on a large-scale, be it parties, formals, or trips. Small groups of friends usually don't have the resources to create similar experiences. These events and the daily routine in the house created invaluable bonds."

ADDITIONAL RESOURCES

www.nicindy.org/index.html (Web site of the North American Inter-Fraternity Conference; links to all national fraternity offices)

www.npcwomen.org (Web site of the National Panhellenic Conference; links to all national sorority offices)

Study Habits and
Time Management
for the College Student

*Spectacular achievement is always preceded
by spectactular preparation.*

Robert H. Schuller

Developing good time management skills and effective study habits is critical to your success in college—not to mention your enjoyment of college life. Fortunately, working out a simple time management system and devising effective study strategies is less about gimmicks than it is about common sense. Follow these simple steps, and we can guarantee that you'll be well on your way to a productive life in college.

GET ORGANIZED AND STAY ORGANIZED

Getting organized and developing a simple system to stay that way are among your first orders of business when you get to college. The first thing you need to decide is what your organizational tool is going to be. For those of us who still love working on paper, it could be a twenty-four-hour day planner, or even something as simple as a desk calendar. For others, it may be a PDA. Whatever tool you choose, it will be the *one* place where you will record all your classes, meetings, assignments, exam dates, and paper deadlines.

As soon as you've decided which classes you'll be taking during your fall semester, it's time to "rip" your course syllabi into this calendar. All your class meeting times go into the calendar, as do the due dates of all problem sets, lab reports, and other assignments. Dates of all quizzes, tests, midterms, term papers, and finals also go immediately into the calendar.

"This is really important," Erika counseled. "As soon as you get your course syllabi, map out on a homework calendar what big tests you have due and when."

"I agree," Lyndsee noted. "I kept a very detailed calendar with all of my class times, exams, papers, projects, and their due dates on it. I also noted social events on the same calendar. This way, I had a long-term picture of what I had coming up and what I had to get done."

If you play a varsity sport, your practice schedule and your schedule of home and away games get overlaid onto this same calendar. This way, you can immediately spot the conflicts and plan ahead about how to deal with them. If you have committed to a couple of extracurricular activities, your meeting dates and times and anything you have committed to prepare for those meetings go into the calendar too. If you have decided to rush a fraternity or sorority, be sure your important dates related to those activities are entered into the calendar. Finally, be sure to plug in other important dates: Parents' Weekend, your campus Octoberfest weekend, the date of the fall formal, or whatever else might be important to you.

Now make us a promise.

From now on, any time and *every* time you make a commitment to be somewhere or do something with someone—be it a meeting with a professor during her office hours, a coffee date with a friend from orientation, or an agreement with the admissions office to house a prospective student in your dorm room—you enter that commitment into this calendar *immediately.*

Capturing *everything* going on in your life in one place should immediately give you a sense of control and organization. It will make your life a hell of a lot more enjoyable and a whole lot less stressful.

This is the first step toward a happy and successful college life. Commit to it.

Once you've finished ripping your syllabi into your calendar, three-hole-punch each syllabus and put it into a separate ring binder. If your professor assigned any course packets or provided any handouts for the course, three-hole-punch those and put them into the binder as well. Using a ring binder makes it easy to keep things safe, in good condition, and all in once place. As you take course notes on your laptop (we'll talk about taking notes later in the chapter), you can print them out and put them into your ring binder so that you'll have everything at your fingertips. If your professor hands out extra things during the semester, you can easily add these as well.

With all the paper that you'll deal with in college, it is easy to misplace things or lose pages from a handout or a syllabus. What you're looking for here is for all of your course materials to be stored in a *single* safe place. This system will help keep you organized and stress-free.

FIND YOUR "STUDY PLACE" ON CAMPUS

The next order of business is giving that "study place" that you found back in Chapter 8 a test drive. It is time to decide *where* you plan to go to get your daily work done. And it shouldn't be your dorm room—even if you live in a single.

Why?

Because there are *way* too many distractions in your dorm room. People will come to visit you or your roommates. You will be tempted to surf the Web, play computer games, download music, or just chill out. Your roommates, suitemates, or hallmates, who may be on a totally different schedule (or have a significantly different work ethic), may draw you into a conversation, a card game, or a television show, or convince you to go out for a drink, a bite to eat, or to do something else on campus.

In short, your dorm room is where you should go to hang out and relax. It is not the place where you should try to study or get serious work done.

So where should you go?

As we discussed back in Chapter 8, our advice is to find a quiet, out-of-the-way place on campus where you know you can be undisturbed. It is completely a matter of your personal preference, so seek out a place where you feel comfortable and empowered to do your best work. For me, it was a particular reading room tucked into the corner of the Yale library. It had little alcoves with comfortable leather chairs with side tables and individual reading lamps, and each alcove had its own window, which made it easy to regulate temperature and get fresh air. It was part of the main library, but isolated enough so as not to get a lot of foot traffic. Other than during reading period, when I usually retreated to a carrel on a high floor in the stacks (when I wanted to be completely undisturbed and unable to be found), I was a regular there on Sunday through Thursday nights.

My roommates and friends knew where to find me if something came up, but I was also tucked away in a place where I could concentrate well.

Eventually, each of my roommates and friends found their own places. One routinely studied in the map room, where no one ever went, but where they had these huge and incredibly ornate desks that you could work at. A couple of others preferred the privacy and quiet of the "loony bins" (soundproof study rooms) in the underground library. Others went to the law school library, which was closer to our suite, had nice, soft lighting, and was open all night; or studied at one of the tables in the main library's great hall—which was a terrific place to see and be seen, but not as great for concentration.

The point is, everyone found his place—and no one lasted for long trying to study in his room. This worked a nice side benefit too, because it meant that when we were *in* our rooms, we never had to worry about whether the TV, the music, or the card game was bothering anyone.

So if you haven't done so already, find your "study place" on campus and make it a habit to go there regularly, at the same times and on the same days. Test drive your chosen spot for several days and don't be afraid to go elsewhere if the place doesn't "feel" right or give you what you need to concentrate and get things done. If you need to mix it up and find two or three different places, fine. Just get into the habit of leaving your room and designating certain periods of your days to be "study times," when you won't be tempted to be distracted away from the tasks at hand.

"You can't just impose all of your old high school study strategies to a new environment without adjustments," Kevin explained. "At home, I studied in the kitchen of my house. In college, there is no kitchen, or dining room, or den. It's all one room. And your bed is in there, too, calling to you.

"It took me a while, but I eventually figured out that studying in my room sucked. You really can't do it well because your bed and your TV and your friends are all there. It takes a lot of willpower to resist that trio. You have to get out, and trust me, the library is your friend."

"The best decision I made freshman year was to begin working in the library rather than in my dorm room," Jim agreed. "I was far more efficient and did better as a result."

MAKE A WEEKLY TO-DO LIST ON SUNDAY—AND STICK TO IT

Speaking of the tasks at hand . . . obviously, you need to know what those are. College presents you with two distinct challenges you probably didn't have to face in high school. The first is the amount of "free time" you have, and the long periods between the times you actually get graded on things (often just three or four exams, or sometimes just a midterm and a final). This situation makes it all too easy to become complacent and to put off until tomorrow (or even the day after tomorrow) the things you really ought to be doing today. The other challenge is the amount of reading you'll have to do in college, which can become overwhelming if you fall too far behind. The way to manage these twin challenges is to try your best to keep on schedule.

At most colleges and universities, some point on Sunday afternoon marks the end of the weekend (which often starts on Thursday night). We recommend that the first thing you do to ease into your new work week is to sit with each of your course syllabi and your calendar and plot out a to-do list for the week. Figure out what reading assignments you have for each class and when they are due; you need to make sure you complete these readings *before* the class meets, so that you'll be able to understand, actively participate in, and enjoy the lecture. Next, do you have any problem sets or lab reports due this week? If you do, pencil these into your calendar for attention at least *two days* before they are due—not the night before. Trying to bang out an econ problem set or a chemistry lab report the night before it is due is just asking for trouble. If you can't figure something out (which will often happen), you end up scrambling around late at night trying to find someone who knows the answer or who can help you—either of which causes you undue stress and makes for a terrible start to the week. With an extra day to play with, though, you can handle these sticking points at any time during the next day—by talking to your friends or classmates about the problems you're having, or even going to visit your TA or the professor to ask questions if need be.

Once you have penciled in all those daily obligations, you should then look long-range at what responsibilities you may have coming down the road in a month, or as you approach the end of the semester. Do you have a term paper that you should start thinking about? If so, and if you have any room in your week to pay attention to some long-range projects, pencil in an hour or two to spend time looking for topics or fishing around in the library for source materials. Again, the long-term planning is to spare you from getting crushed at the end of the semester, which will lead to stress and, most likely, inferior performance.

Now take a look at what you have penciled in for each day. Are these tasks reasonable, or are you likely to get overwhelmed by them? If you see an easy day or a particularly difficult one, try to move tasks around to balance your work better.

Finally, put your work for each day in priority order, so that you will always be working on the most important things first, and the least critical things only if you have time. This way, if your problem set takes you twice as long as you thought it was going to, you'll still get it done; you can put your term paper research off to another day.

"I found that setting tangible daily goals was vital to my academic success," Chase noted. "Every morning, I made out a list of exactly what reading, what assignments, and what classes I had, as well as when I wanted to work out, meet friends, and go to bed. Having clear goals allowed me to work through the day knowing that I had budgeted finite amounts of time for everything that needed to get done.

"I also tried to balance relaxing and social activities with work. So I might meet a friend for lunch after class, then go to the library and knock off a reading assignment, then take a nap on the quad, then work on a paper, then play some basketball. Making a list of daily goals is also very satisfying because you are seeing progress at every point of the day. Remember that goal setting requires looking ahead to foresee bottlenecks in workloads. When work wasn't wholly consuming, I tried to get ahead. Too many students do things at the last minute, and then when several big things have to be done at the same time, their load becomes difficult to manage. Think ahead!"

"Although there will inevitably still be late nights as you try to finish papers or study for an exam, pacing yourself can reduce the frequency of those stressful nights," Lyndsee added.

SETTING REALISTIC DAILY GOALS: AN EXAMPLE

Let's go through an example of how you might look at a typical day's schedule and tasks, and figure out how to set them up—and get everything accomplished.

Wednesday, October 15

9:30–10:20 Chem 115

10:30–11:20 American Literature

Noon (lunch with friend)

1:00–1:50 Poli Sci 110

4:00–7:00 JV soccer practice

Chemistry problem set due Fri 10/17

75 pages of history reading for tomorrow's lecture

Finish chemistry lab report (due tomorrow)

50 pages of psychology reading plus "thinkpiece" due for tomorrow's lecture

Meet Film Club members for 10 P.M. study break to brainstorm ideas for festival

Call Mike [friend from summer camp]

Whoa. It's going to be a busy day. We can't resist pointing out that you would have known about this Wednesday logjam in advance had you gone through your calendar and your syllabi on Sunday night. You might have pushed to finish your lab report on Tuesday or have tried to bang out your history reading on Monday night, instead of watching that *entire* terrible *Monday Night Football* game that was 24–7 at the half. But for the sake of our example, let's assume that you're in this predicament now, and you need to schedule your way out of it.

What to do?

Well, the class times, your soccer practice, and your 10 P.M. meeting are fixed, so there is not a whole lot you can do about any of those things. Remember: we don't want you blowing off the 10 P.M. Film Club meeting just because you chose to watch football on Monday night and put yourself in this jam. That will piss off the people in the Film Club and earn you a bad reputation. Besides, this is workable. You just need to be a little creative about it.

The first thing we're going to do here is get you up early—say 7:00 A.M.

Hey, don't blame us . . . you put yourself in this jam.

Go to the dining hall or the nearest coffee shop, grab some coffee and breakfast, and bring your chem lab report with you. Because you and your lab partner met yesterday and did most of the hard work, all you have left to do is finish the calculations and write up your observations and conclusions sections.

Do that this morning before your chemistry lecture.

Why are you doing this, and not your more enjoyable psych or history reading, which would "ease" you into the day in more enjoyable fashion?

Because the lab report is due tomorrow, and it is graded—and if something were to go wrong with the rest of your day, or if you were to have additional problems in writing up the report, you'd still have some time to deal with those problems. So you knock that off the agenda first.

Happily, you are able to finish up the report without any additional problems, and you go to your chemistry lecture with the lab report finished—and fully jazzed on the two cups of coffee you drank, meaning that you might have some prayer of understanding what the hell is going on with the mean free path equation your professor will be attempting to explain to you today.

From there, you go to your very enjoyable American literature class, for which you completed the reading on a sunny Saturday afternoon lying under a tree on the freshman green—taking advantage of an opportunity to catch some rays *and* get some reading done at the same time. That was a wise use of time!

Because your day was looking hellacious last night when you planned all this out, you postponed lunch with your friend to Friday—which freed up two hours at lunch today to get more done. So when American Literature ends at 11:20, you go by the dining hall, grab a sandwich on the fly, and head over to the library to start banging out your chemistry problem set.

After nearly two hours, you've made good progress, getting about two-thirds of the way through it without encountering any major hang-ups. So you head over to your poli sci lecture at 1:50 P.M., and take that in.

After joking around with a couple of classmates after Poli Sci for fifteen minutes, you get back on track. You need to be over at the soccer field at 4 P.M. for practice, but it's a nice day, so you decide to take your psych book over there now and find an isolated spot to read outside. That way, you won't feel rushed to get over to the fields to make practice on time, and you can max out the rest of the time you have to finish as much of your psych reading as you can.

You get to the soccer field at 2:20, change into your practice gear, and then settle in to your reading. It's 2:30.

By 4:00, you've finished thirty of the fifty pages, but you've read enough to come up with a good idea for the one page thinkpiece you need to turn in at every lecture. So you're on track.

Feeling good about the way your day is going, you have a great scrimmage and push yourself hard. The exercise, coupled with the camaraderie with your teammates, refreshes you and gives you a good break from what has been a strong academic push. Meanwhile, in the time between drills, you give some thought to the movies you'd like to see featured in the campus film festival you'll be meeting about tonight, and you come up with a few ideas.

At 7:00 P.M., you grab a quick shower at the fieldhouse and head to the dining hall for dinner with your teammates. During dinner, you ask them for some feedback about the movies you're considering for the campus film festival, and get some good reaction that you can share with the members of the Film Club at your meeting tonight. After that, you head over to your study spot at the library, where you arrive at 8:00 P.M., finish your psych reading, and knock the thinkpiece out on your laptop.

At 10 P.M., you meet the members of the Film Club for study break, and share your ideas and the reactions of the members of the soccer team. Although a couple of club members are still batting ideas back and forth, at 10:45 you excuse yourself, noting that you still have history reading to do for class tomorrow. You made the meeting and contributed to it, though, so this is not a problem.

The seventy-five pages of history reading still loom at 11 P.M. when you get back to the library, but the good news is that this is just reading, and it's pretty interesting. There is no assignment connected to it, so there is nothing really stressful about it.

You read until 12:30 A.M., at which point you've finished forty-five pages. You're wiped out, though, so you decide it's time to pack it in for the night and head back to the dorm to hang out a little with your roommates and unwind. Fortunately, your first class tomorrow—history—doesn't start until 10:30 A.M., so you can sleep until 8 A.M. and finish up the reading before class.

So you see, with a little advance planning, you can handle even the day from hell. Needless to say, this was a very tough day—and better planning earlier in the week (for example, not watching the entire game on Monday night) would have prevented this crush. Nevertheless, you managed it well—and because you did the assignments with things to turn in first, the end of the day (when you were most tired) wasn't that stressful, and could be spent handling a relatively easy reading assignment.

A failure to plan, though, would be likely to cause you to waste the time between classes and between class and practice—and then force you to skip reading and jam the entire chemistry problem set into tomorrow's column . . . which would have made for a stressful and tough day tomorrow as well.

"Think 'WIN' (What's Important Now)," Erik advised. "You really need to learn to prioritize your time and that often means deciding between multiple conflicting commitments. You need to realistically decide what is the most important thing, then the next most important, and so on, and then formulate a plan as to how you are going to accomplish everything that needs to get done."

"My main strategy was 'work hard, play hard,'" Amanda recalls. "Most weeknights I would study until about 10 or 11 and then socialize. Use your free periods during the day wisely so you can get everything done and still get enough sleep so you're not falling asleep in class or in your books when you're trying to study. If you do find yourself falling asleep in your books, go to bed! You're not accomplishing anything and you're not getting good quality sleep either. Get up early if you need to finish something up before class."

HANDLE YOUR COLLEGE READING ASSIGNMENTS EFFECTIVELY

If you've managed to get through the college admissions process, we're confident that you've learned how to handle reading assignments—but you're in college now, and as we've said, the reading load in college can be very different than what you were used to in high school. If you are not ready for it and don't have a strategy in place for handling the volume, dealing with your reading can often feel like trying to drink from a fire hose.

But fear not: handling college reading is not rocket science. It simply requires an effective strategy and a commitment from you to follow through on it.

If you've followed our advice so far, you will, on Sunday of every week, sketch out your schedule and your assignments for the week. This will help you determine where the big reading assignments for the week fall and how to break them up or otherwise plan to handle them effectively. Proper planning alone, though, is not enough to ensure effectiveness.

First, we hope you've settled in to your "study place" where you have good light, a comfortable chair, and enough quiet and isolation to minimize distractions. The importance of this should be self-evident, as you are looking to get immersed in what you are reading. People stopping by every five minutes to visit, or other distractions will obviously break your concentration, slow you down, and reduce the effectiveness of your session.

Once you've settled in to start a reading assignment, though, there is more to handling it effectively than just plunging in and plowing through it. If you haven't already done so, take a look at the course syllabus as a whole and then at the section containing the reading assignment you are about to begin. Pay special attention to any titles, headings, or other descriptors that your professor has indicated on that section of the syllabus. Consider how your assignment for tonight fits in with what you've been doing and with where you are going in the next several lectures. What you are looking for here is a *context* for your reading, so that you'll know specifically what to be thinking about as you read.

Once you've done that, take a few minutes to flip through the section of the textbook or course packet containing your reading assignment for the night, and get a sense of how it is organized. Scan the chapter titles and section headings to give yourself a framework for organizing the material as you read. Doing this will help you read actively, think critically about what you are reading, and better retain the subject matter.

Once you've done this, go ahead and plunge in. Highlight, underline, or make margin notes in the textbook next to key points. Write any questions triggered by your reading in the margins as well, so you'll remember to ask the professor about these points during or after lecture. If as you read you come across any words, terms, or concepts you do not understand, look them up in the glossary (if there is one), a dictionary, or another secondary source, and write the definitions or explanations right into the textbook so that they'll be there if you need them again. Don't simply read past them—doing so may significantly impede your understanding of the topic.

Finally, force yourself to read actively. Don't simply paint the text with a highlighter, thinking that you'll come back to tease out the important ideas later. Think critically about what you are reading: force yourself to actively relate the subject matter you are covering to the most recent section heading or chapter title and then to the section on the course syllabus you reviewed before you began. If you find your mind wandering or if you find yourself just blindly reading words without thinking about them, stop.

Get up, take a walk, get a drink of water or a breath of fresh air, and then go back to the syllabus and remind yourself again of what you should be looking for. Remember, reading words and simply "covering" the material is not what you are looking for. You are trying to get *an education*—which means you need to be actually processing what you are reading.

When you finish the reading assignment, don't just put it away and move on to the "next thing" you have to do. Take five more minutes and reflect on what the reading assignment was about. Go back and scan the chapter titles, section headings, and all the highlights, underlines, or margin notes you made for yourself. Remind yourself of the section on the syllabus you were covering, where you've been, and where you are going in the course material. Think about where what you have just learned "fits in" to the subject as a whole.

Taking this extra five minutes will have no effect on your daily schedule, but you'll be *amazed* at what it does for your long-term retention and comprehension of the material.

DON'T MISS CLASSES

If you attend the average college or university in this country and take the average course load, you are paying somewhere around $65 *per lecture* for your college education. If you're attending a top private university, the number is closer to $85 per lecture.

Do you routinely go out in the street throwing away fistfuls of twenties? Because that's exactly what you're doing if you skip your class lectures.

I don't care what anyone else tells you. You are always—and I mean *always*—better off going to your classes than you are skipping them. It doesn't matter how hung over you are or how dreadfully bad a lecturer your professor is. It doesn't matter that you haven't started or finished the reading for the class, and it doesn't matter that you might be embarrassed by the professor if you get called on to participate and cannot. It doesn't matter that the class is small and you won't be able to hide the fact that you are unprepared.

You *must not* skip classes unless you are really sick. There are so many good reasons for this, we'll have trouble covering them all in this section. But we'll try. The corollary to this rule is that you must also show up for class on time and not leave class early—and the reasons for the corollary are the same as the ones for the general rule.

"Okay, okay," you say. "But what's the big deal? People have been blowing off class in college since the beginning of time."

True. And people have also been getting needlessly stressed out and have been underperforming in their college classes since the beginning of time, too.

Listen.

The class lecture is where your professors highlight the parts of the reading material that are truly important to the course. Lecture is where professors explain the difficult concepts, provide examples to highlight how these concepts work, and discuss their application to the subject matter and to the real world. Lecture is also where professors make useful offhand remarks like, "I wouldn't get too hung up on this" or "I would pay particular attention to making sure you understand this."

During lectures, professors also frequently provide supplementary handouts, change reading assignments, or announce specific things, such as the format, timing, and permissible materials for upcoming exams.

We hope it is obvious to you why it would be important to hear your professors explain difficult concepts, give examples to help you understand how the concepts work, and drop not-so-subtle hints about what will be on future tests and exams. No amount of attention to the reading material will convey these things to you.

And no, borrowing someone else's class notes isn't going to get you there either. First, most college students are brutally bad note takers. Even if they do manage to get something down on paper, it doesn't mean they recorded it accurately. And because you weren't there to hear it, you'll never know what asterisks, stars, circles, or other flotsam in someone's notes actually means.

Then there is the whole "discomfort thing" associated with missing course lectures. If you are like most students, missing a lecture will make you feel "off balance" for days afterward precisely because of your subconscious concern about what you might have missed or because you feel that you are falling behind in your understanding of the course material compared to your classmates.

Finally, you need to think about class participation. At many colleges and universities, professors are permitted to lower grades or even fail students for not showing up to lectures, or to raise grades for exemplary participation. You'll clearly want to know what your school's policy is on this issue—but remember, the primary reason for going to lecture is not about angling for an upward adjustment in your grade. It is about working hard to achieve a mastery of the material. Even if you pick up only one or two cogent points in each lecture, or clarify one uncertainty from your reading, attending class will be worth it. And we can't overstate the improved comfort level you will experience from simply "being there" to hear everything that is said and discussed.

GET THE MOST OUT OF YOUR CLASS LECTURES

It's important to remember that like your study sessions, your college class lectures are not social occasions. They are short, concentrated information-gathering sessions that warrant your complete and undivided attention.

Yeah, yeah . . . we know that class is one of the best places to flirt and to otherwise banter with people you might like to date. We know that most people sitting in class lecture are engaged in some form of sexual fantasy rather than engaged in the course material.

We were there, remember?

What we're telling you, though, is that there is *plenty* of time for meeting people before class and after class. During the fifty or seventy-five minutes that the professor is actually speaking, we want you locked in on the information he or she is trying to convey—rather than locked in on the rear end of the attractive person in the row ahead of you.

We know it is hard to concentrate, so we offer up the following suggestions to help you along.

Complete Your Reading Assignments and Problem Sets Before Class and on Time

We've already addressed the importance of preparation in the previous sections on organization—but obviously, your going to lecture having read and thought about the material assigned will make the lecture easier to follow, comprehend, and digest, and will naturally make you a more active listener, as you will be on the lookout for any additional nuggets of wisdom you can glean from the lecture and add to the arsenal of knowledge you gained from the reading assignment itself.

Conversely, if you failed to do the reading, you will be off balance and will spend the entire lecture worrying that you might get called on and have your lack of preparation exposed. Even if this happens, however, we say again that you must still *force* yourself to go to class—because not doing the reading and then not going to class merely compounds your mistake, . . . and before long, you will find yourself hopelessly lost and stressed out.

Timeliness in completing your problem sets is also critical. Obviously, you need to turn your problem sets in on time in order to get full credit for them, but the more important reason for finishing your problem sets on time is to keep pace with the class. Problem sets are assigned to help you master difficult material by forcing you to engage the specific concepts presented by that material and to work through how those concepts are used. Further, in many subjects for which problem sets are frequently assigned (such as the natural sciences, math, and economics), mastering the individual problem sets as they are assigned is necessary to help you build skills.

Copying someone else's problem-set answers or simply watching the professor work some exemplars on the board is simply not the same as struggling through the material yourself—relying on such tactics will hurt you in the long run.

Sit Near the Front of the Lecture Hall

We don't care if it means that you're taking a play out of the front of *Dork Handbook* or that all the "cool" people "backbench" in lecture.

You're going to sit in the front—in the center of the lecture hall and within the first ten rows of the professor.

Why?

Because this will make it easier for you to focus on what the professor is saying and to see, understand, and record anything he or she writes on the chalkboard or whiteboard; and, frankly, sitting front and center makes it harder for you to lock in on anything else that might draw your attention away from the matter at hand. You'll be amazed at how well this works in practice. You will also gain the fringe benefit of having the professor recognize and eventually get to know your face. Then, should you ever need to show up in office hours or need a recommendation, the professor will be more inclined to help you, knowing that you are a serious student who always comes to lecture and is not a part of the group of students socializing or surfing the Net in the back of the room.

Take Good Notes During Lecture

Most of the mentors agree that taking class notes on a laptop is the way to go, because most people can type much faster than they can write, but also because it is easier to maintain an outline format and to add, delete, and move text around in your notes as needed. (I always preferred to use the outline function on my laptop to enable the quick organization of the professor's lecture. What's cool, too, is that if you use this function, you can quickly and easily reorganize on the fly if he or she adds additional thoughts, elements, or examples after the fact.) If you don't have a laptop, though, or you prefer to take notes in longhand, the same concepts we describe here apply.

We've already talked about the first important strategy: locking in to the professor once he or she begins speaking, guarding against distraction as much as humanly possible, and listening *actively* to the professor's presentation.

Now let's talk about the substance of what you actually record in your class notes. Instead of trying to take a precise stenographic record of the class by recording every *word* uttered by the professor (and everyone else) during the lecture, focus simply on capturing the significant ideas and all examples conveyed by the professor during the lecture period—including and especially *everything* the professor writes up on the board before or during class.

Be sure to date your notes in your computer or on paper for ease of later reference. If the professor or a classmate subsequently asks a question about something from "last Tuesday's" lecture, you want to have an easy way to refer to it immediately. Similarly, if the professor distributes an article or handout during the lecture, date it and, as soon as you are able, three-hole-punch it and add it to your ring binder for the course so that you'll have everything in one place.

Keeping a thorough and complete outline of the lectures in a particular subject will keep you immersed, interested, and engaged in the class and give you increased confidence about your understanding of and mastery of the material. And after just a few days, you'll be inspired to make it to lectures so that you don't end up with gaps in your work. Having a great set of class notes will make the class more enjoyable, keep your stress level about the class to an absolute minimum, and also put you in the position to help out your less well prepared classmates with notes or explanations of difficult concepts. Helping your classmates—and at the same time building up this kind of "favor equity"—is always a good thing.

At this point, you may be thinking to yourself, "Well, if getting a good set of lecture notes is so important, I'll just tape the class, and that way I can listen carefully and take a good set of notes from the recording later."

We don't encourage this approach.

First, some schools and individual professors will not *allow* you to record lectures. Second, even if taping classes is allowed, employing this approach may encourage passive learning. Knowing that you are recording the lecture, you are far less likely to try to take a good set of live lecture notes and are much more likely to daydream and lose the thread of the lecture. You are also very likely to fall far behind in preparing a good set of notes from your tapes, as using this approach at least doubles the amount of time you must commit to the process.

Many of us have tried both approaches, and we're convinced that locking in and taking a good set of complete lecture notes during the actual, live lecture is the way to go.

To the extent that you have any gaps after taking complete notes, you should follow up with the professor after class to clear up any uncertainties.

PUT IT ALL TOGETHER

The last trick about preparedness is finding the time to put everything together *before* the pressure of an exam strikes. Once you've completed a section of the syllabus, using your lecture notes as the guide, go back and backfill into your class notes relevant details from the readings, including any margin notes, underlines, or highlights—and if applicable, any particularly vexing problems highlighting difficult concepts from your problem sets. What you're looking to do is pull the readings and the lecture notes together into a single, cohesive outline.

Once you've completed this consolidation, studying for tests, midterms, and finals is as simple as mastering this outline.

A WORD ABOUT STUDY GROUPS

Although everyone masters material in different ways, it was our collective experience that college study groups frequently devolved into inefficient social or gossip sessions, rather than effective study sessions. As you have seen, our approach throughout this book has been to make room for study and room for a rich and vibrant life in college. There are, of course, exceptions to every rule—but to us, effective study in college is best done either in isolation or with a single study partner.

ADDITIONAL RESOURCE

Robbins, Anthony. *RPM Planner Kit* (time management system). (www.anthonyrobbins.com)

The Twenty-Three Unwritten Rules of College Etiquette

Good manners will open doors the best education cannot.

Clarence Thomas

All colleges, no matter where they are located and no matter how big or how reputable they are, share some similar "rules of the road." These rules are really more about interpersonal interactions *in* college than they are about college itself. Nevertheless, the failure to abide by these simple rules gets students into heaps of trouble with their peers every year.

To help you avoid this mistake, your mentors have collectively devised the following list of the twenty-three most important unwritten rules of college etiquette. Yes, we're sure there are more, but we agree that these are the most important ones. Think of these rules as your reference guide to playing well in the sandbox with others. Read through the list and make some mental notes to guide your behavior and interactions when you get to campus.

RESPECT AND FOLLOW YOUR SCHOOL'S HONOR CODE

This is at the top of the list, because it is the most important rule of all. Don't cheat.
Period.
Ever.

Even if you don't get caught, nothing will kill your reputation with your classmates faster than hearing, anecdotally or otherwise, that you were willing to cut corners to bail yourself out.

Remember that cheating comes in many forms. Using forbidden materials in an exam room and downloading prewritten papers from online sources are only the most obvious ones. Copying your lab partner's lab report or your roommate's problem-set responses, failing to properly cite reference sources in a research paper, looking at a stolen or hacked copy of upcoming exam questions, and lying about health problems to get more time to finish a paper or a project are all cheating. Establish some clear-cut rules for yourself at the beginning of college so that you don't find yourself rationalizing away behaviors that put you over the line.

"Never hide or steal library books or deliberately reshelve them in the wrong place," Amanda said. "Besides being rude and cheating your classmates, by doing this, you are also giving your major and your college a reputation for being cutthroat."

"And don't put your friends in an uncomfortable place by asking them to tell you about a test or to give you old papers," Chase adds. "When work is piling up and you are stressed, the temptation to use friends as a vehicle for cheating is strong. For example, you may have friends who have taken a test in the morning that you will be taking in the afternoon. Asking them for help is unfair and it *is* cheating. Plus, you're putting your friend in the position to decide between academic dishonesty and turning down a friend."

You should certainly not traffic in rumor—so no, you should not report someone for cheating if you "heard" that so-and-so was using illegal sources in the exam or if "someone told you" that a certain person downloaded his paper for the class. Stay away from hearsay—it can only get you into trouble.

That said, if you *personally* witness someone cheating, you have an ethical and moral obligation to yourself and to your other classmates to report it to your professor. No ifs, ands, or buts. Rules will be respected only when people stand up and defend them when they've been broken.

GO TO CLASS AND GET THERE ON TIME

It is disrespectful to your professor and distracting to your classmates to walk in to a lecture or seminar late. Sure—everyone is going to screw up every now and then, but don't make it a habit. It is rude, and if you do it too often, your professor will notice and may dock your grade for it.

Similarly, you should do everything you can to avoid missing class. If you don't think the professor has something valuable to teach you about a subject and can do so skillfully, don't take the class.

BE PREPARED FOR CLASS AND BE AN ACTIVE PARTICIPANT

A large part of the learning experience in college is what students teach each other, both inside and outside of class. If you have a question about a subject in lecture, raise your hand, wait to be called on, and ask it. Chances are, others are confused on the same point and will be grateful to you for stopping the train.

If it is a seminar or small-group class and your professor routinely solicits your active participation—then participate! Don't be afraid that you'll say something stupid. The only way to learn and gain confidence in learning is to stretch yourself and get out of your comfort zone. Don't assume that the people who *are* talking actually know more than you do. In all likelihood, they are just more confident.

DON'T MONOPOLIZE THE DISCUSSION

Having said that, no one likes the person who doesn't know when and how to shut up. Inevitably, there will be someone in your class missing this social filter—who thinks that his or her opinion on every minor point should be voiced—who has his or her hand raised from the minute class begins until after it ends, and then also monopolizes the professor after class. This is the person who makes every question into one of politics or religion or whatever his or her hot-button issue might be.

Don't be this person.

"You definitely want to be aware of how much you are volunteering in class, and more important, how often what you say enhances (or does not enhance) the discussion," Carolyn advised. "There is nothing more annoying than sitting in class listening to someone monopolizing the class discussion who is speaking only to hear himself speak. When you speak in class, be sure that what you are saying is relevant. In other words, have a point!"

Unless you are in a freewheeling small seminar where discussion is ongoing, a good rule of thumb to follow is not to speak more than twice in a single lecture. There are good reasons to depart from this rule on occasion, but this should be your rule of thumb.

"If you have a question that only applies to you, or one that is probably too specific to benefit the class discussion, don't interrupt the flow of the discussion by asking it," Aaron advises. "Save it for after class."

KEEP A LID ON RELIGION AND POLITICS

Unless you are actually taking a religion or political science or political philosophy class, or have actually been invited to do so, try to keep a lid on your personal political and religious views. Nothing will polarize people to you faster than getting a reputation for being a screeching knee-jerk liberal, an unthinking gun-toting conservative, or a religious zealot (no matter what your faith). And once you have this reputation, it will follow you everywhere—into your other classes, into the dorms, and into your social life. If it is germane to the classroom discussion, then by all means express your views and listen to others. But do so with care.

DON'T EMBARRASS YOUR FELLOW STUDENTS

If a classmate is struggling with an answer to a professor's question, don't be the person hotdogging with your hand in the air to prove that you know what your classmate doesn't. If you do get called on, be circumspect and respectful in your response. Try not to show up your classmates. It is fine to disagree with classmates on points of discussion; without such disagreement, classes would be pretty boring. But always be *respectful* in the way you address your classmates and the points they make. Never preface your responses with snide remarks ("That's stupid") or personal snipes ("That's because you're a tree hugger"). It might be funny for a moment—but that moment of comedy at the expense of a classmate won't make you any friends and will polarize certain members of the class against you.

"And don't ask questions that you already know the answers to just so your professor and your peers will think you are smart," Aaron adds. "That's annoying."

DON'T TALK TO YOUR FRIENDS IN CLASS

You are in class to learn, not to socialize with your friends. If you are going to take a class with a friend or roommate, you'll learn more and focus more on the lecture if you sit apart from your friend and focus on the matter at hand. If you insist on sitting together, though, at least remember this rule. It is rude to the professor and disrespectful to the people around you for you to be whispering and giggling with your friends during class. At a minimum, it will annoy the people around you. At worst, the professor will stop his or her lecture and ask you to stop—which could be very embarrassing and have a negative effect on your grade in the class.

TURN OFF THE GADGETS (CELL PHONE, BLACKBERRY, INTERNET)

The same rule applies for all your electronic gadgetry. It is fine to take notes on a laptop (try to tap quietly so you don't bother your classmates), but it is certainly *not* fine for your cell phone to ring during a lecture, to be seen sending e-mails from your Blackberry during lecture, or to spend the lecture playing Internet poker. Professors aren't stupid—they *will* catch on eventually. Even if they don't, your fellow students will see you, and you'll get the reputation for being a slacker. Then, when you need notes from a lecture you missed, they'll be less inclined to give them to you.

Oh, and if you're going to use a laptop to take notes, turn the volume down so that the *1812 Overture* you assigned as your startup tone doesn't piss off everyone else.

DON'T TALK ABOUT OR COMPLAIN ABOUT GRADES

This is a biggie.

Everyone hates the "gunner"—you know, the student who constantly talks about and whines about grades. The one who is constantly going to the professor's office hours to try to glean what the exam questions are going to be or to brownnose or otherwise suck up to the professor.

Don't be this person.

The best rule to follow here is to treat grades as personal and private. Don't obsess about them, don't discuss them before the fact, and don't compare them after the fact. If someone asks you how you did on a particular exam, paper, or whatever, just tell the person that you make it a policy not to discuss grades. If he or she pushes the point, push back.

The truth is, nothing good can ever come of talking about grades. If you got a better grade, you'll make the other person feel bad. If the other person did, he or she will make *you* feel bad. Comparisons will get you nowhere and typically only engender ill will. So avoid the topic altogether. Learn for learning's sake, do the best you can, and let the grades fall where they may. And when they do, keep them close to your vest.

DON'T GO TO A PROFESSOR'S OFFICE HOURS TO LOBBY FOR A BETTER GRADE

Ugh.

The only thing worse than the person who talks about grades all the time is the more cunning person who goes to his or her professor's office hours after a midterm or paper comes back and lobbies for an upward adjustment. Listen well to this piece of advice. Unless your professor has obviously misgraded your midterm by marking something wrong that was actually correct, don't go to office hours looking for a grade change. All that will do for you is get you a reputation as a gunner among the faculty and among your classmates. And that's a rep you don't want to get.

So what the heck is a gunner?

A gunner is a student who won't hesitate to take shortcuts, pull strings, run over classmates, and beg, borrow, or steal for a grade. This is the person who hides library books needed for community projects, makes off with the only copy of an answer key intended to be used as a teaching tool, and monopolizes the professor's time after class. It is the person who asks for notes when he or she misses class, but won't return the favor. And yes, it is the person who invariably will take papers, midterms, and final exams to office hours in an attempt to lobby for a few more points here or there.

Don't be this person.

KEEP YOUR COMMITMENTS

This is a simple one. There are opportunities to exhibit this trait all over the place in college—in your room, in the dorm or fraternity house, in class, and in your sports and extracurricular activities—and falling down here can have very detrimental effects on your reputation. Make commitments carefully, and once you make them, keep them.

If you are working on a group project and promise to have your part done for Thursday night's group meeting, deliver your part at Thursday night's group meeting. The group doesn't care if you just broke up with your boyfriend, that you had to take on extra hours of work-study, or that you had a midterm the same week. Everyone in college is busy, and everyone has commitments. If you make a commitment, keep it. Otherwise, don't make it.

If it's your turn to take out the trash or sweep the floor, don't wait to be asked or reminded by your roommates. If you said you would pick up tickets to a play or pick up a pizza on the way home from class—deliver on your promise. Most of all, if you promised a friend or roommate that you'd do something with him or her, don't bail for a better offer. The "bailer" isn't a popular person in college. . . .

DON'T BE A MOOCH

. . . Neither is the mooch.

We've all met the mooch. The mooch is the person who asks to borrow money, but always forgets to pay it back. The person who, when you go out to dinner in a group, always throws less money in the pile than he or she owes, assuming that others will overestimate what *they* owe. The person who is always borrowing things, always eating more than his or her share of the pizza, and always taking a couple of beers out of the fridge without ever returning, buying, or replenishing. The person who bums a ride to the airport from you but never offers to pay for gas or parking, and is always late paying his or her share of the cable bill.

The mooch pretty much sucks, because few people ever call the mooch on his or her bad behavior, as annoying and frustrating as it is to have around. I could never figure out how mooches lived with themselves knowing that others were "on" to the way they act. Of course, I never called a mooch on his behavior either. And I have known a few over the years.

In any event, a mooch is another skunk at the garden party. If you're going to borrow, return. If you're going to consume, contribute your fair share. When it's a close call, throw in a dollar more, rather than a dollar less.

CLEAN UP AFTER YOURSELF

You'd think this one would be unnecessary to put in print, but guess what?

Apparently it isn't.

Keep your dirty laundry out of common areas, put your books and papers away after class, and throw out your half-finished sub from the night before. When you get back from the bathroom, stow your toiletries, and don't leave wet towels draped all over everything.

It's really not that hard, is it?

Roommates who fail to clean up their own messes engender serious discontent with their other roommates—so keep this one in mind, or pay for a single and live alone.

"And on a grander scale, be respectful and appreciative of the many, many people employed by the college who help make your life run smoothly by keeping your dorm clean and warm, your stomach full, the campus beautiful, and your paths clear of snow in the winter," Zoe added.

BE A GOOD LISTENER

Listening is truly an undervalued and underappreciated skill.

When a roommate or a friend comes to you with a problem and wants to talk, take it as a compliment that your opinion means enough to him to have been solicited.

And then sit back and *listen.*

Really listen.

Resist the urge to complete sentences or jump in with anecdotes from your own life. No matter how elementary or obvious the problem may seem to you, let your friend speak and get it out. Give her the safe place and the critical ear she came to you for.

To be a good friend, you must learn to be a good listener.

KEEP SECRETS AND DON'T GOSSIP

This is a corollary to the previous rule. Anything shared with you in confidence stays that way. For you to be trusted for your advice and counsel, you must first be seen as someone who can be trusted. That means not trafficking in gossip and never betraying a confidence. Not once.

You won't get a second chance.

People work through a lot of difficult issues during their college years. There are family struggles, financial issues, relationship issues, and questions of personal, religious, and sexual identity. If you are trusted with someone else's confidence during such a struggle, treat it for what it is—a very special gift of trust.

"College is all about exploring, growing, and experimenting," Dan noted, "but be sure you remember to respect your fellow students as individuals going through the same thing."

SHARE EVERYTHING YOU CAN

Share your class notes, clothes, iPod—whatever a roommate, friend, or classmate might need. In college, what goes around comes around. Someday it will be you needing the class notes, the shirt or dress for the big date, or the iPod for your long run when you really need to get away for a while. If you've shared with others, others will share with you. Building up some favor equity with your classmates is always a good idea.

"You reap what you sow," Erik counsels. "It is all about unselfishness and common courtesy. Treat others the way you would want to be treated."

ASK FIRST, BORROW SECOND

To that end, you should *never* borrow anything from a friend or a roommate without asking first. This is how major roommate battles begin. Taking your roommate's iPod for a run without getting the okay first, even if you leave a note, is not okay unless you've worked out an understanding about that ahead of time. The one time you take it without asking will inevitably be the day that your roommate was going out of town and wanted it for the train ride.

CONVEY MESSAGES PROMPTLY

If someone calls or stops by looking for a roommate and you take a message, don't forget to *leave* a message. This is another way that major misunderstandings and roommate battles begin. All it takes to start a problem is one dropped message from the girl or guy whose call was eagerly anticipated but not received.

CONTROL YOUR USE OF ALCOHOL AND DRUGS

Without passing judgment on the advisability of the use of alcohol and drugs generally, an important corollary etiquette issue does come up when you get so hammered or baked that you become a safety concern, a burden on your friends and roommates, or both. As with most things, you may screw up here and there on occasion. But if you find your roommates taking you to the Department of Undergraduate Health to have your stomach pumped or calling the campus police to break into your locked room because they're afraid you've passed out in a dangerous situation—you're taking advantage of these relationships.

Simply put, you should never allow yourself to lose such control of your faculties that you must rely on others for your safety.

Do it once, and assuming that no one dies or is seriously injured, it might be passed off as a funny memory of an indiscretion you got away with. Do it repeatedly, and you'll be viewed as a pain in the ass. (And if you do find yourself in this position more than once, you may want to ask yourself if you might have a substance abuse problem.)

WATCH AFTER YOUR FRIENDS AND ROOMMATES

This, of course, is the flip side of the preceding rule. If you go to a party with some friends or your roommates, keep an eye on each other. Like it or not, bad things *do* happen at college parties, particularly when experienced upperclassmen, inexperienced underclassmen, and drugs and alcohol mix. Talk to each other and reach agreement before you go out about what the rules of the road are going to be. Do you all go home together at a certain time? Do you wait for each other? Is there a certain code you might want to use to express particular sentiments, such as "I like this person" or "This person scares me—get me out of here"?

Whatever your code and whatever your agreement, once you've established it, stick to it. Do not allow diminished faculties to allow you to leave friends or roommates at a frat house or an off-campus party. There is always another night for a relationship to blossom between two people who both want that outcome. The true horror stories happen when friends walk away from each other at the wrong times.

PRACTICE SAFE SEX

You might be surprised to find this mention in an etiquette chapter, but the practice of safe sex is in fact not only an issue of health and wellness but also one of etiquette and respect toward one another. In this era of casual sexual "hookups" on campus, condom use should be the rule and should be assumed. It can sometimes be awkward to initiate a discussion about protection in the heat of passion. Often one partner will wait for the other to start the discussion, and the unfortunate result, many times, is that neither one does start, exposing both partners to the risk of sexually transmitted disease and unwanted pregnancy. Don't wait for the discussion. Assume safe sex to be the rule as a gesture of mutual respect.

DON'T DATE YOUR ROOMMATES' OR FRIENDS' SIBLINGS OR EXES

Perhaps no single thing leads to disaster among friends and roommates faster than dating a friend's or roommate's sibling or ex. This phenomenon is so well known, it should practically be written into the code of conduct at your college or university—but of course, every year, there are you risk takers who throw caution to the wind and do it anyway.

Consider this . . .

Will you be comfortable in a long-term relationship with a person who also dated your roommate? Think that one through awhile. Would you be comfortable in a long-term relationship with your best friend's sister or brother? Visiting them on holidays and vacations? Feeling torn between hanging out with your friend and your boyfriend or girlfriend? Dealing with all the awkwardness of the romance on the one hand, and the friendship on the other?

And if you can somehow navigate all *that,* there are some other realities to worry about: What if he or she cheats on you? What if you cheat on him or her? What if the relationship ends badly? What if it ends *really* badly? You should count on losing both your boyfriend or girlfriend *and* your friend or roommate in that case.

"And never hit on a friend's love interest," Zoe said. "This rule should go without saying but has been broken by most of us more than once. It is virtually never worth it in the end."

RESPECT DIFFERENCES IN TASTE, OPINION, POLITICS, RELIGION, AND SEXUAL PREFERENCE

Although most of us are naturally drawn to people who look, act, and think like we do, college is a diverse world full of people who don't. You may end up with a roommate who is active in the opposing political party, a suitemate who dresses in a way you think is completely ridiculous, and a person across the hall who is thoroughly convinced that she will have failed in her life's mission if she doesn't save your soul from damnation. You may also encounter issues of diverse sexual preference for the first time.

Remember that college is a time of exploration and intense personal growth for almost everyone. Although you may not agree with people's personal choices, you must learn at least to respect their explorations as long as those explorations are legal and don't endanger others. It is precisely *because* college is such a diverse place that it is also such an interesting place.

Embrace this diversity and strive to understand other people's points of view and perspectives, even if ultimately you don't agree with them. Listen more and judge less, and with some luck, your explorations, viewpoints, and voyages of personal growth will be treated the same way by others.

Romance on Campus

Love hurts, no matter how perfect it is.

Anonymous

There may be no subject that provokes a more widespread, passionate, or emotional response than the question of how to find love on the college campus of the twenty-first century.

It seems that everyone has a beef about something related to finding love at college. "The guys are interested only in sex," the straight women insist. "The women don't care about how they look," the straight guys say. "The place is so homophobic, there is no way to make a comfortable pass at someone of the same sex except at a BGLAD dance," some bisexual, bi-curious, and gay students insist. "The culture has become one of random, casual hookups—no one actually dates anymore," other students of all persuasions lament.

It seems that almost every college student has stories of colossal romantic disasters during his or her college years, but there are still some tales of true love that would bring Hollywood calling. There are also some universal truths that those of us who have been through the experience tend to agree on.

So what generalities can be shared about love on the college campus of the twenty-first century? Let's take a look.

CONSIDER LEAVING THE RELATIONSHIP FROM HOME AT HOME

Many college freshman arrive on campus still tied to a boyfriend or girlfriend from high school or summer camp who is now either still at home or off at another college. They limp through part or all of first semester wracked with guilt about not visiting or calling often enough; or, worse yet, they spend most weekends on the road visiting each other or, worse *yet*, cheat on the person with someone else—and then these relationships almost invariably explode. For the lucky ones, this happens within the first few weeks of school, allowing the individuals to go on and have rich and productive college lives. For the less fortunate, the relationships endure long enough to ensure that the individuals have lost out on the early-semester opportunities to bond with their roommates and other freshman new to the campus or, worse, to stigmatize the individuals as people who are "off-limits" due to a girlfriend or boyfriend "from home."

As a collective group, we don't know of very many couples whose relationships began in high school and survived both individuals' attending different colleges. I'm sure there are examples out there, but the chances of your relationship being one of them is very small. Your chance of being one of the thousands and thousands of soon-to-be bitter people who try to make a long-distance relationship work during part of freshman year (or even longer) only to have it fail is very large.

Take our advice.

Have a heart-to-heart with your significant other from high school, summer, or wherever your relationship began. Talk about the realities, talk about the expense, talk about the inconvenience, talk about whatever you want to talk about, but make sure that at the end of the talk, you are free to go your separate ways. At least for first semester.

Trust us—if your relationship is destined to be, you'll have *plenty* of opportunity to get back together later. Coming to college with a relationship from home, however, is like trying to run a road race with your legs tied together—which is to say, restricting and uncomfortable.

"I hate to be the bearer of bad news, but the long distance relationship with your high school boyfriend or girlfriend rarely works out, even between two people who really care about one another and want to make it work," Zoe advised. "In most cases, even if things can survive for a while, a tension develops between the growing need for independence and the desire to maintain the familiar, secure, or meaningful relationship from high school. Usually, the urge for independence, which is a normal part of the college experience, wins out especially because one or both partners is now surrounded by other single people enjoying the freedom of being out 'on their own.' Of course, alcohol is often involved, too, which can lead to impulsive and irreparable choices."

"I was still dating my high school boyfriend at the beginning of freshman year," Amanda added. "We should have parted as friends when we saw each other for the last time the summer before. Maintaining a long-distance relationship during your freshman year can prevent you from a full experience of your own school. I would say about half of the women I knew in the dorm freshman year arrived at college with a long-distance boyfriend—most of them were broken up by the end of freshman year."

Dave agrees.

"No matter how in love you think you are in high school, things change. Although it might be hard to accept that you and your high school sweetheart of six months are not going to spend the rest of your lives together, chances are, you are not. Even though you went to the senior prom together and danced the night away to *Stairway to Heaven,* people change *a lot* when they go to college.

"It is not so much that you acquire new tastes for the opposite sex, it is that you are thrown into this brand new social dynamic where everyone is looking for love, or at least looking to hook up," Dave continued. "In this environment, doing the long distance thing is hard, and can be tiresome. With all the time you spend trying to keep your relationship afloat, you will miss out on a lot of fun nights trying to bond with roommates and dormmates."

"I, too, would strongly discourage having any long-distance relationships because the effort often far outweighs the benefits," Erik noted. "As it turned out, I only dated one girl throughout college. When you do that and you don't ultimately end up spending the rest of your lives together, it seems like a huge mistake in retrospect."

THOSE WHO GO LOOKING FOR LOVE DON'T FIND IT

The next area of consensus seems to be that you shouldn't burst on to campus as a freshman and go "looking" for love—either the serious kind or a casual hookup. It does seem that people can smell desperation a mile away.

The best advice here is to be friendly, outgoing, and approachable and, most important of all, to be yourself. Put yourself out on the "scene" simply by going to parties and other campus events in mixed groups of friends from your freshman dorm. While there, just talk to the people you meet. Forget about using clumsy pickup lines or other clever ploys to "figure out" how to begin a conversation. The best way to start a conversation is just to walk up and start the conversation. If there is one thing we all learned from our social experiences in college, it is that everyone is waiting for everyone else to make the first move.

If you find yourself interested in someone in one of your classes, strike up an easy, stress-free conversation about the course material. Don't worry about "closing the deal" in a single day—you have the whole semester to get to know the person, and the rest of college after that. That's the nice thing about college. You know that anyone you meet there is going to be around awhile.

Intramural sports and your extracurricular activities are other fertile grounds for meeting prospective love interests—and provide easy ways to initiate conversation.

"Most of the women I met in college whom I developed healthy relationships with I met through club activities that allowed us to get to know each other in a nonacademic but not strictly social atmosphere," Jim acknowledged.

RESIST THE URGE TO "COUPLE UP" RIGHT AWAY

The next mistake freshmen seem to make all the time is to look to pair off immediately with the first person who interests them.

Resist the urge to do this.

You're in college now—on a big campus, surrounded by thousands of people of similar age and circumstance. The first few weeks of the first semester of freshman year are the time when new peer groups are forming and when there are the fewest boundaries to meeting new people. No one knows anyone, so the approach can be natural and worry-free. As we discussed in your freshman year goal-setting workshop (Chapter 12), this is also the time to establish your individual identity—and not to become known to some people as "Kristin's boyfriend" or "Brad's girlfriend."

Take advantage of this time to meet a lot of people, bond, have some adventures, and make new friends. Chances are, some of these people will end up staying with you through the rest of college and, if you're really lucky, for the rest of your life. Enjoy your newfound freedom awhile before you become connected to another person. Remember that relationships can be isolating. If you couple up right away and start spending all your time with one person, you may find that if (when?) that relationship expires, you've lost the opportunity to fall in naturally with a group of friends—and you'll then have to work harder to find them.

For many of you, freshman year in college will be the first time you can come and go as you please, keep whatever hours you want, hang out with whomever you feel like whenever you feel like it, and explore anything and everything you might want to explore within the bounds of the law and your own sense of morality.

It truly is a unique time in your life.

You have *plenty* of time to get to know people during college. Don't be in a huge hurry to date or get committed.

"I suggest that as a freshman, male or female, you stay away from serious relationships," Erika noted. "You will either meet a bad influence who steers you away from the most important aspects of freshman year, like developing friendships and excelling in academics, or you will date for a long time, break up, and then wonder why the heck you wasted your college years in a super-serious relationship. In a nutshell, your early undergraduate years are a time in your life when you are still trying to determine who you are and what you are all about. Wait to find a relationship that begins as a friendship, based on common interests, that blossoms into something serious over time.

"My current boyfriend and I have a great relationship because we had similar interests and really got to know each other before we started dating. Now we are in two different time zones, but we have a firm foundation and it isn't a problem. But if we had begun dating early in college, I doubt we would have made it this far."

"I learned, mainly through the observation of friends, that college relationships can be very intense because the couple is basically living together," Lyndsee explained. "That can sometimes be good and sometimes be bad, depending on how much the couple isolates themselves from everyone else. Be sure not to cut yourselves off from your friends and from the activities you enjoy as soon as you find a relationship."

Chase had a specific warning for the guys about perceptions.

"Guys, if you think you might be 'kind of on your way to having a girlfriend,' then you probably already have one. The big difference in college is that the hookup usually precedes the relationship. Instead of dating someone in order to get their clothes off, you get their clothes off first and then date them. This simple change baffles college guys who seem to assume that skipping the initial dating step means that it somehow wasn't important. Wrong.

"I had been with a girl in my freshman dorm for a few weeks, thinking that it was a sort of 'friends with benefits' thing. We had a great time together, but all of our social interactions were with friends, so I didn't perceive of us as a couple. Enter Parents' Weekend and the girl's family. I am out at lunch at a café next to campus with my family and the girl comes over to our table with her mother and father and says, 'Mom, this is my boyfriend whom I told you so much about.' I looked over my shoulder thinking that there must have been someone behind me that she was talking to. I then stood up awkwardly to introduce myself, all the while wondering what was going on. Afterward, my own mother proceeded to lecture me about how I should include her in the important parts of my life. Ouch."

SAFEGUARD YOUR HEALTH, YOUR SAFETY, AND YOUR REPUTATION

As we just said, when you get to college, you are free to explore anything and everything you might want to explore within the bounds of the law and your own sense of morality.

The problem is, not everyone conforms their behavior to the bounds of the law, and people have vastly different senses of morality. Those disconnects can lead to some real perils. Some people are looking for uncomplicated, fleeting encounters without strings or expectations. Some are looking for relationships or even life partners in connection with those encounters. Some people are good communicators and will let you know what their expectations are. Others won't, and it can be hard, particularly in the heat of the moment, to stop to inquire.

You would hope that everyone would respect your expectations and whatever boundaries you set up, even on the spur of the moment. But the truth is, not everybody will. It is therefore up to you, at all times, to make your expectations known and to protect your health and safety.

If you're going on a date with someone you don't know well, stay on campus and in public places. Tell a friend or your roommates whom you are going out with and where you are going. Be sure to bring your cell phone and to make sure that it is fully charged.

Whether you are male or female, carry a condom in your wallet or purse. Although decisions about sexuality are entirely your own, you *always* want to be prepared for the unexpected. In the heat of passion, you'd rather have a condom on hand than not.

"There are more people walking around campus with STDs than you'd think," one mentor explained. "Herpes, genital warts, you name it. It's all out there. And in the current culture of random hookups, it's not always just the people you'd expect. Trust me on this one."

"I made one mistake, one night, and ended up with an STD," another mentor warned. "All it takes is one bad decision."

Oh, and if you're a guy, don't wait to be asked to put one on. Remember that the birth control pill does not guard against STDs; it is therefore both the gentlemanly thing and the expectation that if you are going to have sex, you will use a condom. Taking that affirmative step is the responsible thing to do, and also can stave off a lot of awkwardness.

Although random hookups happen all the time, it is almost never a good idea to hook up with someone you have just met when one or both of you are under the influence of alcohol or other substances. These are the most perilous situations: expectations are unknown, communication styles are unfamiliar, boundaries can become blurred, judgments can become clouded, and trouble can be lurking just around the corner. If you find yourself in such a situation, it is always the prudent decision to err on the side of caution and respect, and to wait for better circumstances to have your first hookup with someone. If it was meant to be, it will happen again another day.

Entire lives have been ruined by people who made the opposite choice in similar circumstances. Remember that.

Finally—and this advice applies equally to guys and girls—remember that your college campus is a small, closed environment, where there is really only one or two degrees of separation between every student. Treat everyone with respect, don't kiss and tell, and be careful about burning bridges that you might someday need to cross again.

Once you get a bad reputation, it is practically impossible to shake it.

COOL COLLEGE DATE IDEAS

If you do start dating someone more seriously, it won't take long before your forays to hear singing groups and see movies at the campus film series will start to get dull. If the Greek scene and the campus party scene are not for you, here are some other creative and exciting date ideas:

- Head to the nearest big city to a concert or game or for dinner or brunch.
- Drive to the mountains and go camping or go for a long hike.
- Head to the lake or to the ocean for the day or a weekend.
- Run, blade, or mountain bike together at a scenic location.
- Take a blanket and go stargazing at the campus astronomy observatory.
- Go to a wine tasting.
- Take a yoga or meditation class.
- Find a building with roof access and bring a blanket and a bottle of wine.
- Get dressed up and go to a nearby casino or charity casino night.
- Find a friend with a kitchen and cook dinner.
- Find a place to go skiing, snowboarding, or ice skating, or to take a sleigh ride.
- Spend a night in the country at a bed-and-breakfast.
- Get tickets to a musical or play at a nearby theater.
- Go to a minor league baseball or hockey game.
- Go skydiving or bungee-jumping.
- Have a tarot card reading together—just for fun.
- Go to the circus or a carnival when it comes to town.
- Go to the state or county fair.
- Find a nearby farm and go apple picking.

- Take a sailing lesson on the nearest large body of water.
- Go to open mic night at a local club.
- Pursue a shared hobby—for example, writing, music, or photography.
- Get dressed up and go to a formal dinner at a fancy restaurant or hotel.
- Spend an evening looking through travel guides at the campus bookstore.
- Spend an afternoon at the career services office to find cool joint summer employment.
- Spend the day at the nearest amusement park or water park.
- Spend an afternoon touring one of the campus or city museums.
- Go to hear a campus speaker.
- Play doubles tennis against another couple.
- Stay in and compete against each other in a board game with "stakes."
- Play Pictionary, Celebrity, or Trivial Pursuit against other couples.
- Hit the road for a few days to support a political candidate.
- Visit and tour each others' hometowns.

HOME FOR THE HOLIDAYS?

Freshman couples frequently find themselves asking when it is appropriate to bring a new boyfriend or girlfriend home to share a holiday with the fam. How you will answer this question is, like many other things romantic, entirely individual, but here are some general guidelines:

If you've been dating seriously for less than three months, it is too early.

If you haven't spent a weekend away together alone yet, it is too early.

If your parents don't yet know you are dating, and if you have not yet met your boyfriend or girlfriend's parents in some other capacity—such as on Parents' Weekend or during some other campus visit—it is probably too early.

If, when you really think about it, you're not sure that you want to be in a committed relationship with this person for a long time, it is too early.

If you've cheated on this person already, or thought about doing so, it is too early.

If one of the reasons you want to invite the person to come home with you is that you want to show him or her off to your high school friends at the Thanksgiving Day game or at church on Christmas Eve, it is too early.

If you're not prepared to face questions from your parents about your sexual involvement and to respect the boundaries they impose with respect to sleeping arrangements in their home, it is too early.

In other words, if you're still a freshman, chances are, it is too early.

SOME FURTHER THOUGHTS ON THE COLLEGE DATING SCENE

"Looking back from the comfortable vantage point of married adulthood, I think the main thing I gained from college romances was knowing that I truly had the time and opportunity to do what I wanted, to look around, and to fall in love without the pressure of making any life-long commitments," Zoe mused. "I had relationships of varying duration and intensity with all sorts of people and I can now say that I have no regrets, no feeling of wanting to go back and have that particular type of freedom again. There's another type of freedom that comes with committed relationships that stand the test of time and the trials of grown-up life, including moves, financial strain, careers, and children. This type of freedom has more to do with knowing that you can be fully yourself with someone and love and trust them without fear. Some people find the right person in college, but most of my friends and I didn't."

"It's alright to have your heart broken," Tiffany added. "You *will* survive it, and as cliché as it sounds, it is a valuable learning experience. I experienced my first real relationship in college and although it did not end pleasantly, I was able to get through it with the help of supportive friends and lots of kickboxing! Being cheated on sucks any way you look at it, but in the end, it taught me a lot about myself and what I want in a relationship."

"I was romantically unfaithful with three different people in college," one mentor explained. "To be honest, it didn't even feel terribly wrong to be cheating on my partner at the time I was cheating. Each time actually felt very electric, maybe because I was with someone very different from my partner. With the benefit of the perspective I now have, I very deeply regret that infidelity. The simple dishonesty of my actions still bothers me to this day. Having said that, I learned a tremendous amount about myself—about making mistakes, about feeling the pain associated with those mistakes, and truly learning from them. It firmly reinforces the grown-up feelings I now have toward the sanctity of commitment, integrity, and honesty. Knowing that I was able to get away with being unfaithful at the time may have made my transgressions easier to deal with then, but it made me learn firsthand that true integrity means doing the right thing even when nobody else is looking."

"In the long run, the more people you make the investment to really get to know in a personal and physical way, the more you will grow as a person," Dan said. "The one-night stand really isn't going to teach you much. However, spending time listening and learning about how another person thinks and feels, and experiencing the growth of a relationship are critical and fundamental skills that you absolutely will carry forward in life. And let's face it—when and if you do decide to settle down into marriage or a committed relationship, it's nice to know that you've tried your hand at a few and found one that really fits."

Coming Out on Campus

Are we ourselves, and do we really know?

The Fixx

As we've noted in various ways and in various places throughout the book, your four years in college will be years of self-discovery and metamorphosis. For some, that voyage of self-discovery may also include a questioning or eventual self-recognition of sexual identity.

The sexual coming-out process, as it is known, is a critical component of gay, lesbian, bisexual, and transgender identity development—but can also frequently present a complex set of circumstances for not only the individual looking to come out but also his or her roommates, friends, teammates, fraternity brothers or sorority sisters, and even classmates more generally. It is important to remember that a closeted gay, lesbian, bisexual, transgendered, or questioning student has likely known, or at least questioned, his or her sexual identity for some time, but has not yet experienced a sufficiently comfortable or mature environment to feel confident enough to come out.

For gay, lesbian, bisexual, transgendered, or questioning students, the campus environment—particularly the perceived views of roommates, suitemates, and people in the same residence hall—can have a significant effect on their comfort in experimenting with or disclosing their sexual identity. If the climate in a room or dorm is hostile, closeted students may feel alone and isolated, and will hesitate to express themselves honestly for fear of stigmatization. These students then often experience feelings of anxiety, loneliness, and depression, which can spill over into their academic work, prompt abuse of alcohol or drugs in an effort to escape the problem, and even provoke attempts to transfer, drop out, or commit suicide.

"Personally, I ascribe to a 'spectrum' theory of sexuality—with one hundred percent homosexual people on one end of the spectrum, and one hundred percent heterosexual people on the other end, and the majority of people falling somewhere in between," Amanda explained. "High school and college are where most people figure out where they fall on that spectrum."

FOR THOSE OUT, WANTING TO COME OUT, OR QUESTIONING

If you are out or if you find yourself wanting to come out or at least to be free to explore your sexual identity, there are several ways, with varying degrees of forthrightness, to address the issue.

For Those Already Out

Students who are already out tend to fall into two groups: those who are eager to lend their support to their classmates experiencing the same questions and anxiety that they did when they came out, and those who don't want to affiliate with their campus's gay, lesbian, bisexual, and transgender association because they don't want their sexual choice to become the focal point of their campus identity. Unfortunately, until gay, lesbian, bisexual, and transgendered students are simply accepted for what they are—just students like everyone else—instead of first being identified by their sexual preference, this dichotomy will likely continue to exist.

If you *are* already out, however, consider doing what you can to help those struggling with the decision you already made—whether this means helping overtly by joining your campus chapter of BGLAD or more subtly by calling people on their homophobic remarks and otherwise helping to promote a nurturing environment to encourage those around you who may be struggling with the decision to come out to feel comfortable doing so. Recognize the challenges you may face, and that your help in promoting a nurturing environment may also require your patience and maturity in helping to educate your classmates and dormmates and promote the cause.

"Freshman year, there were two guys on our floor who were gay, surrounded by about forty apparently very straight guys who loved to play video games, watch football, and brag about hooking up with girls," Kevin recalled. "One of these two guys was readily embraced by the group because he was confident in his homosexuality, did not feel the need to broadcast it, and did not try to proselytize any of us. He knew we were straight, we knew he was gay, and we got along like gangbusters.

"The other guy's behavior quickly made many of the guys on the floor uncomfortable. He frequently commented on how attractive some of the guys on the floor were and was graphic in his description of his sexual activity with some people who were less comfortable hearing about homosexual sex. He was very aggressive about his sexuality and it made many people on the floor uncomfortable and bred resentment.

"My advice is that if you are in close quarters with a gay floormate and you aren't comfortable with him being graphic with his sexuality, then talk about it and draw a parallel he can appreciate. You may not enjoy hearing his graphic stories, but he may, very well, not enjoy hearing yours. The message should be that this is not a gay thing, and it is not a straight thing. This is a respect thing."

"I'm actually a big supporter of gay rights, but I was turned off by the approach my campus gay, lesbian, bisexual group took toward outreach," one mentor explained. "They intentionally scheduled the gay/lesbian awareness days to coincide with the weekend that prospective freshman were visiting the campus, and then welcomed the prefrosh by plastering the campus with blown-up Xeroxed copies of photographs of gay sex. I appreciate the need for greater awareness of gay and lesbian issues, but that approach was a little too 'in your face,' even for me."

For Those Considering: Come Out to Yourself First

Before you can make any progress with others, you must first acknowledge to yourself that you are gay, lesbian, bisexual, or questioning, and try to become comfortable with that notion. For many people, this is the hardest step—and the step that takes the longest, because of relentless pressure to conform to societal expectations, and fear of reprisal from parents, family, friends, and roommates. There are many resources listed at the end of this chapter to guide you on your way to this important level of self-acceptance—but getting there is key. As you will eventually discover, although the initial process might be bumpy, accepting yourself will be much better in the long run than constantly trying to fit in by hiding your identity.

"Learn to accept and love who you are," a mentor suggested. "As you practice this essential life skill, you'll also become more accepting and loving toward others and more able to deal with complexity present in every type of relationship. It can be very unnerving, if not terrifying, to unveil previously undiscovered parts of yourself, but that's what growth is. Aren't you glad you're not exactly the same person you thought you were in junior high?"

If Your Environment Seems Supportive

If your immediate environment (roommates, suitemates, hallmates) seems supportive and you are confident and comfortable enough in your own skin, then you may next want to simply engage your roommates or suitemates in a casual discussion when the opportunity presents itself. Sometimes, putting a rainbow flag or a pink triangle in a conspicuous place can be enough to trigger a discussion if you feel awkward or uncomfortable coming out with, "Brad, I just wanted to let you know that I'm gay[bisexual]," or "Jen, I wanted to let you know, in case you see us around, that I'm dating a woman" right out of the blue. Your sexual identity, after all, is first and foremost your own business—though the ability to have a casual conversation with your roommates and suitemates can help eliminate awkwardness and misperceptions.

Chances are, your roommates will embrace you for the person you are and will care less about your sexual identity. If this is the case, you can then use this support as a springboard to further confidence, safe exploration, and coming all the way out if you choose to do so.

If Your Environment Seems Neutral or Hostile

If your immediate environment (roommates, suitemates, hallmates) seems neutral or hostile, you may want to solicit advice from an upperclassman affiliated with your campus's gay, lesbian, bisexual, and transgender cooperative. You may also want to solicit advice from a counselor at your college or university's Department of Undergraduate Health who can teach you strategies about how to confront and disarm ignorance when you encounter it during your coming-out process or anytime thereafter.

Should your roommate or suitemate situation become physically or emotionally hostile during the process of your coming out, you have a right to expect immediate intervention from your RA, dormitory supervisor, or residential college dean. You would hope, of course, that with some discussion and reorientation of beliefs, your roommates and suitemates could be educated. If the situation does not markedly improve through such intervention, however, you should ask to be expediently placed in a single or a different room to escape the harassment.

FOR ROOMMATES, SUITEMATES, AND FRIENDS OF SOMEONE COMING OUT

If you are the roommate, suitemate, or friend of someone who is struggling with his or her sexual identity and thinking about coming out, there are a lot of things you can do to make that person's struggle easier.

First and Foremost, Be a Friend

Being a friend means making the time to be open and approachable to conversations on the subject, listening carefully rather than simply offering up solutions, and trying to learn about and consider your roommate or friend's concerns about coming out, rather than simply waving them off with bravado. Remember, he or she is the one who will have to deal with any fallout.

"Whether your own evolution in college is sexual, intellectual, or religious, try to show empathy for your friends and acquaintances who are on their own exciting and sometimes frightening paths," a mentor advised.

Promote a Positive, Nurturing Environment

Call people on homophobic or insensitive remarks rather than simply ignoring them and letting them pass. It is not enough simply to support your roommate, suitemate, or friend quietly, in the privacy of your own room. Letting someone get away with a hostile or ignorant remark or an off-color joke is giving your implicit endorsement of the hostile environment such a comment fosters. Staying quiet in those situations will only push your roommate or friend, and countless others, further into the closet.

If You're Not Sure Your Roommate Is Trying to Tell You Something

If your roommate has not yet taken an overt step to communicate to you that he or she is gay or questioning, do not ask, speculate, or gossip. Simply be as open and approachable as you can, and wait for the conversation or the overt signal to be sent.

If that signal comes, recognize the situation as an opportunity to be trusted by another human being, to learn something, and to do some good for your campus and the world in general.

Remember that if your roommate comes out to you, it does not mean that he or she is sexually attracted to you. It simply means that he or she trusts you enough to want to have this hugely important conversation with you. A student trying to come out wants to stop having to hide his or her identity from others, to be relieved of that pressure, and to live the life he or she wants to lead. If you are called on to be the gatekeeper of that opportunity, cherish your chance to make a major difference in someone else's life by doing the right thing.

"Early in my sophomore year, it became clear to me that I had a huge crush on a woman one year ahead of me in college," one mentor explained. "This was initially alarming, not because I had any preconceived prejudices against same-sex relationships, but because I had not imagined that that was something that would ever apply to me. In fact, I remember listening sympathetically to a friend freshman year as she came to terms with that issue and thinking to myself what a relief it was that I wouldn't ever be in that position.

"The first person I remember telling was my closest friend, after dancing around the topic by tearfully asking her, 'do you ever think that maybe you don't really have any idea who you are?' I later wrote in my journal, 'I have shaken the foundation of my soul, but somehow, it's OK. Is it possible to be terrified almost to the point of surrender but feel brave at the same time? Yes. Anything is possible.

"Fortunately, as I told the person I had a crush on, told more of my friends, and within a few months, told my parents, I was fortunate to encounter literally no negative reaction. I always phrased it, 'I think I'm not straight,' and that was actually pretty accurate. Throughout the rest of college, I nurtured what the author Rita Mae Brown described as a 'whimsical disregard for gender,' and had a roughly equal number of relationships with men and women. Sometimes, I think this might have confused my parents a little, but they took it in stride, welcoming each new flame as graciously as the last, regardless of gender. Most of my boyfriends admitted that they thought it was sexy, and my girlfriends never seemed to hold it against me, especially because most of them were exploring their own boundaries in much the same way.

"While some people chose a certain 'look,' or circle of friends, or certain sports activities, or a certain 'identity' that was associated with being gay or bisexual at the time, most did not. You would never have known, looking around a classroom, who was apt to be dating whom. I had straight friends with short hair who played rugby, and gay friends with long blonde hair and immaculate manicures.

"I don't think of that time in my life as just an 'experimental phase,' but as an integral part of who I am," this mentor concluded.

ADDITIONAL RESOURCES

www.dv-8.com/resources/us/local/campus.html (collecting list of college and university campus gay, lesbian, bisexual, and transgender support organizations)

Haward, Kim, and Stevens, Anna. *Out & About Campus: Personal Accounts by Lesbian, Gay, Bisexual & Transgender College Students.* Boston: Alyson Publications, 2000

Huegel, Kelly. *GLBTQ: The Survival Guide for Queer and Questioning Teens.* Minneapolis: Free Spirit Publishing, 2003

Sherrill, Jan-Mitchell, and Hardesty, Craig A. *The Gay, Lesbian and Bisexual Students' Guide to Colleges, Universities and Graduate Schools.* New York: New York University Press, 1994

www.bglad.com (gay, lesbian, bisexual and transgendered general Internet search portal)

www.gaystudentcenter.student.com (online community for gay, lesbian, bisexual, and questioning college and high school students)

Setting Boundaries with Sex, Drugs, and Booze, and Other Legal Issues for the College Student

You are your choices.

Seneca

How the legal system relates to college campuses and to your life on campus is a broad and often complicated subject that is largely dependent on the dictates of state law, the proper treatment of which would consume an entire book in and of itself. Not coincidentally, there have been a couple of books written on the subject, and a good one is referenced for you at the end of the chapter in case you want to read more.

Suffice it to say, though, that most students manage to steer clear of legal trouble in college by taking their lead from upperclassmen and using some basic common sense. Because the letter of the law and the way the law is actually enforced on campus are often very different, your best bet is to trust your instincts and take your lead from those who have come before you.

In the meantime, in the pages that follow, I have endeavored to give you an overview of some of the basic legal issues that you may encounter on the college campus. Some of these, like date rape and possession of drugs and alcohol, are

---

This chapter is included for informational purposes only. It is *not* intended to convey legal advice. If you find yourself in legal trouble, consult a lawyer in your state for advice about your specific situation.

obvious. Others, like downloading music on the Internet, or hazing people in your fraternity, might be less so. Take it from this recent college graduate turned trial lawyer, though—in this unfortunately increasingly litigious society, a drunken fight at a frat party no longer always ends with time and a handshake. Sometimes, it ends in a lawsuit. And sometimes, it ends much worse than that.

Now, more than ever, you need to know what the law is, how to stay on the right side of it, and even beyond that, how to stay out of real trouble, legal or otherwise.

So first, a word about drugs and alcohol. Unless you've grown up under a rock somewhere, you know that the drinking age in the United States is twenty-one, and that sale, possession, or use of drugs like marijuana, mushrooms, ecstasy, cocaine, and the like is illegal everywhere. You probably also know that despite this, underage drinking runs rampant on college campuses and that a great many college students experiment, in one way or another, with drugs. In the pages that follow, the mentors will offer you their own stories and advice on drugs and alcohol. We're not here to preach to you about these issues, because for many of us, it would be hypocritical to do so. We know your conscience will be your guide on these things and that nothing we could say in this book would necessarily change that.

But please give us five minutes for something else.

Before you go off eating a mushroom that someone you barely know just handed to you; before you pop a pill, take a drag, lick a stamp, or snort something; before you find yourself in the middle of a situation you wish you weren't in— please read the sidebar about Joe Sicherman at the end of this chapter.

"And who," you ask, "is Joe Sicherman?"

Joe Sicherman was the guitarist and vocalist in my rock band in high school. He was a very smart guy, a terrific writer, an excellent student, and someone who could make your sides split with his jokes and imitations. He was a good friend and someone who had an incredibly bright future ahead of him. I always pictured him graduating from college and getting a job as a writer for Letterman or *SNL*. You would have, too, if you had known him.

But that never happened.

It never happened because while all of you and your mentors and I have been out building lives for ourselves, Joe made one mistake in his freshman year in the fall of 1989, and that mistake cost him everything.

And frankly, there but for the grace of God, go a lot of us.

Joe's dad, a columnist for the *Minneapolis Star-Tribune,* wrote a piece about Joe that I've kept by my side ever since it happened. And the truth is, Al's column will do more for you than anything that I or your mentors could possibly say on the subject. So when you get to the end of this chapter, please read it. And then, in the inevitable moments to come when you are faced with tough choices about drugs and alcohol, maybe Al's piece will come to mind just at the right time to make a difference to you.

I know it has for me, more than once.

Okay. On to the legal considerations.

ASSAULT AND BATTERY

Assault is the intentional creation, other than by mere words, of a reasonable apprehension in the mind of the victim of imminent bodily harm, or an attempt to commit battery. Battery is the unlawful application of force to another person resulting in either bodily injury or offensive touching. Assault and battery are both illegal and are usually misdemeanors carrying with them hefty fines and the possibility of a jail sentence.

Before you throw that punch in the bar or fraternity basement, remember that if your punch lands, you have committed a battery. Punch the wrong person (or worse yet, punch him and break his nose, a facial bone, or otherwise cause disfigurement), and you can either find yourself (1) looking down the barrel of a loaded handgun in the hands of an angry and irrational person; (2) on the receiving end of a criminal misdemeanor complaint that could earn you a hefty fine or jail time; or (3) on the receiving end of a civil lawsuit by the punchee's parents for the cost of his medical bills and pain and suffering. In addition to that, your instigation of a wild rumpus on campus might well get you suspended or expelled. In other words, fisticuffs are simply not worth it. Sometimes the *wisest* comeback is a good decision to simply walk away

HAZING

If you've been following the news at all, you know that hazing has become a hot-button legal issue on college campuses, due to several highly publicized lawsuits by the families of students killed, seriously injured, or sexually harassed in fraternity and sorority hazing incidents. Keep the following bits of advice in mind: the law applies to fraternity basements, dorms and farm fields the same way it does in ordinary life. A lot of popular hazing activities constitute either assault or battery. All it takes is one litigious person who didn't like your ritual, or one ritual that went too far and prompted a complaint, to get you and your fraternity or sorority into a lot of hot water.

DATE RAPE

Date rape and its commonly affiliated activities (such as lacing drinks) can land you in legal trouble faster than you can possibly imagine. We have dealt with the subject of date rape extensively in Chapter 10. Suffice it to say here that experience has taught us that it is a bad idea to meet and hook up with anyone while one or both of you are under the influence of drugs or alcohol.

"Date rape did occur at Duke, and almost every instance I heard of involved alcohol," Chase noted. "Often, women wouldn't even refer to it as date rape, but instead, would say things like 'I can't believe I drank that much. I don't even remember sleeping with him.' If you do this to someone, that's date rape. Be careful around alcohol. The line between a great evening and a disastrous one is crossed by having only a few extra drinks."

"I heard many personal accounts of uncomfortable situations that could have been avoided," said Amanda, who served as an RA at Cornell. "Most of them involved alcohol use by both parties. Remember, if you are looking for romance and meet someone cool, anyone who is worth kissing will still want to kiss you when you're both sober."

"Although date rape happens a lot on campus, colleges should and *do* take this very seriously when a complaint gets brought against a student," said a mentor with experience on a college disciplinary committee. "That said, the cases often come down to a he-said-she-said situation, with lives and future careers hanging on a bunch of circumstantial evidence. The truth is, a lot of the time, you don't *really* know what happened in that room, and yet an accused can get permanently expelled and prosecuted criminally. Knowing what I know now, there is no *way* I would hook up with someone I didn't know really well if they were under the influence of something and the question of their ability to consent was at all in doubt."

FILE SHARING

By now, if you have an iPod or an MP3 player and have downloaded music on the Internet, you have probably heard *something* about the lawsuits filed by the Recording Industry of America (RIAA) under the Digital Millennium Copyright Act against people who share their music collections on the Internet. Many of these file sharing lawsuits have been filed against college students, and most of them have concluded with the students' having to pay many thousands of dollars to settle the cases to avoid a trial. In fact, the Copyright Act provides for automatic statutory damages of $75 *per song* that you have illegally downloaded. In case you think you can hide your identity behind an anonymous "handle" while engaged in this behavior, remember that your college or university is your ISP and that in almost all cases, each individual computer hooked up to a college network is assigned an individual IP address that can be tracked by your college or university's IT department. So calling yourself "Donkey3438" isn't really fooling anyone.

Keep this in mind if you are in the habit of letting other people use your computer or if you leave your room open and your computer constantly connected to the network without an enabling password. The RIAA has people lurking about in most of the common file sharing rooms with screen-capturing devices that capture the names and numbers of files that you are making available to others for free downloads in violation of the Copyright Act. If RIAA folks come calling, they'll be looking for the registered user of the IP address that was connected to the file sharing room at the time they took the screenshot, and if the incriminating files are on your computer when the federal subpoena arrives, well . . .

As technology has improved, the file sharing issue has expanded from music files to entire motion picture files, and with that expansion, the Motion Picture Association of America (MPAA) has followed the lead of the RIAA and started prosecuting illegal file sharing in much the same way. So you're in the same boat if you download movies.

Rumors abound about ways to beat the RIAA and MPAA "scouts" in the file sharing rooms, and about what is and what is not against the law to do. Bright-line rules are always best in areas like this if you are looking to stay on the safe side of the law. If you are looking to download music on the Internet, go to one of the online music stores that let you preview music for free, such as iTunes or Napster, and download individual songs on a pay-as-you-go basis.

GAMBLING

Gambling laws vary widely from state to state, and with the recent explosion in the popularity of poker games like Texas Hold 'em, more and more state legislatures are moving to regulate these games. The chances of your being prosecuted for gambling with a group of friends in a casual dorm-room game are remote—but such a game *can* get you into hot water with the administration, particularly if it gets big and one of the perennial losers complains to a dean about how you took his financial aid money in a poker game.

Things get considerably more dicey if you start running regular poker games, tournaments, or other such events out of your suite or fraternity house. If you do this, some states may consider you to be running an unregulated gambling hall. Stories abound of these "home games" getting raided by the local police, and people *have* been prosecuted for it. In many other states, it has not yet been resolved whether poker is a game of chance (subject to gambling regulations) or a game of skill. Best you let the "entrepreneurial" types run the on-campus games and take this risk—at least until the still-developing laws in this area become more reliable.

Booking sports bets is a clear violation of state law in most states, and being the campus "bookie" can get you into all sorts of hot water, with both your administration and local and state law enforcement agencies. This one is a clear no-no.

As for Internet gaming—again, state laws are widely disparate in this area, and Congress has not yet figured out what to do with this billion-dollar, largely unregulated industry. So many people gamble on the Internet these days that the probability of your getting prosecuted for doing it is remote—but you are responsible for monitoring changes in the law as it develops. As before, if you connect to the Internet through your college IP connection and transfer money to gambling accounts from your checking account through mechanisms like PayPal, FirePay, or Neteller, understand that your activities can be tracked.

E-MAIL AND INTERNET

By now, most people know and understand that when you surf the Net or send e-mail from an office or university server, you can never really count on those searches or e-mails remaining private. Most colleges and universities have clearly stated privacy statements in their student handbooks, and you should read yours carefully to fully understand what, if any, protections you have. As we noted in the section on file sharing, because your college or university is also your ISP, your school can pretty readily track the sites you visit, and because e-mail is often maintained on a general server rather than downloaded to your individual computer, e-mails can also be fairly readily accessed and reviewed. This is not to say that your college IT professionals are going to sit in their office getting their jollies reading the e-mails you send to your boyfriend or girlfriend—but it does mean that if a subpoena should arrive, your having deleted the e-mail doesn't necessarily mean it is gone.

Oh, and one other point worth noting: under the new provisions of the Patriot Act, if you do something truly stupid, such as communicate terrorist threats or otherwise link yourself to terrorists or terrorist organizations, well . . . good luck to you.

ROOM SEARCHES

Finally we come to the subject of the room search. This scenario typically unfolds when your RA smells something other than garden-variety tobacco wafting out from under your doorway or through your open window and either comes up to investigate or calls the police to do it.

The rule of thumb here is *never* to consent to having your dorm room searched. In most cases, when the police show up, they will have done so without a warrant, which means that unless they are chasing a fugitive or can prove some other form of exigent circumstance, or unless your dorm room lease agreement says otherwise, they are probably not legally permitted to search your room.

Be polite to a fault—but require them to go get a warrant.

In some cases, particularly brazen campus or town police might either ignore your refusal or force their way into your room. As long as the person is a police officer (campus or town), assuming that an exception to the warrant requirement does not apply, and assuming your dorm contract doesn't say otherwise, any evidence found in your room should end up being "fruit of the poisonous tree" (discovered pursuant to an illegal search) and end up being excluded by a judge. Remember, however, that in all cases, you must treat the police with respect or you'll just get yourself into *more* trouble.

If you find yourself in this unfortunate circumstance, be sure to make clear to everyone around that you have *not* consented to the search of your room and that you asked the police to get a warrant. Anyone who hears you make these statements becomes a potential witness in any subsequent legal proceeding.

Remember also that although an RA or your roommate may have standing to allow the police into the common areas of your suite, he or she does *not* have the authority to grant permission to the police to search your personal belongings. Anything that an investigating police officer can see in "plain view" from a common area of your room or suite is subject to seizure, however. So if you have any materials in your room that you would prefer to keep private, these materials are best confined to a locked box or file cabinet under your bed or in your personal (as opposed to communal) space.

SALE OR POSSESSION OF DRUGS AND ALCOHOL

Although laws vary widely from state to state, the unlawful possession of alcohol by a minor is typically a violation or a second-degree misdemeanor punishable by a fine. If you attempt to use false identification to purchase alcohol, though, and someone decides to prosecute you for it, you could be looking at a felony for criminal impersonation or forgery punishable by a jail term and a serious fine.

Penalties for illegal drug possession also vary widely from state to state and are often dependent on the type of drug possessed. Possession of narcotics like cocaine, crack, or heroin is typically treated the most harshly, with long jail sentences and fines into the tens of thousands of dollars even for first offenses not uncommon.

Next up are the dangerous hallucinogens, with first offenses also carrying serious jail sentences and fines into the thousands of dollars. And obviously, possessing any amount of these drugs considered by the authorities to be large enough to constitute a saleable amount rather than a personal use amount will ratchet up the charges to possession with intent to distribute, making the sentences and the fines that much more severe.

Absent an intent to distribute, possession of all other illegal drugs, other than those mentioned above, is typically treated as some form of misdemeanor, punishable by up to a year in jail and a fine in the thousands of dollars. And with prosecutors in counties or districts containing colleges and universities always eager to make a point about illegal drug use, these charges are very often hard to negotiate down.

But the risks can be far more profound than that, and taken together, that's where the boundary decisions come in.

"Peer pressure is everywhere, and if you are not disciplined and grounded enough, you can easily begin to find excuses to party every night," Dave warned.

"I drank socially in college in a pattern technically known as binge drinking. That is, alcohol wasn't a part of my daily life, but on most weekends, many of my friends and I would drink, sometimes to the point of sickness, hangover, or passing out," one mentor admitted. "Because I never combined this with driving, I didn't feel that I was at risk of hurting anyone else, and through sheer luck, I never suffered any real harm to myself other than a hospital visit for dehydration from a terrible hangover. At the time, I thought of it as just plain fun and didn't see my partying habits as any different than those of many of my friends. However, by the end of senior year, I noticed I was drinking a little more often and a little more heavily. When I found myself having a beer before an afternoon class one day, it dawned on me that perhaps I had come to rely too heavily on alcohol."

"Many of my friends became serious drinkers. Some friends fell into smoking a lot of pot. Some experimented further, but BC pretty much stops at coke—and that was the rich kids. A class lower settled for beer and pot," Kevin explained. "Look, if you are the typical college student, you are probably going to have sex while you're in college, you're probably going to drink, and you're probably going to be in a position to at least try one illegal drug. Best to know this is the reality, and, knowing that, to know what the big no-nos are. For this, I always followed what I call the 'Hollywood Rule.' It's not perfect, but for the typical college student it works fine.

"The Hollywood Rule is that whatever is generally accepted as moral for TV sitcom characters and movie protagonists is probably okay for you. They make lots of movies where people drink and smoke pot, and nothing really bad happens to them. But find me a film where people do coke or heroin and don't get into deep trouble doing it. *Blow? Scarface? Pulp Fiction? Boogie Nights?* Hollywood teaches us that these are bad drugs to be avoided. And hey—if you're not ready to adopt the Hollywood Rule, then just be confident with your own rules. There is nothing more cool than a straight-edged person who is neither preachy nor apologetic about abstaining from drinking and smoking."

"I initially acted with reckless abandon, had a lot of fun, made a lot of mistakes, and through it all, became more moderate," Jim admitted.

"Well, I personally did not have issues with boundaries because I breached some of those boundaries in high school," Erika noted. "I had my daughter at sixteen, so when I got to college, I didn't want to make any more mistakes. My advice? Be firm in your convictions and be strong when you say no to something."

"I always kept in mind the larger goals I set for myself before I went to college," Tiffany added. "No one in my family graduated from college, so I knew that I could not let anything get in the way of finishing my four years with a sense of pride and accomplishment."

"The particular challenge, I think, is that college ideally should be an extremely tolerant climate, and it tends to support wild behavior as typical and appropriate," Dan explained. "That's great in many cases, but the reality is that people who may have issues with addiction or destructive behavior might initially be labeled as a 'hearty partier.' As time goes on, though, and the darker sides to alcohol, drug, or even sexual addictions emerge, that supportive environment dissolves and the individual is often left alone and in trouble. I knew a number of folks who really struggled with these issues. It's a terrible thing to watch and a difficult thing to help."

"I think it is fair to say that during my first year in college, I had few boundaries when it came to sex and alcohol use," another mentor explained. "I spent too much time at fraternity parties on the weekends where I drank too much and, on occasion, 'hooked up' with guys I didn't know very well. Although I wasn't interested in having a long-term relationship, I enjoyed the sex and thought it was fun to drink and experiment. By my second year, I had calmed down and found myself wishing I hadn't been so wild my first year. I found that, even though the guys were getting away with it all over the place, as a woman, experimenting with different sexual partners and being pretty liberal and open about it made it difficult to have a more serious relationship later, because 'reputation' can become an issue. It's a completely unfair double-standard, but it exists, so be aware of it."

"Right or wrong, I decided I was okay with sex and drinking in college, but was strongly against trying any drugs," Erik mused. "I tried to use as much common sense as I could to try to avoid putting myself in any situations that might place undue pressure on me, and as such, I was never truly threatened to stray from any of the boundaries I set for myself."

Amanda agreed.

"I can honestly say that I never felt pressured to do anything I didn't want to do, unless you count the occasional blowing off homework to do something fun instead. It may sound crazy, but I think it's all about the people you hang out with and about having mutual and self-respect," Amanda said.

"I just listened to my instincts," Lyndsee stated. "If someone was pushing me to do something that made me uncomfortable or that didn't interest me, it was easy for me to say no. The key is to surround yourself with people who support you."

Whatever your choices about sex, drugs, and alcohol, remember that not everyone is looking out for your best interests. Trouble can be found around every corner, and, as the following column illustrates, it only takes one mistake to cancel out a lifetime of hard work and promise.

TEN YEARS AFTER JOE'S DEATH, GRIEF AND A MESSAGE ENDURE

Al Sicherman/*Star Tribune*

Ten years ago, on November 8, 1989, my column appeared not in the *Star Tribune*'s Variety section but on the newspaper's front page. "Dear, dear friends," it began. "This isn't going to be easy."

In that column I told readers about the death of my 18-year-old son, Joe, who fell from his dorm window after taking LSD. Today, the *Star Tribune* is reprinting the column; I think its message is as relevant now as it was when it first appeared.

Joe was a funny, normal kid who made a bad choice, and I wrote the column to show that the horrible things we read about in the newspaper could happen to any of us—that real, normal people, who have regular lives, full of laughter and hope, are only a lapse of judgment away from tragedy.

I received thousands of letters and cards when this column was first printed, and many more in the long years since. I cannot begin to say how deeply I have appreciated that kindness and support. One note was different: It said, "You wouldn't have written this if it was alcohol."

Of course I would have. It makes no difference what drug it was. Joe took something that seriously impaired his judgment, and in an instant it cost him—and his friends and his family—more than he ever could have imagined.

Alcohol accounts for far more such tragedies than does LSD, and if I were writing this column now I would not make it so focused on the specific drug that was the agent of Joe's death. It isn't about LSD; it's about how a simple bad choice can have a horrible outcome—an outcome whose terrible permanence most people, by the grace of God, cannot fully comprehend.

In sharing this story again, I hope it will give other parents and kids an opportunity to talk to each other about drugs and alcohol—not across the generation that separates them, but through the bonds that unite them, and with a heightened awareness of the fragility of our lives.

A FATHER'S PLEA: BE SCARED FOR YOUR KIDS

Al Sicherman/*Minneapolis Star Tribune*
Editor's note: This column first appeared in the Star Tribune *November 8, 1989.*

Dear, dear friends: This isn't going to be easy.

Nor is it going to be funny.

My older son, Joe, of whom I was very, very proud, and whose growing-up I've been privileged to chronicle occasionally in the newspaper, died last month in a fall from the window of his seventh-floor dorm room in Madison, Wis. He had taken LSD. He was 18 years old.

To say he had his whole life ahead of him is unforgivably trite—and unbearably sad.

I saw him a week before he died. It was my birthday, and he spent the weekend with his stepmother and me. He was upbeat, funny and full of his new activities, including fencing. He did a whole bunch of very impressive lunges and parries for us.

The next time I was with him, he was in a coffin.

He must not have known how treacherous LSD can be. I never warned him, because, like most adults, I had no idea it was popular again. I thought it had stopped killing kids 20 years ago. Besides, Joe was bright and responsible; he wouldn't "do" drugs. It didn't occur to me that he might dabble in them.

His mother had warned him about LSD, though; she knew it was back because Joe had told her about a friend who had taken it. Obviously he didn't listen to her advice. At 18, kids think they're invulnerable. They're wrong.

Joey was a very sweet, very funny kid. And even before he had anything particularly funny to say, he had great timing. When he was about 6, I asked him what he wanted to be when he grew up. He paused, just long enough, and said, "A stand-up physicist."

I went to the mortuary in Milwaukee several hours before the funeral to have a chance to be with him. I spent most of the time crying and saying dumb things like "I would have caught you" and "I would have traded with you." I wish I could say that I sang him a lullaby, but I didn't think of it until several days later. I went ahead and did it then, but it was too late. It would have been too late in any case.

Joe was not a reckless kid. Last summer he turned down my wife's suggestion that the family go on a rafting trip through the Grand Canyon; although he loved amusement-park rides, he thought that sounded too risky. So we went sailing and miniature golfing instead. But he took LSD.

Apparently he figured that wasn't as dangerous.

When he was about 7 or 8, Joey attended a camp for asthma sufferers. When asked "What do you do at asthma camp?" he responded, cheerfully, "Wheeze!"

The coffin is always closed in traditional Jewish funerals, and as I sat with him that morning before the funeral, I minded that. I felt so far from him. I finally decided that I had the right to open it briefly, even if it was against some rule. In fact, I rationalized, Joe probably would like my breaking the rule. So I raised the lid.

He was in a body bag.

I'm not surprised that kids don't listen to their parents about drugs. Adults' standards of risk are different from theirs, and they know it; and they discount what we tell them. But we must tell them anyway.

Joe's aunt, a teacher, says that when you warn kids about something dangerous—something that kills people—they always say, "Name one." OK, I will. Joe Sicherman. You may name him, too. Please.

Joe's first job was in Manchester, N.H., where his mother had moved with him and his younger brother nine years ago. He was a carryout boy in a supermarket. One day he came to the rescue of a clerk faced with a customer who spoke only French and who wanted to use Canadian money. Armed with his two years of high-school French, Joe stepped forward and explained, "Madame, non!" She seemed not to understand. That, he said, was when he rose to the very pinnacle of linguistic and supermarket expertise: "Madame," he said, with a Gallic shrug of his shoulders, "augghhhhh!" The woman nodded and left.

Because the coffin is always closed, nobody expected anyone to look inside. There were blood spatters on the body bag.

It's entirely possible that warning your kids won't scare them away from LSD. But maybe it will. I wish I could tell you how to warn them so it would work, but I can't.

This is the generation gap reduced to its most basic: It is parents' worst fear that something terrible will happen to their kids; it is kids' constant struggle to be free of the protection of their parents.

Joe's next job was in Shorewood, Wis., a Milwaukee suburb, where his family moved just before his junior year in high school. It was a summer job as a soda jerk. He confided to me that he worked along- side "a soda idiot" and that his boss was "a soda &#%@." Actually, I think he enjoyed it. He told me one day that he was "acquiring mean- ingful insights into the Sundae Industry." Like: If you say, "yes" to "Do you want a lid on that?" you're going to get less whipped topping.

Traditional Jewish funerals leave no room for the stage of grief that psychologists call "denial." When you leave the cemetery, you can have no doubt that the person is dead. In fact, you might say that these fu- nerals are brutal. I could avoid telling you about it, and spare us both some pain, but I think I owe it to Joe—and to every parent—to let this be as forceful as possible.

When the graveside prayers were over, workmen lowered Joe's cof- fin into the ground and then eased a concrete cover down into the hole until it covered the metal burial vault. The cover had Joe's name on it. They pulled the green fake-grass cloth off the pile of dirt next to the grave, and the rabbi and the cantor each threw a shovelful of earth onto the vault lid.

Then they handed the shovel to Joe's 15-year-old brother, David.

It occurs to me now that what I might have done is ask Joe what kind of drugs were around. Maybe my genuine alarm at the reemer- gence of LSD would have registered with him. I'm certainly going to be less self-assured about how I deal with this subject with David. He's a wonderful kid, too, and while I don't want to smother him, I don't want to assume anything, either.

I didn't take Joe for granted; I think I encouraged him and delighted in him and celebrated with him. But I certainly took his life for granted. Parents must not do that. We must be scared for them. They don't know when to be scared for themselves.

Although his humor had become somewhat acerbic recently, Joe remained a sweet, thoughtful kid. When, as I often did, I wound up apologizing to him because a weekend or a vacation hadn't worked out the way I'd hoped, he always patted my hand—literally or figuratively—and let me know he loved me anyway.

He took good care of others, too. He spent most of his grandfather's 90th birthday party making sure that his stepmother had somebody to talk to besides my ex-wife's family.

And on that last birthday visit with me in early October, he talked a little about his concerns and hopes for his brother. One of those concerns was drugs.

Then they handed the shovel to me.

Later I overheard my wife say that the expression on my face when I turned away, having shoveled dirt onto my son's coffin, was the most awful thing she'd ever seen.

Whenever I thought about Joe recently, it was about college and independence and adulthood, and his latest involvements: His attempt to produce an English paper that was more interesting than what the instructor had asked for, the raucous rock band he and his friends put together over the summer, his plans to rent a cabin with a bunch of kids at winter break.

Now, suddenly, I'm no longer looking at the moment, but instead at the whole life. And in some automatic averaging-out, in my mind I'm sometimes calling him "Joey," his little-boy name.

He told his mother a year ago that he wanted his senior year in high school to be the best year he'd ever had, and on the drive to Madison to start college this fall, he told her that, despite lots of typical teenage domestic tension, it had been. He said he'd accomplished everything he'd set out to do—except to have a mad, passionate affair with a woman he didn't even know.

She refrained from asking the obvious question.

Then they handed the shovel to his mother.

Even though it is only three weeks since his death, I find that the reality of Joey is beginning to turn sepia. He will be forever 18. And his life will forever stop in 1989. That saddens me so much. It's not just that he won't have a career, maybe get married, have kids, all those things we hope might happen for a promising young person. He won't go out for pizza anymore either, or come into a warm house on a cold night, or imitate Martin Short imitating Katharine Hepburn, or scuff through piles of leaves.

And I won't ever see him again.

Joe had been very involved in high-school journalism. He won a statewide award for feature writing in New Hampshire, and he was news editor of the school paper in Shorewood. He contributed a great deal of that paper's humor edition in May, including a large advertisement that read, in part:

Attention! All available slightly twisted females: Marry Me! I am a nice guy, a National Merit semifinalist, devastatingly handsome, relatively inexpensive, housebroken, handy with tools, easily entertained, a gentleman in the truest sense of the word, and I think I am extremely funny. In fact, I think I am the funniest guy on earth! Please call immediately. Operators are standing by. (I am in great demand.) Kids—Please get permission from your parents before calling.

Then they handed the shovel to his stepmother.

In his sermon at David's bar mitzvah last year, the rabbi used a phrase I'd never heard before. It caused me to weep at the time; I wasn't sure why. It's come back to me again and again recently. It isn't consoling, nor even helpful. But it is pretty, and in an odd way it puts events into a much larger perspective:

"All things pass into mystery."

At one point during that last visit, we went to a craft fair where Joe noticed someone selling hammered dulcimers. He had never played one, but he'd played the guitar for quite a few years, which must have helped. He picked up the hammers and began to fool around, and soon he drew a small crowd with something that sounded like sitar music. He asked about the price; they were expensive. I keep finding myself thinking that it would be neat to get him one. I should have done it then.

Then they handed the shovel to his only living grandmother; it took her two tries to get enough dirt on the shovel. Neither of his grandfathers could bring himself to do it. But many of Joe's friends, weeping, took a turn.

I hope someday to be able to write about Joe again; I probably won't be writing a humor column for a while. In the meantime, I want folks to know how I think he would have turned out. He would have been a mensch—a decent, sincere man, the kind you're proud to know. He already was. Damn drugs.

A year or so ago, the four of us played charades, a vacation tradition. Joe drew "The Sun Also Rises," which he did in one clue. He stretched an imaginary horizon line between his hands then slowly brought his head above it at one end and traversed an arc, grinning from ear to ear. It took us about five seconds to get it. Body bag or no, that's how I want to remember him.

The last thing I wrote about him appeared in the newspaper the morning he died. He told me that he and a friend decided one Saturday afternoon to hitchhike to a rock concert near Milwaukee. He realized, he said, that now that he was away from home, he didn't have to ask anybody if he could go or tell anybody that he was going. He just decided to do it, and he did it. I wrote about what a heady experience that was, to be independent at last.

There's a fair measure of irony in that column. We're told that the rock concert is where he got the LSD, and where he took his first trip.

That trip, I understand, went OK. This one killed him.

Although Joe apparently was with friends most of the evening, the police said he was alone when he went out the window. We'll probably never know exactly what happened in those last minutes, but judging by our own reading of him and by what lots of others have told us, we're sure he wasn't despondent. Many of his friends, including one who spoke at his funeral, said that he was very happy and enjoying his life in Madison.

The likeliest explanation we've heard is that he had the hallucination that makes a person think he can fly. In any case, a little after 1 o'clock Sunday morning, Oct. 15, somebody studying across the courtyard saw a curtain open and then a body fall. Joe didn't cry out.

I have since, many times.

Gratefully reprinted with permission of Al Sicherman.

ADDITIONAL RESOURCE

Lindsay, C. L., III. *The College Student's Guide to the Law.* Lanham, Md.: Taylor Trade, 2005.

Managing Stress, Health, and Well-Being

> *He who has health, has hope.*
> *And he who has hope, has everything.*
>
> Proverb

As we've said in various places throughout the book, a happy and successful life in college depends on achieving balance—balance in the types of courses you take each semester, balance between academics and extracurricular activities, and, of course, balance between work and play. Managing stress, health, and your psychological and emotional well-being in college is also about finding balance.

KEEPING STRESS AT BAY AND STAYING HEALTHY

As you no doubt learned a long time ago, having a *little* bit of stress in your life is a good thing. It keeps you getting up in the morning and moving forward in the direction of your goals and aspirations. Too much stress, though, can wear down your health and cripple your ability to make progress.

Keeping stress at bay in college depends on five primary factors. We discuss each of them here, in no particular order.

Get Organized and Stay Organized

Nothing will get you stressed out faster than being disorganized. Disorganization can lead to missed problem sets and other assignments, forgotten meetings, timing conflicts, and any number of other problems that will send your stress level (and perhaps your blood pressure) shooting skyward. As we recommended in Chapter 17, as soon as you have decided on what courses you'll be taking, transfer the due dates for all assignments, problem sets, and papers, and the dates of all quizzes, tests, exams, midterms, and finals to a single calendar. Every organizational meeting, game, intramural event, party, date, or time you agree to meet someone to study should also immediately make it onto this calendar.

We don't care whether you keep your calendar in a PDA, on your laptop, on your cell phone, or on a good old-fashioned paper calendar. All we care about is that you pick *one* place to keep track of everything and that you do it religiously. Once this becomes a habit, it will be second nature to you to record any commitment that you make. But the confidence you'll have in knowing that you haven't forgotten something or somebody will help you sleep better at night and keep your stress level under control.

Get Some Exercise Every Day

A second component of keeping stress at bay, which you probably also already know, is to get some exercise every day. Exercise triggers a series of chemical reactions in your body that helps you feel relaxed and refreshed and thus makes you better equipped to handle the everyday challenges of college. Whether your exercise comes in the form of grueling two-a-days for the varsity, a simple forty-five-minute walk after class, or anything in between, exercise will serve you well.

If you're pressed for time and you find yourself faced with the question of skipping your daily exercise or cutting something else out of your schedule—keep the exercise. Your daily dose of exercise will make you more focused and more alert, and will give you more stamina to meet the demands of your day.

"All through high school, I danced and played field hockey, so I didn't have to think about staying in shape and exercising. Once I got to college, I was so overwhelmed with everything that exercise was put on the back burner," Lyndsee explained. "I made it a goal to go to the gym three times a week, which I thought was reasonable and manageable. Something that really helps is to go with a friend. That way, it is harder for you to skip it. My friends and I went to the gym together all the time and after we would go get dinner together. Going with them made it something to look forward to."

"I was training for baseball in the fall and winter about three or four times a week," Dave noted. "Our workouts were split among weight training, swimming, and running, and I definitely felt better when I got the chance to go work out."

"I sucked at managing stress and staying healthy," Dan admitted. "In the end, I spent more time than I should have stressing about school work and not enough time exercising. Get in the habit of going to the gym, getting outside with friends, and uncovering new and healthy interests that you can pursue for the long haul. Most colleges and universities have astoundingly good fitness centers that are free and open almost twenty-four hours a day. With the varied schedule of the college day, you should have no excuse for not eating right and getting in shape. Plus, if you make this a consistent part of your daily life now, you will reap the benefits of becoming addicted to health for the rest of your life."

"Exercise and laying off the party scene were helpful to me," Jim added. "I also ate healthy and got a lot of sleep."

Maintain a Healthy Diet

On our busiest days in college, it was almost always easier to grab and nuke a frozen burrito from the quick-mart than it was to walk to the dining hall to get a salad or something out of the pasta bar. Yet these daily choices add up, and a clogging diet of pizza, fast food, and beer, coupled with the rigors of your schedule, inadequate sleep, and exposure to all the germs on campus, will eventually take you down.

We know you're not going to forgo beer *or* pizza, and we know you're going to keep buying and eating processed crap from the quick-mart. We all did—it is practically a rite of passage in college. But make no mistake—it is also where the Freshman 15 comes from.

Try to impose some healthy eating habits on yourself right at the beginning of your college career. If you get in the habit of having a salad at lunch and dinner and trying to eat a balanced diet, eventually these will become second nature to you. Unfortunately, the same holds true if you get in the habit of going back for thirds on dessert every night.

For most of us, college is also where our addiction to caffeine began. Perhaps it was because we really liked coffee. More often, though, it was about staying awake and alert.

Don't panic—I'm not about to tell you to stop drinking coffee or to forget about stopping at Starbucks on your way to class in the morning. I myself have consumed hundreds and hundreds of caffeinated beverages in the process of writing this book. But I want to introduce you to another little secret weapon in the battle to stay awake and alert in college.

No, no—not that little secret. Stay away from the drugs. They're all bad news. I'm talking about water.

Yes, water.

Your body is something like 80 percent water. You can go weeks without food, but without water you'd be dead in only a few days. Water is one of the primary ways your body cleanses itself—and this cleansing process refreshes you and makes you more awake and alert.

The next time you need to push yourself hard but feel really tired or lethargic, pound some water. Go to your sink or run down to the quick-mart and shotgun a pint of water. Then wait about twenty minutes and notice how you feel.

Get Enough Sleep

You know the drill—you're supposed to be getting your eight hours per night.

Right.

We know that's not going to happen on a regular basis. It's more likely to be something like five hours a night from Sunday to Thursday, and then nine or ten hours on Friday and Saturday nights when you go to sleep at 3 A.M. and sleep until noon.

You know that not getting enough sleep will make you less focused and less attentive, and will impede your ability to concentrate. So when you feel yourself getting run down, make sure to get your exercise; have an early, healthy dinner; and then turn off your cell phone and crash early for a couple of nights in a row. Or, as an alternative, if your schedule allows you to do it, grab a two-hour nap for a couple of afternoons.

You'll be amazed at how reinvigorated you'll feel.

"Take one full day off to rest when you are actually sick to try and nip it in the bud, rather than letting a cold drag on for days and weeks," Amanda advised.

Maintain a Proper Work-Life Balance

Finally, we come around to the whole balance issue again. If you don't have a pending exam or paper due, knock off at a reasonable hour every night and take some time to hang out with your roommates, go out for a study break, or talk to a friend on the phone. On Thursday, Friday, and Saturday nights, make sure you are taking some time away from your studies to spend time with friends; see a movie, play, or concert on or off campus; and otherwise "unplug" from the grind.

Making yourself available to these kinds of experiences is one of the most important things you can do for yourself in college. Bonding with friends and roommates is one of the best ways to feel "connected" to your college experience—and feeling bonded and connected is a great way to keep stress at bay.

If you play a musical instrument, lock yourself in a soundproof practice room and have at it. In my college days, I played piano in bars and clubs. When I got stressed, I would often spend some time locked in one of Yale's performance rooms with a Steinway grand piano, belting out favorite songs. Other friends would take their acoustic guitars outside under a tree and play or compose songs.

"I developed a 'work hard, play hard' philosophy, which basically meant that I was involved 100 percent in whatever I was doing, whether it was work or play," Amanda explained. "You need to know how to relax during down time and not continue stressing over what you're not doing. I maintain this philosophy and feel that it keeps me balanced."

"I spent a lot of time with my friends," Zoe added. "In college, especially if you live on campus, it is possible to spend virtually twenty-four hours a day with your friends, eating, studying, working, partying, and sleeping. Even in the shower, there is usually someone you know a couple of feet away in the next stall. Unless you go into the military or join a convent, there really will not be another time in your life quite like this.

"If you're a social person, these intense friendships can be the highlight of your four years. I found that being with friends helped with stress management and staying sane. There was always someone around to laugh with, to keep me company on an all-nighter, to go for a walk, or even to have a good cry. Your true friends will come to know and love you when you're having a beautiful, brilliant day as well as when you're cranky, hung over, unshowered, sleep deprived, and feeling pathetic. Few people in your life outside of your immediate family will ever have the chance to know you so well."

MAINTAINING YOUR EMOTIONAL AND PSYCHOLOGICAL WELL-BEING

Being away at college, managing your own life (perhaps for the first time), making new friends, and trying to find your way in the world all at the same time can be an overwhelming experience. In addition to feeling stressed, you may experience other emotional conditions—from simple and common things like homesickness and anxiety to more serious problems like depression and sleep disorders.

Homesickness

Missing home, things associated with home (such as younger siblings, pets, or family traditions), or things and people left behind at home (typically a significant other or a best friend) is a very common experience of the freshman fall. Fortunately there are easy workarounds for it.

First of all, most colleges and universities have a Parents' Weekend during the first couple of weeks of October, complete with a home football game and a whole series of campus events open to the entire family. If you find yourself missing home, Parents' Weekend usually comes at a good time to cure what may be ailing you. Encourage your parents and, if possible, your entire family to book a hotel room and spend the weekend with you at school. While they're with you, do some things together on campus (possibly in conjunction with one or more of your roommates), but also take the time for a meal or a night *away* from campus to reconnect with your family and get away from the school environment. For most mild cases of homesickness, this dose of your family in early October will probably do the trick.

Homesickness brought on by missing a boyfriend or girlfriend you left behind is also perfectly normal. Getting past this relationship, though (at least for now), will be important to your acclimation to and full engagement in your college experience.

Note that we do *not* encourage you to travel to wherever your former significant other may be. You will probably see each other at Thanksgiving—and if you've broken things off, that is soon enough. You *must* allow yourself the opportunity to move on from that relationship and to become fully engaged in your college experience. Failing to heed this advice can lead to a wealth of distraction, a failure to connect with roommates and others on campus, and a resulting college life that may well be less than what you expected. Read Chapter 19 for more thoughts and advice on this topic.

"I was often homesick during my freshman year," Lyndsee admitted. "One thing I did was talk to my family a lot and tell them about all of the exciting things I was doing. I also brought a lot of pictures with me so I could look at them and show my new friends and talk about my home. I also kept busy, which kept my mind off the homesickness. If you have things to look forward to like parties, lunch dates, and shopping with your friends, by the end of the day, you'll often be too tired to remember how much you miss home."

"Staying busy is definitely a key to dealing with homesickness," Aaron agreed.

Anxiety

As is true of homesickness, a little anxiety in the freshman year is also completely normal. You are likely to experience some anxiety as you approach your first set of midterms and as you write your first substantive college paper, or if you discover that you are having trouble in one or more of your classes. This anxiety may manifest itself in a few nights of disturbed sleep or some disturbance of appetite. Again, staying organized, getting some exercise and reaching out to your roommates can often go a long way toward quelling this anxiety.

"Going to a military school my freshman year, I was anxious about everything, because I had no idea what I was about to get into. I guess my strategy was reminding myself that there were a thousand other students in my exact situation," Aaron counseled.

"The anxiety I experienced came about halfway through the fall semester of freshman year, once the novelty had worn off that I was in college and completely on my own," Dave added. "I became anxious about my school work and felt that I was not as smart as my peers. I felt that in class, what I had to contribute was never as profound or as well-spoken as what my classmates had to say, and I also began to feel a level of stress that I was not accustomed to because everyone around me was always working so hard. It got to the point where I felt that by taking a night off from schoolwork, or taking a relaxing Sunday off to watch football, I was slacking off. In actuality, it was simply a case of having a different schedule than others."

Serious Anxiety, Depression, Sleep Disorders, or Suicidal Thoughts

Obviously, if your homesickness or anxiety develops into something more serious, you should immediately reach out to the appropriate campus service. Your college's Department of Undergraduate Health no doubt has a number of confidential counseling services in place to respond to whatever is ailing you. Your tuition funds these services, and they're there for you.

Instead of turning to drugs, alcohol, or other destructive behaviors to hide from your troubles, give your campus's counseling service a chance to intervene and help you.

Your campus's counseling center will schedule appointments for you, but a counselor is almost always also available for walk-in or emergency appointments.

College students seek counseling services for many different reasons. You may be struggling with the workload, with the adjustment, or with your life after your high school relationship ended. You may be worried about a sick parent or sibling at home. Perhaps you have an untenable roommate situation and need someone away from the dorm to talk it over with. Perhaps you've just learned that your parents are getting divorced and want to talk about it with someone. Maybe you are frightened by some recent addictive behavior with drugs, alcohol, sex, gambling, or your new credit card.

All these reasons, and anything else that is bothering you, are reason enough to schedule an appointment with a counselor. Unlike years ago, when seeking counseling could be stigmatizing, these days it is quite common. Many of us availed ourselves of these resources at one point or another in our college careers, seeking help in dealing with a whole range of issues from stress to depression to sexual identity.

"I took a semester off from school when I felt that my studies would be meaningless and I was feeling too depressed to focus on them," Jim noted. "I went home, tried to deal with it, and got an internship to help provide me with some hands-on experience in the business world. I also experienced some pretty serious depression in my final semester, and worked through it. I basically stopped drinking, forced myself to exercise, and leaned heavily on my close friends and family."

"You should definitely get help when you need it," Zoe agreed. "Early in my freshman year, while I was still in culture shock from leaving the 'small pond' I grew up in and entering a much bigger and more competitive environment, I started to have anxiety attacks. An October journal entry described, 'I don't know what is going on. I can't breathe and I feel nauseous and my hands are shaking. I feel so nervous, but I have no idea why. I can't shake this horrible feeling. I'm literally breaking into a cold sweat. What am I afraid of? My bio exam? My Spanish class? Am I just homesick? What is going on? I feel so out of control!'

"Looking back on that as an adult, it is easy to spot this as a textbook anxiety attack, but at the time, it was truly terrifying. Fortunately, I talked with someone at Student Health who referred me to an excellent campus counselor, and after a few visits, I felt not just back to normal but better and much more in touch with what I was feeling and why. Though I didn't end up in the counselor's office again after that, just knowing there was somewhere to go when needed was invaluable. There is a HUGE amount of pressure to be found in college. If you are struggling, don't be afraid to ask for help!"

Your First Semester Endgame

How to Approach "Reading Period"

Nothing is as far away as one minute ago . . .

Jim Bishop

At the end of both the fall and spring semesters, many colleges and universities feature a span of a few days to two weeks known as "reading period," when most classes have concluded, sports teams stop practicing, and students hunker down to finish term papers and prepare for final exams. Many of us liked to think of reading period as a grace period, or the home stretch, when we had serious, uninterrupted time to concentrate on catching up on unfinished work—and to really prepare for exams.

There are many different ways to approach reading period. A lot depends on just how far behind you have fallen in your classes, how many and what types of exams you have to prepare for, and whether you also have papers to complete. No matter where you stand, however, we approach reading period as an all-out sprint to the finish line. This is not the time to take days off, slack off, or party just because classes are over. Reading period is a tremendous gift of *time* at a period in your life when time is likely to be your most precious commodity. Reading period is the time to squirrel yourself away on the fourteenth floor of the library stacks, in a basement study room at the medical school, or wherever else you can go and *really* concentrate. Reading period is the time to divide up your time by the hour, to schedule your time more carefully than you ever have before, and to ensure that you make the most of the time you have left. Reading period can be your chance to pull a rabbit out of a hat.

SOME GENERAL GUIDELINES

As you consider a study strategy for reading period, a lot will depend on how much time you have and how caught up you are. Having said that, though, we can give you some general guidelines to keep in mind as you design an approach to your first set of finals in college. Use your course syllabus to provide a framework for the material in your head and to organize your study. Review your consolidated lecture notes and affiliated problem sets (if applicable), concentrating most on the concepts you had trouble with and the problems you got wrong. Refresh your memory about why you got hung up on those concepts and how you resolved your confusion about them. Obviously, if you have lingering confusion, you'll want to get yourself to office hours or a review session as soon as possible, or find a classmate who can clear up the problem for you.

As you go through your notes, make a list of all the equations you'll need to memorize, and construct mnemonic devices or other memory aids to help you retain information. Most of all, strive for a big-picture understanding of how the material hangs together. Once you've made a pass through everything once, try to set it aside for a day or so to let it sink in.

Aim to return to the material at least twice more. On your second pass through the material, be sure you have any equations, mnemonic devices, and, just as important, the concepts those equations and mnemonics go with, securely committed to memory. Examine the syllabus for broader themes, and go through your notes for favorite concepts highlighted by the professor within each of these themes. Although you never want to speculate to the exclusion of a thorough and complete review, chances are, this is where the exam questions will come from. Once you've made a second pass through the material, once again set it aside for a day or two to let your second review sink in. If you are still having trouble with equations or mnemonics at this point, write them on note cards and start carrying them around with you until they are committed to memory. The five or ten minutes just before bed or just before a nap are good times to recommit material to memory.

Finally, aim to take a couple of additional summary passes through the material as time allows. When you find yourself in a position to recite concepts and notes virtually from memory and are confident about your understanding of the material, you are ready to roll.

"I found reading period most helpful as a time to collect my broader understanding of a course," Chase noted. "I reviewed all my notes and readings and tried to connect meta-themes. As I read through the material, I would jot down major points on a separate piece of paper and return to areas that seemed unfamiliar at a later time. I also liked to try and anticipate what questions the professor would ask and outline good answers to those probable questions. This method proved to be very successful. If an exam is going to involve a long essay question, it will most likely be a comprehensive issue, and thus, you can make reliable predictions about the topic or topics it is likely to involve. At the very least, doing this forces you to solidify your ideas before the exam so that your writing has good structure."

"I created a final exam study schedule with three-hour blocks of study time in the morning, afternoon, and evening separated by meals and exercise, and stuck to it," Jim said. "I mapped out the time I had during reading period and finals very carefully and used it very efficiently."

"And exercise every day," Carolyn added.

Your effective use of reading period can make letter grades' worth of difference in the outcome of your individual courses. So now that we've gone over the general guidelines, let's look more closely at where you stand and, based on that, talk about your best strategy.

I'M CAUGHT UP—ALL I HAVE TO DO IS STUDY FOR EXAMS

If you've been following the advice in this book, you've kept up with your studies, attended all your lectures, and consolidated all your lecture and reading notes—leaving you with no unfinished reading assignments or uncompleted problem sets to complete during reading period. Congratulations! You've obviously been remarkably diligent during the semester, and you are about to be rewarded for your efforts with a mellow and enjoyable ride through the rest of your semester.

Don't get complacent, though. You must still study hard and make sure that your diligence is displayed where it counts—on your final exams.

Your first order of business is to make a calendar of the remaining days of the semester, place your final exams on that calendar, and then divide up the days leading to your finals according to where you see the greatest need. Pay particular attention to the *format* of each of your final exams. For your open-book exams, it may be sufficient simply to conduct a systematic and careful review of your consolidated lecture notes, review any areas of your problem sets that had previously given you trouble, and tab relevant tables, charts, or other reference points in your books that you'd like to have at your fingertips during the exam. If your professor is allowing you to bring in only certain materials, such as a single-page "crib sheet" or only an "annotated textbook," you will need to spend some time during reading period both preparing these materials *and* studying for the exam itself.

Once you've done this, review your lecture notes to see if your professor has hinted at any potential final exam questions or subject areas, and obviously you should spend the lion's share of your time mastering any such things. If time allows and you can get a copy of some sample exams from past years with model answers, take part or all of these exams to get a sense of the timing and how to handle the subject matter, and review the model answers to get a feel for the level of depth and sophistication expected by the professor. Remember, however, before you get too intimidated, that the model answer is typically an amalgam of a few best student responses to the question, rather than a single wizard's work.

Make sure you spend at least *some* time carefully reviewing your consolidated lecture notes for every class. During reading period, students have a tendency to spend more time studying for the more objective exams, such as those in the natural sciences and math, than they do for exams in subjective areas—literature, religious studies, psychology, and the like. This can be a critical mistake, depending on the nature of each of your exams and your relative state of preparedness. Although it is advisable to spend more time on the classes that gave you more trouble, don't ignore any class trusting that you can skate by on what you have already done. It may be that an afternoon's worth of review is all you need to assure yourself of an A performance on the exam. Be sure to bank those where you can.

Given your position relative to that of most of your peers, you have the luxury of some free time to play with. Be sure to get a workout every day to keep your mind fresh and your spirits high. Keep to your schedule, but get plenty of sleep as well. Your preparedness is your friend—and you want to enter each of your exams as fresh and sharp as you possibly can.

I'M CAUGHT UP . . . WELL, EXCEPT FOR THIS PAPER I STILL HAVE TO WRITE

Unfinished term papers during reading period and finals have been the bane of students' existence for generations. Fortunately, though, in many cases these papers have soft deadlines—"due before you leave for winter break" or "due by the last day of exams." If you have a paper with such a deadline, rejoice. Provided that you have some time remaining before the last day of finals, your job will be to forget about this paper until after you've finished taking your exams—and then devoting two or three days of uninterrupted effort to completing it after your last final.

Yeah, yeah . . . we know this means that you might be arriving home on Christmas Eve. But we're the ones who told you to keep up with your work, so don't curse us now. We're trying to get you through finals with the best grades possible—and your trying to write a paper and study for exams at the same time is *not* the way to do it. Worry about your exams first. If you reach the point where you feel completely and fully prepared for *all* of those, then, and only then, should you turn to your paper. Otherwise, if your paper requirement permits it, plan to knock it out in two or three days of concentrated effort after you finish finals.

"What if my paper is due sooner than that?" you ask.

Then you have no choice but to schedule it into your study time in the same way that you treat your preparation for any other exam. Schedule time for everything during reading period, and force yourself to stick to that schedule. Be very careful, however, that you don't devote an unbalanced amount of time to completing this paper and ignore your preparation for your other finals.

Many students have fallen into this trap. Don't add to their number.

I HAVE SOME CATCHING UP TO DO, BUT I THINK IT'S MANAGEABLE

This is likely to be the situation in which the majority of your classmates who have not read this book, and maybe even some of you who have, will find yourselves as you enter reading period.

Not to worry.

You'll be getting less sleep during the next couple of weeks, but if you make a strong push and stay focused, you'll be fine.

In the semesters when I found myself in this predicament (and yes, there were a few), the first thing I did was commit myself to a reduced or modified sleep schedule. Depending on how much I had to do, I typically resolved to go to an eighteen-hour work schedule, sleeping six hours per night from, say, from 1 A.M. to 7 A.M., and taking a break for a run somewhere in the middle of the day. Yes, this is a totally insane schedule, but it is only for ten days or so, so it is doable.

So what do you do with that time?

Again, budget it across the subjects you have and in the way that makes the most sense to you, depending on what you have left to do. Obviously, if you have any unfinished problem sets or lab reports for which you can get at least partial credit, you *must* get those completed and turned in as soon as possible. Completing those will also produce the side benefit of causing you to go through sections of course material and bring yourself up to speed on what you missed.

From there, take a look at the reading assignments you missed, and review the lecture notes you took for those days. Obviously, if you are missing lecture notes, you'll need to get those from a trusted source right away, because our entire method hinges on knowing what the professor concentrated on in those lectures. Has your professor identified any of the subjects covered by those readings as important? Did he or she spend a lot of time on them or otherwise hint at possible exam questions flowing from them, or was the area largely glossed over in lecture?

If the professor concentrated on any areas covered by readings you missed, then part of your catch-up during your reading period marathon should include doing those readings just as you would have ordinarily done for class. If, on the other hand, the subject area appears to have been glossed over, give the readings you missed a skim, pay particular attention to the notes you took in lecture, and be done with them.

Be careful not to get bogged down spending too much time reading to catch up. The most important use of your time during reading period is to get a sense of the big picture. The best way to do this is to spend a lot of time with your lecture notes, to ensure that you have consolidated these notes with your margin notes or highlights from your daily reading assignments, to ensure that you understand how the concepts fit together to constitute the whole, and then to prepare any of the materials your professor has indicated will be allowed in the final exam.

PANIC BUTTON: I'M TOTALLY F***ED

And now we come to the subset of you who will get back from Thanksgiving break ready to hit the panic button, because you spent most of the semester with fraternity rush or with the hottie from your econ class, and now have suddenly come out of the ether and find yourself completely and utterly . . .

Well, you know.

For you, reading period will be more about damage control than it will be about trying to master material.

Welcome to "cramming."

The first thing you'll need to do is commit to a reduced sleep schedule. Consider something like putting in eighteen-hour workdays, sleeping six hours a night, or going all-out around the clock with three-hour naps interspersed every twelve hours or so, whenever you become too exhausted to continue effectively. You can see that the point of this is to maximize the number of awake hours you have between now and your finals to try at least to become as familiar as you possibly can with the material you covered during the semester.

Your first order of business is to make *certain* that you have a good set of class notes for *every* lecture. Appeal to a trusted friend in the class, talk to your fraternity or sorority friends—do *something* to make sure you have a complete set of class notes.

You will be working from these from here on out.

Have you completed all the assignments—problem sets, lab reports, think-pieces, or short papers—that were due at any time during the semester? Don't give up any of the easy points. Check the course syllabus, but in almost all cases, professors will award at least partial credit for problem sets or papers turned in late. If you fail to turn anything in, though, you will certainly get no credit.

If you have doubts about whether you can get credit for turning something in late, schedule an appointment with the professor during his or her office hours; explain your predicament; *take responsibility* for screwing yourself rather than blame your fraternity, your roommates, or your circumstances; and ask for your professor's advice about how best to proceed.

Trust us—your professor has seen every variety of train wreck before. Yours will not be the worst, just the most recent.

Once you have a clear picture about what you can turn in late, get all of this stuff done and out of the way. Doing this will force you to actively engage the material, and if you are fortunate, you may be tested in one or more of the areas that draw your concentration during this cleanup effort.

Once all your assignments have been turned in, work *solely* off the lecture notes. Try to get a big-picture view of the class. If there are particular areas that jump out at you, or if you and your classmates have identified likely areas of examination, put your eggs in those baskets and do selective readings in those areas. Skim what you can of the rest and then prepare whatever reference materials you will be allowed to take into the exam with you.

I spent one semester in college in this boat, and it was a really scary experience. Not coincidentally, it was also the semester of my metamorphosis—after which I changed majors, changed the direction of my life, and finally got some traction. My memories of the long days in the law school stacks drinking coffee and taking NoDoz as I plowed through many hundreds of pages of undergraduate-level constitutional law reading in preparation for an exam, struggled to understand and complete several multivariable calculus problem sets that had been due weeks before, and familiarized myself with nearly a thousand pages of religious studies reading in order to complete a take-home exam are not fond ones.

Ten years later, I still wake up in the middle of the night in a panic about calculus.

Trust me when I tell you: I've lived in this world. It is not a place you want to be.

If you are reading this section before you get to college or while you still have time to get on the stick and turn your semester around, *avoid this scenario at all costs*. No amount of fun you have during the semester will be worth the discomfort you will feel during the final push under this scenario and the results you are likely to see at the end of it.

Acing Your Final Exams and Term Papers

*The chief pang of most trials is not so much
the actual suffering itself as our own
spirit of resistance to it.*

Jean Nicholas Grou

The coming of the first set of final exams can be a time of high anxiety for many freshmen. Like so many things, though, handling this experience successfully comes down to preparation, organization, and the ability to keep a cool head in the heat of battle.

This chapter is intended to give you a "walk-through" of final exams in order to show you what to expect and to teach you the strategies and tricks, developed through the collective years of your mentors' experiences in colleges and universities around the country, that will make you a more effective test taker. Later in the chapter, we also describe our ten steps to writing successful term papers.

OPENING MOVES

There are no tricks to your preexam preparation. Have a healthy, well-balanced meal and stay well hydrated the night before any exam, to give your body what it needs to be running optimally on exam day. Stop all studying by midevening of the night before the exam to give you time to relax and unwind and to allow the material to sink in. Take a hot shower and retire early to a novel or some mindless television.

Before you go to bed, pack your backpack with all the materials you will need for the exam tomorrow, including all books and reference materials allowed into the exam, your exam ticket or ID, your favorite writing instruments, a set of earplugs, your iPod or Mp3 player, and whatever snacks you intend to bring into the exam with you. (Energy bars or gels, candy, or Lifesavers tend to work well to keep your energy level up.)

Set two alarm clocks (at least one battery operated in case the power blinks) to put your mind at ease that you won't oversleep. Being worried about waking up on time is one of the principal interrupters of your all-important preexam sleep, so don't make this mistake.

On the morning of the exam, get up early, go through your normal morning routine, and plan to arrive at the test location at least fifteen minutes before the exam is scheduled to begin. As soon as you get to the exam room, put on your iPod to avoid listening to the preexam banter of your classmates, which will only make you nervous.

If you have a choice of seats, pick one in one of the front corners of the exam room to minimize all possible distraction. Set your permitted materials (if any) out in front of you in a way that maximizes your ease of access to them during the exam. Be ready to jam in the earplugs at the first sign of trouble. Many a student's final exam performance has been derailed by construction noise, the kid next to her sniffling or grinding his teeth incessantly, union protests, street demonstrations, and the like.

Take no chances.

STRATEGY: SHORT-ANSWER AND ESSAY EXAMS

Short-answer and essay exams, which examine your ability to recall, apply, and synthesize information, are the most common format of exams administered on the college campus. Chances are, you will face *many* of these types of exams as you make your way through college, so developing a consistent and successful strategy for tackling them early on in your college career will suit you well.

Listen to the Professor, Read the Directions, and Then Review the Entire Exam

As the exam begins, the professor may offer some clarifying remarks about how many questions must be answered, whether he or she wants the essay questions answered in separate blue books, and how he or she wants your responses set up. Be certain to listen to these remarks and to follow any directions the professor gives you.

Once the room falls silent, resist the urge to simply plunge right in. Instead, spend the first five or ten minutes of the exam just reading through the directions and learning how the exam is organized and how the time and points are allocated between the various sections of the exam. As you review the various questions, underline the trigger words in the questions (*compare, contrast, explain, criticize, illustrate by providing examples,* and so on) and write down your immediate thoughts for potential responses in the margins. Quickly jot down all your mnemonic devices and equations, and anything else you memorized, to settle yourself and increase your confidence.

Go through the entire exam until you've seen all the questions. This will give your subconscious mind some time to work through the material you covered and begin organizing a response.

Perform a "Data Dump" and Then Outline Your Response Before You Begin Writing

Now, if you have some choices, either about which sections to attack first or which essays to answer, start with the question or section of the exam that you feel most confident about. If you are working out of order, put your answer to each question in a separate blue book, be sure to put your name or exam number on the front of every blue book you fill, and be sure to carefully calculate how much time you have to work on the section and *stick to it!* The most common essay exam disaster (and believe us when we tell you, it happens *all* the time) is the failure to properly allocate your time, resulting in your running out of time before you've answered all the questions. Guard carefully against this happening to you.

"For most of us, freshman year was the first time we encountered an exam that was three or four hours long. I always ran out of time on essay questions, because I kept rationalizing with myself during the exam, 'just five more minutes on this one . . .' If you do that, before you know it, you come to the last question, which is worth 40 percent of the exam, and you only have fifteen minutes left to answer it," one mentor recalled. "Don't screw yourself like this! Budget your time for each question at the beginning and *stop writing* when your time expires."

As you approach answering a question, first grab a spare blue book and brainstorm or "data-dump" everything that you can recall from the course material that might somehow be germane to the question. Pay particular attention to what the question is actually *asking* you to do. Is the professor looking for you to compare and contrast? Explain? Criticize a position? Support a position? Illustrate with examples?

Whatever the case may be, follow those directions and, in your spare blue book, make an exhaustive list of everything you can think of that is responsive to the question.

Once you've emptied your brain of all available knowledge, consult your supplemental resources (if permitted) to fill in the gaps. Otherwise, begin sketching out an outline of a response. Be sure to keep an eye on your time. Although the format of your response is important, the content of it is *more* important.

For each essay, you want to allocate approximately half to perhaps three-fifths of the available response time to reading the question, analyzing it, and outlining a response to it. Spend the second two-fifths to one-half of the allotted time turning your outline into a prose response.

Crafting Your Written Response

When you are ready to begin writing (or when time tells you to begin writing), recast the question asked into a thesis statement that illustrates your conclusion, and argue clearly and forcefully for your thesis, providing examples, explanations, and illustrations from the course material. Take a paragraph to address potential counterarguments or exceptions to your thesis and then get out with a solid conclusory sentence.

Be sure to respond *only* to the question asked. Although it may be interesting to address a tangent raised by the question, you won't get any credit for doing so, and you might seriously impair your ability to collect all the available points elsewhere on the exam.

Write legibly in blue or black ink, on one side of the blue-book pages only. Skip lines and, to help organize your thoughts, use as many headings and numbered or lettered examples as your response permits.

Work your way through all the exam questions this way, until you have crafted an answer for each of them. If you get stuck on a question during your brainstorming session, either skip over it entirely (if you have the option) or save it for last and come back to it after you have collected the rest of the available points on the exam.

Damage Control: What to Do If You Find Yourself Running Out of Time

Every now and then, you will find yourself trapped on an exam: despite your best efforts, you mistimed a section or simply needed more time to work your way through a response. And inevitably, that will come back to bite you at the end of the exam, potentially leaving you only ten or fifteen minutes to answer a thirty- or forty-minute question.

What then?

Divide your remaining time in half. Spend half the time doing your data dump and brainstorming—and spend the remaining time *outlining* a response directly into your blue book, rather than trying to write a prose response.

Why?

Because you'll collect more points jamming information into an outline than you will trying to write good prose. In fact, depending on how charitable your professor is feeling when he or she gets to your exam book, you might even get full credit.

"Remember that professors tend to grade exams quickly," recalled one mentor who served as a TA. "Grading exams is not their favorite thing to do during the run-up to Christmas or as summer approaches. If you convey the responsive information you need to communicate legibly, even if it isn't in essay form, you'll probably do okay. Obviously, you should write an essay response if you can, but if you are faced with a timing issue, get your full outline into the bluebook instead of writing half an essay."

STRATEGY: OBJECTIVE EXAMS

Objective exams, characterized by questions employing the old high school standbys—true-false, multiple choice, fill in the blank, and matching—are much less common in college than essay exams, though you may still see *sections* of exams employing these formats as a mechanism to cover more information on an exam or to give the exam a greater scope.

If you find yourself confronted by an objective section on an exam, use the same general principles you learned in the previous section. First, look over the section of the exam, figure out how much time is allotted to that section, and then calculate how much time you can spend on each question. Then get going, taking the questions in order. Answer the ones you can and skip over the ones you can't answer immediately, putting an arrow or other notation next to them in the margin of the exam paper so you'll easily be able to find the questions you skipped over.

If the exam is multiple choice, use the same strategies you used on the SAT. When you read the question, try to come up with the answer before you look at the responses. Then look at the answers and see if your response is there. If it is, it is almost certainly correct—but take a quick look at the other possible answers to make sure you have not misread the question or fallen into a trap. If you are unsure of the proper response but can eliminate one or two of the choices as definitely wrong, your odds of choosing the right answer, even if you have to guess from among the remaining possibilities, improves dramatically. As you did on the SAT, eliminate polar answers ("never," "always") in favor of more moderate choices ("often," "seldom"), and if you have to guess, choose B or C and stick with whichever letter you choose on all questions requiring a guess where that letter remains viable. Never leave questions blank on a multiple-choice exam.

Finally, don't try to psychoanalyze the professor to detect patterns of responses. If you have seven Bs in a row, so be it.

STRATEGY: PROBLEM EXAMS

You'll find problem exams in your math, statistics, computer science, and hard-science courses. For good reason, these exams seem to promote the most anxiety of any of the college exam formats. There is not a mentor among us who hasn't experienced a "lockup" on a math or science exam. It is the stuff that nightmares are made of, . . . but fortunately there are ways to prevent them from happening and ways to work around them when they are occurring.

Read Through the Entire Exam and Data-Dump Relevant Formulas and Equations

As you do with essay exams, take the first five or ten minutes to read the exam from beginning to end to get an idea of its coverage. Underline the key phrases ("solve for *y*," "express your answer in milliliters"). Data-dump the relevant formulas or equations that you memorized for the exam into the margins next to the problems that call for them.

Take the Easier Problems First

Problem exams can be all about confidence. Get stuck on the first problem you try to solve, and it could be a long day. Nail the first one, and your confidence soars and you get into a groove.

That said, tackle the easier problems first. If you run into a stopper, pass it by until you've earned all the easy points to be had. The mean grade on science and math exams can often be dismally low, and following this one strategy alone can make an enormous difference as to where you end up on the curve.

Show Your Work

Problem exams are one place where you'll want all your calculations and scratch work to actually appear in your exam book. Partial credit can be exceptionally important in these courses—and you can't get any partial credit for your work on scratch paper that got swept up by the janitor after the exam.

Crack the "Stopper"

Most science and math exams have an embedded "stopper" question somewhere in the middle of the exam that is designed to trip you up, stop your flow, and sep-arate students into a workable set of data points on the curve. Those who solve the stopper typically end up with A exams. Those who sidestep it but answer the rest of the exam still do well. Those who hit the stopper and get stopped dead in their tracks by it—well, those are the people who get killed on the exam.

Cracking the stopper question isn't that difficult to do, though, if you have the right approach and the right mind-set.

If you get stuck on a question somewhere in the middle of a math or science exam, the first thing you should do is recall the general themes of the course and figure out which ones have not yet been covered on the exam.

Can you spot the concept being tested now?

If not, go back and recall the things in the problem sets that gave you the most trouble. Remember the tricks that tripped you up on those? Is one of those tricks applicable to the problem stumping you? Could it be that there are two concepts involved in the same question—such that you would first have to substitute a term and *then* solve the equation, or first add a certain reagent to make the reaction workable? Remember that there are only so many possible scenarios that the professor can test—and the chance that you are being tested on a concept that never appeared in a problem set or a lecture is very remote. If you prepared for the exam and are somehow getting stuck, it is probably because there is a trick you need to use to make the problem workable.

Avoid Careless Errors

Careless errors are the bane of students' existence on problem exams. Watch for an exam question that asks you to solve a problem in an unusual unit of measure that requires a conversion at the end. Students who forget to do this final step will lose partial credit, enabling the professor to spread the curve. Also be certain to check your work to make sure that simple calculation errors didn't somehow manage to infiltrate. When you get a final answer, check to see if it actually makes sense in the context of the question. For example, if the question refers to residue remaining in the bottom of a test tube, and the answer you came up with measures the weight of the residue in kilograms, you know there is probably something wrong with your calculation.

STRATEGY: OPEN-BOOK EXAMS

I always preferred open-book exams, because they always seemed to me to be a more realistic examination of a real-world application of the information. After all, in the real world, no one ever calls you with a question and says, "but I want you to give me an answer from memory in the next hour without consulting any secondary sources!" It is also true, though, that mean grades will be much higher on open-book exams, making it harder for you to distinguish your performance from that of your classmates.

The trick to performing well on open-book exams is to attend class; take good notes; integrate the readings with those notes; and then tab the pages in your texts or supplementary readings containing the most relevant charts, equations, or other useful information. Use your syllabus or create an independent subject-matter index to help guide you. For the well-organized and well-prepared student, the open-book exam should be a pleasurable exercise in showing the professor how much you know.

STRATEGY: TAKE-HOME EXAMS

Take-home exams are typically administered by requiring a student to "check out" an exam at a time that will be date-stamped by the departmental office, and to return it twenty-four or forty-eight hours later, when the return time will be date-stamped. Professors like take-home exams because they allow them to ask more intricate and complicated questions and because students typically word-process their responses, making them easier to read.

Take-home exams have advantages and at least one disadvantage. The advantages are that you can work at your own pace and in your preferred environment, consult whatever materials you want, and take time to consider and craft your response. The disadvantage is that if the exam is a twenty-four-hour take-home, some students will spend twenty-four hours working on their answers, which can convert the take-home exam into a marathon, requiring you to put in a similar effort. If the course is in a subject you like, even such a marathon may be an enjoyable, deeply intellectual experience. If not, however, it can feel like sheer torture.

SOME FINAL THOUGHTS ABOUT EXAMS

"Exam preparation begins the first day of class and continues throughout the term," Chase advises. "If learning all the information in a weekend was a realistic goal, then the course wouldn't be taught over a four-month period."

"I think the number-one mistake is definitely poor preparation," Tiffany agreed. "Also, take advantage of study groups, but use them as a means of review at the end, rather than as an actual method of studying. Studying in groups can be distracting and counterproductive. Off-topic conversations can continue for hours."

"And take the whole time allotted to write your exam," Kevin noted. "Double check. Triple check. Brainstorm a few more points. Profs, like parents and bosses, are sticklers for the little stuff. Impress them with your own sticklership."

It is a fact of life that some final exams will go better than others—and that once or twice in your college career, you're going to have an off day or to run into an exam that just catches you off guard. When your day comes, recognize that it is just a part of the experience, and do your best to minimize the damage and get partial credit in as many places as you can.

Whatever you do, though, do not even *think* about cheating on an exam.

Cheating

Cheating can take many forms—from referring to a crib sheet or other forbidden material in a closed-book exam, to craning your neck and stealing answers off a classmate's paper, to taking more time than you are allowed on a take-home exam, to changing your answers after you get your exam back and trying to go back and get credit for the professor's "error."

A subpar performance on a final exam is just that. One bad grade on one bad day. Cheating to prevent such an occurrence, however, can get you suspended or even expelled from college and can derail your future efforts to get into graduate school. Don't take a minor-league problem into the major league by cheating. It is *never* worth it.

Following Up with a Professor If Things Went Badly

If you had a tough day on a final after working hard in the class, find out *why* you did poorly. Go back and get your blue books, work through them, and see if you can spot the problems. If you can't, or if you'd like to get some advice about how to prevent a similar occurrence in the future, make an appointment with your professor during office hours and have a frank discussion about what went wrong and about strategies you can use in the future to spare yourself a repeat performance.

Note that this does *not* mean that you should make an appointment with your professor and go on a grade-grubbing mission. You are looking to gather intelligence about how to improve your performance *in the future*. Your professor is likely to be quite forthcoming with advice and encouragement as long as the meeting is for that purpose. If he or she gets the sense that you are looking for an upward adjustment in your grade though, he or she is likely to turn to stone.

TEN STEPS TO WRITING THE PERFECT TERM PAPER

A term paper can be either a pleasant academic pursuit or a major hassle. Which of those scenarios your paper follows will be largely dependent on how early you start working on it and on whether the topic is one that can sustain your interest throughout the writing process. There are ten principal steps to writing the A term paper. Let's run through them.

Step One: Pick an Interesting Topic

From your first day in the course, be on the lookout for topics that interest you. When you encounter one, talk to the professor before or after class to find out whether he or she can suggest an interesting "open" topic in the area that might give rise to a good term paper. Most professors are more than happy to meet you for coffee to discuss term paper ideas—particularly if you come to them early in the semester. We recognize that it might take you a few weeks to identify what topics in a particular subject you are interested in writing about. As a general rule, though, you should try to choose a paper topic by the end of the first third of the course.

"Do the assigned reading from the beginning," Lyndsee advises. "It is a lot harder to write a good paper if you're not well-read in the subject matter. Ideas for papers come much more freely when you've spent the semester reading and thinking about the material."

Step Two: Limit the Scope of the Topic

A topic that is too broad will overwhelm you with secondary source material and derail your thoughtful, in-depth treatment of the subject matter. A topic that is too narrow may not have enough secondary source material to make for a viable treatment of the subject. When you have tentatively chosen a subject, it is best to run the topic past your professor to confirm that the scope of your topic is broad enough to ensure an interesting paper, but narrow enough to allow you to treat with the material in some depth.

Step Three: Spread Out the Work

Once you have chosen a topic, take advantage of the lulls in your academic schedule to make progress on the paper. If you have a light week of reading across your courses, or a week off from submitting a lab report or a problem set, use the extra time that week to conduct some research. As you will see in step five, conducting *proper* research is the key to an A paper—but conducting proper research takes time.

Step Four: Ask Your Professor to Define "Proper Citation Format" for Your Paper

Most colleges and universities subscribe to particular manuals of style and citation format. Ironically, there are several different accepted compilations of these conventions. Before you actually begin your research, ask your professor to define what he or she considers to be "proper" citation format—and whether he or she expects to see citations in footnotes or endnotes, or directly embedded in the body of your paper. Different professors will have different preferences—and the earlier you find out what the expectations are for your paper, the fewer adjustments you will have to make later on.

Step Five: Research the Hell out of Your Topic

It is a fact of life: professors are impressed by exhaustive and well-performed research. It is, after all, what they do when they're not teaching you.

Before you begin researching your term paper topic, get yourself a ring binder with a notebook in it that will enable you to track and capture all your research in one place. Scour the Internet and the online card catalogue and other online journal databases at your university library for source material—mindful that you may have to place recalls or requests for an interlibrary loan in order to acquire certain materials. Start too late, and you'll never receive these materials in time. Start early, and you'll probably be able to get everything you want.

As you print off lists of resources, three-hole-punch them and put them in your ring binder so that you won't lose threads of work. Sometimes you'll find yourself tracking down a particular line of material and then needing to retrace your steps to the place you broke off on the current avenue of pursuit. Without a road map, you can get completely turned around and waste a lot of time. By taking and *keeping* some simple notes on what you've explored and what you haven't, you can keep your research trails clearly delineated.

Step Six: Clearly Define All Source Material

As you begin to photocopy or download source material, make certain that you acquire all the necessary source information about that material to allow you to cite it properly. There is nothing more frustrating than having to spend hours and hours during reading period tracking down publication years of earlier editions of the source materials you used simply because you failed to practice proper record keeping when you initially consulted the materials.

"Be very careful about plagiarism," Erika states. "Although you get most of your ideas from other sources, you need to properly credit those sources."

Step Seven: Develop a Detailed Outline of the Paper

Once you have your research completed and all source materials in hand, work up a detailed outline of the paper. What is your thesis? What are your primary, secondary, and tertiary supporting arguments? What are the examples you intend to use to make your points? What are the responses to critics of your thesis? What are the supporting materials you intend to use to defend each point?

If you've created your outline properly, the paper should practically write itself.

Step Eight: Work Up a First Draft

Take a pass through your source materials and develop a working first draft of your paper. Use headings and subheadings as necessary to break up the text into a series of complementary sections, which will give the reader a framework for following and processing your argument. Be *especially* careful to properly cite all source materials; it is at this stage of the writing, when you may drop a source or two as you add text to a draft, that unintentional plagiarism typically occurs.

As you know, plagiarism—even accidental plagiarism—is punishable by suspension or expulsion from college, so this is not something to take lightly.

Step Nine: Edit Your Draft

Once you have a finished draft of your paper in place, complete with footnotes, endnotes, or text citations, set it aside for several days to give yourself some time away from the document. Then, with a fresh eye, edit the paper for style and grammar, and look for places where an additional reference or source might shore up a sagging argument. This is the time to make the little additions and adjustments that separate the B paper from the B+ paper. Once you've edited your draft, it's time to set it aside again.

"When you think you're done, let the paper sit for a day or two before you go back to edit it one last time. This final polish is an important step," Carolyn notes.

"Right," Chase said. "Rushing a paper and not having the time to review your grammar and syntax can doom an otherwise good paper."

Step Ten: Polish Your Final Draft

After another day or two away from it, come back to your second draft. Take it to a place where you can read it through completely without being interrupted. Are all your citations in the right places and in the right format? Have you accidentally left any citations out? Have you properly credited all arguments and ideas that are not your original thoughts?

Once you've assured yourself about these kinds of things, take one final pass through the paper, tightening up your sentence and paragraph structure. See how it reads.

When the paper represents what you think clearly constitutes your very best work, turn it in.

SOME FINAL THOUGHTS ABOUT TERM PAPERS

"It was so difficult to get myself to do this, but if possible, try to write papers in advance of the deadline," Carolyn advised. "It really makes a noticeable difference in quality."

"Start them as early as you can and then hand them in early, too," Aaron added. "Professors tend to give favorable grades to the papers that are handed in early."

Chase takes this approach one step further.

"I would start early and then give a rough *draft* to your professor during office hours. Take his or her comments on your draft and then diligently incorporate them into your final paper. Do this well before the deadline. Then, when you submit the paper, the professor will know you worked hard on it. Perhaps more important, if you made the changes the professor suggested, you *know* they will be well-received. I used this method for writing papers throughout college, and it was *gold*."

"Have fun with it," Dave concludes. "Remember you are trying to write something original. Take a chance. Take a firm stance on an issue and use the class materials to defend it well. Draw your arguments from a diverse and wide array of sources and be sure to make room for and address potential counterarguments."

"Finally, don't just write what you think the professor wants to hear," a mentor added. "That's a sycophantic, chicken way of going through college. Push the limits a little bit. Challenge some well-established principles. Embrace and defend some controversial positions. Dare to be different.

I wrote a college paper espousing the legalization, regulation, and taxation of all controlled drugs, and using the billions of dollars we would save to improve the educational infrastructure in this country. I supported my thesis with studies from other countries and a lot of good secondary source material. The theory went flatly against what my professor believed, but I got an "A" on the paper because I executed it well. You don't have to be a suckup to do well on college papers."

Looking Behind and Looking Ahead

Assessing the Damage and Charting the Course for Your Second Semester

> *An error, gracefully acknowledged,*
> *is a victory won.*
>
> Georges Gascoigne

In many different ways, thriving and succeeding in college is about adjustment. Adjustment and readjustment.

And re-readjustment.

There is no more important time to make some adjustments than after you take your first set of final exams. Most students fail to take advantage of the lessons their first semester exams and papers can teach them.

Lessons about adjustment.

THE PERFORMANCE SELF-EXAMINATION, PART ONE

Before you leave for winter break—no matter how tired, fed-up, or anxious you are—you need to force yourself to sit down for a few minutes and indulge in the exercise we describe here.

Using the chart that follows, fill in the name of each of your first-semester classes in the spaces provided and then, as soon as possible after you finish an exam or term paper for a particular class, answer each of the questions in the chart in the column for that class. Be as complete and as honest as possible. Put your responses right here in the book, in the spaces provided. Spill over into the margins if you need to, or photocopy these pages, blow them up, and put your responses directly into your *Campus Confidential* workbook. Remember, this is *your* book, so scribble at will.

Once you've taken all your exams and completely filled in the chart, the notes you have put here serve as a testament to your preparation for and execution of each particular exam. Then, when your grades come out, you'll put those into the chart and be able to compare how you did in each class to the way you prepared, in the hopes of making some distinctions about what worked and did not work for you.

First Semester Performance Evaluation (Part One)

Name of class				
Grade received				
Number of classes missed				
Percentage of reading assignments completed on time				
Duration of class period and time of day it met				
Male or female professor?				
Did you sit in front of lecture hall?				
Did you sit next to friends or other distractions during class periods?				
Did you rely on a study group?				
Number of times you went to office hours				
Did you attend a review session?				
Did you make your own outline?				
Did you complete all problem sets or other assignments?				

Was exam open- or closed-book exam?				
Was exam essay, multiple-choice, or mixed exam?				
Was exam a take-home or in-class exam?				
How did you spend night before exam?				
How many hours of sleep on night before exam?				
Did you wake up feeling well rested?				
What did you have for your preexam meal?				
Did you eat or drink anything during exam?				
Where did you sit in exam room?				
Were you bothered by any distractions in exam room?				
Did you take time to read questions carefully and outline response before writing?				
Did you organize exam answers well with headings, letters, and numbers?				
Did you write in blue or black pen?				
Did you skip lines and write on only one side of page?				

Did you print, type, or write legibly?				
Did you have problems with time?				
Any other relevant observations?				

For each class, consider what you brought with you into the exam room. What did you depend on the most? The least? What did you never look at? What *would* have been helpful to you if you had had it in the exam room? How might you have been better prepared for the exam? Write down your responses to these questions here.

Name of class: _____

_____

_____

_____

Name of class: _____

_____

_____

_____

Name of class: _____

_____

_____

_____

Name of class: _____

_____

_____

_____

Good.

Now you have a permanent record of the strategies you used while they are fresh in your mind; when your grades come out, you'll be able to come back to the chart, put them in at the top of each column, and try to make some distinctions based on your results.

For now, though, go home and relax. Have a good time. Indulge yourself in the holidays, the company of friends and family, bad television, trashy novels, sun, skiing, or whatever else suits you. Don't dwell on your exams—they're history now, and there's nothing you can do to change them. You'll take part two of this performance self-exam once you have all of your first-semester grades in hand—at the beginning of next semester.

THE PERFORMANCE SELF-EXAMINATION, PART TWO

The first thing we want you to do, if you haven't already done so, is to go to the departmental offices of each of your first-semester courses and pick up your graded papers and exam blue books. Don't just leave them sitting there in the cardboard box outside your professor's office until they finally get thrown out. Your goal is to *learn* from them.

You can't continue with this chapter until you have your exam books and papers back, so if don't have them, take a walk and go get them.

Yes, right now.

Okay!

Once again, we're about to get interactive. What we'd like you to do is close your door, turn off your cell phone, and pull out your first-semester grades and your exam books and papers. Assuming that you took our advice about not overloading on courses during your first semester, you should have received grades in four or five classes. Write the grades you received in the appropriate spaces in the chart you filled in earlier. Whether your grades were perfect, perfectly awful, or anywhere in between, you have something to learn from the following exercise. Answer the questions as truthfully and completely as possible.

If there were differences among your grades, look at the different variables in the table and highlight any differences in your responses between the classes you did well in and the classes you struggled in. What do you notice about the classes you did well in? What did you do differently in the classes where you faltered? Answers to these questions might not be immediately obvious. There might not seem to be any correlation. This *can* be very frustrating—sometimes it just seems as though the grades were handed out randomly. But perhaps there is something hiding in the chart. Look for any distinctions you can make.

Did your professors make any particular comments about your exam answers in your blue books? Is there anything broadly applicable that you can learn from those comments?

If you were very disappointed with a grade you received, make an appointment with the professor during his or her office hours to discuss your exam—*not* for the purpose of lobbying for a higher grade (which, as we told you in Chapter 18, is a no-no), but for the purpose of *learning* what went wrong and how you can improve your performance in semesters to come. Maybe there was something about the way you organized your exam answer that your professor didn't like or had trouble following. Maybe it was something about your writing style. Maybe you got off track or went off on a tangent. You can't find out unless you ask—so ask! Whatever it is, you can learn from it—and then move on.

Grades *are* important, but they are also just checkpoints. They do not define who you are. If you didn't do as well as you had hoped you would, you have the unique opportunity to learn from your mistakes and show a trend of improvement in your transcript in semesters to come. That kind of trend is one that *everyone*, be it grad school admissions committees or potential employers, will be looking for.

What Did You Learn?

"At the end of my first semester, I realized I needed to work a lot harder," Chase admitted. "In high school, people did well because they were intelligent. In college, people do well because they work hard. It doesn't take a genius to go to the library nightly, keep up with the reading, and study thoroughly for tests . . . but it does take a good work ethic. So at the end of first semester, I changed my academic priorities. Instead of thinking about being prepared for tests and papers, I made my goal being prepared to make intelligent contributions in class, every day. This required careful reading and extra work, but it paid dividends."

"I learned that I did not know how to study for an exam," Dave admitted. "I was simply reading over the material and thought that by some magical force, I would soak it up. But I learned that reading is not studying. Reinforcing major ideas, identifications, or equations over and over again and applying concepts until they are second nature—that's good studying. I also learned that it isn't the quantity of studying, but the quality and effectiveness of your studying that makes the difference."

"I learned not to simply accept that I was weak in a particular subject," Erika noted. "Because I knew that I was not that interested in history, I did not expect to do as well in that class, and therefore, did not try as hard either. Don't get psyched out! If you know you are weak in one subject, you should work even *harder* in that class to account for it."

"I agree totally with that," another mentor said. "I got four 'As' and a 'D' my first semester in college. The 'D' was in chemistry, because I hated the class, hated the professor, and never really engaged the subject. I saw this coming all semester long because we had three exams and a final, but I just couldn't get myself to do anything about it, because I didn't like the subject and my repeated bad performances psyched me out. What I should have done is prioritized this class because it was clearly a weakness for me."

"I was preoccupied with trying to discover all that New York has to offer, so my first semester grades weren't all that great," Tiffany added. "If I had it to do over again, I would have devoted more time to studying. Learn to balance your social life and academic life early on."

Now you face a new semester—clean textbooks with uncracked bindings, new notebooks, and a fresh start. Take one more look at the chart you filled out to remind yourself of the things you learned from last semester, the distinctions you made about which study methods worked and which ones didn't, and the new approaches you are going to bring with you into the new semester. Get out your *Campus Confidential* workbook and write down these distinctions so that you don't forget what they are—and be sure to implement them immediately!

Now leave the story of first semester behind. It's time to turn the page.

Transferring to Another School

The foolish man seeks happiness in the distance,
the wise grows it under his feet.

James Oppenheim

Sometimes things just don't work out the way you expected.

Perhaps you didn't do your due diligence about your college before you decided to attend. Maybe you went to the place that offered you the most money in scholarships, the place that was closest to (or farthest from) home because you were running away from something, or the place that offered you a starting spot on the varsity as a freshman.

Whatever the reason, when your college experience doesn't feel like a good fit, it can be cause for significant concern—perhaps enough to make you think about pulling up roots and movin' on.

Transferring to another college or university is no easy task. At your target schools, your class has been previously selected, and unless the attrition rate is significant, there typically isn't a whole lot of space in the class for extra students coming in from the outside. Recognize that transferring will require you to go through a modified admissions process, complete with applications, essays, interviews, and a whole lot of bureaucracy as you try to transfer credits and your financial aid package.

So how do you determine whether transferring to another school is a wise choice or whether you ought to stay put, redoubling your efforts and making things work out where you are?

Read on.

THE FIVE MOST POPULAR BAD REASONS TO TRANSFER

Let's look first at some of the bad reasons to transfer.

I Had a Bad First Semester

Yeah, and as you've already seen, so does about 50 percent of the college population out there. There is a lot of adjustment associated with going off to college, packing up and moving to a new place, living with a new roommate, and being more or less completely responsible for your own life and academic progress. First semester typically confronts freshman with an astounding array of difficult choices—about alcohol, drugs, sex and sexual identity, friends, life, and, oh yeah—all that academic stuff too, such as what classes to take, what to major in, and when and how much to study.

Having a tough first semester is no reason to transfer to another school.

If you had problems first semester, be they personal or academic, take stock of what went wrong and *why* it went wrong. Seek help from an RA, an academic dean, a coach, or a trusted upperclassman. Adjust, and try to work things out. You have to give yourself at *least* part of the second semester to see if things get better.

"The best decision I made during freshman year at West Point was not transferring right away when I realized I was unhappy and wanted to leave," Aaron recalls. "I'm glad I gave it a chance and stayed until the end of sophomore year, because although I did end up leaving, by that time I was positive I was making the right decision."

I Miss My Boyfriend [Girlfriend] from Home

Time to echo the familiar refrain again: if it was *meant* to be, it will wait—and to be honest and blunt, chances are, it wasn't meant to be. Almost every college campus has someone who transferred in from somewhere else to be closer to a boyfriend or girlfriend who then almost inevitably dumps him or her within a year of the transfer. You want to talk about putting pressure on a relationship?

That's pressure.

Most relationships are not ready for this kind of pressure during freshman or sophomore year of college. Yeah, yeah . . . we know you think you're different and that you and your significant other are more mature and have really thought this out and all that.

Listen.

It's a bad idea.

If you can't bear the thought of being apart, start making plans to spend the summer in the same place so that you can test things further. But don't pull up roots and move your life somewhere else just to be closer to a significant other at this stage of your life. There will be plenty of time for incredibly difficult choices like that later in your academic life—such as when you're trying to decide whether to give up your dream job to follow a significant other to the city where he or she got into medical school, or when you are forced with the decision to leave the great outdoors of Colorado to move to inner-city Cleveland because your significant other got a job there.

Those decisions can be excruciatingly hard during senior year and after college, even when they come with engagements and other serious expressions of commitment. Few people are in this kind of place during freshman or sophomore year of college.

I Hate My Roommate(s)

Yes, this can make for a tough year—but it is still not a reason to transfer. First, read the chapter on roommate relations (Chapter 9) and do everything you can to work things out. Remember that the roommate relationship is a two-way street and that you have part of the responsibility to make things work out.

If you've done all you can on that front and things just can't be worked out, then take your complaints to the next level. Maybe your roommates truly *do* suck. If they do, spend a lot of time out of the room studying in the library, hanging out with friends from outside your dorm, or throwing your energy into an extracurricular activity, athletics, or something else.

If you are being physically or emotionally abused by your roommates due to race, religion, sexual identity, or some other significant factor, seek the help of your RA, who should immediately intervene in the situation. If he or she does not, work your way up the college's chain of command until you find a sympathetic ear. Chances are, if your situation really *is* that bad, you will be moved to a different room, and your situation should then resolve itself.

Having a bad relationship—even a disastrous one—with your freshman roommates is not a valid reason to transfer to a different school. There are much simpler workarounds to that problem.

I Haven't Found Any Friends Here

How hard have you tried? And what have you actually done to find a group of people with similar interests? Have you talked to people in your classes and in the departmental office of your subjects of greatest interest or your intended major?

Have you joined an extracurricular activity or two that reflect your interests? Have you reached out to the other people participating in those activities? Have you engaged in some form of athletic activity—be it at the varsity, junior varsity, club, or intramural level—and tried hanging out with those people? What about a religious or spiritual group, where people will be likely to embrace you? Have you explored Greek life on campus?

Some people fall in with a good group of friends right off the bat. For others it takes time and integration into the campus culture to find a good group of people with similar interests. Once again, getting halfway through freshman year is not enough of an experience to determine that there is no one on campus with similar interests.

Stop in and chat with your dean of residential life, your RA, or a counselor at your Department of Undergraduate Health. Feeling alone and isolated can be a debilitating experience that can lead to depression and physical manifestations, so it is not something to be simply ignored, either. You probably just need a few ideas about where and how to meet new people and some coping mechanisms to bridge the gap in the meantime.

Remember, there are thousands and thousands of college students out there right now who feel exactly the same way you do.

But those feelings aren't a reason to transfer. Not yet, anyway.

I'm Homesick

This is another incredibly common experience for college freshmen—but not a reason to pack it in and move closer to home. If you're homesick on campus, chances are you're not keeping yourself connected enough or busy enough to overcome those feelings. Dive into your coursework, join an activity or two that you really enjoy, bond tightly with your roommates and new friends, and try to keep your mind off what you left behind at home. Soon enough, it will be Parents' Weekend or Thanksgiving or winter break or spring break or summer. You are rarely more than a month or two away from a significant opportunity to see your family and friends from back home—and in today's world of low-cost air travel and increasingly convenient transportation options, it is becoming easier and easier to do so.

If things get really bad, make an appointment to see a counselor at your Department of Undergraduate Health. You'll be surprised to hear how many other students seek the same assistance and how easy a fix these issues tend to be.

SOME EVEN WORSE REASONS TO TRANSFER

Some of these may seem ridiculous, but hey—we're not making this stuff up. These are reasons your classmates are coming up with!

The Weather Sucks

You *knew* this when you chose Bates over Stanford, or Oregon State over Arizona State—and if you've been reading us all along, there must have been a reason why you made the choice you did. So stock up on long underwear or buy an umbrella (respectively), but forget about transferring because of the weather.

The Food Sucks

Please. The food sucks almost everywhere.

The Campus Is Too Liberal [Too Conservative]

Listen to the counterarguments, then speak your mind anyway—this is what college is all about. Whether you are a defender of liberal causes on a very conservative campus, a conservative on a very liberal campus, or a moderate who feels like a man or woman without a country, you have an important role to play in the dialogue on your campus. Don't run from that—embrace it. If you are willing to listen to others and conduct that dialogue with grace and principle, you will ultimately be respected for it.

Our Sports Teams Suck, and the Campus Has No School Spirit

No doubt it is fun when your football team is kicking ass and the stadium is full of a rowdy mass of people cheering them on. Unless you're planning a career in football or cheerleading, though, chuckle at the fact that men's soccer lost both ends of its home and home series with the junior high all-stars from across town, and keep your eye on the ball.

SOME GOOD REASONS TO TRANSFER

Of course, not all reasons to transfer are bad. As we noted at the outset, sometimes things just don't work out the way you expected. If you are in any of the following situations (or something similar to them), then you may in fact be a candidate for transfer.

I've Discovered a Legitimate Interest in a Discipline Not Offered by My College

Perhaps you've discovered a gift for the stage, improvisational comedy, or screenwriting, for example, but your school does not have a workable major in any of those areas, and it can't satisfy your academic interests through independent studies, offering you visiting-student status at another school, or the junior year abroad program. As long as your interest in this discipline is legitimate—and is not simply a pretext to, say, move closer to your girlfriend at Columbia by attempting to transfer to NYU—then this is a reasonable rationale for pursuing a transfer to a school more suited to your academic interests.

My College Just Cut My Major

You went to this college or university with the express intent to study Tibetan philosophy, but due to state budget cuts and other cost-saving measures, and the departure of the two visiting professors who headed up the program, it is no longer offered—and now the school is just like any of the others you turned down to come here.

Again, as long as your continued interest in Tibetan philosophy is legit, and not a rationalization to escape from a psychotic roommate, you're justified in pursuing greener pastures.

I Have a Family Emergency

Chalk this one up as a "maybe," because you do actually have some options in such a case. We hope you'll never face the circumstance where you need to consider transferring due to a family emergency, but we know that it sometimes happens. If a family member is terminally ill but you otherwise like the experience you've been having in college, consider asking the administration for a semester or year's leave of absence to go home and attend to your family during its time of crisis. Chances are, your attention will be divided anyway, and spending time memorizing equations when your dad is dying is not something you'll care much about.

If the situation is more protracted, however, as in the case of a more debilitating illness that will require more long term but less intense participation on your part, moving to a campus closer to home may be the best option. Before you make a decision, talk things over with your family and your dean of student affairs, who may be able to offer you additional options or solutions.

I Can't Make Ends Meet

Your inability to fund your college education in your present circumstances should rarely have to be the impetus for a transfer. If you find yourself in such circumstances, you should first consult your college or university's financial aid office to see what changes might be made to your financial aid package. Bringing your situation to the attention of the financial aid officials at your school is often all that's necessary to bring about the change in circumstances that will make your remaining at school a possibility.

Even if this initial step does not solve your problem, though, you need not give up. Work your way up the chain of command. Talk to your dean of students to see if he or she can offer any suggestions. If you still get nowhere after that effort, make an appointment and take your case to the college president. How many people do you think take that extraordinary step?

If despite all these efforts you still come up empty and cannot make ends meet, then, and only then, a transfer for financial reasons might be in the offing.

I Think It's a Bad Fit—After a Full Year of Effort

Sometimes it's not the unavailability of a major, the departure of key professors, or financial issues that derail you. Sometimes it really is a question of fit.

If you've given it a year and you can articulate specific and legitimate reasons why your college or university is a bad fit for you—*and* you have identified one or more schools that you know would be a better fit—then proceed to the next section.

THE NUTS AND BOLTS OF THE TRANSFER PROCESS

If you've gone through the analysis and you are certain that transferring is the right option for you, your next step should be to contact the admissions offices of your target schools, establish a relationship with one of the admissions officers at each of those schools, and determine what will be required of you as a transfer applicant.

Although every school's transfer process is a little bit different, you will almost certainly be asked to submit a certified transcript from your current college or university, a statement from your current college or university registrar's office establishing that you are a current student in good standing, and at least one essay justifying your interest in transferring out of your present school and into your target school.

You are also likely to be asked to come to campus for an interview or to interview by telephone. If this is the case, be ready to discuss how you erred in choosing to attend your current school, what is motivating your interest in transferring, and what actions you took at your current school to try to resolve your dissatisfaction. Establishing that you made efforts to make things work out at your current school will show your maturity and may help convince the admissions committee at your target school that you have thought your decision through carefully and warrant one of the precious few transfer slots that come available each year.

ENSURING THAT YOUR FINANCIAL AID TRANSFERS WITH YOU

A complete discussion of how to handle financial aid transfers is beyond the scope of this book. Suffice it to say that you will have to file a new FAFSA and CSS Profile form (if applicable) for your new school, because if the cost of your new school is either higher or lower than your old school, the size of your aid package is likely to change. Keep in close touch with a financial aid officer at your new school, as this person will be in the best position to help you navigate the transfer and reconfiguration of your federal aid package. Also be sure to inform all federal, state, and local scholarship sources of your change of schools to ensure that any renewable annual awards end up in the right place.

"After my sophomore year at West Point, I transferred to UMass-Amherst," Aaron noted. "I transferred because prior to college, I wasn't exactly sure what I wanted to do. Through lacrosse, I was offered the opportunity to attend West Point after completing one year of their preparatory school. It was a great opportunity athletically, educationally, and economically (you get paid military salary to attend), so I decided to give it a shot. After three years in the program, I decided I was tired of not having any personal freedom and I was unhappy with being away from my friends and family for such long periods of time. The experience just wasn't right for me.

"I left in the spring and took the following fall semester to work and decide what I really wanted to do. I decided to attend UMass the next spring semester. I had it relatively easy because I was recruited to go to UMass for lacrosse, so they did most of the nuts and bolts work of getting me in. You definitely want to find out which of your class credits are going to be accepted by your new school and which classes you'll have to retake, as this can be a major issue."

"A good friend of mine transferred to Yale during the spring semester of his sophomore year," Tom noted. "One obvious drawback to transferring to a school in midstream is that you have virtually no control of the on-campus housing situation. Although my friend did not fit in well with his assigned roommates (not surprising, because he essentially just filled an open single wherever the open single was), he soon befriended my group of friends, and has stayed a core member of our 'family' ever since. Even for transfer students, social interactions still can develop quite naturally. This story illustrates that despite its challenges, transferring colleges *can* work out quite well."

Planning a Meaningful Freshman Summer

The Brainstorming Workshop

*Summer is the time when one sheds one's tensions
with one's clothes, and the right kind of day is
jeweled balm for the battered spirit.*

Ada Louise Huxtable

Your freshman summer will present you with a unique opportunity: a *looong* period of time—perhaps as much as fifteen weeks or, in other words, the equivalent of an *entire school semester*—away from academics.

For most of you, this will be the first time since you first went to kindergarten thirteen or so years ago that you will have this much time off.

What are you going to do with such an incredible opportunity?

On the afternoon in December that I was writing this chapter in my local Borders bookstore, I took an informal poll of a group of college freshmen—old high school friends who had just returned home for winter break and gathered for coffee. After introducing myself as an author writing a book about college, inquiring about their college schedules, and learning that the shortest summer break among the students in the group was fourteen weeks (in other words, no one was on the quarter or trimester schedule), I asked the group what their plans were for the upcoming summer. Although the responses they gave me probably won't surprise you, they are eye opening in terms of what they can teach you about taking advantage of opportunities.

Here are a few of the responses I heard:

"Uhh, I dunno . . . I haven't really thought about it. I guess I'll head home and, uhh, try to find a job."

"Well, I need to make some money, so I guess I'll just go work for my uncle's company."

"I'll probably get a job lifeguarding."

"Well, I made varsity soccer, so I'll be training all summer, and then I have to get back to campus by the end of July for practices. I'll probably try and waitress a little on the side to make some cash."

"I'll probably try and waitress down at the beach, you know, so I can work on my tan."

"Hang out at my lakehouse and sleep. A lot."

"Come home and hang out with my boyfriend."

"No clue."

"Hey—do you need someone to help type and edit your manuscript? I'm available."

Yikes.

We're here to tell you that the three summers you have during college are some of the greatest gifts you will get in your entire lifetime—extended periods of time where most of you will have few, if any, responsibilities or obligations. Even if you have to make money during the summer, have you ever considered thinking adventurously outside the box about different ways that you could accomplish this *and* do something interesting or exciting at the same time?

Probably not, right?

Well then, you've come to the right place. Welcome to your freshman summer brainstorming workshop—where you're going to come up with the antidote to a long, boring summer spent scooping ice cream at your local high school hangout, waitressing at the same club or restaurant where you worked when you were in high school, or otherwise doing the exact same things you did for the last four years.

You're in college now, and the world is your oyster. All it takes is a little bit of research, a little creativity, and a sense of adventure to ensure that you have three amazing summers while you are in college.

Come along.

REVIEW YOUR GOALS FOR FRESHMAN YEAR

The first thing you need to do is take a look at the work you did in your freshman year goal-setting workshop and, if you followed our suggestions, at the eighteen or so "most important" goals you set for your freshman year.

What did you identify as the things you hoped to accomplish during your freshman year? How many of them have you actually accomplished so far? Which ones might be things you could work on this summer?

Yeah, yeah . . . we know that you need to make money this summer. We all either needed to or wanted to make some money during our college summers. The trick is that some of us figured out how to do that in really fun and interesting ways or in ways that furthered our academic, social, personal, or career goals (or a combination of these). You really *can* do both at the same time. Many of us did.

We want you to be one of us.

So think about what you had hoped to accomplish during your freshman year and about which of those things might be worthwhile summer pursuits.

Explore Your Academic Interests

What have you learned about your academic interests this year? Are there possible related careers you might want to explore this summer? For example, if you are interested in pursuing a career in medicine, do you want to try to get a job working on a research team in a laboratory this summer? Or working in a hospital? Or working for a rehabilitation center or a hospice care agency? Even if all you do is deskwork, you will be making important contacts and spending your time in furtherance of your interests and goals.

Have you identified a particular subject as a likely major? Is there a particular professor in that major whose work sounds interesting to you? Maybe someone with whom you might someday take an independent study, or whom you might use as your senior thesis adviser? Is this person hiring a research assistant for the summer? Even if he or she isn't, there might be other professors in the department who have books coming out or important articles in process that need research help. Again, this is a great way to forward your goals and interests while making money at the same time.

Are there any prerequisite courses that you might want to get out of the way during the summer to help advance your academic career? Perhaps you have longed to study one course intensively, maybe a science or a topic in literature, without being distracted by a bunch of other courses. Does your college or university allow you to take that course intensively over the summer? If it does, might you do that, sublet an apartment with a friend or two over the summer, *and* pick up a part-time job in the evenings or during the day on the weekends to pay the freight and make some dough?

Did you crush the SAT? Could you offer private tutoring in the city of your choice—or work for the Princeton Review or Kaplan and at the same time explore a city or place that interests you? These organizations have offices in foreign cities too, so don't limit yourself to the United States!

Are you thinking of taking your junior year or at least a semester abroad? Do you want to *really* master the native language of that country before you get there? Perhaps a summer studying the language is the way to go. You could do this during the day by taking the language as a single course, whether on campus, at your local college, or even on CD-ROM, and make money doing whatever else you want to do in your spare time. Again—you'd be furthering your goals *and* making money.

Or if you are *truly* adventurous, maybe you and a friend or two could just up and leave for that country right now—and work *there* during your freshman summer. Lots and lots of our friends did all sorts of interesting things—working on farms, building houses, working in the retail, restaurant, and entertainment businesses—in foreign countries. By doing this, you'd be making money, learning a foreign language, *and* seeing the world all at once.

"I spent the majority of my freshman summer traveling with my best friend in Europe," Dan recalled. "We were living on the cheap, but have many happy memories of dive hotels and cheap beer across the world."

Sure beats a long summer working at the Frosty Freeze in suburban Peoria, doesn't it?

Explore Your Extracurricular Interests

Like music? Are you proficient in an instrument or in voice such that you could make a bunch of money teaching at an upscale summer tourist destination, such as Nantucket, the Hamptons, or the Outer Banks? If you are a huge fan of a particular band or musical artist who is touring this summer, have you given any thought to trying to get a job as a roadie or T-shirt salesperson with the band? Life on the road is full of adventures . . .

Are you a varsity athlete? What about offering one-on-one skills lessons in a sport like golf, tennis, soccer, or basketball at one of those tourist spots, where well-heeled parents are always willing to spend money to help their kids develop skills?

Explore Your Social Interests

If you determined that you want to try to become more social, you could take a summer job somewhere new, away from your hometown, where you will be *forced* to be social—working as a concierge at an inn or hotel somewhere, working as a waiter or waitress in a crowded tourist spot, leading tours of your college campus, or doing *anything* that will force you to speak in front of people and interact with strangers. Feeling comfortable in new social settings is a learned skill. If it is one you want to improve, dedicate some time to practicing it. Note that if you work as a waiter or a waitress for *this* reason, you are making money and advancing one of your goals at the same time.

Explore Your Interests in Travel, the Outdoors, or Physical Development

Do you love the outdoors and want to become more skilled in this area? Perhaps you could make some money this summer working as a national forest ranger or a fire monitor in a remote wilderness location, or working on a trail crew or for any of a number of wilderness preservation societies that are always looking for part-time summer help on specific projects.

If money is less of an object, might you want to combine your love of the outdoors with a spiritual quest or an effort to really get back in shape, by hiking part of the Appalachian Trail or the Continental Divide or any other part of the country?

If money isn't an issue, might you want to explore taking an NOLS or Outward Bound course to sharpen your skills and to mature and grow as a person? Or might you want to find a cheap airline ticket and travel to a remote international location, such as Peru, Argentina, Africa, or the Himalayas, to do some trekking or other adventuring?

You'd be a long way from spending Saturday night loitering at the mall, hanging out at the Regal Cineplex, or getting bombed in a field somewhere, right? You can *actually do* these things for not a lot of money if you do some research and advance planning, share living costs with a friend or two, or "rough it" by living in tents or hostels.

If you identified working on your physical body as a goal, maybe you want to use part of this summer to train for a marathon or a triathlon, or simply to become a better runner, biker, swimmer, hiker, tennis player, or whatever. Obviously, this goal can be worked on practically anywhere—and can be combined with just about any other goal at the same time.

"I was a camp counselor at my old summer camp for the first three years out of college," Kevin notes. "It was, looking back, not a great way to spend my time as far as scoring a job after graduation, but I had some of the best times I can remember in my life. I certainly don't regret doing it."

Chase agreed.

"I spent all of my summers during and immediately after college working as a leader at Camp Belknap in New Hampshire. During my freshman year, I had to evaluate what I might lose by not pursuing certain internships or academic opportunities. I gathered information by talking with professors and consulting members of the career center, and ultimately decided that, given my desire to go to law school, there would be no adverse opportunity cost in my going back to camp for the summers. The decision was certainly the right one."

Explore Your Interest in Politics or Administration

Are you a likely poli sci, history, or government major? Are you interested in attending law school or interested in a particular political or social issue? Or are you just a political junkie? Is this a campaign year? Could you hook up with a political campaign as a policy analyst, speechwriter, advance person, researcher, campaign worker, or media adviser, or in any of a virtually unlimited number of other capacities? If it isn't a campaign year, perhaps you could to look toward Washington, D.C., where you might land a summer job working alongside thousands of other college students as an aide, page, researcher, or policy assistant.

Do you love your college and have visions of becoming an admissions officer someday? If so, a summer working in the admissions office as an interviewer is a common first step to that popular post.

Are you interested in a social issue that is addressed by a particular local, state, regional, or national agency? Might you want to work there this summer to explore your interest in the subject?

BRAINSTORM

So now that you've had a chance to review your goals and interests and to kickstart your imagination, it's time to brainstorm. What is it that you want to accomplish with your freshman summer? Grab a pen or pencil, haul out your trusty *Campus Confidential* workbook, and list a bunch of ideas. Then rejoin us to learn about a way to make sure you actually take *action* with respect to these ideas.

Okay. Now look at the ideas you brainstormed, pick four or five of them, and put them in an order of priority from highest (1) to lowest (4 or 5) by just writing a number in a circle next to them. Go ahead, do it now.

PUTTING IT ALL TOGETHER

Now I want you to think really creatively here. How could you accomplish three, four, or all five of these goals at the same time in the same summer? And how amazing do you think you would feel if you could actually pull this off?

Let's Look at an Example

Suppose you identified the following as your freshman year summer goals: (1) making money, (2) getting in better shape, (3) spending some time in the outdoors, and (4) finding some time "away from it all" to contemplate the meaning and direction of your life. What could you possibly do with your freshman summer that would make you feel fulfilled and would further the pursuit of your goals?

Obviously, procrastinating about this decision and then defaulting to working as a file clerk at your mother's law firm, though it may pay some bills, is not going to advance your personal agenda very much. At most, you will be deferring the decision about what you want to do, which may increase your anxiety and put more pressure on you next year; you will also be subverting your desires to get back in shape and be outdoors to your desire to make money. And chances are, you end up feeling miserable and unfulfilled.

So get creative. What if you got a job working on a mountain trail crew in the Rockies? Instead of filing paper, you would spend your days hiking, clearing brush, repairing washouts and preventing erosion, and working outdoors in the wilderness. Nights would be spent in remote cabins, in tents, or under the stars. Because your meals and accommodations would be provided, your expenses would be limited to the costs of getting out there and back, and whatever incidentals you chose to incur. Now, instead of meeting a single goal, you'd be addressing all four of your priorities in a single job in a single summer.

How good would that make you feel?

You say you're not into cutting trails? What about working as a forest ranger? Or as a fire spotter? Or as an attendant at one of the cabins run by the Appalachian Mountain Club? Any one of these positions would allow you to meet all four of your stated freshman summer goals. And there are countless other jobs that would do it too.

"I worked at a dude ranch in Wyoming and had a *blast*," Carolyn recalls. "I spent part of almost every day hiking in some of the most beautiful mountains in this country. Honestly, my advice for the summer after freshman year would be to do something fun that can also earn you some money. I would not necessarily advise getting a job designed to help you get a job out of college. There is plenty of time for that later."

"I think something meaningful is something that does one of the following things for you," Jim noted. "One: something that makes you feel good by helping others; two: something that helps you make a career decision or helps you better define what you want to do; three: something that contributes significantly to your financial ability to attend school; four: something that helps establish contacts and experience that will help you land the job you want after school; or five: something, like summer study abroad, that enables you to have an experience that you may never again be able to enjoy."

"For me, what was meaningful the summer after freshman year was to go *home*," Zoe concluded. "I worked at an inn ten minutes from home, saved some money, lived with my parents, hung out with old friends, and pursued some romantic adventures. Just before school started, I flew out to Illinois and drove back to Maine with my roommate-to-be. Did I contribute to the greater good of the world or 'broaden my horizons'? Probably not. But I did have a great, stress-free time, and returned for sophomore year feeling rejuvenated and grounded."

NOW DO SOME RESEARCH

Once you've established your goals, thought about ways to make a few of them work together, and brainstormed a bunch of possibilities to produce the blueprint for an immensely satisfying freshman summer, now armed with this blueprint, head on over to your college career planning and placement office to find the ideal position for you. Don't just settle for something run of the mill. You have plenty of time to devote to this activity. Yes, it will take some time, but finding the right way to combine your goals and your interests will ensure that you'll spend a well-adjusted, meaningful, and happy freshman summer.

Moving Off-Campus and Managing Other Housing and Roommate Decisions

*A house is a home when it shelters
the body and comforts the soul.*

Phillip Moffitt

As your freshman spring semester draws to a close, you will face one of the biggest decisions of freshman year—and one of the decisions that is likely to have a significant impact on the rest of your college career: where and with whom you are going to live next year.

For students moving into a fraternity or sorority house next year, this choice is not a choice at all, as both your accommodations and your roommates have been decided for you. Similarly, for those of you attending colleges where rooming on campus is mandatory until the junior or senior year, the choice is easier. At a great many colleges and universities, however, students have the option to move off-campus after their freshman year—and this is where the choice becomes considerably more difficult.

How do you make this important decision? And how do you decide whom to live with?

ON OR OFF CAMPUS?

There are a few factors to take into consideration when you are trying to decide whether to live on campus or off. As the two experiences can be radically different from one another, it pays to do a bit of research on this issue up front.

Majority Rules

The first thing to consider is what choice predominates on your college campus. Do most students live on campus in dorms, or off-campus in the surrounding community? Remembering that ready exposure to other students both in class and around campus is one of the most important parts of college, you are generally safe following the trend of the majority on your campus. If almost everyone stays *on* campus, you should too. If many or most students move *off*-campus and into the surrounding neighborhoods after freshman year, then there is less holding you to the campus, and you should feel free to join the exodus yourself.

Financial Aid

You should also consider what your financial aid package will cover. If you are getting an allotment for room and board, does this allotment require that you live on campus, or is it transferable to off-campus housing? Be sure to get a definitive answer to this question before you commit to moving off-campus. You will also want to check with your college or university to determine whether you will still be eligible for some iteration of the campus meal plan (if you want it) if you move off-campus, and whether or not you will be required to pay a premium for this privilege because you are not also living on campus. Do the math and figure out if the economics make sense.

Living Conditions

The advantages and disadvantages of living off-campus are very dependent on your particular college or university. At some schools, on-campus housing is expensive and overcrowded, in which case there can be a distinct financial and comfort advantage to finding an apartment just off campus to share with a few friends. In other cases, off-campus housing can be very expensive and no more spacious than that available on campus, in which case the hassle of having an absentee landlord responsible for your maintenance issues may not be worth it.

Legal Considerations

Obviously, living off-campus frees you from any rules governing conduct in your dorm rooms. It does *not*, however, free you from the rules of conduct of the university as a whole, as you are still a student no matter where you choose to live. Although you may be liberated from the watchful eye of a tyrannical RA or an overzealous campus police force, you will be trading in that oversight for the jurisdiction of the city or town police. Note well that campus police are often much more forgiving of lapses in judgment than the town or city police will be.

Distance from Campus

If you are considering a move off-campus, think carefully before you choose accommodations too far away (read: beyond walking distance). Remember that you will often have meetings on campus at odd times, including late in the evening, and even if you move off-campus, you will almost certainly want to continue to study somewhere on campus—necessitating your late-night travel to and from wherever you choose to live. If this distance isn't walkable, or isn't at least accessible by reliable and safe all-night public transportation, think twice before committing to such an arrangement.

Leases

Finally, if you are considering off-campus accommodations, remember that local landlords are going to be renting by the *year,* not the school year. You will therefore be responsible for rent year round, including the summer months. Be sure that any lease you sign includes the right to sublet your space during the summer—but understand that you will be responsible for finding a trustworthy and reliable sublettor and that if you do not do so, you will still be on the hook for your share of the rent. Annual leases are also subject to rate increases at the whim of your landlord every year unless you lock in a multiyear obligation at the time you sign your lease. Committing to a multiyear obligation can save you money, but it also limits your flexibility if your roommate situation sours or if the space ends up being inconvenient or unworkable for whatever reason. Remember also that you may be taking a semester or year abroad.

OUT WITH THE OLD AND IN WITH THE NEW: CHOOSING NEW ROOMMATES

The other piece of the puzzle that you have to face is *whom* to room with. For those of you who had no real connection with your freshman year roommate(s), the decision to move on may be easy. For others, though, particularly those of you facing the prospect of keeping *most* of the group together but ditching one or two of your current roommates, this can be an awful time.

There is really no magic formula about how to "break up" with one or more of your roommates. There are all sorts of valid reasons why you might need to jettison one or more of your present group. Maybe you need to break into triples or quads. Maybe you're merging two rooms together, but don't have room for everyone. Or maybe it's because you just don't want to tolerate the habits or personality quirks of one or more of your present roommates any longer.

It is your right, after all, to choose with whom you want to room. Roommate breakups can be done the right way or the wrong way, though. Even done well, they may cause some temporarily hurt feelings or bruised egos, but these can and will be overcome with time. Done badly, however, roommate breakups can become the stuff of legend.

"Be honest about your plans from the beginning," Lyndsee warns. "I ended up losing some friends over housing choices. It can be hard not to hurt someone's feelings in the process."

"One of the biggest mistakes I made in college had to do with choosing a roommate for sophomore year," Zoe agreed. "In our first freshman semester, my roommate and another friend and I decided that we would all live together. As the year wore on, the roommate and I grew apart, and eventually the other friend and I told her that we didn't want to share a triple. This was a very painful conversation, probably not handled well, and created a rift between my freshman roommate and me that was never healed. In fact, we almost never spoke again during the next three years. It is something I still regret."

"Roommate decisions for sophomore year are very much a continuation of the rooming combinations, and new friendships from freshman year," Tom explained. "The simple advice here is to establish strong foundations for friendships in your freshman year. Then, rooming situations will take care of themselves."

"Choose someone who has similar study habits, sleep habits, and interpretations of cleanliness, in addition to being a friend," Jim added. "Traveling with someone over a break can really help you to decide whether you get along well enough to live together."

The best advice we can give you about this is to communicate clearly, directly, and *as soon as possible* with those who will be left behind. Choose one or two people from the suite to have the conversation with the roommates who will be left behind, rather than convening a summit meeting to announce the news. Having everyone there heightens the tension, formalizes the discussion, and makes the whole thing seem more like an inquisition than a conversation.

If you are one of the people chosen to talk to the roommates who will be leaving, downplay the reasons for the breakup unless you are asked directly for an explanation—but be sure to provide *plenty* of time for your spurned roommate(s) to make other housing arrangements for next year. Doing this allows you to soften the blow by saying something like, "I just wanted to make sure you had plenty of time to talk to some of your other friends about rooming with them next year"— and will likely make the truth easier to take. The *last* thing you want to do (and, remarkably, it happens all the time) is to put off telling your fourth roommate that she is out of the suite for next year because no one wants to have the tough conversation, and then ambush her with the news on the eve of the sophomore year housing draw—giving her no time to make alternative arrangements. Doing this is likely to condemn those left behind to "psycho singles" in patchwork suites composed of strangers thrown together by the administration.

You know you would not want to be faced with such a situation, so if you're lucky enough to be on the inside, don't do it to someone else. As hard as it may be, having the conversation early goes a long way toward mitigating the damage.

PART THREE

Considerations for Sophomore Year

Your Sophomore Year Goal-Setting Workshop

A goal without a plan is just a wish.

Larry Elder

ongratulations! You're over the hump.

No longer a freshman, and no longer the least experienced person on your college campus, you no doubt returned to campus with more confidence and less anxiety than you did last fall. Nevertheless, you face a significant challenge as you start your sophomore year.

Last year, it was passable and, yes, even justifiable to want to explore all sorts of new things. You may have taken several large survey courses, dabbled in some smaller seminars, and sampled from a bunch of extracurricular activities. The transcript of your coursework last year may look a bit schizophrenic.

That was okay—last year.

This year, however, is a little different.

By your sophomore year, the expectation is that you will have determined at least a general direction for your studies from all that exploration. Indeed, for some majors, particularly those in the hard sciences, you need to start knocking down requirements and prerequisites by the fall of sophomore year, as many of these requirements, such as physics, organic chemistry, and physical chemistry, are full-year courses.

Enter the sophomore year goal-setting workshop.

We're hoping that if you've been following along with the chronological advice we've been providing so far, you have kept weekly or even daily tabs on your eighteen or so goals from freshman year and have achieved a great many of them. We also hope that doing so empowered you and armed you with the information, direction, and resolve you need to avoid getting caught in the sophomore slump (see Chapter 31). Now, it's time to set some new goals for the coming year to follow up on what you've already learned about yourself and your wants and needs.

Once again, we've divided the workshop into six categories: (1) academic and career goals, (2) social goals, (3) extracurricular goals, (4) physical goals, (5) financial goals, and (6) spiritual goals.

For now, do *not* look back on the goals you set last year. You want to come to this experience with a fresh perspective, motivated by what drives you now—not what drove you a year ago. The differences you see will be instructive. We'll send you back to check on last year's goals *later* in this process. Don't cheat!

Once again, remember not to censor yourself. Just write down everything that comes to mind. You'll have a chance to go back through the ideas later to decide on your priorities, and you *will* cross-reference your list from last year to catch anything you didn't complete last year that is still relevant to you. For now, though, you just want to dump your pent-up thoughts down on paper. As you did last year, try to keep writing in each category for at least five minutes.

Let's begin.

YOUR SOPHOMORE YEAR ACADEMIC AND CAREER GOALS

So what did you learn about yourself academically last year?

What courses did you take and love, and what classes did you have trouble dragging yourself to attend every time? What distinctions can you draw from those experiences? Did you love your large lecture classes or hate them? Or did your enjoyment depend on the subject area or the professor? What introductory courses or subjects did you enjoy that you might want to explore more intensively? Did you hear about any other subjects that your roommates or friends explored that you might want to check out?

This is the semester when you really ought to be thinking about choosing a major. Are you there yet? If not, think about which courses and subjects really *moved* you last year. Were you engaged by your political science class, but utterly uninterested in your philosophy class? Fascinated by psychology, but bored by economics? In love with a foreign language and desperate to explore more about it and its affiliated culture? What courses were you excited to read for, and what were the classes you didn't want to miss? Draw every distinction you can from your experiences last year, and write them down. Worry about the practical application later. Let's try and find your passion!

Do you want to learn to speak another language? If you want to go abroad next year, this is the year to study a language intensively. Make your plans.

What possible careers do you find turning around in your head? Which ones have you now discounted? Are you premed? Or did you take a couple of premed prerequisites last year and hate them? What about law or business, or becoming an entrepreneur? What subjects would you need to take to properly explore these fields? What about a career that lies more off the beaten path, such as working for a nonprofit, a think tank, or a political organization? Did you enjoy reading and writing? Maybe you'd like to explore life as an editor, an agent, or a writer. Or if you are more into photography or visual arts, perhaps you'd like to explore working for a museum or a magazine. What steps will you need to take academically to begin setting yourself up for a trial run in one of these jobs (or some other)? Get these thoughts down on paper.

If you find yourself undecided or completely without direction, know that you are not alone—but have you consulted the available resources on campus to help you think about potential career paths? Have you talked to your academic adviser? To your dean of students? To your academic dean? To a counselor in your college or university's career planning office? Do you want to schedule such an information-gathering meeting? Or maybe more than one? There are tremendous resources out there to help you.

Are you into art or music? Do you want to study an instrument or learn to sing, draw, paint, or sculpt? Or learn more about art and art history? Don't forget about these courses!

Did you uncover any noticeable academic weaknesses in yourself last year? What about strengths? What kinds of skills do you want to continue to develop or master during your sophomore year? Do you want to learn to be a more analytical writer? A more creative writer? Do you want to become a more careful reader? Or just someone who can read more or for longer without tiring?

Do you want to learn to be a better note taker or develop more critical listening skills so that you can get more out of your lectures? Do you want to learn how to be better organized?

What kind of academic life do you think would give you the greatest satisfaction? What did you prefer reading last year: novels, nonfiction books, or analytical texts? Did you enjoy writing papers, essays, and other thinkpieces, or did you dread your writing assignments? Did you enjoy your science courses and laboratory work?

What about class size? Did you prefer larger lectures or smaller seminars? Do you learn more effectively by reading and by absorbing lectures or by interacting with your professors and peers in a small-group setting?

Did you establish effective study habits last year? Were you well prepared for exams, or did you find yourself cramming at the last minute? Are there any goals you want to set about your study methods? What about papers? Did you write them far enough in advance to have time to edit and polish, or were they last-minute jobs delivered at the deadlines with no time to spare? Is there anything you want to do with respect to time management or procrastination this year?

What academic things do you want to get out of this year and out of college generally? Write down everything that you'd like to try this year or at some point during college.

You have five minutes. Keep your pen moving.

Go!

If you've reached the end of your five minutes and you want to keep going, by all means do so. If you've written a good list of at least ten or twelve items and you've listed everything you can think of right now that qualifies as an academic goal for this year or for college generally, then go ahead and move on to the next section.

During the next day or two, more things will come to mind. As they do, be sure to add them to the list. Don't just let them wander into and out of your consciousness. Capture your thoughts so that you can turn them into goals!

YOUR SOPHOMORE YEAR SOCIAL GOALS

Did you spread your wings and "become you" last year? Who was it that emerged from the cocoon of high school or prep school and burst on to the college scene as a freshman?

What did you learn about yourself? And what do you still need to work on socially? Are you as confident as you want to be? Did you express yourself? Did you learn to be a good listener?

Did you find a good group of friends? Did you meet the people you wanted to meet? Did you get out enough, or did you go overboard and go out too much? Do you want to set any new goals or ground rules for your social interactions on campus this year? Did your social life swallow your academic life, such that you need to rein it in this year and get serious about your studies? Or did you spend too much time in the library and not meet as many people as you had hoped to meet? Remember that success in college is about balance. Do you need to work on maintaining a proper balance?

Did you join a fraternity or a sorority last year? Did it add value to your life socially, or was it more of a drain or a bad influence? What impact, if any, do you want Greek life to have in your sophomore year?

Did you make empowering or disempowering choices about drugs, alcohol, and sex? Do you need to think about a new approach to any of these things as you embark on your sophomore year?

Are there any other aspects of who you are or what you discovered about yourself last year or this past summer that you'd like to move front and center now? Do any of your attributes, characteristics, or interests need more expression than they had last year? Maybe you just want to try to have a little more fun or to take life a little less seriously. Or maybe you need to buckle down and get more serious about life now.

Write for at least five minutes, listing everything you'd like to try and everything you'd like to explore socially this year or at some point during college.

Go!

YOUR SOPHOMORE YEAR EXTRACURRICULAR GOALS

We hope that you sampled several different activities last year and found a few things that you enjoyed doing and that both supplemented and rounded out your freshman year experience. Which of those activities do you think you might want to commit to for the long term? Are there any in which you would ultimately like to assume leadership positions? Which ones didn't really work out the way you had hoped?

Think about your extracurricular experiences last year, and think about the experiences your friends and roommates had. Did you sample too many activities last year, such that you didn't get a concentrated experience from any of them, or did you hang back and really not get involved at all? Do you need to pare down the list of things to get involved in, or do you need to find one or two things to commit to? Or were your activities a disappointment, such that you need to find some *different* ones this year?

Was there an organization or an activity that one of your friends participated in that seemed really fun, really interesting, or really rewarding?

Did you make a JV or varsity team? If you didn't, and you were an athlete in high school or prep school, the transition can be hard. What about club sports or intramurals? Is there a sport you'd like to learn or get more involved with on a social level? Don't just abandon all sporting activity altogether!

Did you see a student play or a student film last year? Is the idea of working in one of these productions, either behind the scenes or out in front, enticing to you?

Did you explore politics or religion? Are you interested? If so, maybe the campus political unions or the campus chapter of the Young Republicans, Young

Democrats, or Green Party still needs to be paid a visit. Thinking of switching religions, exploring a new religion, or simply becoming more devoted to your own? You can think about checking out the local congregations or groups.

What about working in the community? Community outreach is a great way to develop career ideas while doing good at the same time. Want to explore teaching by volunteering in an underserved school for an afternoon a week? Or explore medicine by "candy striping" at the local hospital? Or use your skills by teaching languages, sports, or other skills to area kids? What kind of community activities might you want to get involved in?

Want to write for the campus paper? Or the literary journal? It's not too late to sign up for these things if you discovered a love of writing, editing, journalism, or criticism last year.

Want to interview prospective applicants, give campus tours, or help run your college's recruiting effort? If you love your college or university, this is a good way to plug into the energy, get connected to the individuals who run the place, and meet and talk with prospective applicants.

The sky's the limit as to the extracurricular activities you can do in college. Sophomore year, though, is the year that you need to start establishing some roots in various organizations if you hope to assume leadership roles as an upperclassman. So brainstorm a good list of things you might want to be involved with this year. Let your mind wander—and write down everything it finds in its travels.

You have five minutes.

Go!

YOUR SOPHOMORE YEAR PHYSICAL GOALS

So what happened to you physically last year? Did you stay committed to an exercise program, try to eat healthily, sleep enough hours most nights, and otherwise take good care of yourself?

Or were you like most of the rest of us?

Things definitely tend to get a little out of control during your freshman year. Everything is so new, the sense of freedom is so overwhelming, and the degree of control you have over your own life is so complete that it is very hard not to lose your balance. So think of this section as your checkup in that regard—and chances are, you probably have some work to do to restore that necessary balance to your life.

First of all, let's check in on your diet. Are you eating enough? Are you eating too much? Has your weight dropped or ballooned significantly? Are you eating healthily most days, or does your diet comprise mainly pizza and beer and whatever you pick up at the campus quick-mart? What do you want to do about that this year? Be sure to write down some dietary goals for the coming year.

While you're at it, let's check in on your actual physical condition. Eating disorders affect both sexes, and are especially common during the freshman and sophomore years. Are you engaging in any destructive behaviors that might characterize an eating disorder? Has anyone told you that you are looking especially thin or maybe even unhealthy? If you are concerned at all about these issues, check in with your campus health center, check out the National Eating Disorders Association Web site at www.nationaleatingdisorders.org, or call its toll-free hotline at (800) 931-2237.

What about exercise? Are you getting any on a regular basis? If not, might you want to set some goals in that area for this year? Do you want to take up mountain biking, rollerblading, or running? Chances are, your college or university has clubs or informal groups that organize these activities daily. Do you want to do some research to find one?

What about taking a weightlifting class, taking up yoga or meditation, learning a martial art, or learning to play tennis, golf, squash, or racquetball recreationally? Any of these activities would add a necessary physical component to your day. Do you need to do some research to find out what is available? Do you need to set up a schedule or make arrangements with a friend or a roommate to hold you to a workout regimen?

How have you been sleeping? Are you on a fairly regular sleep schedule, or do you find yourself up until all hours of the night socializing, playing poker, surfing the Net, or working? All-nighters and nights with very little or irregular sleep take a toll on your immune system, bring down your mood, and make it harder to concentrate and perform at your optimum level. That's not to say we haven't all pulled them! Nevertheless, you should work hard to get enough sleep so that you don't become run down this year.

What are some things you might do to ensure that you are getting enough rest? Maybe it's as simple as taking an hour-long power nap in the afternoons after class or trying to contain the nights you stay out until 3 A.M. to Fridays and Saturdays and to give yourself Sunday morning to catch up on sleep.

What else do you want to do for yourself physically this year? Do you feel alone or depressed, such that seeking out a few hours of counseling from your campus health center might be constructive? Have you noticed any other physical changes in your body, your energy level, or your mood that might warrant a checkup at the Department of Undergraduate Health?

Remember that sophomore year is the transition year between the thrill and excitement of freshman year and the significant strides in personal development and increased workload and responsibility of junior and senior years. It is a year that can either serve you well or really drag you down. Staying physically active, fit, energized, and healthy this year is critical.

Spend the next five minutes setting some goals in these areas for this year. Go!

YOUR SOPHOMORE YEAR FINANCIAL GOALS

Another area of life in which things tend to get a little out of control during freshman year is your finances. Many of us had our first experience holding a credit card—and for many of us, that experience led to overspending, and blowing our budgets.

Chalk it up as an educational experience, but get your spending under control now, before things really get out of hand.

So how *did* things go for you financially last year? Chances are, you discovered that college is even more expensive than you thought it would be—and that opportunities to spend money are around every turn. How are you going to deal with those discoveries this year? What financial guidelines do you want to set for yourself?

Are you on a budget? Should you be? Have you now realized that you really *do* need to draw it up so that you'll know what kind of plan you need to stick to?

Are you on a work-study plan again this year, or for the first time? Have you figured out how you're going to fit those hours into your week so as to minimize the disruption of your academic and social schedule?

Do you want to get a part-time job somewhere to make some extra cash? Maybe you could tutor someone in one of your strong subjects or become a teaching assistant. What are your other marketable skills?

Don't be afraid to think outside the box here—but if you find yourself with a lot of short-term credit card debt because of some bad choices you made last year, you really do need to do something about that. Don't let that debt grow and hang around your neck like an albatross for the next several years. Find a way to work it off and get rid of it.

Have you closely examined your cell phone plan and other monthly expenses to make sure that you are optimizing your expense-to-use ratios? Is there a better plan that you ought to be using?

Do you really need to have your car on campus? If so, might you want to work out some sort of car-sharing arrangement that would produce some additional income for you, or at least help defray the expenses of insurance, gas, and parking fees? If you do pursue this kind of arrangement, be sure that you have proper insurance on the car and that anyone who uses your car is insured as well.

Take the next five minutes and set out your financial goals for sophomore year. Remember that managing your finances requires you to play offense and defense. Think creatively.

Go!

YOUR SOPHOMORE YEAR SPIRITUAL GOALS

As we've mentioned before, sophomore year is a time of transition. Once the thrill, excitement, and newness of freshman year have faded, the reality begins to set in that college is a significant undertaking that requires vision, responsibility, and commitment. For many of us who lacked that vision or that commitment, sophomore year became a time of deep introspection and varying levels of concern ranging from mild stress to serious depression.

And for many of us, connecting to some sort of spirituality during these times of transition was very comforting.

Again, spirituality does *not* necessarily mean religion. For some people, though, connecting to their religion provides the necessary grounding and direction. (It didn't for me.)

Maybe for you, being spiritual means taking a few hours each week to practice yoga or meditation.

Maybe it means taking a long walk in the woods one morning a week to be alone with your thoughts and to reflect.

Maybe being spiritual means reading introspective writings or listening to music and letting your thoughts wander away from the mundane and the everyday.

Maybe it means volunteering to help the less fortunate at an area shelter or soup kitchen, or working at an animal shelter.

October of my sophomore year at Yale found me slumped in the hallway of my dorm in a state of depression and panic—caught between a premed program that I was committed to but hated and the vast expanse of "other" opportunities out there that seemed so enticing but so completely overwhelming as to be entirely unnavigable. I sought wisdom not through religion per se, but through advice imparted by several of my favorite books. I read some transcendental philosophy and took the time to nestle myself away from the hustle of campus to try to develop a vision and a direction for my life.

And it worked. Within several weeks, I had worked out a potential transition plan in my head away from medicine and toward my growing interest in psychology. I paid attention to "coincidences" that seemed to be encouraging me down this new path, and relied on my inner strength and the conclusions I had reached during my period of reflection to carry me through.

They did, and although I didn't make the clean cut until after I took Orgo (Organic Chemistry) after sophomore summer, this period of intense reflection was clearly the tipping point of my college career.

Whatever spirituality means to you, do not underestimate its power to enrich your life. In your campus world, where people will often seem very id-driven or self-absorbed, maintaining some perspective can be really helpful. And whether that means you'd like to get to church or synagogue once a week or simply that you want to read *The Celestine Prophesy* this semester, don't forget to pay some attention to your spiritual side. You'll be amazed at how refreshed and centered it will make you feel.

Think about a few ways to nurture your spiritual side during sophomore year and write them down.

Resist the urge to just dismiss thoughts about this topic out of hand.

Think about it for a minute and jot down a few ideas.

Go!

NOW WHAT DO I DO WITH ALL OF THIS?

If you're still with us, you should now have an abundance of good information written down to help ensure that your sophomore year is as productive and satisfying as you hope it will be.

But you're not done yet.

If you've followed our directions, you should have written down a stream-of-consciousness list in each of the six areas. We hope you didn't censor your thoughts as you were writing. If you didn't, your lists may be quite long.

You also have your list of goals from freshman year, and now is the time to look back at the lists you made last year in each of these areas and take stock. Which goals did you achieve, and which ones did you not achieve? Think about the ones you did achieve: *How* did you make them happen? What specific things did you do to make sure you achieved those goals? How can you replicate that activity to help you achieve your new goals?

Really take the time to think about this. Knowing what motivates you to get things done and what specific actions lead you to accomplishment is immensely valuable, because they can be replicated in any number of scenarios. So think about why and how you achieved the goals you did and write down any distinctions you can draw.

Okay!

Now go through your lists from freshman year again, to see if there are any unmet goals that you think are still worthy of your attention this year. Maybe there are some things from these lists that you forgot about, but still think are important enough to add back in to your sophomore year lists. Do that audit now and update your sophomore year lists accordingly—then come back here to continue.

Do it now. Don't just keep reading. Go ahead, we'll wait.

All right.

You now need a way to manage all those ideas you've recorded and to go through them and cull the ones that are most critical to you—to choose the ones that you think will give you the most bang for your buck, so to speak.

Here's what you're going to do next.

As you did last year, go back through each list and read what you've written down. Think about each item and see how it resonates with you. Some of the ideas will get you fired up as soon as you think about them. Others, upon reflection, may not seem that important or that exciting after all.

It's all good. That's part of the goal-setting process.

Go through each list and pick the three things from that area that you are absolutely committed to accomplishing during your sophomore year or, if you want to think more long term, during college as a whole. Pick the three things that you feel are most critical to making your experience a success—three that would make you feel great about yourself if you were to accomplish them.

Circle those items in each list.

Feeling really ambitious? Want to pick four or five? That's fine, but don't feel that you have to. You want to keep the number of goals manageable—so that you'll actually follow through and complete them. Three in each category is fine. More in some categories and less in others is fine too, but make sure you have at least one goal in each category to maintain some balance.

Remember: pick the ideas from each list that excite you the most or that, on reflection, seem to make the most sense or to be the most important.

Go ahead and make your choices now.

ONE MORE STEP . . .

Okay.

You should now have chosen somewhere around eighteen goals for your sophomore year or perhaps for college in general.

But you're not done yet.

Setting goals is one thing. Following through on these goals is quite another.

So now, for each one of these goals, we want you to articulate at least one very good reason why it is *essential* for you to follow up and to achieve that goal during your sophomore year. Make sure your reason compels you—that it lights a fire under you and propels you toward meeting the goal.

Articulating a powerful rationale makes it far less likely that you will simply forget about these goals once you conclude this exercise and close this chapter. So really take the time to do this well. Amend and edit your reasons. Choose powerful language and drill down into the real motives compelling you to achieve these goals.

Create a master list of each of your goals and your rationales for achieving them, and keep it somewhere where you can refer to it often.

Tape your list of goals up to the wall over your desk or on the mirror in your closet. If you don't have that kind of privacy, keep it in your desk drawer or your day planner—but refer to it at least once a week. Daily is even better.

If you did this last year, you've no doubt reaped the benefits of the process. If you're starting now, do this for your entire first semester, and we bet you'll be hooked for life. You won't believe the progress you'll make.

A FINAL NOTE FOR STUDENTS INTERESTED IN STUDYING ABROAD

It may seem very early to be thinking about this, but if you are interested in studying abroad in either your sophomore spring, sophomore summer, or for any part of next year, you need to start planning that experience *now*. It takes a lot of work and advance planning to get an experience abroad off the ground. If this is something that interests you, skip ahead and read Chapter 34 in its entirety now and then check in with your college or university's travel abroad office to determine the necessary steps.

Congratulations on completing the sophomore year goal-setting workshop!

ADDITIONAL RESOURCES

Robbins, Anthony. *Awaken the Giant Within*. New York: Free Press, 1992.

Robbins, Anthony. *Personal Power* (audio series). Robbins Research International. (www.anthonyrobbins.com)

Robbins, Anthony. *RPM Planner Kit* (time management system). (www.anthonyrobbins.com)

Robbins, Anthony. *Unlimited Power: The New Science of Personal Achievement*. New York: Free Press, 1997.

Choosing a Major and Designing a Course of Study

I will study and get ready, and
perhaps my chance will come.

Abraham Lincoln

Choosing your undergraduate major is without question one of the two or three most crucial decisions you will make during your college years. This decision will affect literally everything that happens to you from this point on—from what courses you will take, to what people you will see in your classes, to possibly even what career path you will embark on. Yet despite the obvious importance of this decision, many students simply fall into a choice of major without reflecting on the reasons for their choice.

True, many colleges ask you to declare your "intended" major on your application. Yale asked me to do this when I applied, and I declared myself to be a premed biology major. On the day I graduated, I had taken exactly *one* biology course. So you see how predictive that declaration can be.

Maybe you'll be one of the approximately 20 percent of college students who come in to college committed to a major and actually stick with it. Even if you think you are one of these people, though, you owe it to yourself to explore your motives.

Why have you chosen the major you have? Did you choose biology, as I originally did, because you are premed, and biology is the "typical" premed major? If so, you owe it to yourself to do some more meaningful analysis than that. Even if you *are* premed, you don't *have* to major in biology! As long as you complete your premed requirements, you can major in American literature, French, or Renaissance art for all the medical schools care. In fact, majoring in one of those subjects will actually help you stand out from the horde of thousands of biology majors.

"I chose geology, and specifically marine geophysics," says Dan, the doctor on our mentoring team. "It was a bit of a random major for a kid out of Colorado, but it suited my interests well, particularly at the time. I did work in the field for several years and parlayed my skill set into jobs in software engineering and environmental remediation. Ultimately, I switched gears entirely and headed toward medicine, but never once have I regretted the time I spent or the many adventures I had pursuing marine geophysics. I firmly believe that choosing your college major should be less about preparing yourself for a career and more about pursuing your interests and seeing where they take you."

The same holds true for law school, business school, or whatever the hell else you think you want to do with your life. There is no *one* correct way or one correct major that will put you on the Yellow Brick Road.

Let that reality wash over you and liberate you from yourself.

"I thought about pursuing a long list of different majors, ranging from economics to creative writing," said Chase, who is now in law school. "Considering my own experience and those of my friends, the pivotal factor in determining a successful experience in the major seems to be the amount and quality of the interaction you have with faculty."

"I always wanted to go to law school, so I decided I wanted to major in something that was law-related. It was either political science or criminal justice and I chose the latter," Erika explained. "Before you go choosing a major based on what you *think* you should be majoring in, get some advice from your adviser or from someone in the field. I made the choice to major in criminal justice, but if I had bothered to talk to any of the attorneys I know, or my adviser, who was also an attorney, I would have found out that a major in English would have been more helpful to me than criminal justice."

Having said that, we now need to push back a little. Too many students approach college one semester at a time, without a grand design or vision for the experience as a whole. You know the type—the people who are always scrambling for classes at the last minute, flipping through the course guide and choosing classes based on what their friends are taking or what time the class meets (making sure to avoid early mornings or Friday classes). These will be the same people who end up choosing a major at the last minute in a field they find only marginally interesting, writing a senior thesis or completing a senior project that is about as enjoyable as a root canal, and then graduating and looking back on their college years with regret.

You don't want to be that person.

"I ended up majoring in history and Spanish because these were the subjects I enjoyed," Carolyn, the senior lawyer on our panel of mentors, explained. "I'm glad that I chose to major in Spanish and to spend a year abroad in Madrid. I became conversationally fluent in Spanish and that was really the only tangible 'skill' I left college with. I would advise students to pick at least one major or minor that leaves them with a skill. I believe that as a history major alone, I would have had fewer options after graduating from college than I did as someone who was conversational in Spanish as well."

Erik agreed.

"I do think it is helpful to try to envision what field you see yourself *most likely* to pursue after graduation and then to choose a major or course of study that will at least assist you in developing the knowledge and skills necessary to pursue that field. Even though many students will certainly *not* know the answer to that question, I still think it is important, at the beginning of sophomore year, to muster a best guess based on what you know so far and to proceed from there," Erik advised.

CHOOSING YOUR MAJOR

As a college student about to begin your sophomore year, you have your entire future ahead of you—and the chance to make the well-reasoned, thoughtful decisions that will ensure that your college experience is a rich and memorable one.

"Okay," you say. "So what about it? How am I supposed to decide which major is right for me?"

We suggest choosing a major based on the following four criteria—and in this order: (1) pick a subject you're passionate to learn about; (2) pick a subject that allows you to do the things you enjoy doing academically; (3) pick a subject that relates at least somewhat to your likely career track; and (4) pick a subject that has some potential real-world applicability for you now or later in life. To give you a better idea of how to undertake this analysis, we'll address each of these criteria in turn.

Pick a Subject You're Passionate to Learn About

This idea is so obvious, you'd think we wouldn't even need to mention it, but, as Erika just pointed out, you'd be shocked to learn how many people major in subjects they think they're *supposed* to major in rather than the subjects they *want* to major in.

Forget the *supposed to*'s. What do you *want* to study?

No idea? Then go now and get your college's course selection guide.

Yes, we're serious. Go get it. We're going to figure out what your major ought to be.

Chances are, the guide is organized by majors. Start reading! Each section probably starts with a summary of the major and a section on its core requirements. Does the summary catch your attention? Do you feel the stirrings of a passion to get up at 8 A.M. in the middle of the winter to trek up Science Hill to learn about the cracking and distillation of petroleum in Inorganic Chemistry 101? No? Then keep reading. It's okay to skim the sections about majors in which you *know* you have no interest, but do take the time at least to skim them so that you'll have some familiarity with what is offered, how the majors are organized, and what is generally required of a student in a particular major.

Eventually you're going to find one or more subjects that give you some pause. "Hey, that sounds pretty interesting," or "Wow, I could get into studying that," you'll catch yourself saying.

Be careful, though. Introductory summaries can be seductive. I remember thinking that majoring in astronomy would be really cool, until I found out that the astronomy major was composed almost entirely of high-level math and physics courses.

"Next!"

When you find a major that sounds interesting, stop and write it down, but keep going until you work your way through the entire guide. By the time you're finished you'll probably have three or four possibilities. For me, they were American literature, history, political science, American studies, and psychology.

Now go back to the respective sections of the course selection guide and investigate further. Grab a highlighter and read through all the courses offered in each of those majors, highlighting all the courses in the major that you are excited to take. Are there three or four courses, or are there seventeen? If there are only three or four, you'll probably want to keep looking at other majors. If you found seventeen courses that sounded cool, you've probably found a viable candidate for a major.

Take the time to do a thorough job on this. As you'll see, we're going to come back to this work later in the chapter.

Once you've completed this task, go on to the next step.

"I majored in what interested me," Lyndsee said. "I didn't even think about what I would do with Japanese or East Asian studies or what kind of career that would lead to. I didn't care. I wanted to learn about what I enjoyed, and I knew my life would fall into place if I just did what made me happy.

"Think about what you what to learn about right now. There really is no way to predict the exact path that your life will take, so instead of trying to plan for ten or twenty years down the road, concentrate on *now*. College is about finding yourself and figuring out what your passions are."

Dave agreed.

"I, too, chose my major because I was simply the most interested in that subject area. Find the major that intrigues you and piques your interest. Be honest with yourself and don't choose a major for anyone else but yourself," Dave advised. "At Middlebury, my major, American civilization, had a reputation of being an easy (jock) major. I had to get over that stigma and realize that this was really what I was interested in studying. The truth is, it probably *was* one of the easier majors at Middlebury, but that's not why I chose it, and I didn't treat it that way. I made my course of study within the major very challenging and engaging. Your major is what you put in to it, not what labels other people try to attach to it."

"Don't be afraid to choose the major you like, rather than the major you think best fits a projected career path," Tom advised. "The workplace is more flexible than you think and the career path you ultimately embark on is far more dependent on the work experience you accumulate later in life, as well as the networking you do, rather than your choice of college major."

Pick a Subject That Allows You to Do the Things You Enjoy Doing Academically

Are you a paper writer or a problem-set person? Do you prefer reading novels and historical texts or working in the laboratory? What would you like to spend the next three years doing?

I wish I had asked myself these questions a lot sooner than I did. If I had, I would have seen some clear warning signs. I hated *all* my science classes *and* hated the labs. I couldn't have been more bored by them, and no matter what little tricks I used to try to get myself excited to understand and memorize the formula for the cracking and distillation of petroleum (who cares?), the steps of photosynthesis (again, who cares?), or the concept of chirality in organic chemistry (one more time—WHO CARES?), I kept finding myself reaching for the assignments in my other subjects.

Now you'd think I would have seen the light and made my clean break from premed sooner than the beginning of my *junior* year in college—but I didn't. I even gave up my sophomore summer to spend nine weeks in New Haven, Connecticut, taking the intensive Organic Chemistry (Orgo) summer program. It wasn't enough to hate the subject during the school year when I had other things to distract me—I had to study it intensively in a summer program, where it was the *only* thing I had to do.

When the summer was over, I still hated Orgo, and I was bitter. But that was when I finally understood that I was in love with the *idea* of being a doctor, rather than the practical realities of being a doctor. As soon as I let go of that idea—and started pursuing the courses I was really interested in, three very interesting things happened.

First, I felt really, really happy—happier than I had ever been in college—as though a giant burden had been lifted. Second, doors started opening to me left and right, such that it seemed as though exciting opportunities were everywhere. Third, my GPA took off like a rocket.

Learn a lesson from my density. If you *hate* what you're doing in college, stop doing it as soon as you feel you've given it a fair opportunity. The ends do *not* necessarily justify the means. Do not hesitate to change your path if you know, instinctively or otherwise, that the one you are currently on is not the right fit for you.

"I started off as a music major, but eventually decided to pursue communications studies," Tiffany explained. "Music will always have a place in my heart, but I was looking for a different way to challenge myself intellectually. I had taken some communication courses to supplement my music courseload and I found them to be extremely interesting, so I made the change."

"I started college as a chemistry major for two reasons," Tom added. "I liked the subject and I wanted to leave open the possibility of going to medical school. Half way through college, my passion for music grew and I decided to take more courses there. By the spring semester of my junior year, I saw that I was only a few credits shy of completing majors in *both* chemistry and music, so I took a couple of extra courses my senior year and was able to complete a double-major."

"If your college offers double-majors, minors, or concentrations, look into the requirements early on and do whatever paperwork is necessary to make it official," Amanda suggested. "You might as well get official credit for having pursued other interests."

Pick a Subject That Relates at Least Somewhat to Your Likely Career Track (If You Know What That Is . . .)

Just as not all prospective medical students need to major in biology, not all future lawyers need to major in political science or history, not all teachers need to major in education, and . . . well, you get the message. At the same time, however, as Erik noted earlier, it *will* help you down the road if your major bears some relation to what you end up doing for a living.

Obviously, that's a broad statement—which is okay, because the premise is broad. If you want to be a teacher and you major in history, you might be more inclined to teach history—but you could also major in English, chemistry, sociology, or any of a number of other subjects and teach any of those. Could someone who wants to be an entrepreneur or a corporate CEO major in something other than business? Of course she could. Psychology, sociology, history, philosophy, political science, and foreign languages are all possibilities. The same holds true for lawyers. Some of the most sought-after lawyers these days are those who majored in mechanical or electrical engineering or biochemistry and used their background in those subjects to pass the patent bar and emerge into the world of intellectual property law.

Having said that, we might still ask if there are some majors that don't make a whole lot of sense for certain career tracks. Sure there are. Will a major in Renaissance art help a doctor in medical school? That's probably a stretch. Is there a reason for someone who wants to be a jazz musician to major in genetics? Unlikely. Should a would-be poet major in physics? Umm . . .

You've no doubt picked up on the point by now. If you are trying to decide between two majors, one of which dovetails nicely with one or two of your likely career choices, the other of which bears no relation to them whatsoever—you're probably better off going with the major that could help move the ball for you.

Remember, doing a major in college is like having a full-time job. You're going to end up taking anywhere between twelve and sixteen classes in your major, and you're going to end up an expert in one or more aspects of it. It is certainly important that you love the subject. But it is also important that the subject matter do some work for you down the road—either for your career or for something else that you love to do . . .

Pick a Subject That Has Some Potential Real-World Applicability for You Now or Later in Life

Maybe you want to become an accountant, but you have a passion for art history and have always dreamed of traveling the world to see the great museums. Maybe you're going to become a marine biologist, but you're engaged to someone from Japan and want to learn Japanese. Maybe you're into hotel management, but you also love gardening, and opt to major in botany. Maybe you're just a political junkie and want to study politics, or you love history and feel that every good student should learn from history so as not to repeat it. Those are all good reasons for choosing a major. There are many reasons why your career track and your major may not coincide, and no one says they have to—including us.

If you do choose a major with little or no relation to your likely career, just make sure that you can enunciate some rationale for doing what you're doing. Your four years in college will pass like a shadow, and when they're gone, they'll take with them a unique opportunity to study a subject in depth—perhaps the only such chance you'll ever have.

Don't blow your chance to do something meaningful with your four years. Think about your choices carefully and choose wisely!

Other Considerations

Here are just a couple of other dos and don'ts with respect to choosing a major.

Do talk with a number of students at your school who are presently studying in the major you are considering. How happy are they with their choice? Are they finding the subject matter interesting, the professors exceptional, and the work enjoyable? Is there unanimity of thought within the department as to what the major should entail, or is the department characterized by a lot of infighting between warring factions, such that the rules of engagement might change on you midstream? What does the department require to graduate? A senior thesis? A senior project? A departmental exam? Are you okay with that requirement?

Don't just pick a major because you've done well in the subject. Acing Psych 101 does not mean you are going to enjoy majoring in psychology, nor is pulling an A in Single-Variable Calculus a guarantee of future success.

Oh, and there's one more.

For the love of God, *don't* pick a major because your parents think you should major in it. Chances are, your parents have no idea what you're interested in studying, and unless you've been really honest with them, they're still telling everyone you want to be a doctor or a lawyer, even though *you* know you don't. Do not, under any circumstances, allow yourself to be pressured into majoring in something that doesn't interest you. That is the road to misery.

And yes, this advice pertains even if your parents are paying for your education. Trust us—you'd rather incur the debt and study what you want than spend four years studying for free a subject that doesn't interest you. You're only going to pass this way once. Make your own decisions—and let the chips fall where they may.

Make It a Double . . .

If you're really ambitious or you can't decide between two favorites, perhaps you'd like to double major. Be warned, however. Double majoring is not for the faint of heart. Most colleges and universities do not lower the bar for you just because you've decided to double major. In most cases, you'll be required to fulfill the full number of courses in each major—and yes, you may have to write a thesis or do a senior project in *both* majors.

Unless you are *truly* a masochist, though, there ought to be *some* common thread running through the two majors that might afford you the ability to have one or more classes count toward the requirements of *both* majors. Likewise, if you're clever, you ought to be able to come up with a thesis topic that spans both majors; if you're also persuasive, you might be able to convince your department chairs or your academic dean to permit you to do a single, extended-length thesis or senior project that will count for both majors. The possibilities here are limited only by your imagination, the extent of your persuasive powers, and the mood of the decision makers at your college or university.

Keep in mind that if you choose to double major, you are seriously limiting the number of electives you will be able to take outside your majors, because between the core curriculum and your two majors, you will have a great many requirements to fulfill. Nevertheless, choosing a thoughtful and meaningful double major can produce huge academic satisfaction for you. Just know what you're getting yourself into up front!

Okay. You've read through the course guide, evaluated the various course offerings, considered your options, and talked to other students. You've chosen a major.

Congratulations!

But you're not done yet . . .

Not by a long shot.

DESIGNING YOUR COURSE OF STUDY

Now it's time to actually *design* your course of study for the rest of your college career to ensure that you will (1) satisfy the requirements of your school's core curriculum; (2) satisfy the requirements of your major; (3) satisfy any and all prerequisites for the upper-level courses you identify as likely targets for your junior and senior years; (4) avoid the annoying scheduling conflicts that can prevent you from taking the classes you want *when* you want them; and (5) ensure that you still have the time for the athletic, extracurricular, and social commitments that will round out your college experience.

You're going to need about an hour for this activity, so turn off your cell phone and find a quiet place where you can work undisturbed for a little while. Trust us—the time you spend on this activity will pay huge dividends later.

Review Your Core Curricular Requirements

The first thing you need to do is go back to Chapter 11 ("A Brief Overview of the Typical 'Core' Curricular Requirements") and recall exactly what it is that your college requires as part of its core curriculum. If you did your work in Chapter 11, you should have mapped out the core curriculum in your *Campus Confidential* workbook, so haul out your workbook and revisit that information. Now cross out any of the core courses you fulfilled last year. Once you've done that, what remains is what's left of your core curricular requirements.

By the way, if you have any ideas about what courses you'd like to take to satisfy these curricular requirements, you should jot those down right next to the listed requirement so that you'll capture all your ideas in one place.

List the Requirements for Your Major

Now that we've taken care of the core curriculum, let's turn to your major. Grab your course selection guide, because we're about to go digging through that again.

Turn to the pages in your course selection guide where the general discussion of your major can be found. In it, you will no doubt find discussion about the requirements for the major, including the number of courses you need to take; any distributional requirements *within* the major that you need to satisfy (for example, a certain number of courses in social, cognitive, and developmental psychology); any laboratory, research, or practical components that may be required; and, of course—the biggie—what kind of grand finale, if any, is required during the senior year. Read the section on your major requirements carefully, and write down all the requirements in your workbook. If you are double majoring, you'll need to do a list for each major.

List Courses in Your Major That Interest You

Now that you know exactly what is required of you, the real treasure hunt begins. Go back to the part of the course selection guide where you highlighted the various courses in your major (or majors) that you were excited to take at some point during your college career. In your workbook, you're going to make a four-column list of the following: (1) all those courses, (2) the quarter or semester they are offered, (3) who is teaching them, and (4) whether the course has any prerequisites that you'll need to take in order to qualify for admission—including whether they are attendance-capped or open only to members of certain classes (for example, seniors only).

Yeah, yeah . . . we know that course offerings might change a little bit from year to year. Don't worry about that—do this exercise anyway. For the most part, you'll find the offerings in your course selection guide to be fairly reliable from year to year—enough so that this activity will have substantial benefit for you.

So let's get to it. Make your list of the courses in your major that interest you. To the extent that a course fulfills one or more of any distributional or other requirements within the major, note that somewhere on the list as well—so that you'll know what the various courses are doing for you.

Review Your Lists

You now have the makings of a blueprint for your college career. You know what core requirements you *have* to take, and you've jotted down some ideas about how you're going to fulfill those requirements. You know the distribution of courses in your major that you *have* to take, and more important, you've now identified the courses in your major that you are excited to take. You know what prerequisites (if any) those classes have, you know generally when they are offered (fall or spring, and at what time), and you know who teaches them and if there are multiple professors who teach the course.

Now scan your list and take note of the information you have.

Do you see any obvious order in which one or more courses should be taken? Do the prereqs for certain courses suggest an order to you? Are there any obvious conflicts (two classes that meet at the same time, for example) that warrant some advance planning? Make some notes to yourself to capture those thoughts so that you can revisit them at the start of each semester.

Okay, there's one more list to make.

List Electives That Intrigue You

Electives are the courses outside your major that you've been dying to take—the art history class that everyone raves about, the poli sci class on the American presidency with the guy from the State Department, or the writing course with the famous author in residence. Whatever your passion may be, you want to make sure there is room to explore it—and the more you can plan for that in advance, the more room for it you will have in your schedule. So once again, go back to your course selection guide and revisit those meanderings you took when you were first considering what your major might be. There were courses that caught your eye—remember?

They go on the list.

There are courses that your RA, your upperclassman friends, and everybody else has told you that you have to take.

They go on the list too.

Write your elective classes down so that you won't forget to consider them as you round out your schedule each semester.

Put Together a Blueprint for Your Course of Study

There's only one thing left to consider: how you're supposed to cram all of this into your three remaining years in college. Obviously, how many electives you take and how many courses you end up taking per semester (or per quarter) is up to you, within the limits set for you by your college or university. There are some universal truisms about this subject, though, and we'll share those with you here before we wrap up the chapter.

First, do not wait until you are an upperclassman to start knocking off core requirements. The last thing you want is to spend your senior year completing your language requirement and your two required hard-science courses. Remember that a lot of the coolest courses—the upper-level classes in your major and the small seminar classes—either have prerequisites or have their enrollment restricted to juniors and seniors (or in some cases, just seniors). It would be a real shame if you couldn't fit in one or two of these courses because you had to knock off core classes that you procrastinated about taking . . .

"Knock off your core distributional requirements early," Chase advises. "Though I took a large swath of courses during my first year, I still made sure that they all chipped away at the required curriculum. The electives at higher levels are far more interesting, so don't waste your last semesters, when you are eligible for the best seminars, filling in core requirements."

"I kept a list of everything I had to get done, and mapped it out over the four years," Lyndsee explained. "I didn't list every class I was going to take, but I made general notes like 'I need a science class this semester,' or 'I need two more politics classes to complete my major.' Each semester, I would choose classes that interested me, but would still fit the descriptions of courses I needed to take in order to satisfy the core curriculum and the requirements for my major."

"I should have taken overloads more often," Jim lamented. "I could have handled the work, and it was no more expensive to take more classes. Finally, I made some choices to take classes I heard were 'easy.' This was stupid. The courses were usually easy, but they were also typically unhelpful in my life and a waste of time, money, and opportunity."

The best thing you can do for yourself is, as Lyndsee suggests, to sketch out a blueprint for your course of study. To do this, you're going to chart your three remaining years, broken down by semester or quarter, depending on your school. In your *Campus Confidential* workbook, label three pages "Sophomore Year," "Junior Year," and "Senior Year." On each page, create separate list headings for each semester or quarter of that year. Now, referring to the work you've done so far in this chapter, write out a prospective course of study. By engaging in this activity, you'll force yourself to see how the pieces fit together—which courses you'll need to take in what order—and how many core courses you'll need to get out of the way in order to free up your junior and senior years for your major and for interesting electives.

So go ahead and do this activity now—and see where you stand!

A WORD ON "CLOSED ENROLLMENT" OR LIMITED-ENROLLMENT COURSES

Every now and again, you'll come upon a course that you really, really, *really* want to take that for one reason or another has a limited enrollment. Maybe it is just that the professor wants to keep the class size small. Maybe the course is being taught by a visiting luminary. Whatever the reason, you should not allow yourself to be excluded from a course simply because the enrollment is limited. Don't be discouraged even if there is a lottery for the course and you lose or if enrollment is capped to seniors only and you are a junior. If you can enunciate a strong reason why it is important for you to take the class, take a shot at getting in. Figure out who the professor for the class is and how to get in touch with her. Call the professor *before* the first meeting of the class and make your pitch. Be prepared for at least *some* stonewalling by the professor—but be politely persistent. Explain your rationale passionately, and emphasize that you don't want to let the serendipity of a lottery keep you from your academic goals. If you are still getting nowhere, ask the professor if you could audit the class for no grade. That way, at least you'll get to be in the class and learn the information conveyed in it.

Chances are, you'll be allowed at least to audit the class. And if after you've diligently shown up for a couple of classes you approach the professor and pitch her again, chance are you'll win her over. Professors love students who are passionate and engaged—as long as they are also polite and respectful.

Remember that if you are trying to crash a capped class, there is most certainly a right way and a wrong way to do it. If you approach the situation as though it were your divine right to be in the class and you will not be denied the opportunity— you most certainly *will* be denied the opportunity, and you'll get a nasty reputation among your peers and the faculty to boot. If, in contrast, you approach the situation respectfully and make a good case for yourself that goes beyond "I don't want to wait until next year to take the class," you may well win over the professor and get what you want.

As with most things in life, success or failure turns on approach.

KEEP COMING BACK HERE!

The purpose of creating this blueprint is to get you thinking about how to manage your course selection process and to *design* a course of study for yourself. The more you think about this and plan it out, the more satisfying your college experience is likely to be. So keep coming back to this chapter and your blueprint as you select classes at the beginning of each semester—and be sure you stay on course!

Avoiding the
Sophomore Slump

chapter
3 1

*Slump? I ain't in no slump.
I just ain't hitting!*

Yogi Berra

For many of you, by the time you reach sophomore year, the thrill of being "away" at college and the newness of the experience have faded, leaving in their place a sense of growing urgency about deciding on a major, choosing a career path, and finding a group of friends or a romantic interest. Sophomore year is often characterized by confusion, soul-searching, motivational problems, and, occasionally, flat-out rebellion against parents, professors, or friends. You may find yourself feeling depressed and alienated, and studying listlessly or skipping classes because you feel that your coursework has no meaning for you.

Welcome to the Sophomore Slump.

If you find yourself huddled up somewhere staring blankly at a wall or out the window, wondering about your destiny and the meaning of life, and wanting to just let loose with a primal scream, know that you're not alone . . . but resolve to do something before things get worse.

"Eventually, the bloom comes off the college rose," Dan says. "At some point, your classes start to seem arbitrary and the entire college experience seems a bit contrived. I think this is a normal, perhaps even vital, realization. It is probably the push that makes you realize you can't spend the rest of your life in college, so you'd better get something out of it and move on."

"The four-year college career has a life cycle, much as a relationship or a new career does," Zoe explained. "At first, there is the excitement of newness and small flaws are easily overlooked. As time wears on, you invariably arrive at a point where taking stock is necessary, and suddenly, minute details about your college (or partner, or boss) start to bother you—sometimes a lot. It's natural to feel some disillusionment and anxiety when the honeymoon ends. Most students weather it with time."

The best antidote for the sophomore slump is activity. But not just any activity. We mean *goal-centered* activity—activity that has you exploring the areas that you have decided are of interest to you and that propel you forward toward a set of longer-terms goals that you've established for yourself.

To avoid the sophomore slump, be sure to work through the sophomore year goal-setting workshop (Chapter 29). Be sure that you have identified what you hope to explore this year in all areas of your life and have decided on two or three specific, tangible activities that will motivate you in each of those areas.

A SPECIAL WARNING FOR PREMEDS

Some of the most common victims of the sophomore slump are premeds who don't want to major in a science but who find themselves bound up in a seemingly endless array of science and math prerequisites and their associated laboratories. Forced to take a bunch of classes they don't want to take, these people often become depressed, disinterested, and aimless—going to class and working through the material, problem sets, and labs without any real conviction, and often putting off these classes until all their other work is done. Then, after a couple of unfortunate exam performances, they find themselves reevaluating their commitment to medicine and feeling increasingly anxious about college and about life in general.

If this sounds like you, rest assured—you're not alone.

One of the best strategies here has to do with careful management of your course schedule. Do *not* load up on premed prerequisites in an effort to "get them out of the way" if you know you aren't going to enjoy them. Stacking up too many of these courses at a time can lead to feelings of disconnectedness, alienation from the things you enjoy, and, eventually, depression.

At most colleges and universities, the premed prerequisites include a year of biology (with lab), a year of inorganic chemistry (with lab), a year of organic chemistry (with lab), a year of physics (with lab), and a semester of calculus. You can place out of one or more of these required courses with sufficient scores on the AP or SAT II exams you may have taken in high school, which can work to your significant advantage in terms of scheduling. If you want to proceed directly to med school after college without taking a year off, you will need to complete your premed prerequisite courses by the end of your junior year in order to begin your preparations for the MCAT in a timely way.

Let's assume that you did not place out of any premed prerequisites. You can see that this means you will need to take a couple of courses (plus labs) each year in order to complete your requirements on time. The key here, however, often lies in the *combination* of courses you take, and when you take them.

Most premeds say that Organic Chemistry is the "gatekeeper" course—the single course that more than any other tends to knock people out of the med school race. Knowing this, try to isolate the course during your sophomore year or sophomore summer, so that you can devote the proper time and energy to it. Assuming you will do that, we work backward because you need to take Inorganic Chemistry before Organic Chemistry, you'll need to take Inorganic simultaneously with Biology during your freshman year or you could push one of them off until your sophomore year if you decide to isolate Orgo for summer study Then you can fit in your Calculus course somewhere, and push Physics off to junior year.

This bears repeating: we do *not* recommend overloading. Balance is key, and spreading out your tough, distasteful course requirements will make everything more palatable. Jamming too many required courses into the same semester is asking for unhappiness.

Don't do it.

OTHER WAYS TO AVOID THE SLUMP

Others who fall victim to the sophomore slump typically point to the same root causes: (1) a failure to find a major that provides sufficient intellectual stimulation and interest; (2) a failure to connect with a network of friends; (3) a failure to "plug in" to a meaningful extracurricular activity or two outside the classroom to give texture and relevance to their experience; and (4) the feeling of bloat, lethargy, and lack of energy that comes from poor diet and a failure to exercise.

Obviously, each of these causes has a remedy, and some of them even tie in with each other. If your proposed major "just isn't doing it for you," don't be afraid to toss it overboard and start anew. If you haven't found your way yet, don't panic. Many of us didn't declare a major until the very end of sophomore year. What you need to do, though, is spend some time with your college's course catalogue and go back through the recommended exercises in Chapter 30 on choosing a major. Look around for course titles and subjects that pique your interest as you browse the catalogue, and sit in on a lecture or two, even if you're not registered for the classes. Taking little steps like these can quickly confirm a new direction in your coursework for you—and put you right on track.

If you have thus far failed to connect with a group of people on campus, perhaps it is because you are not being social enough. Are you spending your days in the classroom and your nights in the library, without getting out some or getting involved in any of the goings-on out on campus? If so, force yourself to engage more with your roommates, your classmates, and the people around you. At no other time in your life will you ever again be surrounded by so many people of similar age with such similar goals, fears, aspirations, and concerns. There are natural connections to be made all over the place. All it takes is a little courage.

If your roommates or classmates aren't presenting you with any obviously attractive options, seek out an interesting extracurricular activity or two to get involved with on campus. Perhaps working for a social service organization, teaching inner-city kids, writing for the newspaper or one of the campus magazines, or getting involved with a theater group or one of the nearly infinite number of clubs on campus is just what you need to inject some meaning and enjoyment into your life. If you played a sport in high school but opted not to play in college, perhaps you could get involved with that sport on the club or intramural level. This will allow you to meet new people, exercise, and have some fun—providing three antidotes to the slump in one shot.

"The secret to avoiding the Sophomore Slump is breaking away from your routines and trying new things," Dave suggests. "People get so caught up in their schedules that they forget that there is a whole community out there that they have never reached out to. It could be as simple as taking a class you wouldn't usually take or maybe it is having a night every week where you get together and cook dinner with a group of people. Whatever it is for you, beginning to develop new and innovative twists that get you outside of your little bubble is a good way to change it up and keep things interesting and exciting."

If you're feeling down, there is no quicker remedy for that than exercise. Become involved with something that forces you to get out and move every day. Go to the gym every day. Start running, biking, or blading, and get hooked up with one of the many groups on campus that do the activity daily. Take up yoga, Pilates, or meditation. Go to the campus bookstore and pick up a book on diet and nutrition—and impose some changes.

Shake things up a bit. Don't allow yourself to descend into a rut.

And of course, there is no remedy for the slump like love. Have the courage to date. If you want to get to know someone, ask him or her to have a cup of coffee, catch a movie together on campus, or ask one of your roommates to set you up at the next "Screw Your Roommate" dance. Finding a love interest on campus, even for a short time, can really inject some new life into your experience.

The sophomore slump is real, but it is beatable. If you find yourself bummed out at any time during your sophomore year, see if it isn't because one or more of the aforementioned causes has taken root in your life. Root them out and get back on track.

Planning a Meaningful Sophomore Summer

The Brainstorming Workshop

> *The bee, from her industry in the summer,*
> *eats honey all the winter.*
>
> Proverb

We're ba-ack!"

We hope you found this workshop worthwhile last year in preparing for last summer. . . . If you did, we trust you'll take the time to work through your goals and the possibilities for harmonizing those goals again this year. But even if you blew us off last time, give it a try this year.

As you discovered last year, your college summers present you with a unique opportunity: a *looong* period of time—perhaps as much as fifteen weeks or, in other words, the equivalent of an *entire school semester*—away from academics. And we hope that last year you learned just how much, in terms of your goals, wants, needs, and desires, can be accomplished in this period of time.

What are you going to do with this incredible opportunity this summer?

Welcome to your sophomore summer brainstorming workshop—where you're going to come up with the antidote to a long, boring summer spent scooping ice cream at your local high school hangout, waitressing at the same club or restaurant where you worked when you were in high school, or otherwise doing the exact same things you did in the past.

You're in college now, and the world is your oyster. All it takes is a little bit of research, a little creativity, and a sense of adventure to ensure that your two remaining college summers are amazing in what they do for your goals, dreams, and desires.

Come along.

REVIEW YOUR GOALS FOR SOPHOMORE YEAR

The first thing you need to do is take a look at the work you did in your sophomore year goal-setting workshop and, if you followed our suggestions, at the eighteen or so "most important" goals you set for this year.

What did you identify as the things you hoped to accomplish during your sophomore year? How many of them have you actually accomplished so far? Which ones might be things you could work on this summer?

Yeah, yeah . . . we know that you're spending money like water in college and that even more than you did last summer, you really, really, *really* need to make money this summer. So did we. Yet despite these increasing financial pressures (which will be even worse next year—trust us), some of us figured out how to make money in really fun and interesting ways or in ways that furthered our academic, social, personal, or career goals (or a combination of these). You really *can* do both at the same time. Many of us did.

We want you to be one of us.

So think about what you had hoped to accomplish during your sophomore year and about which of those things might be worthwhile summer pursuits.

Explore Your Academic Interests

What have you learned about your academic interests this year? Chances are, you chose a major this year. Are there possible careers you might want to explore this summer? For example, if you chose to major in poli sci with an eye on working for a policy think tank, getting into politics, or applying to law school sometime after graduation, might there be something you could do this summer that would further illuminate that career path? Could you intern for a senator or member of Congress in Washington, D.C., doing research, shaping policy decisions, writing policy memoranda, or answering constituent letters and phone calls? Paid jobs are available doing such things, but even if you had to volunteer, you could further your career goals by doing so and then work part-time doing whatever to pay the bills. Even if all you do is deskwork, you will be making important contacts and spending your time in furtherance of your interests and goals.

If you chose a major, do you know of a particular professor in that major whose work sounds interesting to you? Maybe someone with whom you might someday take an independent study, or whom you might use as your senior thesis adviser? Is this person hiring a research assistant for the summer? Even if he or she isn't, there might be other professors in the department who have books coming out or important articles in process that need research help. Again, this is a great way to forward your goals and interests while making money at the same time.

Are there any prerequisite courses that you might want to get out of the way during the summer to help advance your academic career? Perhaps you have longed to study one course intensively, maybe a science or a topic in literature, without being distracted by a bunch of other courses. Does your college or university allow you to take that course intensively over the summer? If it does, might you do that, sublet an apartment with a friend or two over the summer, *and* pick up a part-time job in the evenings or during the day on the weekends to pay the freight and make some dough?

Did you crush the SAT? Could you offer private tutoring in the city of your choice—or work for the Princeton Review or Kaplan and at the same time explore a city or place that interests you? These organizations have offices in foreign cities too, so don't limit yourself to the United States!

Are you thinking of taking your junior year or at least a semester abroad? If you are, this is your last chance to *really* master the native language of that country before you get there. Perhaps a summer studying the language is the way to go. You could do this during the day by taking the language as a single course, whether on campus, at your local college, or even on CD-ROM, and make money doing whatever else you want to do in your spare time. Again—you'd be furthering your goals *and* making money.

Or if you are *truly* adventurous, maybe you and a friend or two could just up and leave for that country right now—and work *there* during your sophomore summer in advance of your upcoming semester or year abroad. Lots and lots of our friends did all sorts of interesting things—working on farms, building houses, working in the retail, restaurant, and entertainment businesses—in foreign countries. By doing this, you'd be making money, learning a foreign language, *and* seeing the world all at once.

Sure beats a long summer measuring feet at Stride-Rite or stocking shelves at Home Depot, doesn't it?

Explore Your Extracurricular Interests

Like music? Are you proficient in an instrument or in voice such that you could make a bunch of money teaching at an upscale summer tourist destination, such as Nantucket, the Hamptons, or the Outer Banks? If you are a huge fan of a particular band or musical artist who is touring this summer, have you given any thought to trying to get a job as a roadie or T-shirt salesperson with the band? Life on the road is full of adventures . . .

Are you a varsity athlete? What about offering one-on-one skills lessons in a sport like golf, tennis, soccer, or basketball at one of those tourist spots, where well-heeled parents are more than willing to spend money to help their kids develop skills?

Explore Your Social Interests

If you determined that you want to try to become more social, you could take a summer job somewhere new, away from your hometown, where you will be *forced* to be social—working as a concierge at an inn or hotel somewhere, working as a waiter or waitress in a crowded tourist spot, leading tours of your college campus, or doing *anything* that will force you to speak in front of people and interact with strangers. Feeling comfortable in new social settings is a learned skill. If it is one you want to improve, dedicate some time to practicing it. Note that if you work as a waiter or a waitress for *this* reason, you are making money and advancing one of your goals at the same time.

Explore Your Interests in Travel, the Outdoors, or Physical Development

Do you love the outdoors and want to become more skilled in this area? Perhaps you could make some money this summer working as a national forest ranger or a fire monitor in a remote wilderness location, or working on a trail crew or for any of a number of wilderness preservation societies that are always looking for part-time summer help on specific projects.

If money is less of an object, might you want to combine your love of the outdoors with a spiritual quest or an effort to really get back in shape, by hiking part of the Appalachian Trail or the Continental Divide or any other part of the country?

If money isn't an issue, might you want to explore taking an NOLS or Outward Bound course to sharpen your skills and to mature and grow as a person? Or might you want to find a cheap airline ticket and travel to a remote international location, such as Peru, Argentina, Africa, or the Himalayas, to do some trekking or other adventuring? You can *actually do* these things for not a lot of money if you do some research and advance planning, share living costs with a friend or two, or "rough it" by living in tents or hostels.

If you identified working on your physical body as a goal, maybe you want to use part of this summer to train for a marathon or a triathlon or simply to become a better runner, biker, swimmer, hiker, tennis player, or whatever. Obviously, this goal can be worked on practically anywhere—and can be combined with just about any other goal at the same time.

Explore Your Interest in Politics or Administration

Is this a campaign year? Could you hook up with a political campaign as a policy analyst, speechwriter, advance person, researcher, campaign worker, or media adviser, or in any of a virtually unlimited number of other capacities?

Do you love your college and have visions of becoming an admissions officer someday? If so, a summer working in the admissions office as an interviewer is a common first step to that popular post.

Are you interested in a social issue that is addressed by a particular local, state, regional, or national agency? Might you want to work there this summer to explore your interest in the subject?

WHAT I DID ON MY SUMMER VACATION

"I stayed on campus at M.I.T. the summer after my sophomore year," Erik recalled, "and worked in my dorm making a very high hourly wage doing menial work in a position affectionately known as 'grunge.' It was essentially a dorm maintenance position, as the dorm turns into a hotel of sorts over the summer. A team of four to six students remain on staff for forty hours a week to serve as glorified housekeepers for the guests of the dorm. So that was me.

"When those housekeeping duties were fulfilled, we performed maintenance and repair functions throughout the building. Again, it was as basic a summer job as was humanly possible on the M.I.T. campus, but it paid very well and a few of my friends were staying to do the same thing, so I acquiesced. Of course, I would not at all consider this a summer spent wisely, nor would I recommend that *you* work any job known as 'grunge' during *your* sophomore summer.

"Instead, I would strongly recommend that you seek a relevant internship or apprenticeship within your field of interest, even if it means having to work for free. The experience you will get and the contacts you will develop, along with your ability to impress your superiors by working hard even though you are working for free, is extremely valuable if you are looking to set yourself up."

"I left West Point at the end of my sophomore year," Aaron noted. "That summer was a major transition time for me. I needed to take time to regroup and figure out what I wanted and what my next step was going to be, so I got a job as a carpenter, and at the same time, worked on transferring to UMass Amherst. It was a summer well spent because I used it to reevaluate how things were going in my life and I used the time to set goals for myself and to begin taking the steps to achieve those goals. I think the most effective and valuable way to spend your summers in the college years is to use them to constantly examine your life and how happy you are and to use the built-in breaks to make any necessary changes."

"I waitressed at a restaurant back out in Wyoming," Carolyn said, "but I wish that I had spent the summer more wisely. I should have used the summer to explore potential career options either through volunteer work, an internship, or something of the sort in a field I might have been interested in pursuing as a career. This summer was a wasted opportunity for me."

As you are seeing, sophomore summer is a kind of netherworld. You're not yet an upperclassman focused on "what comes next," but you're not still an underclassman who can claim naivety and inexperience either. And the result is that a lot of us got caught up in this indecision and failed to take advantage of what might have been a valuable learning opportunity.

"I took the low road, too," Zoe admits. "Perhaps as an extension of my Sophomore Slump, I procrastinated on deciding what to do for the summer, and at the last minute, made a weak decision. I had a job interview scheduled for a position working with migrant farm workers doing translating and support activities with a nonprofit. This fit in perfectly with a lot of my interests and skills and would undoubtedly have been an opportunity to learn a lot and make some good contacts. Inexplicably, the morning of the interview, I called and cancelled, and later that week moved to a resort town in Maine to waitress. Although I made good money waitressing, I wasn't very happy or fulfilled. Worse, I was plagued with the sense of having copped-out and missed a great opportunity. The silver lining was that I recognized what a lame series of decisions I had made and I don't think I've made the same mistake since."

"So," you may now be wondering . . . "did *any* of the mentors actually do something that furthered more than their goals to make money during their sophomore summers?"

Well, we do have one winner—although his experience ended up driving him in another direction!

"I did a Summer Undergraduate Research Fellowship (SURF) at Cal Tech," Tom said. "Although it was a very good experience, the fact that I didn't go into chemistry might make it seem like a wasted endeavor. But it wasn't at all!

"For better or for worse, it would be smart to get deeper, hands-on experience, and do something to help you decide on a possible career choice during the summer after your sophomore year. This is a good time to do this because on the one hand, you've gained enough exposure to and experience in a certain field to make such an experience meaningful, but on the other hand there is still enough time should you opt to change course, as I did."

And then, there is my story.

As I headed into my sophomore summer, I was mired in an incredible Sophomore Slump. I was taking a bunch of premed classes that I absolutely *hated*, I was miserable as a biology major, I was slipping out of shape, and I was determined to figure out what the hell I wanted to do with my life before any more of my college career slipped by. I had discovered a love of psychology, but didn't know enough about it, as

I had only recently discovered it and had taken only two courses (both of which I loved). So I decided to bite the bullet and spend the summer in New Haven to determine, once and for all, whether or not I *really* wanted to go to medical school.

How?

I enrolled in the obligatory Organic Chemistry and laboratory summer course at Yale that I would have otherwise had to take during the regular school year (when I knew there were countless other courses I would rather be taking); shared an apartment (and costs) with a roommate and good friend of mine who was doing research at Yale-New Haven Hospital that summer; did some tutoring to pay the freight; resolved to run every day; and promised myself that if I was still miserable at the end of the summer, it would be a sign that I didn't want to go to medical school—and that I should choose a different major and a different direction in my life.

So what happened?

The summer absolutely, totally, and unequivocally sucked.

I eked out a B in organic chemistry, but hated every day of it and, to be frank, never really understood much of it. Concepts like acid-base reactions and chirality still make me wake up in cold sweats more than a decade later. I did run every day, and by doing so managed to get back into really good shape. And in a state of complete and utter despair one night in late July, having already decided that I was done with Orgo, done with premed, done with *any* class that met on Science Hill, and couldn't *wait* for the summer to be over—I caught a rerun of a television show (ABC-TV's *Life Goes On*) that gave me the idea that would become my junior project, my senior thesis, my ticket to a year off traveling the country after graduation, and the genesis of my career as a writer.

All in one night.

And all because I had intentionally and purposefully put myself into a position to really examine what the hell I was doing with my life.

I wish for each of you the opportunity to do the same thing . . . whatever that may be for you. Because as much as my sophomore summer sucked, it was the turning point between the life of confusion and dissatisfaction that had characterized my first two years at Yale and two of the most amazing years in college anyone could ever ask for.

More on that later.

BRAINSTORM

So now that you've had a chance to review your goals and interests and to kick-start your imagination, it's time to brainstorm. What is it that you want to accomplish with your sophomore summer? Grab a pen or pencil, haul out your trusty

Campus Confidential workbook, and list a bunch of ideas. Then rejoin us to ensure that you actually take *action* with respect to these ideas.

Okay. Now look at the ideas you brainstormed, pick four or five of them, and put them in an order of priority from highest (1) to lowest (4 or 5) by just writing a number in a circle next to them. Go ahead, do it now.

PUTTING IT ALL TOGETHER

Now I want you to think really creatively here. How could you accomplish three, four, or all five of these goals at the same time in the same summer? And how amazing do you think you would feel if you could actually pull this off?

Let's Look at an Example

Suppose you identified the following as your sophomore year summer goals: (1) making money, (2) furthering your knowledge in your new major (art history), (3) traveling, and (4) becoming fluent in a foreign language. What could you possibly do with your sophomore summer that would make you feel fulfilled and would further the pursuit of your goals?

Obviously, procrastinating about this decision and then defaulting to working for a college painting company in your home town of Albany, Georgia, might make you some money, but you won't learn much about art history (unless you *really* stretch the definition), won't advance your goal to travel (you could have at *least* gotten out of Georgia to do this), and won't help with your fluency in anything except profanity when you're up on a ladder in mid-July in 100-degree heat surrounded by mosquitoes.

So get creative. What if you got a job working as a docent, security guard, or gift-shop clerk at the Louvre? Sure, unless you landed the docent job, your work would be pretty boring—but so too would be painting houses. You *would,* however, have unlimited access to the Louvre (where you could *easily* spend an entire summer) and be living in Paris, immersing yourself in the French language and culture. Now, instead of meeting a single goal, you'd be addressing all four of your priorities in a single job in a single summer.

How good would that make you feel?

Not an art history major, you say? Okay. Let's do it for another major.

Let's say you're a psychology major with the same interests. In asking around the department, you discover that one of your favorite professors is starting a new study of the origins of love with a colleague at the University of Rome. Your professor needs a research assistant to coordinate the development of the instruments for the study, the translation of those instruments from Italian to English and English to Italian, and the initial trials of those instruments on Italian university students in summer session. Bingo. You apply for and get the job (because it is in perfect harmony with your goals), and you spend the summer getting paid by your professor's grant to crisscross the Atlantic and spend part of your summer in Italy, speaking Italian and gaining invaluable experience in your major.

Either of these experiences would allow you to meet all four of your stated sophomore summer goals. And there are countless other jobs that would do it too.

NOW DO SOME RESEARCH

So you've established your goals, thought about ways to make a few of them work together, and brainstormed a bunch of possibilities, to produce the blueprint for an immensely satisfying sophomore summer.

Now, armed with this blueprint, hop on the Internet and head on over to your college career planning and placement office to find the ideal position for you.

Yes, all this will take some effort. But the payoff will be well worth the time you put in.

PART FOUR

Considerations for Junior Year

Halfway Home

The Midpoint Assessment and Junior Year Goal-Setting Workshop

Ordinary people think merely of spending time.
Extraordinary people think of using it.

Anonymous

So you've reached the midway checkpoint of your college career. How does it feel? Are you happy with where you are, or are you still drifting around looking for direction?

By the beginning of your junior year, you should be committed to a major, and you should have made at least some rudimentary decisions about where your life may be headed after college. If you are planning to go to medical school straight out of college, you'll need to have your basic premed requirements completed by the end of this year so that you can begin your MCAT preparation in earnest during the spring term. If law school is in your future, you'll need to make plans to prepare for the LSAT this spring. If you're hoping to get a job out of college, but don't know what that job is, this is the year you familiarize yourself with your career services office and all that it offers.

"But wait a minute," you say. "How did we get here so quickly?"

Remember at the beginning of the book, where I told you that your college career would fly by and that sooner, rather than later, you'd find yourself facing important life choices that you wouldn't feel prepared to make?

Welcome to that time. That time is now.

There is, of course, an off-ramp to escape this madness . . . and for many of us, it was clearly the right decision to take that exit and park awhile. That exit is called "time off after college," and there is a whole chapter later in this book (Chapter 43) devoted to just that. But the bottom line for our purposes here is this: if you aren't going to be taking time off between college and *whatever* it is you're planning to do after graduation, you need to start getting your house in order *right now*.

Yes, it seems ridiculously early. But that's the reality . . . and getting your house in order is what the junior year goal-setting workshop will help you accomplish.

We're hoping that if you've been following along with the chronological advice we've been providing so far, you have kept weekly or even daily tabs on your eighteen or so goals from freshman year and have either achieved all of them or actively determined to abandon some of them. Similarly, if you kept weekly or even daily tabs on your eighteen or so goals from sophomore year, you should by now have achieved most or all of those. We also hope that setting and achieving those goals last year empowered you and armed you with the information, direction, and resolve you needed to avoid getting caught in the Sophomore Slump. It's now time to do it all over again—to say goodbye to the experimentation of the first half of college and to zero in on some new and critically important goals for the second half of college and the coming year in particular. These goals, believe it or not, will begin to affect your postcollege plans, so part of this process will involve figuring out, right now, what those plans are.

Once again, we've divided the workshop into six categories: (1) academic and career goals, (2) social goals, (3) extracurricular goals, (4) physical goals, (5) financial goals, and (6) spiritual goals.

For now, do *not* look back on the goals you set last year. You want to come to this experience with a fresh perspective, motivated by what drives you now—not what drove you a year ago. The differences you see will be instructive. We'll send you back to examine those differences later. But for now, don't cheat.

Once again, remember not to censor yourself. Just write down everything that comes to mind. You'll have a chance to go back through the ideas later to decide on your priorities, and we *will* cross-reference your list from last year to catch anything you didn't complete last year that is still relevant to you. For now, though, you just want to dump your pent-up thoughts down on paper. As you did last year, try to keep writing in each category for at least five minutes.

Let's begin.

YOUR JUNIOR YEAR ACADEMIC AND CAREER GOALS

So what have you learned about yourself academically during the first half of your college career?

What courses have you taken and loved, and what classes have you had trouble dragging yourself to attend every time? What distinctions can you draw from those experiences? Did you love your large lecture classes or hate them? Or did your enjoyment depend on the subject area or the professor? What introductory courses or subjects did you enjoy that you might want to explore more intensively? Did you hear about any other subjects that your roommates or friends explored that you might want to check out?

Unless you are exploring a new area of interest, this is the year you will be leaving the large survey courses behind and starting to take smaller, more specialized classes, particularly in your major field of study. At many colleges and universities, it is also the year you first begin to qualify for certain seminar courses open only to upperclassmen or you first have the option to take independent study courses one-on-one with a professor in an area of interest to you. Have you yet encountered a professor with whom you might want to work in that capacity? Have you encountered a particularly interesting academic question or subject that might be the impetus for such an arrangement?

This is also the year you may be spending a semester or even the full year abroad. If you are going abroad for some or all of your junior year, or perhaps are already abroad as you are completing this activity, what are your goals for your time overseas? What do you want to accomplish? What do you want to learn, do or see? Where do you want to go? What experiences would you like to have?

How are you doing with your core curricular requirements, as we first discussed in Chapter 11? The last thing you want to do is forget about your math requirement or your foreign language or science requirements, and end up having to jam them in during your senior year. Pull out your *Campus Confidential* workbook and confirm for yourself that you will have fulfilled all your core requirements by the end of this year.

What possible careers do you find turning around in your head? Which ones have you now discounted? What steps will you need to take academically to begin setting yourself up for a trial run in the field you are now considering? Get these thoughts down on paper.

If you still find yourself undecided or completely without direction, it is now time to take more serious action to do something about that—because time has ceased to be on your side. Have you consulted the available resources on campus to help you think about potential career paths? Have you talked to your academic adviser? To your dean of students? To your academic dean? To a counselor in your college or university's career planning office? If you have not yet decided on a major, or if you still have no idea whatsoever what you want to do with your life after graduation, now is the time to take some meetings and explore the resources available to you.

Are you into art or music? Did you want to study an instrument or learn to sing, draw, paint, or sculpt? Or learn more about art and art history? Don't forget about courses outside your major.

Did you uncover any noticeable academic weaknesses during the first half of college? What about strengths? What kinds of skills do you want to continue to develop or master during the second half of college? Do you want to learn to be a more analytical writer? A more creative writer? Do you want to become a more careful reader? Or just someone who can read more or for longer without tiring?

Do you want to learn to be a better note taker or develop more critical listening skills so that you can get more out of your lectures? Do you want to learn how to be better organized? Remember that the more you practice a skill, the more you'll own it.

Have you established effective study habits during the first half of college? Were you well prepared for exams, or did you find yourself cramming at the last minute? Are there any goals you want to set about your study methods? What about papers? Have you been writing them far enough in advance to have time to edit and polish, or were they last-minute jobs delivered at the deadlines with no time to spare? Is there anything you want to do with respect to time management or procrastination this year?

Finally, junior year is the time to begin thinking about a thesis topic if your major requires you to write a senior thesis. As we will discuss in Chapter 36, if you can identify areas of interest early on during your junior year, you may be able to write a seminar paper junior year that can serve as a launching pad for your senior thesis—which can make your life much easier and also allows you to really explore an area of academic interest in depth. Have you identified any such areas of interest in your major yet? Brainstorm for some ideas.

What academic things do you want to get out of this year and out of the second half of college generally? Write down everything that you'd like to try, and everything that you'd still like to explore this year, or at least before you graduate.

You have five minutes. Keep your pen moving.

Go!

If you've reached the end of your five minutes and you want to keep going, by all means do so. If you've written a good list of at least ten or twelve items and you've listed everything you can think of right now that qualifies as an academic goal for this year or for the rest of college generally, then go ahead and move on to the next section.

During the next day or two, more things will come to mind. As they do, be sure to add them to the list. Don't just let them wander into and out of your consciousness. Capture your thoughts so that you can turn them into goals!

YOUR JUNIOR YEAR SOCIAL GOALS

Have you found a good group of friends? Have you met the kinds of people you wanted to meet? Has your group of friends developed some habits that disempower you such that you might want to limit your exposure to them? Are you dating someone, either on campus or somewhere else? Do you want to be? Maybe now is the time either to approach that person you've been thinking about or at least to be open to the idea of dating someone more seriously.

Consider whether you want to set any new goals or ground rules for your social interactions on campus this year. Has your social life been swallowing up your academic life, such that you need to rein it in this year and get serious about your studies? Or have you been so serious about your studies that you are spending too much time in the library and missing the broader experience of college? Remember that success in college is about balance. Is your life in balance?

If you are in a fraternity or a sorority, is it still adding value to your life socially, or has it been more of a drain or a bad influence? Do you want to continue your affiliation with your fraternity or sorority? Might you want to seek a leadership position in the organization?

Have you been making empowering or disempowering choices about drugs, alcohol, and sex? Do you need to think about a new approach to any of these things as you embark on your upperclass years?

Are there any other aspects of who you are or what you discovered about yourself last year or this past summer that you'd like to move front and center now? Do any of your attributes, characteristics, or interests need more expression than they had last year?

Write for at least five minutes, listing everything you'd like to try and everything you'd like to be socially this year.

Go!

EXTRACURRICULAR GOALS

This is the year that you make the transition from sampling a bunch of different extracurricular activities, or "dabbling," to making more serious commitments to the two or three things that you really like. What are those things? What activities or organizations have meant something to you during the past two years, such that you are now ready to make a more serious commitment to them?

Did you make a varsity team? If you did, is it still meaningful to you, or are you finding the time commitment, the travel, and the impingement on the rest of your college calendar to be too much? Does it look like you're going to get to play a lot, or are you going to be primarily a bench player? There is nothing that says you *have* to continue to play your varsity sport—and yes, that's true even if you have an athletic scholarship. There is more than one way to pay for college, and if you are going to mortgage a significant part of your experience to play a sport you don't enjoy anymore, you should at least consider your alternatives.

If you were an athlete in high school or prep school, but either did not make the varsity or gave up your sport when you got to college, is there a sport you'd like to participate in again, or to learn on a social level? If so, perhaps now is the time to get involved with your school's club sports or intramurals.

Did you see a student play or a student film last year? Is working in one of these productions, either behind the scenes or out in front, enticing to you?

Have you explored your campus's various takes on politics or religion? Interested? If this is an election year, perhaps you'd like to get involved in a political campaign.

Thinking of switching religions, exploring a new religion, or simply becoming more devoted to your own? Check out the local congregations or groups.

What about working in the community? Community outreach is a great way to develop career ideas while doing good at the same time. Could you tutor at an inner-city high school or serve as a mentor to a child who needs one? Might you want to get involved in a volunteer project building or renovating housing for the neediest members of your community? Perhaps you might want to run for political office? What kind of community activities might you want to get involved in this year?

Want to interview prospective applicants, give campus tours, or help run your college's recruiting effort? If you love your college or university, this is a good way to plug into the energy, get connected to the individuals who run the place, and meet and talk with prospective applicants.

Remember, you're now at the midway point of your college career. It is a good time to take stock of where you are and where you hope to go socially and with your extracurricular involvements. Are you overcommitted and finding yourself unable to give any activity your full attention? If so, now is a good time to evaluate what each of your activities lends to your life in college and to decide which ones you're going to commit to for the next two years.

You have five minutes.

Go!

YOUR JUNIOR YEAR PHYSICAL GOALS

For many of us, junior year brought the first real understanding that college was having a negative effect on us physically.

Things definitely tend to get a little out of control during the first couple of years of college. So think of this section as your checkup in that regard—and chances are, you probably have some work to do to get back in shape.

First of all, check in on your diet. Are you eating enough? Are you eating too much? Has your weight dropped or ballooned significantly? Are you eating healthily most days, or does your diet feature mainly pizza and beer and whatever you pick up at the campus quick-mart? What do you want to do about that this year? Maybe it is as easy as having a salad from the salad bar every day and taking a piece of fruit with you to class after breakfast and lunch. Maybe you have more to do than that. Be sure to write down some dietary goals for the coming year.

Another thing that tends to get lost during the first couple of years of college is exercise. Chances are, if you're not an athlete and you weren't already committed to a regular program of exercise before you got to college, you're not exercising. But you ought to be! At no other time in your life will you have as much flexibility and opportunity to commit yourself to a regular exercise program as you have right now. Might you want to set some goals in that area for this year? Do you want to take up mountain biking, rollerblading, or running? Your college or university no doubt has clubs or informal groups that organize these activities daily. Do you want to do some research to find one?

What about taking a weightlifting class, taking up yoga or meditation, learning a martial art, or learning to play tennis, golf, squash, or racquetball recreationally? Any of these activities would add a necessary physical component to your day. Do you need to do some research to find out what is available? Do you need to set up a schedule or make arrangements with a friend or a roommate to hold you to a workout regimen?

How have you been sleeping? Are you on a fairly regular sleep schedule, or do you find yourself up until all hours of the night socializing, playing poker, surfing the Net, or working? All-nighters and nights with very little or irregular sleep take a toll on your immune system, bring down your mood, and make it harder to concentrate and perform at your optimum level. That's not to say we haven't all pulled them! Nevertheless, you should work hard to get enough sleep so that you don't become run down this year.

What are some things you might do to ensure that you are getting enough rest? Maybe it's as simple as taking an hour-long power nap in the afternoons after class or trying to contain the nights you stay out until 3 A.M. to Fridays and Saturdays and to give yourself Sunday morning to catch up on sleep.

What else do you want to do for yourself physically this year? Do you feel alone or depressed, such that seeking out a few hours of counseling from your campus health center might be constructive? Have you noticed any other physical changes in your body, your energy level, or your mood that might warrant a checkup at the Department of Undergraduate Health?

Remember that your junior year is a year of heavy workloads and serious personal growth. Staying physically active, fit, energized, and healthy this year will be critical to optimum performance.

Spend the next five minutes setting some goals in these areas for this year. Go!

YOUR JUNIOR YEAR FINANCIAL GOALS

Finances are another place in which things tend to get a little out of control during the first couple of years of college. Chalk it up to an educational experience, but get your spending under control now, before things really get out of hand.

Chances are, you've now discovered that college is even more expensive than you thought it would be—and that opportunities to spend money are around every turn. Obviously, you take this trip only once, and you don't want to deprive yourself of *everything* in the name of financial responsibility, . . . but you also don't need to buy every new CD that comes out or drop a hundred bucks a week on clothes. What financial guidelines do you want to set for yourself this year?

Are you on a budget? Should you be? Have you now realized that you really *do* need to draw one up so that you'll know what kind of plan you need to stick to?

Are you on a work-study plan again this year, or for the first time? Have you figured out how you're going to fit those hours into your week so as to minimize the disruption of your academic and social schedule?

Do you want to get a part-time job somewhere to make some extra cash? Maybe you could tutor someone in one of your strong subjects, or become a teaching assistant. What are your other marketable skills?

Don't be afraid to think outside the box here—but if you find yourself with a lot of short-term credit card debt because of some bad choices you made during the first half of college, you really do need to do something about that. Don't let that debt grow and hang around your neck like an albatross for the next several years. Find a way to work it off and get rid of it.

Have you closely examined your cell phone plan and other monthly expenses to make sure that you are optimizing your expense-to-use ratios? Is there a better plan that you ought to be using?

Do you really need to have your car on campus? If so, might you want to work out some sort of car-sharing arrangement that would produce some additional income for you, or at least help defray the expenses of insurance, gas, and parking fees? If you do pursue this kind of arrangement, be sure that you have proper insurance on the car and that anyone who uses your car is insured as well.

Take the next five minutes and set out your financial goals for your junior year. Remember that managing your finances requires you to play offense and defense. Think creatively.

Go!

YOUR JUNIOR YEAR SPIRITUAL GOALS

As we've mentioned before, junior year is a time of intense personal development. Gone is the newness and carefree feeling of being an underclassman; in its place is the growing sense that "real life" is looming and that this is the year you'll need to start making decisions about that. For many of us who still lacked a clear vision or purpose for our lives, junior year became a time of even deeper introspection and varying levels of concern ranging from mild stress to serious depression.

And for many of us, connecting to some sort of spirituality during these times of transition was very comforting.

Again, spirituality does *not* necessarily mean religion, and I am not suggesting that you need to find religion in order to find vision or purpose. For some people, though, connecting to their religion can provide the necessary grounding and direction.

Maybe for you, being spiritual means taking a few hours each week to practice yoga or meditation. Maybe it means taking a long walk in the woods one morning a week to be alone with your thoughts and to reflect. Maybe being spiritual means reading introspective writings or listening to music and letting your thoughts wander away from the mundane and the everyday. Maybe it means volunteering to help the less fortunate at an area shelter or soup kitchen, or working at an animal shelter, and reminding yourself that although you may lack vision, others lack much more than that.

Whatever spirituality means to you, do not underestimate its power to enrich your life. In your campus world, where people will often seem very id-driven or self-absorbed, maintaining some perspective can be really helpful. And whether that means you'd like to get to church or synagogue once a week or simply that you want to read a thought-provoking book for pleasure this semester, don't forget to pay some attention to your spiritual side. You'll be amazed at how refreshed and centered it will make you feel.

Think about a few ways to nurture your spiritual side during your junior year and write them down.

Resist the urge to just dismiss thoughts about this topic out of hand.

Think about it for a minute and jot down a few ideas.

Go!

NOW WHAT DO I DO WITH ALL OF THIS?

If you're still with us, you should now have an abundance of good information written down to help ensure that your junior year is as productive and satisfying as you hope it will be.

But you're not done yet.

If you've followed our directions, you should have written down a stream-of-consciousness list in each of the six areas. We hope you didn't censor your thoughts as you were writing. If you didn't, your lists may be quite long.

You also have your lists of goals from freshman and sophomore years, and now is the time to look back at the lists you made in each of these areas and take stock. Which goals did you achieve, and which ones did you not achieve? Think about the ones you did achieve: *How* did you make them happen? What specific things did you do to make sure you achieved those goals? How can you replicate that activity to help you achieve your new goals?

Really take the time to think about this. Knowing what motivates you to get things done and what specific actions lead you to accomplishment is immensely valuable, because they can be replicated in any number of scenarios. So think about why and how you achieved the goals you did and write down any distinctions you can draw.

Okay!

Now go through your lists from freshman and sophomore years again, to see if there are any unmet goals that you think are still worthy of your attention this year. Maybe there are some things from these lists that you forgot about, but still think are important enough to add back in to your junior year lists. Do that audit now and update your junior year lists accordingly—then come back here to continue.

Do it now. Don't just keep reading. Go ahead, we'll wait.

All right.

You now need a way to manage all those ideas you've recorded and to go through them and cull the ones that are most critical to you—to choose the ones that you think will give you the most bang for your buck, so to speak.

Here's what you're going to do next.

As you did last year, go back through each list and read what you've written down. Think about each item and see how it resonates with you. Some of the ideas will get you fired up as soon as you think about them. Others, upon reflection, may not seem that important or that exciting after all.

It's all good. That's part of the goal-setting process.

Go through each list and pick the three things from that area that you are absolutely committed to accomplishing this year or, if you want to think more long term, during the rest of your college career. Pick the three things that you feel are most critical to making your experience a success—three that would make you feel great about yourself if you were to accomplish them.

Circle those items in each list.

Feeling really ambitious? Want to pick four or five? That's fine, . . . but don't feel that you have to. You want to keep the number of goals manageable—so that you'll actually follow through and complete them. Three in each category is fine. More in some categories and less in others is fine too, but make sure you have at least one goal in each category to maintain some balance.

Remember: pick the ideas from each list that excite you the most or that, on reflection, seem to make the most sense or to be the most important.

Go ahead and make your choices now.

ONE MORE STEP . . .

Okay.

You should now have chosen somewhere around eighteen goals for your junior year or perhaps for college in general.

But you're not done yet.

Setting goals is one thing. But as we noted earlier, a goal without a plan is just a wish.

So now, for each one of these goals, we want you to articulate at least one very good reason why it is *essential* for you to follow up and to achieve that goal during your junior year. Make sure your reason compels you—that it lights a fire under you and propels you toward meeting the goal.

Articulating a powerful rationale makes it far less likely that you will simply forget about these goals once you conclude this exercise and close this chapter. So really take the time to do this well. Amend and edit your reasons. Choose powerful language and drill down into the real motives compelling you to achieve these goals.

Create a master list of each of your goals and your rationale for achieving it, and keep it somewhere where you can refer to it often.

Tape your list of goals up to the wall over your desk or on the mirror in your closet. If you don't have that kind of privacy, keep it in your desk drawer or your day planner—but refer to it at least once a week. Daily is even better.

If you did this last year, you've no doubt reaped the benefits of the process. If you're starting now, do this for your entire first semester, and we bet you'll be hooked for life. You won't believe the progress you'll make.

Congratulations on completing the junior year goal-setting workshop!

ADDITIONAL RESOURCES

Robbins, Anthony. *Awaken the Giant Within*. New York: Free Press, 1992.

Robbins, Anthony. *Personal Power* (audio series). Robbins Research International. (www.anthonyrobbins.com)

Robbins, Anthony. *RPM Planner Kit* (time management system). (www.anthonyrobbins.com)

Robbins, Anthony. *Unlimited Power: The New Science of Personal Achievement*. New York: Free Press, 1997.

The Junior Year (or Semester) Abroad

The world is a book, and those who
do not travel read only a page.

Saint Augustine

There are two primary schools of thought with respect to the junior year abroad. Some students swear by it, noting that an international experience is a critical element of a college education; that it allows you to really master a language while steeping in the life, ideas, and politics of a culture other than that of the United States; and that it produces a measurable degree of maturity and perspective that students who don't go abroad simply don't have. The other school of thought on the year abroad is that there will be plenty of time to travel and experience life overseas, including schooling if desired, but that taking a semester or a year away from your life in college is simply not a trade-off worth making.

Obviously, deciding whether or not to spend a semester or year abroad is going to be a personal choice, driven by your own wants and needs and your own feelings about the experience you are having on your college campus. For this reason, most of this chapter will be devoted simply to mentor advice on the pros and cons that animated their decisions to go or not to go abroad during the academic year. There are, however, a few housekeeping issues to get out of the way before we do that.

SUBJECTS FOR CONSIDERATION

If you are interested in going abroad, you will need to do a lot of work and advance planning to ensure that your time overseas is both successful and *recognized* by your home college or university. To that end, there are a few important things to consider.

Acquire Language Proficiency

First, you should be aware that most study abroad programs that award course credit for your work will require you to have taken two years of college-level instruction in the foreign language in which your curriculum will be delivered overseas—or to otherwise be able to demonstrate proficiency in that language. Thus, if a year abroad is in your college plans, you must think ahead and ensure that you attain proficiency in the language of your host country no later than the end of your sophomore year in college.

Arrange for Course Credit

You should realize that most colleges and universities have a Junior Year Abroad Committee that oversees students' applications to various overseas programs, coordinates arrangements, and makes determinations about the portability of course credit from those programs back to your original school. If you are interested in going abroad during your junior year, attend the information sessions provided by your college's JYA Committee and apprise yourself of the deadlines governing your application to foreign study programs. At most schools, interested students must actually apply to the JYA Committee for permission to go abroad, in addition to separately applying to the overseas program(s) they intend to attend. This application package will typically require the following: a generic application form and a personal statement outlining your proposed course of study, an authorization from the department head or director of undergraduate study in your major, a certification that you are carrying at least the designated minimum GPA to go overseas, proof of your proficiency in the language of your host country, and proof of acceptance into a program recognized by your college or university.

Financial Aid

If you are receiving financial aid, this money may or may not transfer to the program you are selecting for time abroad. Before you make any commitments, check in with your financial aid office or have your JYA Committee work with your financial aid office to assist you.

Passport and Immunizations

Before you will be allowed to go abroad, you will need to have an up-to-date passport and, for many countries, a schedule of your inoculations. If you are seriously considering time abroad, do not wait until the last minute to gather these required documents—as it can take six to eight weeks to get your passport back if it needs renewal.

Deciding Where to Apply

For those of you looking to go abroad in the fall term of your junior year, your applications to these programs are typically due in March of your sophomore spring. For those of you looking to go abroad in the spring term of your junior year, the application deadline is usually in mid-October of your junior year. This of course presupposes that you have already conducted your own independent research and identified and applied to the program(s) overseas that you would like to attend.

If you are wondering, at this point, how you are supposed to identify such programs . . . don't panic. Your college or university probably has a study abroad office (or something similar) that gathers reams of data on all the programs that your college will recognize for course credit. Approved study abroad programs typically fall into two categories: (1) programs sponsored by colleges and universities in the United States and (2) programs that involve your direct enrollment as a "visiting student" in a foreign university. We have compiled a list of resources at the end of this chapter to help get you started.

If you are interested in pursuing study abroad, attend one of the many information sessions that will be held on your college campus, and ask your dean or JYA Committee for the names of upperclassmen who studied abroad—preferably in the programs or at least in the country you are considering. Obviously, first-hand feedback is the best preparation for what to expect.

OUR THOUGHTS ON OUR TIME ABROAD

"I spent my entire junior year in Madrid, through the Tufts in Madrid Program," Carolyn explained. "I took half of my classes at a Spanish university and the other half of them at the Tufts in Madrid program with other American students from Tufts and Skidmore.

"I went abroad because I wanted to become truly fluent in Spanish. Going for the entire year was one of the smartest decisions I made in college. I became proficient in a foreign language by speaking it every day to native speakers, I learned about another culture, I learned about the United States through the perceptions of non-U.S. citizens, I gained confidence in my ability to adapt and take care of myself, and I had a *ton* of fun.

"I would advise anyone who wants to go abroad to be very careful about the program they choose," Carolyn continued. "The Tufts in Madrid Program had a well-deserved reputation for excellence. It was extremely well organized. All students lived with host families and took classes at both the university and at the Tufts program center. We had scheduled day and weekly trips to other parts of the country that were well-organized and highly educational. We also attended a number of lectures and cultural events organized by the program. Because this was a Tufts program, I did not have to worry about transferring course credit, as it was all done automatically. I have heard some horror stories from friends at other colleges and universities about the disorganization of their study-abroad programs, and the difficulties they had getting credits to transfer—so I would just caution you to work with your college or university to make the arrangements and be sure everything is in order before you leave campus at the end of sophomore year."

"I went to Aix-en-Provence in southern France," Jim explained. "I went through a Vanderbilt University program and studied French history, art history, the European union, and French language. I lived with a seventy-one-year-old widow and a French college student. It was a fantastic experience. I would, however, recommend that students going abroad try to avoid programs in which they will be spending a significant amount of time with other Americans, as I believe that lessens the utility of the experience."

Kevin had some specific advice for students considering going abroad for only one semester.

"If you are in a situation in which you are going abroad for one semester of your junior year *and* you are planning to live off campus, try to go abroad *first* semester," Kevin advised. "Leaving first semester means you miss the stress of finding an apartment, assembling roommates, finding furniture and kitchenware, and worst of all, finding a subletter come second semester and the summer. If your name is on the lease, you have to do all of that and many students end up paying a lot of cash they shouldn't have to pay.

"If you go abroad first semester, you will be returning to a great wide world of housing opportunities. Everybody will be looking desperately for someone to fill a vacant room in their off-campus apartment. You get your pick of the litter in terms of rooms, roommates, location and amenities, and when the semester is over, you're home free. No worries about the summer, about subletters, or anything else. You just walk away.

"As for actually going abroad, I went to London and had a wonderful time," Kevin said. "Going abroad is a great opportunity that should not be passed up. If you are going to a European country for your first-semester travels, though, I would recommend traveling early. England and the Mediterranean stay warm through November, but much of the continent gets unpleasantly cold by the end of October. It's a world of difference between Paris in November and Barcelona in November."

Other mentors went abroad at nontraditional times or to nontraditional places.

"Although junior fall is certainly the norm at Duke, I went abroad my sophomore spring," Chase noted. "There were a couple of major reasons for deciding to jump ship and go abroad a semester early. First, 'I had to see about a girl.' She was older, went to another school, and I wanted to be with her. Romance in Italy is pretty hard to beat. Second, as if that weren't enough, there were opportunities on campus that I wanted to take advantage of and could only do so if I remained for the year. I became the president of my a capella group, and was able to lay the groundwork to become the vice president of the student government. Both of these things were contingent on my being at school for the entirety of my junior year.

"I opted to go to the New York University Program in Florence, Italy. I wanted to be in an active city, have quality language courses, and make sure my credits would transfer. NYU fit all those criteria. I took an Italian language class, two Italian history courses, and a course on European law. The classes were interesting and the Italian lessons were helpful, but the value of my time abroad came outside the classroom. I had the opportunity to travel to Switzerland, Tunisia, Croatia, Slovenia, France, Germany, Greece, and all over Italy. Nearly every weekend, I hopped a train to a new Italian city.

"These adventures are where I truly learned to speak Italian. Being in a new town, looking for food and a bed and having to speak a foreign language is a bit of a sink-or-swim experience. I would not trade a day of my time abroad for any other day of my life. The experience was spectacular and invaluable."

"I went abroad in the second half of my sophomore year, too," Lyndsee said. "I went to Paris and studied French, French art, French literature, and French history. It was one of the best experiences of my life. I lived with a host family whom I now consider part of my immediate family. I made amazing memories and I think about my time there often, wishing I could do it over and over again.

"I chose not to spend as much time enjoying the Parisian night life as some of my classmates, choosing instead to spend a lot of time getting to know my host family and building a relationship with them. That is something that no one else in my program accomplished. I learned more about French culture in their home than I did in class or exploring the city on my own."

"I initiated an independent study in Beijing and Hong Kong during the *summer* after my sophomore year," Tiffany explained. "Because I had switched majors, I would not have been able to fulfill my curricular requirements if I had gone abroad for a whole semester. The project was a unique experience, as I traveled to both Beijing and Hong Kong where my professors engaged students in more active and spontaneous dialogue. We visited different media venues in both Beijing and Hong Kong. I was able to visit media institutions including TVB, Radio Free Asia, and CCTV. The intimate learning environment also served to revitalize a natural curiosity in my cultural heritage."

And finally, there was Dan's trip.

"I had enough AP credits from high school that I could graduate in seven semesters. I used the extra semester to take the junior spring of college off from classes and spent that time preparing for my research cruise in Antarctica in May. It was a once-in-a-lifetime opportunity to spend five weeks in Antarctica on an ice-breaker doing research. Who could say no to that?"

ADDITIONAL RESOURCES

www.iiepassport.com (Institute of International Education study abroad search engine and informational Web site)

www.studyabroad.com (study abroad search engine that collects data on programs for the semester and academic year, as well as summer programs, intensive language programs, intersession programs, and programs for short-term study or work abroad)

www.iie.org (Institute of International Education Web site—search for scholarships, awards, and grants)

http://travel.state.gov/passport (U.S. Department of State Web site with information regulating issuance and renewal of passports)

http://travel.state.gov/travel (U.S. Department of State Web site—click on "Studying Abroad" link in left column to bring up U.S. government advice on studying abroad, including any applicable travel warnings in place)

Looking Ahead
to Graduate School

School is like a lollipop.
It sucks until it is gone.

Anonymous

It seems like only yesterday that you went through the application process.

You're just hitting your stride.

You have half your college career still ahead of you.

So why in the world, you ask, are we already talking about graduate school?

The fact is, if you are committed to going straight to graduate school after college without taking any time off, you must begin the planning process at the start of your junior year.

Yes. Right now.

Trust us when we say this. The reality catches a *lot* of students by surprise and leads to a lot of stress, heartache, and unintended years off for those students who don't start the process on time.

Yeah, yeah . . . we know that you aren't yet sure whether or not you actually want to go to law school.

Or med school.

We know you haven't decided whether that Ph.D. in psychology is right for you. We know that despite your love for the subject matter, you haven't yet been able to figure out what you would actually *do* with a master's in American studies.

And we *know* you haven't figured out what you're going to do if you eventually want to earn an MBA, as getting into business school straight out of college and without any real-world business experience is a statistical improbability.

It's okay . . .

The reason we're tackling this subject early is for precisely those reasons. You need the appropriate lead time to actually *think* about these things before you get ambushed by application season. By then it will be too late to do any serious thinking about whether the degree or the program is right for you. You'll be too busy studying for the entrance exams, completing applications, and traveling the country interviewing to figure out whether that next great ladder you're about to climb is leaning against the right wall.

"The main thing I should have done differently was to look more carefully at what courses I needed to complete in order to get into (and out of!) grad school in a timely fashion," Zoe said. "I decided to go to nursing school but didn't actually bother to research what programs I wanted to apply to and what the prerequisites were until after my college graduation. As a result, I spent extra time and money taking some core classes through the University system here in Maine and while at Penn that I could just as well have completed while I was at Wellesley."

APPROACHING THE DECISION

The first thing you really need to decide is whether you actually *want* to go directly from college to graduate school, or whether you will want to take some time off in between to explore other interests, travel, or just decompress and reflect on what your college years have taught you about the world and your potential roles in it before you commit to your next journey. That decision is an intensely personal one—but one that nevertheless tends to be influenced by factors that many people experience. We'll look at a few of these factors here.

Countering the Will of Your Parents

The primary influence is likely to be the will of your parents.

"We never took any time off after college," they will argue. "You had four years of college to screw around and find yourself. It's time for you either to get your graduate degree or to go out and get a job and start earning some money."

Sound familiar?

Or how about this one: "If you don't go directly to med school [law school, grad school], you'll get bound up in something else in the world and you'll never go back." (To which we have to be restrained from yelling out, "*Yeah, so?*")

Or this one: "If you go now, we'll pay for it. If you take time off, though, you're on your own."

Whatever the argument used against you, remember one thing—and one thing only. It is *your* life, and this is *your* decision. Once you make the decision to apply to graduate school and you get in, the direction of your life will become much more certain and much more immutable. Each graduate school experience comes with an enormous set of commitments and a well-worn path of expectations that will consume your weekends, your vacations, and your summers.

There won't be any time to write a novel once you're in med school.

There won't be an opportunity to hike the Appalachian Trail, spend a summer (or longer) backpacking across Europe, or drive across the United States with your friends. You can't go back to your old job as a summer camp counselor, work in the Peace Corps, do Teach for America, try to make it with your rock band, or follow your dream to perform Shakespeare in summer stock theater.

When you commit to graduate school, you are setting your course for the future. And closing the doors to a lot of other things you've always wanted to do.

Are you ready for that?

If you *know* you're not, no amount of parental influence, pressure, or bribery should push you to the contrary decision. You need to *know* you are ready to go to graduate school. And you'll *know* when you know. If you're not charged up to spend the next four months holed up studying for the GMAT, MCAT, or LSAT, you're not ready.

"I would advise people to *not* rush into grad school," Carolyn warned. "I think it is valuable to gain some real world experience before going back to school."

Ignoring Your Peers

Familiar with lemmings, are you?

Lemmings are little half-blind rodents that burrow underground and blindly follow each other. In some places, entire families of lemmings are wiped out when the lead lemming goes right off a cliff and all of the others just follow that guy right off the same cliff without ever looking up.

Hmm . . .

So if seventeen of your friends have all decided to sign on to a two-year management consulting gig on Wall Street, . . . or your two best friends have decided to take the LSAT, . . . or your boyfriend has decided to apply to medical school . . .

That's right. It should make absolutely *no* difference to you.

Listen up. This is your *last* chance to get it right.

If you're not sure what you want to do for the rest of your life or you are haunted by a burning desire to do something "crazy" before you settle down, listen to those longings and page ahead to Chapter 43, where we'll take you through the thought processes and the justifications for taking some time off to do something else before you decide on a next step.

Recognize that the world is *full* of unhappy successful people—doctors who should have been teachers; lawyers who should have been writers; and middle managers, clawing their way up the corporate ladder, who would have been much happier taking their college rock band to the Jersey Shore for the summer in an effort to test the appeal of their music. All these people got to their junior or senior year and grabbed the ladder, propped it up against the wall, and just kept right on climbing.

And you guessed it—much later, they discovered that the ladder was propped up against the wrong wall.

Instead of ending up divorced and lying on a psychologist's couch in the throes of a midlife crisis twenty years from now, take the time to hear the call of your life and to answer it. Forget what you're *supposed* to do. Figure out what you *want* to do—and go do it.

Graduate school will *always* be there for you.

The only reason to continue with this chapter is if you are satisfied in your heart of hearts that you're ready to take the next step into your future.

Gathering Information

Even if you *think* you're ready to go off to law school, med school, business school, or grad school, don't just sign up for an LSAT, MCAT, or GMAT prep course and dive right in to your preparation. It is not enough to have simply taken your premed requirements, come from a long line of lawyers, or done well in your psychology major so far to justify a decision to go to med school, law school, or graduate school (respectively).

You need to actually *test* the hypothesis.

Taking you through that analysis for law school, medical school, business school, or graduate school is beyond the scope of this book. Fortunately for you, however, we can provide you with a direct handoff from here to our sister publications *Law School Confidential, Med School Confidential,* and *Business School Confidential.* Each of these books contains an entire section to help you test your readiness for each of these respective schools, along with interactive exercises to help you explore whether or not you would be better suited to take some time off first. If you think your path will take you to one of those schools, we strongly encourage you to pick up a copy of the relevant one of these books and to follow the instructions and complete those exercises *before* you commit to a prep course for one of the entrance exams.

If you are thinking about graduate school in a different area, your best bet is to avail yourself of the advisory materials available in the relevant undergraduate departmental office. Each of these offices is likely to have a whole set of materials to help you explore whether an advanced degree in the subject is the right choice for you, what exams you will need to pass in order to apply, how long it will take to earn a master's or Ph.D. degree in the subject, and what you can reasonably expect to do with each degree once you complete it. Naturally, the director of undergraduate studies in the particular subject area is also an excellent resource on the subject. Make an appointment during his or her office hours to further your knowledge *before* you throw yourself into the application process.

PREPARATION FOR ENTRANCE EXAMS

If you've made the decision to apply to graduate school directly out of college, you will need to be extremely vigilant about meeting the various application deadlines for your chosen discipline. Medicine and law impose the greatest burdens, as you will need to begin preparing for the LSAT and MCAT no later than December of your junior year. This means you'll need to assure yourself of your readiness to apply *before* then—and then decide on your method of preparation for either of these two exams by the time you take your fall semester finals during junior year. Proper preparation for either the MCAT or the LSAT takes *months*, not weeks— and you need to stay on top of things to ensure that you have proper time to prepare. Once again, our sister publications *Law School Confidential* and *Med School Confidential* each contain multiple chapters to walk you through the application process—including complete chapters with suggested strategies on how to prepare for the LSAT and the MCAT.

If you are applying either to law school or med school, you should avail yourself of a copy of the relevant book now to guide you from here.

If you are interested in going to business school, remember that the vast majority of successful applicants have actually worked in the business world for several years prior to applying. It *is* possible to go to business school directly from college—but you will be facing an uphill battle to do so. You also need to score very solidly on the GMAT to give yourself any shot, and as with the MCAT and the LSAT, proper preparation for the GMAT will take time. Consult a copy of *Business School Confidential* to apprise yourself of a suggested study strategy and timeline for taking the GMAT.

If you have decided to go to graduate school, chances are you will need to take both the general GRE *and* the specific exam for the subject you are going to study on the graduate level. For example, to apply to graduate school in psychology, you must take both the general GRE and the subject-specific GRE in psychology. So you will need to study for not just one but *two* entrance exams. We recommend using a study schedule for the general and subject-specific GREs similar to those we recommend for the LSAT and the MCAT—meaning that your preparation for these exams must begin immediately after finals in the fall semester of your junior year if it is your intent to go straight through from college to graduate school.

RESEARCHING SCHOOLS

So you're in the second semester of your junior year, studying hard for the graduate school entrance exam of your choice. Guess what? You have more work to do.

You need to figure out what graduate schools you're going to apply to!

You *can* put this off for a little while—say, until after you take the exam . . . but you can't wait forever. Before you leave campus at the end of your junior year, you'll need to have researched all your schools and decided which ones you'll be requesting applications from.

Why?

Because if you are applying to med school, you need to file what is called your standard primary med school application "in the Js" (June or July) after your junior year in order to maximize your competitiveness in the application process. Wow—see what we mean about sneaking up on you?

You'll have a little bit more time for law school, business school, and most grad programs; if you are applying to law school or business school, you'll want to have all of your applications in by the end of October of your senior year to maximize your competitiveness. The same is true for most graduate programs, though you should check with your individual programs to be certain of the deadlines, as your mileage may vary. What this means, obviously, is that if you intend to apply to law school, business school, or graduate school right out of college, you'll need to do your homework over the summer and request your applications before you return to college in the fall. A *general* treatment of the admissions schedules for these various programs appears at the end of this chapter.

Trust us—if you are already back on campus for senior year and you're just starting to think about applying to graduate school, you're too late for this application cycle.

REQUESTING APPLICATION MATERIALS

The last piece of the preparation puzzle involves requesting your application materials. In this age of the Internet, most schools now have their application materials available in downloadable form on their Web site. Therefore, once you have chosen the schools to which you intend to apply, monitor their Web sites for the first date that the new season's application materials will be available.

On the designated date, download away and get started. Applying to grad school can be even more time-intensive than applying to college was—and you have to do it while writing your senior thesis and finishing your major requirements.

GENERAL CALENDARS AND ADVICE FOR GRAD SCHOOL APPLICATIONS

Med School

Your first step in applying to med school is to familiarize yourself with the application process. Almost all medical schools use an initial "universal" application produced and managed by the American Association of Medical Colleges (AAMC) and its American Medical College Application Service (AMCAS). You can review the list of AMCAS member schools that use this universal application on the AMCAS Web site (www.amcas.org). This universal online application provides a common format for detailing all your academic and extracurricular credentials, and can then be distributed to all the AMCAS member schools of your choosing.

Individual schools then review this primary application and determine whether they wish to send you a secondary application. Thus, the "first cut" in the medical school admissions game is whether or not you get a secondary application.

Each medical school crafts its own secondary application. Once your prospective schools receive your secondary application (and, yes, an additional application fee), they decide whether to offer you an interview. This is the second cut in the process. Getting an interview puts you in the final round of applicants under consideration. After the interview, schools will admit, reject, or wait-list your application.

The table here is a visual outline of the road ahead.

Med School Application Calendar

Month	Activity
Summer after sophomore year (or one year prior to application)	• Start researching Web sites and blogs to get the lay of the land and the latest tips and trends. • Pick up a copy of *Med School Confidential* and read Part One to determine whether med school is the right choice and to develop application strategies.
August before junior year (or one year prior to application)	• Evaluate AMCAS requirements, identify personal weaknesses, and begin pulling materials together.
September of junior year (or one year prior to application)	• Go to AAMC Web site and gather information about MCAT. • Consult premed adviser for list of recommended resources. • Develop personal MCAT study plan. • Enroll in MCAT review course (if chosen).
December of junior year (or in year prior to application)	• Research test centers for MCAT administration on AAMC Web site. • Identify and record MCAT registration date. • Scope out various test centers and choose one.
January of application year	• Register for MCAT.
March of application year	• Meet with premed adviser to discuss application process. • Solicit letters of recommendation from faculty.
April of application year	• Take MCAT.
May of application year	• Begin researching medical schools.
June of application year	• Evaluate MCAT scores and begin finalizing application list. • Begin drafting personal statement.
July of application year	• Ensure that all faculty letters of recommendation have been received by college premed committee.
August of application year	• Upload completed AMCAS universal application.
October of application year	• Complete all secondary applications.
Fall and winter of application year	• Conduct interviews.
Fall and winter of application year	• Evaluate and rank acceptances. • Keep in touch with schools where wait-listed.
Winter of application year	• Make a final decision and celebrate!

The AAMC Web site (www.aamc.org) provides a bewildering array of tools and tables to help you assess your strengths and weaknesses as a candidate (for example, how your undergraduate GPA stacks up nationally or at a particular school), and also allows you to search and compare the attributes of every program in the country (for example, how innovative the curriculum is at your favorite school). Spend some time exploring this Web site and get familiar with it. As you march through the application process, it can be a very useful resource.

As noted earlier in the book, the AAMC also produces a book called *Medical School Admission Requirements* (also known as the MSAR). This is a fairly comprehensive collection of both the general requirements for medical school admission and all the individual, school-specific requirements, which will be very helpful to you in preparing your spreadsheet of individual application requirements and helping you stay organized. Purchase a copy, or at least consult a copy in any college library or career services or premed office. You can order your copy from the AAMC's Web site (www.aamc.org/medicalschools.htm).

There is a wealth of information available to you on the Internet. Helpful hints, application tips, and information about various medical schools and their cultures can be found on list-servs and in chat rooms and blogs. One particularly helpful and stable site is the Student Doctor Network (www.studentdoctor.net). Here you will find a wide array of forums detailing everything from premed classes to choosing your residency. Web sites like these attract an online community of would-be physicians and provide a welcome opportunity to share ideas, ask questions, learn from each other's misadventures, and otherwise commiserate about the process.

A complete treatment of how to navigate the application process successfully and then thrive and succeed in medical school is available in our sister publication *Med School Confidential.*

Law School

For applicants to law school, the big rate-limiting step in the admissions process is preparing for and taking the LSAT (Law School Admissions Test). The LSAT is offered four times a year, in June, October, December, and February, and you really want to take the June administration if you're planning to apply in the fall. Yes, you *can* get away with taking it in October, but because it will take about six weeks to get your scores back, you won't have a complete application until sometime in late November—about a month into the application season. It also won't give you a fall-back in case you take ill during the exam or otherwise have a mishap that requires you to cancel your score. Because most law schools use rolling admissions, you really want to have a complete application in the door on the first day that applications are considered, so as to give yourself your very best shot of getting admitted.

Why?

Because applicants to law schools, like those at most schools, are getting more and more credentialed and impressive every year. Admissions standards at most competitive law schools in the United States are trending up. It will take admissions committees a month or two into the admissions season to get a good sense of what the admissions pool looks like. If you present to them on day one with solid numbers and a good application, you may well get through the filter—whereas a similar candidate two months later might get held up if the pool has trended up in LSAT scores and average GPA from the year before.

To prepare adequately, you'll need somewhere between three to six months of lead time, depending on how much time you are devoting to exam prep each day. This means that if you're looking to go straight through, your preparation for the LSAT should begin around the time you return from winter break in your junior year as shown in the law school application calendar below

Law School Application Calendar

Month	Activity
Summer after sophomore year	• Start researching law school Web sites to start identifying schools of interest to you. • Pick up a copy of *Law School Confidential* and read Part One to determine whether law school is the right choice and to develop application strategies.
December of junior year	• Register for LSAT prep course (if you have decided to take one).
January of application year	• Identify registration dates for the LSAT and pick test center strategically. • Begin LSAT preparation.
June of application year	• Take LSAT.
Late July of application year	• Get LSAT score back and refine list of law schools based on your score.
August 1 of application year	• Most applications are available online. • Download them, assemble the components and deadlines into a spreadsheet, and begin working on essays.
Late August of application year	• Solicit two faculty recommendations and an outside recommendation immediately upon your return to campus.

Month	Activity
September of application year	• Request certified transcripts and begin compiling financial aid info.
November 1 of application year	• Strive to have all applications submitted and complete. Verify "completed" status of all applications.
Fall and winter of application year	• Keep in touch with schools where you were wait-listed. Supplement your application with any additional grades or honors received.
Winter of application year	• Make a final decision and celebrate!

Business School

As we noted earlier, most business schools are looking for people with three to five years of business experience. Although exceptional undergraduates with significant business experience acquired prior to or during college may be considered by upper-echelon business schools, that is the exception rather than the rule.

For further information about how to properly position yourself for application to business school, including information about whether your background makes you a viable candidate to apply directly out of college, consult chapters 4 and 5 of our sister publication *Business School Confidential,* which features a lengthy and in-depth interview with Kristine Laca—the director of admissions for the top-ranked Tuck School of Business at Dartmouth College.

For those of you considering applying to business school directly out of college, a general timeline for the process follows in the next table. As is true of the med school and law school entrance exams, the business school entrance exam, the Graduate Management Admission Test ("GMAT"), is a rate-limiting step, although because the GMAT is computer administered, you can time the administration of your exam according to your own schedule. Proper preparation for the exam still takes two to four months, however, so plan accordingly.

Business School Admissions Calendar

Month	Activity
Summer after freshman, sophomore, and junior years	• Develop in-depth business or entrepreneurial experience in an existing company, or start and operate your own enterprise.

(continued)

Month	Activity
	• Pick up a copy of *Business School Confidential* and read Part One to determine whether your experience makes you a viable candidate for applying directly out of college.
December of junior year	• Register for GMAT prep course (if you have decided to take one).
January of application year	• Begin GMAT preparation. • Register with GMAT computer-administration center for test administration date.
Spring of application year	• Take the GMAT and begin researching business schools to find schools that emphasize your area of interest. • Get scores back, determine whether to take the test again, and refine list of schools based on result.
June of application year	• Finalize list of schools and determine application schedule for schools offering early action or application "rounds." • Strive to apply early action if you can identify a top choice; otherwise apply in the first application round for best chance of success.
July of application year	• Most applications are available online. Download them, assemble the components and deadlines into a spreadsheet, and begin working on essays.
Late August of application year	• Solicit two faculty recommendations and an outside business recommendation immediately upon your return to campus.
September of application year	• Request certified transcripts and begin compiling financial aid info.
October of application year	• This is the early-action deadline at some business schools.
November of application year	• This is the first application round due date at most schools.
Fall and winter of application year	• Conduct Interviews and receive decisions.

Month	Activity
	• Keep in touch with schools where you were wait-listed.
	• Supplement your application with any additional grades or honors received.
Winter of application year	• Make a final decision and celebrate!

Grad School

Finally, we come to all other graduate programs, including master's and Ph.D. programs. For these programs, again the rate-limiting step is typically the standardized entrance exam, called the Graduate Record Exam (GRE), which comes in two stages. The first stage is the general GRE, which has been referred to as an SAT on steroids—because it contains math, verbal, and analytical writing components that are similar to, but more complex than, those found on the SAT. The GRE general test got a major overhaul in 2006: it has been expanded to four hours in length; is now an Internet-delivered, computer-based linear exam administered on approximately thirty fixed test dates rather than on ongoing dates throughout the year; and uses an entirely new scoring system. Some of these changes were still evolving when this book went to press.

Stage two of the GRE is the subject test—which measures undergraduate achievement in eight disciplines: (1) biochemistry and cell and molecular biology, (2) biology, (3) chemistry, (4) computer science, (5) literature in English, (6) math, (7) physics, and (8) psychology. Subject-specific GRE scores are used by some programs as a common measure to compare the qualifications of applicants from diverse schools and undergraduate programs. The subject-specific exams are still delivered on paper three times a year in November, December, and April.

If you are a candidate for admission to a graduate program in any of the aforementioned eight subject areas, you may be required to take both the general test and the subject test for your particular discipline—although requirements vary from program to program. As always, your best bet is to check the Web sites of the programs that interest you to make these determinations.

Whether you must take just the general test or both the general test and a subject test, we encourage careful preparation, because your scores will be carefully considered by the programs to which you apply. Plan for two to three months of prep time to get ready for the general GRE. As is true of most other standardized exams, you can prepare for the general GRE through one of the commercial test preparation centers, such as the Princeton Review or Kaplan, or by using test preparation guides available online or from your local bookseller. Subject test preparation is still primarily book based—with preparation guides available from commercial test preparation centers or online and local booksellers.

For more information about the GRE exams and how they changed in 2006, hop on the Net and surf to www.ets.org or www.princetonreview.com/grad and click on the respective links to the sections on the GRE.

Because application deadlines across graduate programs vary so much, it's impossible to give you a chart showing a general set of deadlines. Suffice it to say that if you are required to take the subject test in your chosen discipline, you should do so in April to ensure that your scores reach your graduate schools well in advance of their application deadlines. Taking the November administration of the subject tests will put you right up against department deadlines—you can do it, but you leave yourself no room for error.

Because the general test is computer administered, you will receive your scores immediately; you should therefore choose an administration that (1) will give you time to regroup and prepare to retake the test if you get a subpar score and (2) will ensure that your scores are in place by November 1 of your application year.

Applications generally become available on your department Web sites in July or August of your application year—so bookmark and monitor these sites closely in order to allow yourself maximum preparation time.

Beyond that, application procedures are specific to each discipline and school, so leave plenty of time to research these different procedures and get them all into your application spreadsheet to ensure that you keep track of the different requirements and deadlines.

The Junior "Thesis"

*There is always one moment when
the door opens and lets the future in.*

Deepak Chopra

Although few American colleges and universities still require a
junior "thesis," there are a lot of very good reasons why, whether
it is required or not, you should still aim to complete a significant piece
of academic scholarship or research before the end of your junior year.

CONFIRM WHAT YOUR MAJOR REQUIRES

Do yourself a favor. When your undergraduate course catalogue arrives during the
summer before your junior year, spend some time reading the introductory section about your major. At many colleges and universities around the country, and
for a great many majors at those colleges, a significant senior thesis or senior project is required prior to graduation. What does your major require?

I mean specifically. Is it a research project? A piece of written scholarship? A
performance project? A significant laboratory experiment? Who needs to super-
vise your work? Does the topic need to be approved in advance? How long does it
have to be? Most important, when is it due?

START LOOKING FOR A THESIS TOPIC NOW

Once you have the answers to these questions, you should immediately begin thinking about what you might want to explore through this important and memorable

experience. Writing a senior thesis or embarking on a senior project can be a very exhilarating and eye-opening experience, or it can be the bane of your existence for most of your senior year. Which way you land on this issue generally depends on how excited you are about the subject matter. So don't wait until your senior fall to start thinking about a thesis or project topic.

Start thinking and looking now.

Senior thesis and project topics are everywhere. Think back to the general survey courses you took for your major. You know, the introductory classes with a thousand people in them. What topics struck you? Did you find anything particularly interesting? Was any reading assignment especially memorable or fascinating?

What about the coursework you've taken since? Has there been a seminar that proved to be especially fertile ground for discussion or a particular subject that really caught your interest?

If so, now—before you select your fall class schedule—go back through the table of contents of those textbooks or reading materials, and review the syllabi for those classes. Does anything stand out? What might make good subject matter for further pursuit this year?

If you have no idea, or if nothing from your previous coursework was especially memorable, spend a good long time with the course catalogue this summer. Read through the available classes in your major, paying particular attention to smaller classes and seminar opportunities. Look for compelling subject matter— something that makes you excited to shop the class and is likely to sustain your interest over the semester.

If you're an English major, maybe you know that your real love is American literature, and you want to focus in on a particular time period by taking a couple of intensive seminars on the works of the period. While doing so, maybe you want to cross-register to study the history, politics, philosophy, or art of the same period; maybe through such exploration, a topic will jump out at you.

If you're a poli sci major, perhaps a certain period of political history intrigues you, or maybe there is a specific incident, war, or school of thought that you'd like to explore.

If you're a science person, opportunities for experimentation in the laboratory abound—and chances are, there is someone at your university working on the subject matter of greatest interest to you.

If you're more artistically inclined, perhaps there is a particular discipline you'd like to focus on, a type of music you really want to study and master, a play you'd like to write, or something you'd like to compose.

Whatever your major and whatever your interest, be on the lookout, starting now, for something that could sustain your attention over the better part of a year. And then start thinking about how you could leverage that opportunity into something much bigger this year.

Permit me an example.

Try to Kill Two (or More!) Birds with One Stone

As I've already told you earlier in the book, I did not decide on a major (psychology) until the very beginning of my junior year. That put me seriously behind the eight ball, as I needed to take thirteen classes and complete a thesis in the two years I had remaining. While reviewing the course catalogue after its arrival in mid-summer, I discovered a seminar called "Television and Human Behavior," which looked interesting. The course was taught by a professor named Dorothy Singer, who was the codirector of Yale's Family Television Research and Consultation Center. Having had a long interest in television's ability to convey messages of persuasion, and having recently thought about possibly going into a career in advertising, I decided to take the seminar.

That decision would literally change the course of my college career and the direction of my life. I was absolutely enthralled by the subject matter and devoured the reading assignments. I knew, almost immediately, that I had found a passion.

Around the same time, ABC television was featuring an hourlong television drama called *Life Goes On,* written and directed by Michael Braverman and starring Patti LuPone, Kellie Martin, and Chris Burke. The show was the first to feature a full-time actor (Burke) with Down Syndrome, but even more important, it had just embarked on a story line featuring an HIV-positive teenager (Chad Lowe) as Kellie Martin's love interest at a time when AIDS and the risks associated with it were not part of the everyday dialogue in American culture. It was a revolutionary concept that had network executives buzzing and reviewers raving.

As mentioned previously, I had caught an episode of this show in summer reruns completely by accident one night while I was still studying Orgo during my sophomore summer in New Haven and it had given me a really interesting idea for a possible senior thesis. The producers of the show were clearly trying to teach their target audience (teenagers) about AIDS and how it is (and is not) transmitted in an effort to promote cultural awareness of the disease and empathy for those afflicted by it.

What I wanted to know is whether the producers of the show, by embedding their factual and cultural content in a television drama, were succeeding in teaching their target audience about AIDS and changing certain risky sexual behaviors in their target audience—and if they were, whether dramatic television would be a better vehicle for teaching teenagers about these things than simply lecturing to them about it in health classes or requiring them to read about it in a textbook. In other words, would television prove to be the best mechanism for teaching kids in this area?

It was, admittedly, an ambitious project, and at the time I had no idea how to pull it off. But the idea *really* fired me up, and obviously, I'm telling you this story more than ten years after it happened for a reason . . .

Dr. Singer's television seminar required a long research paper in lieu of a final exam, and after consultation with her, I decided I was going to use the paper requirement to review the seminal studies of how television effects changes in human behavior. Although this was hardly a revolutionary topic, I explained to her that I needed to understand the basic studies that had already been done in the area, and how they had been done, because I wanted to conduct one of my own. I then came clean about the whole *Life Goes On* idea.

She loved it, and immediately offered to become my adviser. This was September of my junior year. And we were off to the races.

Dr. Singer helped me apply for grants to help fund the research, and helped me contact the show's executive producer, Michael Braverman. On receiving my letter explaining my research idea, Mr. Braverman invited me to come to Hollywood to review upcoming scripts, talk to the actors, and develop the testing instrument I would use to examine the show's effectiveness. Yale produced several thousand dollars in funding for the project, and we were on our way.

To make an already long story a little shorter, I completed the paper for Dr. Singer's seminar. I would later adapt that paper into the first twenty-plus pages of my senior thesis—providing the theoretical background on which my research was predicated. I did two additional independent study courses with Dr. Singer for credit, during which I completed the instrument and used it to test my hypothesis on more than five hundred high school sophomores and juniors using a couple of episodes from the television series. I knocked off another psychology credit by taking a course in research statistics, which I needed to analyze my data. In the end, I pulled all this research together into my senior thesis, spending all of my senior year coding and analyzing the data and writing it up as a study that ultimately was nominated for a couple of Yale's prestigious prizes for the most outstanding work of undergraduate scholarship.

It didn't win, but it wasn't a bad result for someone who had no idea what he was doing with his life only two years earlier.

I tell you this story for its potential motivational effect and as a possible blueprint for you to follow. Remember, I didn't even have a clue what my *major* was until the course catalogue arrived in the summer before my junior year.

FIND YOUR *LIFE GOES ON* MOMENT

So what's the point of all this?

Be on the lookout for your *Life Goes On* moment: when all of a sudden, everything comes together for you in a moment of clarity, and you become really passionate about some subject matter, a research idea, or a particular curiosity. Everyone has a moment like this at some point during college. The trick is to be on the lookout for it and to embrace it when it comes and not let go of it. Once it happens to you, you need three basic things to make it succeed.

Find a "Champion" for Your Idea

First, you need to get someone on the faculty energized about your idea and committed to help you. That's usually the easy part. College professors, by and large, are passionate, curious people who love it when their students get juiced up about a particular topic and come to them for help and guidance. It also goes without saying that once you have this person on board, he or she becomes valuable to you in many other ways as well: as a supportive member of your departmental faculty when you go looking to have independent research credits approved or when you need to get funding for your project; as a thesis adviser; as a friend; and as a steward and your most relevant and important recommender for your graduate school applications should you choose to go that route.

Dare to Be Great

Second, you need perseverance and guts. It's not all going to come together magically for you in one made-for-TV moment. You need to be willing to push for what you want, to believe in your idea, and not to take no for an answer. If someone shoots down your idea as "too ambitious" or "too advanced" or "too complicated," work with that person to gain his or her acceptance. If you need funding, go knock on some doors and ask for it. As I discovered in college, a passion for intellectual scholarship and a desire to follow through on an idea, especially when the passion is backed by a faculty member, can open a lot of unknown coffers.

But for me, there was still a hurdle to overcome.

When I arrived at the Warner Brothers Studios for my first meeting with Mr. Braverman, it was clear to me that there had been a misunderstanding in the communication between us. I was a twenty-year-old college junior, and he had expected me to be a professor. He expressed some initial dismay at this misunderstanding and at having a "college kid" running around his set talking to his writers and actors.

It was another turning point. If he had sent me home, the story would probably have ended there, and I might be driving a taxi today instead of writing this book.

Thinking quickly, I reassured Mr. Braverman by telling him that Yale had put its imprimatur behind my research by funding it, and that as a result, my age or status was entirely irrelevant. I argued for the merit of the idea, explained how passionately I felt about it, and implored him to let me see it through. He looked me over for a few long moments, and then shook my hand, welcomed me to California, and, to his credit, worked closely with me for the rest of my visit. It was, I'm sure, a leap of faith for him—but again, if you're on the right path, I firmly believe that the universe will conspire to open doors for you. It certainly did for me that day!

Confirm Your Passion in Your Idea

Third, you need to be certain that your idea is *the* question you want to spend the next year researching, thinking, and writing about. The path to the completion of your senior thesis is a long and complicated one. If you enjoy your subject, it will be the most exhilarating experience of your academic career. On the flip side, if you grow bored with your topic, completing your thesis can be sheer hell.

HOW IT PLAYED OUT FOR ME

As I've already mentioned, though it came to me all of a sudden and very late in the game, my senior thesis topic changed the course and direction of my life. After meeting and working with Mr. Braverman in furtherance of my thesis research, and tinkering around behind the scenes of a television show, I got bitten by the writing bug. Wanting to explore that further, I would take a couple of senior screenwriting seminars in which I wrote two teleplays (one for *Life Goes On* and one for another short-lived *Fox* show called *The Class of '96*) for course credit! Although neither script was produced, one of them did land me my first agent and launched me on my writing career, which obviously continues to this day.

Dr. Singer also steered me into her course on psychology and law, which ultimately spurred my interest in law school. And when I decided I wanted to take a couple of years off before going to law school, I spent one of those years in New Haven doing research for Dr. Singer on one of her research projects on television and human behavior, which explored many of the same things that my study had done.

So what are you supposed to take from all of this?

Remember my story.

In July of my sophomore summer, I was still a miserable premed student with no certainty about the direction of his life, without a declared major, and with no idea how to really extricate myself from those circumstances.

Four months later, I was living in a hotel in Hollywood doing psychology research of my own design, funded by Yale, and completely on-track, with certainty about where I was going and how I was going to get there.

It can all turn around in a moment for you. When your moment comes, pounce on it, and hold onto it for dear life.

So get excited about the prospect of your senior thesis, and if your major doesn't require one, you might want to do one as part of a series of independent study courses anyway. . . . Be on the lookout for your topic this year, and look for opportunities to leverage the work by spreading it out over several courses or course credits. The bottom line is, you never really know where your senior thesis topic can or will take you. What you can be relatively certain of, however, is that the work will place you in close proximity with a professor and, if pursued ambitiously, can open doors to you that you can't yet imagine.

Planning a Meaningful Junior Summer

The Brainstorming Workshop

*Life is not divided into semesters. You don't get
summers off, and very few employers are
interested in helping you find yourself.*

Bill Gates

It's us again . . . your conscience on paper reminding you that you
had a bunch of goals for your junior year—at least some of which
are probably staring back at you, unfulfilled, from wherever you taped
them up.

This is your chance to make them happen.

Will you be abroad this summer? If so, you have a once-in-a-lifetime chance
to spend the summer traveling and experiencing life overseas. Even if you won't
be, your junior summer will present you with a unique opportunity: a *looong*
period of time—perhaps as much as fifteen weeks or, in other words, the equivalent of an *entire school semester*—away from academics. Remember, the summers
you have during college are some of the greatest gifts you will get in your entire
lifetime—extended periods of time where most of you will have few, if any, responsibilities or obligations. Even if you have to make money during the summer, have
you thought outside the box about different ways that you could accomplish this
and do something interesting or exciting at the same time?

Welcome to your junior summer brainstorming workshop—where you're
going to come up with the antidote to a long, boring summer in some God-
forsaken place, doing some mind-numbing job that has nothing to do with your
wants, your hopes, and your dreams of becoming something bigger than you are.

You're an upperclassman in college now, and the world is your oyster. All it takes is a little bit of research, a little creativity, and a sense of adventure.

Come along.

REVIEW YOUR GOALS FOR JUNIOR YEAR

You probably know the drill by now. The first thing you need to do is take a look at the work you did in your junior year goal-setting workshop and, if you followed our suggestions, at the eighteen or so "most important" goals you set for your junior year—you know, the ones that are haunting you right now because life has gotten away from you, and you haven't done enough to achieve them.

What did you identify as the things you hoped to accomplish during your junior year? How many of them have you actually accomplished so far? Which ones might be things you could work on this summer?

Yeah, yeah . . . we know that you're now hopelessly in debt, that you have spent *much* more money in college than you budgeted for, and that you've hit the wall in terms of what your parents are willing to do to indulge you. We know—we were there too. Yet some of us figured out how to make money *and* further our academic, social, personal, or career goals (or a combination of these). You really *can* do both at the same time.

So think about what you had hoped to accomplish during your junior year and about which of those things might be worthwhile summer pursuits.

Explore Your Academic Interests

What have you learned about your academic interests this year? By now you should be well into your career exploration. Are there things you can do to further the depth of that exploration this summer? If you think you're headed to med school, law school, business school, or graduate school directly out of college (and are you *sure* you want to do this—if not, be sure to read Chapter 43 now), this is the last summer you will have to explore, define, and confirm those interests. Time to pick up your copy of *Law School Confidential, Business School Confidential, Med School Confidential,* or any other career-specific resource containing chapters that explicitly walk you through the relevant career-choice analysis; read it thoroughly and ask yourself the hard questions. If you're still on course after doing so, choose to do something this summer that will in some way enhance your application process next fall.

By now you should also be well on your way to completing the requirements of your major. Have you chosen a thesis topic yet? If you have, and you are really into your topic or the task of completing the thesis is likely to be monumental (or both), perhaps this is the summer to take an independent study course for credit with the professor you would like to be your thesis adviser. And yes, we know you need to make money, so you should also try to hook up with either the same professor or another professor in the department to help him or her do research. Again, this is a great way to forward your goals and interests while making money at the same time.

Are you running out of time to take all the courses you had hoped to take while in college? If you are double majoring, are you running up against scheduling conflicts or time constraints? If so, might you want to pick up a course or two this summer, sublet an apartment with some friends who are staying in town to do research, *and* pick up a part-time job in the evenings or during the day on the weekends to pay the freight and make some dough?

Explore Your Interests in Travel, the Outdoors, or Physical Development

Are you abroad? When your semester or year abroad is complete, perhaps you and a friend or two will want to stay were you are or travel to a different part of the world you learned about, and work *there* during your junior summer. Lots and lots of our friends did all sorts of interesting things—working on farms, building houses, working in the retail, restaurant, and entertainment businesses—in foreign countries. By doing this, you'd be making money, learning a foreign language, *and* seeing the world all at once.

If you can afford to (and even if you can't), if you are already abroad, we encourage you to do everything you possibly can to see the world. If you are creative and enterprising enough (and willing to do whatever menial labor is required to make enough dough to keep you on the road), you'll find ways to make ends meet.

Is this the summer that you combine your love of the outdoors with a spiritual quest or an effort to really get back in shape, by hiking part of the Appalachian Trail or the Continental Divide or any other part of the country?

If money isn't an issue, might you want to explore taking an NOLS or Outward Bound course to sharpen your skills and to mature and grow as a person? Or might you want to find a cheap airline ticket and travel to a remote international location, such as Peru, Argentina, Africa, or the Himalayas, to do some trekking or other adventuring? You can *actually do* these things for not a lot of money if you do some research and advance planning, share living costs with a friend or two, or "rough it" by living in tents or hostels.

If you identified working on your physical body as a goal, maybe you want to use part of this summer to train for a marathon or a triathlon, or simply to become a better runner, biker, swimmer, hiker, tennis player, or whatever. Obviously, this goal can be worked on practically anywhere—and can be combined with just about any other goal at the same time.

Explore Your Interest in Politics or Administration

Is this a campaign year? Could you hook up with a political campaign as a policy analyst, speechwriter, advance person, researcher, campaign worker, or media adviser, or in any of a virtually unlimited number of other capacities? If it isn't a campaign year, but you're majoring in history, poli sci, or government or are thinking about applying to law school, perhaps you could look toward Washington, D.C., where you might land a summer job, working alongside thousands of other college students as an aide, page, researcher, or policy assistant.

Do you love your college and have visions of becoming an admissions officer after you graduate? If so, this is the summer that you should be working in the admissions office as an interviewer.

Are you interested in a social issue that is addressed by a particular local, state, regional, or national agency? Might you want to work there this summer to explore your interest in the subject?

BRAINSTORM

So now that you've had a chance to review your goals and interests and to kick-start your imagination, it's time to brainstorm. What is it that you want to accomplish with your junior summer? Grab a pen, haul out your trusty *Campus Confidential* workbook, and list a bunch of ideas. Then rejoin us to learn about a way to make sure you actually take *action* with respect to these ideas.

Okay. Now look at the ideas you brainstormed, pick four or five of them, and put them in an order of priority from highest (1) to lowest (4 or 5) by just writing a number in a circle next to them. Go ahead, do it now.

Amanda used her junior summer to set up a job during her senior year and beyond.

"The summer after my junior year, I stayed on campus at Cornell, continued my work-study job from the prior school year, and was a resident adviser in a dorm of high school students on a program called 'Summer College,'" Amanda explained. "This was direct preparation for being an RA in a college dorm the following year, but even better prep for being a teacher at a boarding school, which is something I knew I wanted to do, and was my first job after college."

Lyndsee fulfilled a dream, and brought her academic life full-circle.

"I spent the summer as an intern at the St. Paul's School Advanced Studies Program—an intensive summer program for public high school students in New

Hampshire," Lynsdee added. "I was an assistant teacher in the Japanese language program as well as a dance coach and a resident adviser in a dorm. I chose that job because as a high school student, I attended the same summer program, and that is where I had my first introduction to Japanese language and culture. It was that exposure that prompted me to major in East Asian studies in college.

"I remembered my experience at St. Paul's fondly, and I always knew that I wanted to work as an intern there when I was old enough to go back in that capacity. I wanted to be able to share my knowledge and excitement about my chosen course of study with young students who were eager to learn. I wanted to have fun over the summer, but also to do something creative that I had always wanted to do and that I knew I would enjoy."

Aaron used the summer to make some money and explore a potential post-college career.

"A good way to spend the summer after your junior year is to try getting a job that is related to something you might want to pursue after college," Aaron advised. "This is the last summer you have before you leave college for the working world, so it is a good idea to use this time to get into the field, meet some contacts, and start developing skills that you might later put to use in your career. It's a good time to start laying out a path to follow after graduation.

"I worked at a carpentry and construction company that I had worked with previously when I was home for the summer," Aaron added. "I chose to go back to the carpentry job because it paid well and I wanted to save money for school. I also decided to go back because I enjoy working outside and learning carpentry skills."

And Dan, back from his research cruise on the Antarctic icebreaker, used the summer to get a jump start on senior year academic requirements.

"After I got back from the cruise, I returned to Middlebury and continued my thesis research for a good portion of the summer before resuming classes for my senior year," Dan said.

PUTTING IT ALL TOGETHER

Now I want you to think really creatively here. How could you accomplish three, four, or all five of these goals at the same time in the same summer? And how amazing do you think you would feel if you could actually pull this off?

Let's Look at an Example

Suppose you identified the following as your junior year summer goals: (1) making money, (2) continuing your year abroad, (3) connecting with your college friends who are also abroad, and (4) having some outrageous adventures. What could you possibly do with your junior summer that would make you feel fulfilled and would further the pursuit of your goals?

Obviously, procrastinating about this decision is likely to lead you nowhere: you'll run out of money and be forced to come home early, which would really suck, especially considering you may *never* again have the opportunity to go gallivanting across the globe in the carefree and responsibility-free way that you can this summer.

Now get creative. What if you did your research and discovered that there are organic farms all across the world that take in workers for a few days at a time and provide room and board and a small stipend? What if you IM'ed your roommates, made a list of such farms, and spent the summer crisscrossing the globe, working and staying at these places to make some cash and then traveling around sleeping in hostels or on beaches while you have your series of unforgettable adventures? Now, instead of meeting a single goal, you'd be addressing all four of your priorities (and creating a bunch of amazing memories) in a single summer.

How good would that make you feel?

What if you're not abroad? Okay—let's take the opposite perspective and say that life has dealt you a bad hand this year. Maybe one of your parents has taken ill, the family business is in trouble, or for some other reason you have been *forced* to return home and focus on a bunch of issues not of your own making.

You can *still* make the most of the summer and use it to advance your life.

Take a look at your list of stated goals for this year. Obviously, if you have to be home working or caring for a sick family member, your time may be limited. But there may still be windows of time during the day—early in the morning, late at night, and on weekends—when you can steal a couple of hours to focus on the things that are important to you.

If you had hoped to get a jump on your thesis, could you do research on the Internet to advance the ball and make things easier for yourself come fall? If you wanted to get back in shape, surely you can find an hour every day to go for a run or to engage in some other form of physical exercise. If you wanted to write a short story, start a screenplay, or pick up guitar, guess what? You could do all those things.

NOW DO SOME RESEARCH

So you've established your goals, thought about ways to make a few of them work together, and brainstormed a bunch of possibilities, to produce the blueprint for an immensely satisfying junior summer.

Now, armed with this blueprint, hop on the Internet and head on over to your college career planning and placement office to find the ideal position for you.

Yes, it will take some effort. But the payoff will be well worth the time you put in.

PART FIVE

Considerations for Senior Year

Your Senior Year Goal-Setting Workshop

A good goal is like a strenuous exercise.
It makes you stretch.

Mary Kay Ash

Well, you've rounded third and are headed for home. This is the year you take over the campus, captain your sports team, run your fraternity or sorority, lead your extracurricular organization, write your thesis, and start making some really important decisions about your future.

This is your last go-round on campus. Your last spin through the course catalogue. Your last chance to take that art history class you kept putting off because it conflicted with courses in your major. Your last chance to date that person from your freshman econ class you kept wanting to get set up with.

By the beginning of your senior year, you should have most of the requirements of your major completed, and you have firmed up your plans about where your life is headed in the year after college. If you are planning to go to medical school straight out of college, you should be taking the MCAT this fall. If law school is in your future, you should be taking the LSAT no later than this October. If you're looking to get a job right out of college, you should be deep into your search at the career services office by now.

It's the fourth quarter, and whether you are winning and just need to keep running the plays in your playbook, or losing and need to stage a memorable comeback, the clock is ticking.

We're hoping that if you've been following along with the chronological advice we've been providing so far, you have kept weekly or even daily tabs on your eighteen or so goals from junior year and have either achieved them or made the active determination to abandon them. Now, it's time to do it all over again—one more time—to establish one last set of critically important goals for your senior year. Obviously, these goals will be informed by and will significantly affect the direction your life will take this year and on into the future, whatever that may hold for you.

Once again, we've divided the workshop into five categories: (1) academic and career goals, (2) social goals, (3) extracurricular goals, (4) physical goals, (5) financial goals, and (6) spiritual goals.

This time, because it is the last time, go back and reread the goals you set for last year *before* you engage in this activity. Pick up anything that got left behind that you still want to do, and plug it in. In fact, look back over the goals you set for freshman year, sophomore year, *and* junior year, to see if there is anything you listed that you still want to go back and do.

Remember, this is your last chance.

Now think about what else you might want to do during your senior year. What experiences do you want to have? What places would you like to go, and who would you like to go there with? Once again, remember not to censor yourself. Just write down everything that comes to mind. You'll have a chance to go back through the ideas later to decide on your priorities. For now, though, you just want to dump your pent-up thoughts down on paper. Try to keep writing in each category for at least five minutes.

Let's begin.

YOUR SENIOR YEAR ACADEMIC AND CAREER GOALS

What requirements for your major are left to complete?

Do you need to write a thesis or complete a senior project? Do you have a topic yet? Have you at least identified possible subject areas that interest you? If you haven't, do you remember a few things from the classes that you've already taken that seemed to resonate with you? What were they?

Do you have any distributional requirements left to complete? Have you completed your language requirement, if your college has one?

Are you a candidate for departmental or college honors? Do you know what you need to do in terms of grades this year to achieve those honors? Do those things matter to you?

Now for the fun part. Are there any upper-level senior seminars that you might want to take? What elective classes have you identified in past years that looked interesting or fun? Are they still being offered? Can you fit one or more of them into your schedule?

Are you planning to do some traveling after college or during your senior year? Might there be a history class that you could take that focuses on one of the places you are planning to visit?

Is there a particular book you've always wanted to read that you could study in depth in an independent seminar this semester? Do you want to write a novel or a screenplay for credit? Have you always wanted to explore acting? Is there another subject area of interest that you might explore? Is there anything at all that you might want to learn about, read about, or write about in an independent study course? Can you identify a particular professor with whom you might want to study? Did you hear about any other subjects that your roommates or friends explored that you might want to check out?

Might you want to cross-register for one or more courses in one of the graduate schools at your university? Have you taken a spin through any of the graduate school course catalogues to see if you can find anything to interest you?

Have you decided on a career path? Are you intending to go to graduate school? If so, do you need to establish a schedule for the application process? Do you need to find a job for next year?

If you still find yourself undecided or completely without direction as to what you are going to do after college, have you consulted the available resources on campus to help you think about potential career paths? Have you talked to your academic adviser? To your dean of students? To your academic dean? To a counselor in your college or university's career planning office? If you have not yet decided what you want to do with your life after graduation, now is the time to take some meetings and explore the resources available to you.

What academic things do you want to get out of your last year in college? Write down everything that you'd like to try and everything that you'd like to explore in your last year of college.

You have five minutes. Keep your pen moving.

Go!

If you've reached the end of your five minutes and you want to keep going, by all means do so. If you've written a good list of at least ten or twelve items and you've listed everything you can think of right now that qualifies as an academic goal, then go ahead and move on to the next section.

During the next day or two, more things will come to mind. As they do, be sure to add them to the list. Don't just let them wander into and out of your consciousness. Capture your thoughts so that you can turn them into goals!

YOUR SENIOR YEAR SOCIAL GOALS

This is the last year that you will be surrounded by thousands of unattached people your own age. Have you found a good group of friends? Have you met the kinds of people you wanted to meet? Are you dating someone, either on campus or somewhere else? Do you want to be? Maybe now is the time either to approach that person you've been thinking about or at least to be open to the idea of dating someone more seriously.

Maybe this is the year you resolve to break out of your shell and become more socially confident. You are, after all, in the senior class on campus!

Consider whether you want to set any new goals or ground rules for your social interactions on campus this year. Has your social life been swallowing up your academic life, such that you need to rein it in this year, pull up your GPA, and really get serious about knocking your thesis out of the park in order to finish strong? Or have you been so serious about your studies that you've missed out on the "fun" part of college?

Is your life in balance?

Have you been making empowering or disempowering choices about drugs, alcohol, and sex? Do you need to think about a new approach to any of these things or clean up your act before you enter the real world?

Are there any other aspects of who you are or what you discovered about yourself last year or this past summer that you'd like to move front and center now? Do any of your attributes, characteristics, or interests need more expression than they had last year?

Think about what you achieved socially during college, and what you had hoped to achieve. Take a look at the lists you made during the previous three years. What goals did you achieve, and where did you fall short? Which goals deserve to be renewed for another year, and which ones have you moved beyond or do you want to discard because your wants and needs have changed?

Write for at least five minutes, listing everything you'd like to try, everything you'd like to explore, experience, do, or be socially this year.

Go!

EXTRACURRICULAR GOALS

If you are in a fraternity or a sorority, this is the year you get to run the show. Do you want to seek a leadership position in the organization?

If you've devoted time to one or more extracurricular activities and attained a position of leadership for this year, have you determined what you want the organization's agenda to be? Have you set some goals for the organization or for your participation within it?

Are you a varsity athlete? If you are, is it still meaningful to you, or are you finding the time commitment, the travel, and the impingement on the rest of your college calendar to be too much? Does it look like you're going to get to play a lot this year, or are you going to be primarily a bench player? There is nothing that says you *have* to continue to play your varsity sport—and yes, that's true even if you have an athletic scholarship. There is more than one way to pay for college, and if you are going to mortgage a significant part of your experience to play a sport you don't enjoy anymore, you should at least consider your alternatives. This is the year you should be a starter. Are you? If you're not, do you want to stay with the team?

If you were an athlete in high school or prep school, but either did not make the varsity or gave it up when you got to college, is there a sport you'd like to participate in again or to learn on a social level? If so, is this year finally the time to get involved with your school's club sports or intramurals?

Have you explored your campus's various takes on politics or religion? Interested? If this is an election year, perhaps you'd like to get involved in a political campaign.

Thinking of switching religions, exploring a new religion, or simply becoming more devoted to your own? You can think about checking out the local congregations or groups.

What about working in the community? Community outreach is a great way to develop career ideas while doing good at the same time.

Want to interview prospective applicants, give campus tours, or help run your college's recruiting effort? If you love your college or university, this is a good way to plug into the energy, get connected to the individuals who run the place, and meet and talk with prospective applicants.

This is the last year for you to get the most out of college.

You have five minutes.

Go!

YOUR SENIOR YEAR PHYSICAL GOALS

How badly out of shape have you gotten in college?

Check in on your diet. Are you eating enough? Are you eating too much? Has your weight dropped or ballooned significantly? Are you eating healthily most days, or does your diet *still* feature mainly pizza and beer and whatever you pick up at the campus quick-mart? Remember that unless you are going to graduate school next year (and maybe even if you *are* going to graduate school next year), this is the last time you are going to be able to take all three of your meals in a dining hall. Although you may think that is cause for rejoicing, keep in mind that this means that next year you're going to need to shop for groceries and learn how to cook, unless you plan on spending a lot of money eating out.

Might you want to work on developing some good eating habits this year? And what about exercise? If your academic schedule is under control, is this the year you actually try to get some exercise *every* day?

What about taking a weightlifting class, taking up yoga or meditation, learning a martial art, or learning to play tennis, golf, squash, or racquetball recreationally? Any of these activities would add a necessary physical component to your day. Do you need to do some research to find out what is available? Do you need to set up a schedule or make arrangements with a friend or a roommate to hold you to a workout regimen?

What else do you want to do for yourself physically this year? Do you feel alone or depressed, such that seeking out a few hours of counseling from your campus health center might be constructive? Have you noticed any other physical changes in your body, your energy level, or your mood that might warrant a checkup at the Department of Undergraduate Health?

Spend the next five minutes setting some goals in these areas for this year. Go!

YOUR SENIOR YEAR FINANCIAL GOALS

Another area of life in which things tend to get a little out of control during college is that of finances. Chalk it up to an educational experience, but get your spending under control now, before things really get out of hand.

Chances are, you've now discovered that college is even more expensive than you thought it would be—and that opportunities to spend money are around every turn. Obviously, you take this trip only once, and you don't want to deprive yourself of *everything* in the name of financial responsibility, but you also don't want to graduate with an unnecessary mountain of short-term debt.

If you are heading out into the real world next year, remember that unless you're going to graduate school, you're going to have to start paying back your student loans. Have you figured out what those monthly payments are going to look like, and whether or not the year you are planning for next year is going to permit you to make those loan payments? If you also have a bunch of short-term credit card debt, it may seriously limit the kinds of things you are able to do.

Mindful of that, what financial guidelines do you want to set for yourself this year?

Are you on a budget? Should you be? Have you now realized that you really *do* need to draw one up so that you'll know what kind of plan you need to stick to?

Are you on a work-study plan again this year, or for the first time? Have you figured out how you're going to fit those hours into your week so as to minimize the disruption of your academic and social schedule?

Do you want to get a part-time job somewhere to make some extra cash and try to knock down some of your debt to free you up for whatever you have in mind for next year? Is there any aspect of your status as a senior on campus that you could take advantage of to make some extra cash? Could you tutor someone in one of your strong subjects or become a teaching assistant? What are your other marketable skills?

Don't be afraid to think outside the box here, but if you find yourself with a lot of short-term credit card debt because of some bad choices you made during the first half of college, you really do need to do something about that. Don't let that debt grow and limit what you can do for the next several years. Find a way to work it off and get rid of it.

Are there any other ways to limit your expenses? Do you really need to have your car on campus? If so, might you want to work out some sort of car-sharing arrangement that would produce additional income for you, or at least help defray the expenses of insurance, gas, and parking fees? If you do pursue this kind of arrangement, be sure that you have proper insurance on the car and that anyone who uses your car is insured as well.

Take the next five minutes to set out your financial goals for your senior year. Remember that managing your finances requires you to play offense and defense. Think creatively.

Go!

YOUR SENIOR YEAR SPIRITUAL GOALS

Senior year is a time of freedom and of confidence, but also of change. For the many of us who still lacked a clear vision at this stage of our lives, senior year became a time of intense contemplation, nostalgia, and perhaps even some regret.

And for many of us, connecting to some sort of spirituality during these times was very comforting.

Again, spirituality does *not* necessarily mean religion, and I am not suggesting that you need to find religion in order to find vision or purpose. For some people, though, connecting to their religion can provide the necessary grounding and direction.

Maybe for you, being spiritual means taking a few hours each week to practice yoga or meditation. Maybe it means taking a long walk in the woods one morning a week to be alone with your thoughts and to reflect. Maybe being spiritual means reading introspective writings or listening to music and letting your thoughts wander away from the mundane and the everyday. Maybe it means volunteering to help the less fortunate at an area shelter or soup kitchen, or working at an animal shelter, and reminding yourself that although you may lack vision, others lack much more than that.

Whatever spirituality means to you, do not underestimate its power to enrich your life. In your campus world, where people will often seem very id-driven or self-absorbed, maintaining some perspective can be really helpful. And whether that means that you'd like to get to church or synagogue once a week or simply that you want to read a particular book this semester, don't forget to pay some attention to your spiritual side. You'll be amazed at how refreshed and centered it will make you feel.

Think about a few ways to nurture your spiritual side during your senior year and write them down.

Resist the urge to just dismiss thoughts about this topic out of hand.

Think about it for a minute and jot down a few ideas.

Go ahead.

NOW WHAT DO I DO WITH ALL OF THIS?

If you're still with us, you should now have an abundance of good information written down to help ensure that your senior year is as productive and satisfying as you hope it will be.

But you're not done yet.

If you've followed our directions, you should have written down a stream-of-consciousness list in each of the six areas. We hope you didn't censor your thoughts as you were writing. If you didn't, your lists may be quite long.

You also have your lists of goals from freshman, sophomore, and junior years that you should have consulted for any lost sheep that you might want to recapture. Look again at these lists, though, and reflect on which goals you achieved and which ones you didn't. Think about the ones you did achieve: *How* did you make them happen? What specific things did you do to make sure you achieved those goals? How can you replicate that activity to help you achieve your new goals?

Really take the time to think about this. Knowing what motivates you to get things done and what specific actions lead you to accomplishment is immensely valuable, because they can be replicated in any number of scenarios. So think about why and how you achieved the goals you did and write down any distinctions you can draw.

Okay! You now need a way to manage all the ideas you've recorded and to go through them and cull the ones that are most critical to you—to choose the ones that you think will give you the most bang for your buck, so to speak.

Here's what you're going to do next.

Go back through each list and read what you've written down. Think about each item and see how it resonates with you. Some of the ideas will get you fired up as soon as you think about them. Others, upon reflection, may not seem that important or that exciting after all.

It's all good. That's part of the goal-setting process.

Go through each list and pick the three things from that area that you are absolutely committed to accomplishing this year. Pick the three things that you feel are most critical to making your last year of college or your college experience as a whole a success—three that would make you feel great about yourself if you were to accomplish them.

Circle those items in each list.

Feeling really ambitious? Want to pick four or five? That's fine, . . . but don't feel that you have to. You want to keep the number of goals manageable—so that you'll actually follow through and complete them. Three in each category is fine. More in some categories and less in others is fine too, but make sure you have at least one goal in each category to maintain some balance.

Remember: pick the ideas from each list that excite you the most or that, on reflection, seem to make the most sense or to be the most important.

Go ahead and make your choices now.

ONE MORE STEP . . .

Okay.

You should now have chosen somewhere around eighteen goals for your senior year.

But you're not done yet.

Now, for each one of these goals, we want you to articulate at least one very good reason why it is *essential* for you to follow up and to achieve that goal during your senior year. Make sure your reason compels you—that it lights a fire under you and propels you toward meeting the goal.

Articulating a powerful rationale makes it far less likely that you will simply forget about these goals once you conclude this exercise and close this chapter. So really take the time to do this well. Amend and edit your reasons. Choose powerful language and drill down into the real motives compelling you to achieve these goals.

Create a master list of each of your goals and your rationale for achieving it, and keep it somewhere where you can refer to it often.

Tape your list of goals up to the wall over your desk or on the mirror in your closet. If you don't have that kind of privacy, keep it in your desk drawer or your day planner—but refer to it at least once a week. Daily is even better.

If you did this in previous years, you've no doubt reaped the benefits of the process. If you're starting now, do this for your entire first semester, and we bet you'll be hooked for life. You won't believe the progress you'll make.

Congratulations on completing your senior year goal-setting workshop!

ADDITIONAL RESOURCES

Robbins, Anthony. *Awaken the Giant Within.* New York: Free Press, 1992.

Robbins, Anthony. *Personal Power* (audio series). Robbins Research International. (www.anthonyrobbins.com)

Robbins, Anthony. *RPM Planner Kit* (time management system). (www.anthonyrobbins.com)

Robbins, Anthony. Unlimited Power: The New Science of Personal Achievement. New York: Free Press, 1997.

Five Ways to
Avoid Senioritis

*Short as life is, we make it still shorter
by the careless waste of time.*

Victor Hugo

Senioritis is just as common in college as it was in high school, if
not more so, and is characterized by the same listlessness, lack of
motivation, sleeping late, skipping classes, road tripping, and perpet-
ual partying as it was if you had it four years ago. And just as in high
school, senioritis can roll in like a fog, afflict everyone around you,
and sabotage what should otherwise be the absolutely best year of
your college career both academically and socially.

You must do all that you can to prevent senioritis from taking you down and
robbing you of the incredible opportunities that senior year will offer you. To that
end, we offer you five tried-and-true strategies to ensure that when the plague hits,
it will stop at your door.

GET *REALLY* INTO YOUR SENIOR THESIS OR SENIOR PROJECT

If you are academically oriented at all, there must be *some* aspect of your major,
or something you can at least tangentially relate to your major, that you would like
to read about, research, and study in depth. Take whatever time you need to come

up with the idea that really, really excites you—and once you have it, don't stop until you locate a faculty member who can share your enthusiasm for the subject and who will agree to guide you on your path.

From there, the sky is truly the limit.

Perhaps you'd like to go completely nutty with your senior thesis, as Dan and I and many of your other mentors did. Petition your department for double or even triple credit for your project, write the magnum opus on your subject area, and try to get it published. If your project is in the arts, don't just stop at the bare minimum—composing a piece of music, completing an original work in oils, or writing a one-act play. Compose something unbelievable and then stage it for performance on campus, go wild and put on an entire exhibition in oils, or write a three-act play and direct it for performance in the spring term. If you're in the laboratory, find a faculty adviser who will let you really spread your wings and delve deeply into a particular research question that interests you and who will agree to help you publish a paper on your results.

The senior thesis is something that you can simply do to get credit and get it done, or it can become the capstone of your college career and something you look back on with pride and nostalgia for the rest of your life.

This is the single best way we know to stave off senioritis. You will simply be too excited and too busy with your work to get bored and disenchanted!

TAKE AN INDEPENDENT STUDY

Or you could *really* get crazy and write your thesis *and* do an independent study with a professor in an area completely outside your major. Maybe you've always wanted to read a particular novel in depth, use secondary sources to deeply explore its meaning, and then write a paper about a particular aspect of the book. Maybe there is a particular historical event that holds some significance for you that you would like to give some concentrated study. As for me, I wanted to write a teleplay—so, rather than either just talking about it or simply doing it in my spare time, I went to the film studies department, found a professor knowledgeable about screenplays, and registered for independent study with him, for credit. Needless to say, when you're doing what you love to do, it doesn't feel like work—and senioritis doesn't have a shot at you.

Again, the sky is really the limit here. Almost every college and university will embrace an ambitious student interested in exploring some academic area in depth for credit. The thing is, most students just aren't ambitious enough to take such initiative.

Trust me when I tell you that there is no greater joy than a semester full of courses that you love.

Make this your reality.

GET CREDIT FOR EXPLORING A NEW HOBBY

In a similar vein, you may have noticed at one time or another that your course catalogue is full of interesting courses in such areas as athletics, photography, nature, art, music, and writing. Do any of these things interest you? Perhaps you'd like to explore a new hobby for credit.

What could be better than learning how to play acoustic guitar, to play tennis, to take stunning pictures, or to cook—and getting credit for doing so?

You've spent most of your college career—and you're probably stocked up pretty well during at least your first semester of senior year as well—taking serious, academic coursework. There is nothing wrong with dedicating a class or two during senior year to some interesting elective subjects.

Take a spin through the course catalogue, find something that interests you, and enroll. This breath of fresh air might be just the thing you need to keep you engaged for the entirety of senior year.

DEVOTE YOURSELF TO YOUR EXTRACURRICULAR ACTIVITIES

As you make the turn into senior year, chances are you will be in one of the positions of power for whatever extracurricular activities you have engaged in throughout your college career. Throw yourself into this work—and make a lasting impact on the organization.

Most seniors who ascend to positions of power simply act as placeholders—keeping the organization running and doing the same things in the same order this year that they have been done in past years.

Why not shake things up?

If this is an organization you truly care about, try to schedule a new event that will dramatically increase the exposure of the organization; have a retreat to evaluate and change the organizational structure of the organization, write a mission, or decide on a strategic plan; or figure out a way to raise some real money to leave a lasting legacy.

Sure, you could do what countless seniors before you have done: simply keep the organization flying on autopilot. Or you could do something radical and actually make a real difference.

DO ALL THE THINGS YOU STILL WANT TO DO
BUT HAVEN'T DONE

Finally we come to the catch-all suggestion that will help you fill those random afternoons and evenings without definitive plans. As you have no doubt learned by now, your college is an incredibly vibrant place—alive with the social, political, musical, and creative rhythms of its students.

Have you drunk fully from the experiences it offers?

Have you been to a singing group concert? Have you heard the college orchestra? Have you been to a debate in the political union or gone to hear any of the people who come to the campus speaker series? Have you gone to a game of any of the less well known varsity teams—such as a fencing meet or an equestrian event? Have you been to a campus play or to hear the campus comedy troupe?

Have you gone to the Parents' Weekend football game with your family, participated in your campus Octoberfest activities, or gone to the fall, winter, or spring formal dances? Have you allowed your roommates to "screw" you at a "Screw Your Roommate" dance? Have you gone caroling during finals or participated in your campus's primal scream?

Have you appreciated your campus in fall, with the leaves ablaze in color, or in winter, buried under a blanket of snow? Have you taken pictures of your roommates and friends engaged in their favorite activities? Have you been to Florida, Texas, or Mexico for a proper celebration of spring break with your roommates or friends from college?

Have you been to all the college museums? Walked through all the different campus buildings and libraries?

Have you thoroughly explored the city or town where your college sits?

Have you taken that art history course you've been meaning to take since sophomore year?

Believe it or not, this year is your last shot.

Take stock of where you are, and think about what you have "left" to do on campus that you haven't yet seen, tried, or done.

Don't leave campus with regrets about things left undone.

Drink deeply now, while you still can.

Choosing and Completing the Senior Thesis or Senior Project

A carelessly planned project takes three times longer to complete than expected; a carefully planned project takes only twice as long.

Anonymous

The introductory courses began your journey. The intermediate courses focused your study and allowed you to explore a few areas or concepts in greater depth. The upper-level seminars narrowed the focus even more, taking you on a concentrated tour of a particular area or concept.

Now it's your turn to take it the final step.

The senior thesis or senior project.

If your college or university requires you to complete a senior thesis or a senior project in order to graduate, then this is the big moment you've been working up to for four years—your chance to pick the subject or area of greatest interest to you and, perhaps, to become one of the country's foremost experts on that subject.

Yes, you read that right. One of the *country's* foremost *experts* on the subject of your choice. This is the Superbowl of your collegiate academic experience.

For most college students, the process of writing a senior thesis is either exhilarating or intolerable. When you talk to students about their experiences, you learn that there isn't much in between. And you learn the one critical element that usually decides which school of thought people fall into:

Pick a topic that fascinates you.

Got that?

If we told you nothing else in this chapter, that would be enough. If you pick a truly compelling topic, you'll be mesmerized by the experience, and the writing process won't feel like work at all. If you procrastinate to the point where you have to hurry to pick a topic, and end up choosing something that is of only marginal interest to you or choosing something that has been beaten to death by countless others—you will have fumbled what is, in all likelihood, the most meaningful academic opportunity of your college career.

So join with us as we consider how to choose a bulletproof topic for your senior thesis and then how to lay out the work schedule to ensure that the experience is an enjoyable one for you the whole year through.

CHOOSE YOUR TOPIC

Understand, first of all, that choosing your thesis or project topic is not something that you are going to do over dinner one night in the dining hall, or on the way back from class on Friday afternoon. If you've followed our advice in this book (see, for example, Chapter 36), the process of choosing your thesis topic will have had its roots in those introductory courses you took as a freshman or sophomore—when a particular subject or topic you came across gave you pause or made you stop and reflect.

Any recollections of something like that?

From there, whether you realized what you were doing then or not, you probably migrated toward a further investigation of related topics around one of those early concepts. Maybe it was a course title that seemed just to jump out of the course catalogue when you looked through it, or it was a course description that made you want to rearrange your entire academic schedule just to make room for the class.

Sound familiar?

And then—perhaps after taking such a course and writing a good general paper on the subject matter—you've identified one or more things that just linger in your mind and won't go away. If you're a chemistry student with designs on medical school, maybe you are wondering why the rate of heart disease in France is so much lower than it is in the United States, despite the fact that the French eat a diet so high in fat. Could something in the copious amounts of wine they drink with their meals inhibit the binding of cholesterol on the walls of their arteries or facilitate its elimination from the body?

Or maybe what keeps you up at night is a fascination with the nine "gams" in Melville's *Moby-Dick,* the telltale names given to the ships in each of those gams, and what the whole series of events might have been intended to symbolize in the context of the larger novel.

Maybe it is a nagging interest in a particular Civil War battle.

Or maybe it is a piece of music that you wake up hearing in your head that you seem destined to compose, or a story you can see in your mind's eye that you seem fated to write.

If nothing immediately jumps out at you, go back through your old syllabi and textbooks searching for the things that compelled you in the early years of college. Look for the general themes at first. Then look for patterns or themes in the courses you subsequently chose to take. Does anything in those syllabi jump out at you?

Look at the courses you are taking now. What are the concepts or ideas that compel you? What interests you or makes you linger over a question you come across in your evening reading?

Is there anything from your larger life experience that intrigues you and might be converted into a workable thesis idea? By way of example, I can remember being forever fascinated with society's persistent belief in the existence of Bigfoot. As a boy, I can remember checking out and reading every available book on the subject and being riveted to television specials on the subject. I spent many a late night on the lodge porch during my summers at Camp Belknap discussing the "Bigfoot myth" with a good friend who was then a graduate student in geography (and is now a professor at West Point) and shared my interest in the subject. We were both fascinated by how the concept of Bigfoot or Sasquatch had survived by oral tradition from Indian times, and why, if Bigfoot really is a myth, it had managed to survive as a myth for so many generations. How had the myth managed to "have legs" for such a long time? And what possible benefit could the North American Indians possibly have realized in perpetuating this story through their oral traditions if it weren't true? Our discussions grew so serious, in fact, that we considered trying to get a publisher to underwrite an anthropological, psychological, and geographical examination of the subject—culminating in our spending a summer in the Pacific Northwest on a legitimate search for this mythical(?) creature.

Had I been an anthropology student, or perhaps even a history or American studies student, I'm quite sure the Bigfoot myth would have been right up there at the very top of my list of potential thesis topics.

Maybe you are rolling your eyes and thinking, "what a completely absurd topic!" But the specifics don't matter. I'm just trying to show you how a closely held fascination can give rise to a really interesting project that will keep you riveted to your work. I'm sure an examination of the Bigfoot myth, through a close reading of American Indian oral tradition and the subsequent writings of early American and

Canadian settlers, would have compelled me to research tirelessly and stay up late in my quest.

And that passion—whether it is for television, Bigfoot, chemistry, writing, or music—is what you're looking for.

"I wrote about the influence of music in the politics of the 1960s," Jim explained. "I chose the topic because of a personal interest in the music and history of that era and the availability of Dean Gerald Wilson, who agreed to advise me and was a mentor who made the project more fun."

"I wrote about the effect teen pregnancy has on the likelihood the mother will be abusive to the child," Erika noted. "I also looked at factors that might lessen that possibility, such as help from family or the child's father, levels of education, and so forth. I chose the topic because I was a teen mother and I wanted to research something that would shine some light on the difficulties of raising a child at a young age. I really enjoyed writing my senior thesis, because it was a topic that was both interesting and educating for me."

"We were looking at the pace of climate change in the critical Antarctic Peninsula, where the zone between the frozen polar world and the slightly less-frozen subpolar climate is in constant flux," Dan explained. "My work involved tied sediment core samples we recovered with seismic profiles of the ocean floor. The general subject matter fit will with my interests and I would have done just about anything to go on that cruise, so I wasn't about to be picky!"

FIND AN ADVISER

Once you have a topic that makes you want to talk to everyone about it (yes, it should be *that* compelling), your next job is to find an adviser to guide your quest. As a first stop, try the professor whose course most closely tracks your subject, while also keeping in mind that this relationship will be the most important one you will have with a professor as an undergraduate. If the professor is completely antisocial, you may want to keep looking. But if you can establish a rapport, the more closely aligned your academic interests are, the more synergy you will have in your relationship, and the richer your experience is likely to be.

If the professor you choose can't accept the role because he or she is going on sabbatical or taking a post as a visiting professor at another school next semester, ask him or her for a recommendation of someone else you could ask—and ask for permission to say that the professor referred you. If the professor you have chosen declines because he or she has already taken on too many advisees, politely probe a little harder. Explain your interest in the subject matter and why you think he or she is a natural fit for the role. Enthusiasm is contagious and can often make a professor take on an extra student—particularly one who is likely to be self-guiding and motivated.

"I chose my major adviser as my thesis adviser," Zoe explained. "I had known her since sophomore year, had taken several of her classes, and respected her work. She had expertise in the political and social aspects of contemporary economics and a particular interest in Marxist and cooperative economic theory, which was an excellent fit for my chosen topic—examining the transformation of the Cuban economy after the break-up of the Soviet Union. I was also confident that we could get along well. The experience did turn out to be an enjoyable one."

For me, the natural choice for an adviser was Dr. Singer, who, as I explained earlier, had taught the seminar on television and human behavior that marked the beginning of my thesis work. When she heard my idea, her interest in the subject was immediately apparent. You want your professor to show enthusiasm. If you see it, as I did in Dr. Singer, you know you have a match.

AGREE ON A SYLLABUS AND INTERIM DEADLINES

Once you've found your professor, hold an initial meeting very early in the fall of your senior year to set out a "syllabus" and a schedule for your thesis research and writing. Make sure that your professor holds you to a series of interim deadlines (source list, source materials, materials read, outline, first draft, second draft, and final draft) spread out over the year to keep you on track. Most senior thesis projects are worth one semester of credit, but if your idea is ambitious enough, with your adviser's blessing you can often successfully petition your department chairman or director of undergraduate studies to approve the project for double credit—or full-year status.

START YOUR RESEARCH RIGHT AWAY

Picking a compelling topic is certainly the most important factor in ensuring that your thesis experience is a happy one. The second most important factor, though, is getting a jump on your work so that the project never becomes a burden on you. As we noted in the chapter on writing a good research paper (Chapter 24), doing good research takes a *lot* of time, and this is particularly true with research for your senior thesis. Because your subject is likely to be a relatively narrow one, you will probably have to request certain materials from interlibrary loan, and if these materials are relatively obscure, there might be only a few libraries in the world that have them.

And they may be lost. Or out. So you might have to make multiple requests. You get the point.

Assemble Your Source List

The first milestone you're headed toward is a completed source list: the complete list of secondary sources that you will use in drafting the paper. You know you have a complete source list when all the sources you consult start referring to each other, but getting to this point will take some time. Creating a good source list will include scouring the online card catalogue at your college or university library, the Internet, and all available collections of journals and periodicals. Be sure to consult both your thesis adviser *and* the reference librarian for help in this process.

Obtain Your Sources

Search the stacks and all the affiliated libraries in your university system. Collect everything and bring it to a central place. Recall any materials that have been taken out by someone else, and request an interlibrary loan of any item that is not in your own library's collection. Finally, search the online card catalogues of one or two larger reputable colleges in your area to see if you can uncover more source material. This is a treasure hunt, and the more treasure you find, the happier you'll be.

Keep Your Research in a Thesis Binder

As you conduct research, keep careful notes of your research trails. Collect printouts of source lists, write notes directly on them, and capture everything in a thesis ring binder so you won't lose any of these materials. There is nothing more frustrating than finding a promising source, getting distracted by something else, and then not being able to find your way back to it.

Collect and Photocopy Source Materials—Including All Identifying Information

As you begin to build your body of research, you are going to start wanting to cross-reference and make notes about certain concepts or ideas. Because you can't write directly in the books, and because Post-its can fall out and start to become unwieldy, you will want to photocopy source materials so you can highlight important passages and write all over them.

As you photocopy these materials, be sure to collect all relevant identifying information about them, including authors' names, publishers' names, and the publication date of the edition of the source you are using. Remember that you will need to collect, list, and properly and carefully cite all your source materials in your final paper. A little bit of care up front will save you a lot of headaches later.

OUTLINE YOUR ARGUMENT AND HOW YOUR SOURCE MATERIALS FIT IN

Next, work up an outline of the paper, complete with your introduction and the layout of your various sections, including the source materials you intend to use for each section. When you've finished sketching out the parameters for the paper, take a step back and see how it hangs together and where you might need some additional resources. When you've completed this process, it's time to check in once again with your thesis adviser.

WORK UP A FIRST DRAFT

Armed with a solid outline, you should feel as though the first draft is writing itself. If you experience this phenomenon, you are probably on your way to a wonderful paper. If you don't, the problem is likely to relate to your organizational structure. Try to move one or more of the sections of the paper around and see if that doesn't produce a breakthrough.

Be *especially* vigilant about crediting any sources you use for arguments, even if you are not quoting them directly. If the ideas or arguments in your paper are not original to you, you need a citation. As you begin the drafting process, particularly if this is the first major paper you've written in college, discuss proper citation methodology with your adviser, who no doubt will be quite familiar with your university's policies on the subject.

EDIT TO A SECOND DRAFT

When you have a first draft in place, it's time to put the paper in a drawer for a week or so. Ideally you'll complete your first draft before spring break, which will serve two purposes. First, your spring break will be a hell of a lot more enjoyable, and you'll have something tangible to drink to. (As if you needed that.) Second, and more important, the break will give your brain some important time away from your work and enable you to come back with a fresh eye for the editing process.

The process from here on in often separates the B papers from the A papers. Those who run out of time will have to rush through the editing process, and it will show. Those who have planned properly will have time to shore up any weak points in their argument with supplementary support, tighten up the prose, and ensure that the citations are right and the formatting looks good on paper. This is the point at which to go back to your adviser for any final thoughts.

POLISH TO A FINAL DRAFT

After another week in the drawer, the paper is ready for a final look. It shouldn't take more than a word or two here or there to take this into the end zone. When the paper represents the very best you have to offer, reflect for a moment or two on its importance in the development of your education—and then turn it in.

Congratulations! The capstone of your college education is now in place.

CELEBRATE—AND CONSIDER PUBLICATION

Time to celebrate. But before you hang up your hat, check in with your thesis adviser and see whether he or she sees any possibility of trying to get part or all of your work published in an appropriate academic journal or a magazine of wider circulation. You've done the work, and a publication credential coming out of college is a nice feather in your cap. There may also be opportunities to present your research at conferences or meetings. Again, your professor will guide you in this regard, but he or she may not appreciate how far you'd like to pursue the project, so make your desires known and see how far your work will take you.

WAIT A MINUTE, DUDE . . . I DIDN'T WRITE A PAPER; I DID A PROJECT INSTEAD

The scope of possible senior theses and senior projects is virtually unlimited. The vast majority of students who do a senior thesis or senior project end up writing a paper, so that's why we've focused on that discussion. We appreciate, however, that your project may have been a piece of sculpture, a public performance of a play or a piece of music, or a series of biochemistry experiments. Obviously there is no specific advice we can give you about these many different projects other than the three points we made at the beginning of the chapter: (1) pick a project that you know will hold your interest for as long as it takes to complete; (2) find an adviser who is both a good match for the project and a good match for your personality, as this person is almost certainly destined to become the most important faculty connection you have at the college or university; and (3) begin your project promptly and work steadily so that you can enjoy the process and never feel burdened by it.

SOME FINAL THOUGHTS

We really encourage you to complete a senior thesis or senior project if you have the chance to do so. Properly planned and executed, the project can be an extremely fulfilling way to complete your college experience.

"Any student considering graduate work should strongly consider doing a thesis or project in the subject they plan to continue studying," Jim advised. "This will be the single best way to get a taste of what graduate work would be like and will help you decide if the path is appropriate for you."

"The thesis was a great experience for me," Dave adds. "I highly recommend writing one if you have the opportunity. I grew ten-fold as a writer, as a researcher, as an editor, and as a thinker during the process. My advice, though, would be to be sure you choose to write about something you truly care about. Your thesis will become your life, and at times, there will be nights that you can't go to sleep because your head is exploding with ideas about different angles that you might want to explore."

"Taking on a large project like this requires a new level of organization, dedication, and perseverance," Dan explained. "It is excellent training for subsequent work in a career and certainly can be a shining component of your portfolio as you approach future employers. Focusing that long on a single topic will also help you assess your level of interest in the field and whether it is something you want to pursue long term."

Working After College

> *Work and play are words used to describe the*
> *same thing under differing conditions.*
>
> Mark Twain

If you have determined, after thoughtful reflection, that rather than taking a year off *or* applying to graduate school, you actually want to become a productive member of society (imagine that!) after graduation—hie thee to your college's career planning and placement office as soon as you get back to campus for your senior fall. Browse around and become familiar with the resources available to you, and schedule an appointment with the career services director or one of his or her staff members as soon as you can get one.

BEFORE YOUR APPOINTMENT

In order to get a jump on your employment search and maximize the efficiency of your meeting with the career services director or staff person, there are a few things you should do prior to your meeting.

Update Your Résumé

Make sure that your résumé is up-to-date and in proper form to send out to the business world. Your résumé is your calling card, and the career services people are going to hammer you over and over again to get your résumé into perfect—and we mean *perfect*—shape.

You might as well get a jump on the process.

Make a List of Your Strengths and Weaknesses

We know this sounds corny, but it is another thing that the career services people are likely to ask you to do. If you are an ace at math and economics but fear the written word, you are going to be in the market for a different job than the person who loves to write but can't calculate proper change. As you construct this list, though, go beyond the simple things.

Do you like to work with people, or are you more comfortable alone with your thoughts as you read, write, or engage in research? What were the subjects you liked best in college? Which ones did you hate? Are you better working alone or as part of a team? Are you a better leader or a better follower? Do you take constructive criticism well, or do you tend to be defensive?

So make up a list of your strengths and weaknesses. Just do it. The career services people will use this information to help suggest possible jobs that you might not even have thought of.

Describe Your Ideal Workday in a Paragraph

Remember, we said *work*day—so lying on a beach reading a novel doesn't count. But if reading a novel would be part of your ideal workday, perhaps working as an editorial assistant at a publishing house or as an agent's assistant at a literary agency would be in the cards for you. And if your being outside in the sun is the important part of the equation, knowing that will help the career services people steer you in the direction of jobs that will have you working outside in the great outdoors where you can enjoy the sun, rather than the glow of fluorescent lights.

See how it works?

Make a List of Jobs That Interest You—and Why

Don't worry about whether or not you could actually *get* the job—just make a list of jobs that interest you, and include a line or two about *why* they interest you. Again, you're looking to trigger ideas in the minds of the career services people. It may be possible to get one of the jobs on your list. If it isn't, maybe you can get something like it, or at least get into the same industry, where you can network with people and put yourself into position to get the job you want a year or two down the road after you've proven yourself and paid some dues.

DURING YOUR APPOINTMENT

Remember that your career services office serves hundreds, if not thousands, of students every year—and the staff's goal is to get you employed. Your job is to make sure they get you employed where you *want* to get employed. The way to do this is to take ownership of your job search (which is why we suggested the pre-meeting legwork we just described) and to take control of your appointment.

If the career services director or staff person starts suggesting things that don't interest you, it is okay to politely interrupt and say so, rather than letting him or her waste ten minutes telling you about something you know you're not interested in. At the same time, though, it is important at least to listen to the person's suggestions and ideas offered in response to your materials. Although an initial suggestion may not hit the mark, a later one might.

Make the appointment a *conversation;* don't just sit there and expect the person to deliver you the ideal job on a silver platter. The most successful appointments are ones that begin as conversations, and both people help narrow the field of possibilities until you collectively and cooperatively generate a list of four or five viable opportunities.

Once you have a list of options, ask for advice and suggestions about how to pursue the jobs you seek. See if the career services office maintains a contact list of alumni working in the fields that interest you, a list of open jobs in the industries that interest you, or any other reference resources. Avail yourself of every available resource. In the campus job search, as in the real world, initiative pays dividends.

AFTER YOUR APPOINTMENT

After you've had your appointment, spend the necessary time working through the available resources in the career services office. When you get a lead, follow it through by phone or on the Internet. Be polite but firm. If you are initially spurned or rejected, try someone else at the same organization. Write letters and e-mails. Make polite phone calls. Show persistence and initiative. All it takes is one "yes" to get the job interview you are looking for.

WHAT SOME OF US CHOSE TO DO

A number of the mentors decided to teach, either to explore the profession as a possible vocation or to give something back.

"I took a job through Teach for America teaching Spanish to sixth, seventh, and eighth graders at a public middle school in the Bronx," Carolyn explained. "I was *thrilled* to have the opportunity. I spent two years teaching at the same school, and although I ultimately decided that I did not want to stay in teaching, my experience during those two years was truly invaluable and taught me a great deal about the world and about myself."

"I got a job in a teaching apprentice program after college," Dave said. "I wanted to test the waters in education and this program gave me a unique opportunity to be a second teacher in a classroom with an experienced mentor teacher. I went about getting this job through personal connections and a teacher recruitment firm. In the end, it was a personal connection that helped to get my foot in the door. I think the same can be said across the board: you can have the best résumé and interviewing skills in the world, but if you know someone on the inside, it can take you far."

"From the time I left high school, I knew that I wanted to go back to my school and teach for a year after college," Amanda echoed. "My high school had a cool one-year program for 'rookie' teachers. Senior year of college, I applied according to the deadlines. A teacher I had known when I was a student was in charge of the program. That job was something that I knew I wanted to do, even if I didn't continue teaching after that."

Jim used the year after college to bankroll his later adventures through-hiking the Appalachian Trail.

"I started looking in the beginning of my final semester through on-campus recruiting," Jim noted. "I ended up getting the job by responding to a recent graduate's e-mail. He had started working for a large project that needed additional staff. The job was not what I wanted, but I did not want to move home, so I took it and worked for a year. After having saved some money up, I decided to do some traveling and walked the Appalachian Trail."

Erik followed his heart (and his girlfriend) to Phoenix, and learned a lesson about the inherent difficulties in trying to balance two people's interests at the very beginning of adult life.

"Ugh. Well to continue the long saga that was my college romance, I had a decision to make early in my senior year," Erik explained. "My girlfriend had interned with the same company for two straight summers, and they offered her a full-time job after graduation. She knew she was going to take the job back in Phoenix. So I had to decide between moving to Phoenix to be with her and trying to find a job out there, or proceeding with the 'normal' recruiting route and accepting the best job I could find regardless of its location. I loved my girlfriend and wanted to try to start a life with her after school, so I chose the former. I also wasn't sure exactly what I wanted to do for work at that point, so it was a pretty easy decision for me to make at the time.

"We had a tough time once we moved to Phoenix. I was unhappy because I wasn't making any progress in a job market that was supposed to be 'hot.' I ended up working a handful of odd jobs just trying to contribute to our household income while I tried to figure out what I *really* wanted to do. I somehow ended up trying to sell insurance full time about eight months after we arrived in Phoenix, and that lasted for only three months because I was completely miserable doing it.

"My lack of confidence in finding my way in the workforce caused me to be very unhappy and our relationship ultimately suffered greatly as a result of it. I ended up moving back home after only a year out there."

As for me, I took a job working for Dr. Singer as the national coordinator of her research study examining the prosocial effects of the *Barney and Friends* television show on three-, four-, and five-year-olds. I traveled the country to our various research sites, administered questionnaires, and managed a fleet of psychology doctoral students who were helping us with the study around the country. I scored and coded questionnaires, kept the databases, and did some of the statistical analysis and project writing.

And I got to hang out with *Barney* a lot.

He really is a wonderful, nurturing, and educational resource for young children. The research bore that out, and my own three-year-old son will tell you that himself. When you have kids, you could do *much* worse than allowing them to watch *Barney.*

As much as I love Dr. Singer, and loved working with her, though, the repetitiveness of the job, and more particularly, having to spend so much time watching, testing, and hanging out with *Barney* often made me want to blow my brains out.

And that's when I concluded that a job in psychology research was not for me and I started thinking more seriously about law school. And that, and graduate school more generally, not coincidentally, is the subject of our next chapter.

Applying to Graduate School

Grad school: it's not just a job, it's an indenture!

Graffiti

Applying to graduate school during your senior year in college, or sometime thereafter, is a significant undertaking that will require a serious commitment of time and a particular attention to organization.

We hope you have been following the chronological advice we've provided in earlier chapters of this book—most notably, Chapter 35 ("Looking Ahead to Graduate School"); if you have, by the time you return to campus for your senior year, you will already have compiled a final list of the schools to which you will be applying, you will have downloaded or received each school's application materials, and you will be well on your way to completing these applications.

Obviously, your application process will be driven by different deadlines depending on the graduate field you have chosen and, even within that field, on which individual graduate schools to which you are applying. Still, there are general application schedules that you should become familiar with, and there is some basic advice that will help you navigate *any* of these application processes. This chapter is intended to help you with both. The next section will discuss some general strategies to help you manage your application process; the rest of the chapter will provide generally applicable schedules to help keep you on track.

GET ORGANIZED AND STAY ORGANIZED

Applying to graduate school while at the same time taking a full course load, trying to complete the requirements of your college major(s), and trying to write a senior thesis or complete a senior project can be a very challenging undertaking. Obviously, staying abreast of your individual application deadlines, keeping track of essays and other application materials, and distributing and tracking your recommendations are all critical tasks. As always, organization makes the difference between a smooth and relatively stress-free application process and a process that is wrought with chaos. Consider the following strategies to help you stay organized as you apply to graduate school.

Compile a Spreadsheet or Table of Schools, Application Components, and Deadlines

As soon as you have either downloaded or received applications from the schools on your list, compile a spreadsheet or table collecting all the necessary components of each application, with their deadlines, in one place. Keep this master list in a safe place. As you complete the various components of a particular application, check them off on this master list, such that you will always know at a glance *exactly* where you stand in your journey through the application process. The figure here is an example of a spreadsheet for an individual school.

UNIVERSITY OF PENNSYLVANIA LAW SCHOOL

3400 Chestnut Street

Philadelphia, PA 19104

admissions@law.upenn.edu

Phone: (215) 898-7400

Early Notification: Due 11/1; notification 12/31 (nonbinding)

Rank on My List of Schools: 4

ACTION ITEM	Date Due	Date Completed
Download online application form (available 8/1)	8/1	✔ 8/1
Request recommendation 1	8/15	✔ 8/15
Request recommendation 2	8/15	✔ 8/15
Request certified undergraduate transcripts	9/1	✔ 9/1

ACTION ITEM	Date Due	Date Completed
Request LSAT/LSDAS score report	9/1	✔ 9/1
Personal statement draft	9/15	✔ 9/10
Optional essay A draft	9/15	✔ 9/5
Optional essay B draft	9/15	✔ 9/10
Optional essay C draft	9/15	✔ 9/10
Follow up with recommender 1	9/20	✔ 9/20
Follow up with recommender 2	9/20	✔ 9/20
Receive LSAT/LSDAS score report	10/1	✔ 9/21
Complete financial aid worksheets/compile data	10/1	✔ 9/15
Personal statement complete	10/7	✔ 9/27
Optional essay A complete	10/7	✔ 9/29
Optional essay B complete	10/7	✔ 9/22
Optional essay C complete	10/7	✔ 10/4
Receive certified undergraduate transcripts	10/15	✔ 9/23
Receive completed recommendation 1	10/15	✔ 9/7
Receive completed recommendation 2	10/15	✔ 9/30
Application fee: $70 ("Trustees of the University of Pennsylvania")	10/15	✔ 10/15
Application signed and FedEx'ed	10/15	✔ 10/15
Application deemed "complete" by admissions office	10/25	✔ 10/22
Financial aid package deemed "complete" by admissions office	10/25	✔ 10/22
Decision	12/31	✔ 12/2!!

Choose a System to Keep School-Specific Materials Organized

Once you have your overview organizational system in place, you will still need a system to keep track of the materials for each school. For that, I recommend the system I used: I had a different file folder for each school; I taped the spreadsheet of that school's individual requirements and due dates to the inside of the folder and stored all school-specific documents inside that folder. So, for example, when I completed essays for that school, they went right into the folder, both for safe-keeping and to ensure that the right essay went to the right school. In the blizzard of paper that characterizes the graduate school application process, it is easy to mix things up accidentally. Having a clear organizational system in place for each school can be very helpful.

FOLLOW UP WITH RECOMMENDERS AND THE ADMISSIONS OFFICE

Remember that almost everyone these days has a busy life, so it is more essential now than ever before that you *follow up* on every piece of your application. Once you have chosen your recommenders (and given them plenty of time to complete your recommendations), be sure to follow up with them about a month ahead of your deadline to make sure they haven't forgotten you. A simple reminder call is all that is required to keep you on schedule.

The same is true when you submit your application materials. Always do so two weeks before the deadline, to ensure that loose ends or missing pieces can be taken care of in advance of any "drop dead" date. Take *nothing* for granted. Admissions staffs do an amazing job tracking and documenting the incredible volume of information they deal with each year—but mistakes do occasionally happen. Call the admissions office of each school about ten days after it should have received your information to ensure that the office deems both your application materials and your financial aid materials complete.

There is a lot of important and specific advice to convey about applying to graduate school. We recommend that you consult one of the resources referenced at the end of the chapter to guide you further.

ADDITIONAL RESOURCES

Miller, Robert H., and Koegler, Katherine. *Business School Confidential.* New York: St. Martin's/Griffin, 2004.

Miller, Robert H. *Law School Confidential (Revised Edition).* New York: St. Martin's/Griffin, 2004.

Miller, Robert H., and Bissell, Dan. *Med School Confidential.* New York: St. Martin's/Griffin, 2006.

Peters, Robert. *Getting What You Came For: The Smart Student's Guide to Earning an M.A. or a Ph.D. (Revised Edition).* New York: Farrar, Straus and Giroux, 1997.

Finding Yourself

The Case for Taking Time Off After Graduation

*Your time is limited, so don't waste it living someone else's life.
Don't let the noise of others' opinions drown out your own
inner voice. And most importantly, have the courage to
follow your heart and intuition. They somehow
already know what you truly want to become.*

Steve Jobs

Going to college today isn't like it was when your parents went (*if* they went) a generation ago. For one thing, getting *in* to college is a much trickier game today than it was a generation ago. Everything has gotten more competitive—and with that, the experience itself has become much more fast paced and goal driven—as you've seen from the advice provided in the pages of this book thus far.

For many of us, college is a moving sidewalk that takes us in as children and deposits us, four years later, into the world—where we are immediately bombarded with the relentless message that it is time to get started building a life, finding a spouse, settling down, and becoming "responsible" members of society. And many of us dutifully accommodate that expectation, coming out of college and going right on, with our heads down, to the "next big thing," or in order to "make someone proud of us," to "live up to expectations," or whatever it is.

Whoa there, doggie. Hold on just a minute.

Nobody believes in the power of goal setting or longitudinal thinking more than I do. That's why I built four goal-setting workshops into this book for you, and included a whole team of über-mentors to give you the benefit of their longitudinal wisdom.

It might surprise you to learn that I am also one of the most vigorous proponents of taking some time to explore all of your possible options after college before you make a real commitment to the "next thing," whatever that is.

"Wow," you might be saying. "That's a pretty stark contradiction. . . . First, this guy has me setting goals and designing a strategy for my major, my core curriculum, and even my summers off . . . and now he's telling me to explore something different after graduation?"

That's exactly what I'm telling you. And it's not a contradiction at all. If you've done college "right"—which is to say, milked the experience for all it's worth by taking as many courses as you could responsibly jam into your schedule; salting your free time with lectures, extracurricular activities, and sports; and spending the wee hours bonding with your roommates, classmates, and new friends—you're going to make the turn into senior year pretty exhausted by it all.

And then you need to write a thesis. And worry about finding a place in the world where you can actually get paid enough to survive or, in the alternative, apply to graduate school and postpone that inevitability a little bit longer.

Or for some of us, much longer.

Slow down! Why is it that so many of us are in such a hurry to "get started" on a career track at twenty-one or twenty-two?

"Money," you say. "I've just incurred all this debt, and I need to start paying it back."

Or . . .

"Responsibility," you say. "Once you graduate from college, it is time to go out into the world and start doing something with your life."

Or . . .

"My parents," you say. "They helped pay for college, and now they're expecting me to go get a job and act like an adult."

Okay, so start paying it back. Go out and do *something* that will allow you to start doing that. I'm not suggesting you should take a one-way trip to Jackson Hole, take up permanent residence in the ski dorm there, and drink yourself into oblivion every night. I'm not saying you should go down to Key West with your acoustic guitar and become a burnout.

All I'm encouraging you to do is to slow down in your haste to grow up.

Take a look at Steve Jobs's quote at the top of this chapter. You know who Steve Jobs is, right? The cofounder of Apple Computer. Father of the iPod. Brilliant businessperson and gazillionaire.

Yet look at what he is asking you.

"Are you living your own life?"

Well, are you? Or are you trying to measure up to an older sibling or doing what you think your parents want you to do?

"Are you listening to your inner voice?"

Is your inner voice telling you that you want to become a chef and open your own restaurant? If it is, then for the love of God, don't go to law school! That's a recipe for misery!

"Are you following your heart and your intuition?"

Well?

When was the last time you sat down and asked yourself, "If I could invent my world and make it perfect, what would I be doing for a living?"

What would you be doing?

Teaching? Then why the hell don't you go do it now, instead of enduring twenty years of misery on Wall Street and a divorce before you do it?

Founding a nonprofit? Then go DO it. I interviewed a candidate for admission to Yale last week who founded a thriving nonprofit organization when she was fifteen years old!

Want to be an artist or a musician?

Then go *do* it.

Don't live someone else's life. Life your own life. Do it now, before you have kids and a mortgage, and it is much harder.

So where are you in your thinking? Do you know for certain that you want to go to law school? Are you absolutely sure? Even if you are, do you feel mentally and physically ready to start down that road next fall? It's an incredibly grueling intellectual experience that requires you to be at your mental, psychological, and physical best in order to perform optimally.

Ditto for med school.

You think Wall Street or one of those management consulting firms is going to be any easier? Think again.

A master's or Ph.D. program? Same deal. Huge commitment.

Starting your own business? Hah! That's the biggest commitment of them all.

Now imagine trying to accomplish one of those things in a state of mental exhaustion and with only a halfhearted commitment to it. We see it all the time, and the story almost always ends the same way. You end up miserable, you underperform in comparison to your true ability, and then you shortchange yourself in the opportunity department.

And for what?

All in the name of haste—of hurrying to grab the next brass ring.

Permit me another story.

As I've told you earlier in the book, I came to my choice of major late in the game, and for that reason, my last two years at Yale were jam-packed full of activity. As I hit the turn into senior year, I was so busy working on my thesis and trying to fulfill course requirements that I missed all the off-ramps into life that many of my classmates were taking. At some point in there, a lot of people were interviewing for those Wall Street and management consulting gigs—the two-year commitments with the big paydays that everyone seems to lust after.

Funny how very few of my friends who were in such a hurry to rush off into that world actually stayed there.

Then there were people all around me freaking out about the MCAT and the LSAT. Trying to write their senior thesis, take courses, do test prep, and apply to med school or law school all at the same time.

It was madness.

If I hadn't had my head down, and if I had seen an advertisement for an LSAT prep course at around that time, I probably would have taken it—and might have applied to law school directly.

That would have been the biggest mistake of my life, because I wasn't ready to go to law school at that point. Not even close. But I don't think I would have known that then, so I'm thankful for my good fortune in missing the bus on that one.

Anyway, the rest of us blissfully ignorant people trudged on with our coursework, enjoyed a more leisurely pace in completing our senior theses and senior projects, and, I think, really enjoyed our senior year of college as a result. I can remember spending hours and hours in the library with my roommate Joel reading source materials for our theses—and marveling at the true pleasure of learning for learning's sake. Without the pressures of deciding what we had to do with our lives *right now,* we were liberated to steep in the academic environment of college, to make our own schedules, and to revel in the experience.

As I mentioned, I took a couple of elective screenwriting seminars and got hooked on writing.

The rest, as they say, is history. But I would never have had the time to take those classes if I was pushing hard to enter graduate school that fall. My schedule would have been blocked full of musts, leaving no time for shoulds, wants, or wishes. And that would have been a tragedy.

When it came time to graduate, I knew I was going back to Belknap for the summer, but I had no idea what I was doing after that. I loved writing, and thought seriously about packing up the car after camp and driving to Los Angeles to try to make my way as a writer out there. And then I thought about the thousands of other people who did the same thing every year, only to burn out or wash out a decade later with nothing to show for themselves. That choice, I thought, was a little too seductive and a little too high-risk for me.

I was unresolved about psychology as a vocation; although I had enjoyed my coursework immensely, I didn't know if a lifetime of research, writing, or clinical practice was what I really wanted to do. Applying to Ph.D. programs in psychology would require taking the GREs and then embarking on the lengthy, expensive, and extremely time-consuming task of completing applications and interviews. It was a commitment I didn't feel ready to make at the time.

I started thinking more seriously about law school, and resolved that when the summer ended, I would drive out to my aunt and uncle's camp in the Adirondacks and hole up for a couple of months to prepare for the LSAT and, at the same time, get to work on a screenplay. I knew I would take the LSAT in the middle of October. And I had no plans after that.

By late September, after a month of daily running and concentrated study for the LSAT in a distraction-free environment (no TV or radio and only a party-line phone!), I was hitting my target scores on my practice LSATs, and felt ready. I think there is a lot of value in using this "total immersion" method to study for the LSAT or the MCAT, by the way, as a number of the mentors in *Law School Confidential* and *Med School Confidential* agree. In any event, it was nice to have the opportunity to do it that way.

Around that same time, my college thesis adviser called me with news that she had just received a grant to study the prosocial teaching effects of *Barney* and asked me to come back and act as the national coordinator for the research. The school-year-long position gave me a real opportunity to evaluate psychology as a possible profession, gave me chance to do some traveling, and provided an income stream to pay for room and board in New Haven and get me through the rest of the year. And, of course, it gave me the chance to learn more from Dr. Singer!

Although I will never again be able to be in the same room when *Barney* is on television, the year served its purpose. After working on this grant for the year, administering the tests across the country, and collecting and analyzing the data, I realized that a life in academic psychology was not a perfect fit for me. I spent a terrific year with my adviser, lectured on some of my thesis research, and applied and got into law school.

So, one would think, my exploration was done, my path determined.

And one would be wrong.

There was still the whole writing thing. Because the grant research, coupled with applying to law school, had taken so much time and had been so demanding, I had written less than half of my screenplay.

And I was haunted by that.

As the summer passed, I became more and more restless and uncertain about my decision to enroll at Penn for law school that fall. I began to get cranky and irritable, and eventually found myself at another one of those defining crossroads in life. I knew that if I went to law school that fall, I would probably never finish my screenplay—at least not for the foreseeable future, and I would therefore never really know what writing might have done for me.

Eventually the relentless nagging in my gut became too much to ignore. I called the dean of admissions at Penn and asked her how she would feel if I deferred my admission for a year. As it turned out (and when a decision is the right one, it often does), the first-year class at Penn was oversubscribed, and she was *looking* for people to take one-year deferrals. The coincidence was remarkable, and I signed up then and there.

But then there was the little issue of explaining this decision to my parents—who were part of the process because they were *paying* for it.

It didn't go well.

My dad flipped out, calling the decision "irresponsible" and wondering when I was going to "start acting like an adult."

My mom cried.

But I knew from what I felt like inside that I was making the right decision, so I did not allow them to shake my resolve.

My dad asked me what I planned to do for the year. I told him I was going to spend it writing, though I did not yet know where.

He told me that because he disagreed with the decision, he would not support it financially; I would have to make it on my own. That seemed fair to me, so we shook on it and agreed to disagree. I headed back up to Belknap feeling as though a huge weight had been lifted from my shoulders. I don't think I have *ever* felt as free as I felt on that drive back, and for many months after that.

I knew I was doing exactly what I wanted to do with my life. And the feeling was amazing.

After turning back several offers to spend the winter with friends at various ski towns in Colorado (so tempting—but remember, the point was to spend the year really exploring writing, not perfecting my mogul skills), I found myself on a ferry to Martha's Vineyard, which I had always wanted to visit, and where I knew no one. I spent the first ten days living out of my car and in the youth hostel, making a few bucks playing cards at night and pounding the pavement by day looking for an affordable place to live and somewhere to work. I ended up getting a job working at a gourmet coffee place called Espresso Love, and after befriending a local realtor, house-sitting a multimillion-dollar oceanfront retreat for a friend of hers.

I paid my way; finished, shopped, and *almost* sold the screenplay; taught a screenwriting course on the island; read my way through about 20 percent of my list of the top one hundred books of all time; and got in really good shape. I had gotten some very positive feedback from a well-known screenwriting agent in California, who agreed to read anything else I wrote. By the time the year was over, though, I recognized that writing alone would not satisfy me for a lifetime. It was a lonely life, and there were a lot of hours to fill every day.

And, thus, with all paths explored, *that's* when my life path finally crystallized for me. I would go to law school and continue to write on the side.

When the year ended, I left Martha's Vineyard with a few scars from the espresso machine on my arms, a lot of stories, and peace in my soul for the first time ever.

After a terrific final summer at Belknap, I said my good-byes, packed up my car, and headed for Philadelphia and the rest of my life—where I would approach law school fresh, energized, and clear that it was what I was *supposed* to be doing with my life at the time.

I met my wife, Carolyn, there during the first week of school.

I made some really good friends.

I made *Law Review.*

I got the job I wanted.

And it's all worked out pretty well since then.

For me, finding inner peace and my life's direction was the benefit of taking time off after college—and even my parents came (with time) to appreciate how important that process was for me.

Others of you may be haunted by other things. An urge to travel and see the world. A desire to teach in the inner city. A need to help the less fortunate in a Third World country or to work to save the environment.

Maybe you just want to spend some time with a relative who isn't well, or just need to take a time-out to refresh.

Whatever your motivation, as long as you can articulate it to yourself, a year or two off will probably do you a lot of good. Just be sure you actually do some thinking and soul-searching during your time off, as opposed to just partying yourself into oblivion every night. Remember, we can't all be Jimmy Buffett—and even he plays a guitar for a living.

Whatever you choose to do, resist the lemming mentality—blindly going down the moving walkway of life, grabbing at brass rings without knowing why you're doing so. If you want to go to get your Ph.D. in astrophysics because you just can't imagine ever doing anything else with your life, or you want to go to med school right out of college because it is going to take you seventeen years of residency, internship, and fellowships to get where you want to go—then by all means, do so.

Just please know why you're doing it.

"I have also found that when I've taken time out to ponder life's bigger issues, solutions tend to fall into place almost effortlessly, and the world is suddenly full of signs and hints," Zoe agreed. "For example, prior to writing my grad school essays, I took a short oceanside camping trip alone. It rained nearly the whole time and I tended the campfire constantly. One gray morning, as I started to crumple up an outdated newspaper, I noticed an article related to a migrant health program in a town about 90 minutes from where I grew up. It also happened to be the program that I talked about earlier that I had almost taken the internship position with the summer before.

"Reading that article gave me a vision of somewhere I could actually imagine myself going when I completed my master's degree, which, at the time, was then still four years away on the horizon.

"Now, nine years later, I work for the very health center that was in that article in that old newspaper, doing work remarkably similar to what I envisioned that day, and I live in the town where I took that camping trip. Did I consciously *choose* all those things? No, in fact, it wasn't until I had signed the contract for my current job that I even remembered the whole 'coincidental' chain of events. However, it is clear to me now that on that rainy morning nine years ago, I unwittingly took the first step on the twisting path that has led me home—and that I was drawn here by an unconscious but knowing part of myself."

Your Graduation Planning Guide

There is a good reason they call these ceremonies "commencement exercises." Graduation is not the end. It is the beginning.

Orrin Hatch

Graduation from college is a bittersweet time.

It will be one of the proudest times of your life. You have applied yourself for four years, satisfied the requirements of your major course of study, perhaps written a thesis or completed an extensive senior project, and earned a degree. This experience will serve you well for the rest of your life, not only for what it has taught you but also for the friends and contacts you have made during your college years.

And that's where the sad part lies.

For four years, you have lived on a campus, in a dynamic, alive environment in close proximity to many friends and people your age. If you've done it right, it was the best four years of your life so far.

And now it's all about to change.

Your class, as a group, is about to be flung from the confines of your campus, out to the four corners of the world. Never again will you all be assembled in the same place as you are now. That realization can produce a strong emotional reaction, and if you have had a good time in college, you are likely to experience that reaction, so be ready for it.

At the same time that you are dealing with these grave feelings of imminent departure, however, you will need to be planning for the arrival of your family.

And that, depending on your relationship with your family, can either be a lot of fun or a real pain in the ass.

In the hopes of helping you make your experience as pleasant as possible, we offer here a few things to remember.

MAKE RESTAURANT AND HOTEL RESERVATIONS *WAY* AHEAD OF TIME

Needless to say, graduation time is the busiest time of the year on any college campus—because it is the only time of the year when members of the extended families of nearly every graduating senior will descend on the campus at the same time and be looking to stay overnight. That will put a lot of pressure on available hotel rooms and seats in area restaurants.

You'll need to be proactive.

First, call the registrar's office at your college and find out the date of your graduation. Remember, graduation usually involves events spread out on both Saturday and Sunday—so ask that question to make certain that you have complete information.

Find out when area hotels will open up reservations for your graduation season. Often it will be a year in advance—and the rooms in the best hotels and the hotels closest to campus will sell out almost immediately. Because parking around campus at graduation time is also a complete nightmare, you will score *huge* points with your family if you can get them housed within walking distance of the campus and all the graduation festivities.

Target two or three of the closest hotels and make some calls to find out when they will start taking reservations and whether you can get on a waiting list or a call list. Talk to your parents and extended family and try to determine how many hotel rooms you're going to need—and book as many rooms as you're going to need *right away,* as soon as they become available.

The same holds true for restaurant reservations—although restaurants will usually wait until a few months before graduation week to open up reservations. Pick two or three of your favorites and make reservations as soon as the restaurants begin taking them. If you have a particularly close relationship with your roommates, fraternity brothers or sorority sisters, or teammates, you might want to try to organize a community dinner for everyone's families by renting a function room or even an entire small restaurant for the occasion. We did this with great success at my graduation—everyone had a good time, and the size of the group allowed for a lot of intermingling and took pressure off a couple of my roommates who had uncomfortable family situations to deal with.

"One of the best nights I had in college came on the evening of our graduation," Chase recalled. "My best friend and I got a table at a great restaurant and invited our families and our favorite professors. We told stories, gave toasts, drank wine, and let the night slip away. The night was a beautiful culmination of college, combining friendship, the gained adulthood, and the academic growth into one special night."

Whatever your approach, keep in mind that the best restaurants will often take nonrefundable deposits to guarantee seating to avoid the problem of last-minute cancellations during their busiest time of year. Pay up—it's standard operating procedure in many places.

TICKETS

Many schools will allocate a certain number of graduation tickets per student and distribute these tickets during the winter term of your senior year. Although doing so will seem like a hassle to you, make a big deal out of them. Send them to the people you are inviting to your graduation with a little note. Grandparents in particular will save things like this and show them to all their friends.

If your family is enormous and you need additional tickets, this is rarely a problem. First, talk to your friends and roommates and see if they have extras; these tickets are almost always transferable. If you can't find any extras, pay a visit to your registrar's office and ask for more. Tickets are usually allocated equally to all students in the graduating class. Because many students come from abroad or have smaller families, however, the folks at the registrar's office *know* that they have over-estimated attendance and will almost always provide you with additional tickets.

SELL YOUR THINGS TO UNDERGRADS

Unless you and your roommates have grown particularly attached to your rugs, couches, and other furniture, sell as much of your stuff as you can to undergraduate students during the waning days of spring semester when people start liquidating their rooms and suites. The last thing you want is to get stuck with a huge couch that you have to dispose of before you leave campus. Although you may have sentimental feelings toward some of these items, those feelings will wane quickly once you have to try to pack everything up and move to wherever you're going after graduation.

WHEN GRADUATION DAY ARRIVES

Graduation weekend puts a lot of pressure on families—particularly divided families in which one or both parents have remarried. It is one of the few occasions (baptisms, marriages, and funerals being the others) where people who may not like to be around each other are forced into close quarters.

If your family falls into this category, try to be proactive in your planning to avoid conflicts that will mar your enjoyment of the weekend. If a meal all together is out of the question, try to allocate your time equally between parents by doing a dinner with each. If your parents have paid for some or all of your college tuition or expenses, remember to thank them for it with a little token of appreciation—be that a good bottle of scotch or an official college sweatshirt for your dad, or a college blanket for your mom.

Regardless of how often your family has been to campus, they are going to want to "experience" college life with you there on graduation weekend. Knowing this, your college will schedule a number of social events on campus to accommodate the families of graduating seniors. Get the schedule of these events ahead of time and snap up tickets to anything where attendance will be limited. Grab tickets to a singing group, to the president's or dean's reception, and to whatever else is going on that weekend. Doing this will give you things to do with everyone—and will make your family feel that you put some effort into the weekend too.

Remember that graduation weekend is primarily for your family. Even though you are the one who's graduating, and the weekend may represent the last opportunity for you to hang out with your friends, roommates, or teammates, it is not cool to leave your family on their own on graduation weekend so that you can spend one more evening partying. Schedule those sessions for late at night, after your parents and grandparents have retired to the hotel for the evening.

PACKING UP AND MOVING OUT

Once the speeches have been given, the diplomas have been given out, and the caps have been tossed, the reality will begin to set in.

It's time for you to go.

And there is definitely a good way and a bad way to handle your departure from campus.

If your move involves a drive, consider whether you'll need to rent a truck, trailer, or other vehicle to get your belongings home. Doing so can be a much easier, more relaxing and sane alternative than trying to cram all your things into various cars while your family is around. If you *are* going to rent a vehicle, though, remember to reserve one well in advance of graduation, as they too will sell out quickly.

Moving out a day or two after graduation will make the process markedly easier on a number of fronts. Stairs or elevators will be readily available, curbsides will be far less congested, and campus police will be far more relaxed about your taking your time loading a vehicle.

If your move involves air travel, you'll need to box everything up and send it via UPS or some other interstate carrier. If you find yourself in this situation, it is especially important that you sell everything you can before you graduate. Remember that it costs a lot of money to send things via interstate transport. Think about whether you really want to haul your microeconomics textbook with you—or whether you'd rather take the $20 buyback you can get for it from the campus bookstore.

If you are in no hurry, and if your college will allow you to hang around for a day or two after graduation, opt to do so. Although it can be depressing to be one of the last people in your class to leave campus, it can also be comforting to be able to say good-bye to your family and then take some time adjusting to the coming change by taking a walk around campus after the crowds have gone, or having a beer with a friend or roommate who has chosen to linger. Doing this will also allow you to take your time packing your things, so that you can throw away the accumulation of debris you have collected during your four years and make decisions about which mementos you want to take with you—rather than having to throw everything into boxes in a rush to finish packing before graduation.

Hanging around for a day or two can provide you with some closure during what may well be a very emotional time.

Our Parting Thoughts

*There will come a time when you
believe that everything is finished . . .
and that will be the beginning.*

Louis L'Amour

T he world is an astoundingly diverse and exciting place," Dan says. "And college is your first opportunity at truly independent exploration. It is the ideal crucible in which to test your interests and abilities, and to try new things you haven't even imagined. Yes, you need to be pragmatic enough to make it all fit into some sort of degree and course of study, but within those confines lies a wide world to explore. Fill your sails with passion and curiosity and see where they will take you. And the freedom and inquisitiveness that you have felt in college need not end at graduation."

"My growth as an explorer, as a friend, as a student, and in romance expanded tremendously while I was in college," Tiffany said. "Some people see college as a means of just having a good time, but it really is so much more than that. I wanted to discover myself, and challenge myself, and take myself to new heights. I searched for answers regarding relationships, academics, and personal interests. What do I want from someone who loves me? How will globalization further affect how we live our lives? Where do I see myself in ten years? Although I did not find all the answers to these questions, in those four years, I came just a little bit closer to knowing exactly who I am and what I want out of life."

"As someone who currently has a rewarding career in experimental music, who fifteen years ago, started as a chemistry major, it might be easy to wonder whether my four years at Yale were a total waste," Tom noted. "However, that thought could not be further from the truth—for college is not fully about the courses you take, the major you choose, or the grades you get. Yes, college *is* those things, but it is really so much more. In terms of education, Yale gave me the ability to think *critically*—a far more important skill than the ability to think *correctly*. But it also gave me all of the people I now call friends, who, at the time, challenged my thinking. The experience contributed to my growth as a person, and provided me with a good foundation to address, confront, and resolve the personal and professional complexities of life."

"Don't get overwhelmed with studying to the exclusion of everything else," Lyndsee noted. "Although undergraduate education is important, undergraduate personal development is, I think, equally if not more important. Growing as a student, a person, and a friend are critical experiences in college. Make sure the experience doesn't pass you by before you can make some lasting memories with your friends doing things other than academics."

"It was a truly spectacular time," Erik observed. "It was a slice of all that is good in life. I played college athletics—winning championships and losing heartbreakers in overtime. I partied with teammates and celebrated great times with an inordinate number of friends. I got paid to play blackjack with other people's money as part of the now-fabled M.I.T. blackjack team. I shared special, intimate moments with loved ones, and I truly learned something new every single moment of every day I was there. That it all happened at one of the most prestigious private universities in the country is both humbling and very gratifying, and something that I know I will benefit from for the rest of my life."

"College offers people an incredibly wide array of academic and social possibilities," Jim noted. "The experience will help you prepare for a career, better define who you are, and give you the opportunity to live life with a great deal of independence. It often involves periods of intense ups and downs, clarity and confusion. People that approach college thoughtfully, explore their options fully, evaluate friendships and experiences deeply, and take care of their health and well-being will exit their four years with fond memories and skills to tackle their life ahead.

"It took a while for me to find my niche in college, both academically and socially. I had fun throughout college and was always surrounded by people I enjoyed, but I didn't find real meaning in what I was doing initially. I left college with a deep appreciation for the outdoors, a desire to teach, and many different experiences to draw on. And I came to understand that I could change direction when I made a mistake and still land on my feet."

"Because I am happy where I am now and so many important things came my way as a direct result of all the decisions (sometimes crazy, sometimes uninformed) I made along the way, I am tempted to say that I would not change a thing about my college experience," Amanda said. "However, I am not sure that I got all that I could have out of my undergraduate education, so as a mentor, I would advise doing a few things differently than I did. First, be informed about what's out there and be proactive, rather than letting yourself be carried by the tide. Take a summer (or several) or even a whole year before college to do some kind of exploration of careers—and not just the ones that everybody's heard of.

"Did you know that there are people who actually make wine or make beer for a living? Did you know that there are engineers who inspect roller coasters for a living? Did you know that there are statisticians who determine the cost of living in other countries (which usually requires *traveling* to those other countries) for a living? I use these examples because they are some of the careers that I had no idea even existed when I was in high school.

"Think about what you might want to do for your first career, but always bear in mind that it probably won't be your only career. Keep your options open," Amanda concluded.

"I went to boarding school (Taft) for high school, where every minute of my day was programmed with activity, as I'm sure is the case for most of you," Carolyn noted. "Then, when I got to college, I found myself with a *ton* of free time and initially, I didn't know what to do with it. I felt lost and overwhelmed by the breadth of opportunity. I was hesitant to get involved in too many activities for fear that I would later get swamped by academic demands. I eventually figured out the proper balance and was able to more confidently throw myself into the college experience during my last three years. If I had it to do over again, though, I would have gotten involved in more volunteer work, would have been more politically active, and would have taken advantage of more of the cultural events and community activities that college had to offer. Try a ton of new things, find your passion, and take advantage of every minute."

"Go hard," Chase agreed. "Never again will you be surrounded by such a remarkable mix of people and opportunities. The minute you leave college, you'll forget all the sleep you missed, the struggles to finish papers, the television, and the visions of PS2. What you will remember are the professors, the friends, the classes, the parties, the games, and the conversations."

"College helped me to grow up a lot," Dave said. "I was a completely different person when I left. The experience humbled me. It made me think on a whole new plane and it empowered me as a human being. I made some great friends and really gained an appreciation for learning that I did not have previously. Living on my own forced me to make big decisions and to take ownership and responsibility for my actions. College is a four year rollercoaster that comes with its fair share of ups and downs, corkscrews and climbing anticipation, joy and fear. When it's over, you can't believe how fast it went by. I envy those who are lucky enough to be at the beginning of their journey through the experience. To you, I say, 'buckle up, hold on, and get ready for the ride of your life!'"

"For me, college was an intense and meaningful time in terms of getting to know, test, and trust myself," Zoe said. "After four years surrounded by intellectual challenge, great people, and incredible diversity, I feel that I was able to embark on the adult phase of my life with confidence and enthusiasm. By graduation, I had come to feel so at home at Wellesley—so happy and so alive—that I was genuinely afraid that life later on could not possibly compare. A good friend, twenty years my senior, reassured me that life would change, yes, but my definition of happiness would too, and that joys I couldn't imagine at twenty-one were yet to be discovered.

"Fortunately, he was right.

"Allow yourself to grow and change. Challenge yourself, but be kind to yourself also. Know that what you do is important, but it is nothing compared to *who you are.* Breathe in and breathe out. Temper periods of intense drive and activity with periods of reflection and rest. Above all, make peace with the fact that no one, including those of us in this book, can actually tell you what your own journey will be like, or how you are meant to navigate it.

"Each of us gets to learn that as we go.

"Be brave."

ROBERT H. MILLER graduated with distinction from Yale University with a B.A. in psychology. After taking two years off to travel, serve as the national coordinator of a Yale study on the prosocial effects of Barney the Dinosaur on three- to four-year-olds, write a screenplay, and decide on the future direction of his life, he matriculated at the University of Pennsylvania Law School, where he was senior editor of the *Law Review*, an H. Clayton Louderback Instructor in Legal Writing, and Chair of the law school's Executive Committee on Student Ethics and Academic Standing. After law school, he served as law clerk to the Honorable Chief Judge Paul Barbadoro of the United States District Court for the District of New Hampshire and then joined the New England law firm of Sheehan, Phinney, Bass & Green, where he is now a trial lawyer and an equity partner in the firm's Manchester, New Hampshire, office.

A rabid baseball fan and an avid skier and outdoorsman, Miller lives in Hopkinton, New Hampshire, with his wife, Carolyn, and their two children. This is his fourth book.

INDEX

391–393; and Graduate Record
Exam (GRE), 397–398; looking
ahead to, 385–398; and peers,
387–388; requesting application
materials for, 391; researching, 390;
and will of parents, 386–387
Graduation: and applying to graduate
school, 447–450; planning guide,
461–465; taking time off after,
453–460; working after, 441–445
Grants: Barnett-Miller research,
63–64; federal, 58; private, 63–64;
state, 61–62
GRE (Graduate Record Exam), 397
Grou, J. N., 277
Guidance counselors, 14–15

H

Hartman, H., 29
Hatch, O., 461
Hazing, 247
Health, 261–268
Hobby credit, 429
Hollywood Rule, 252–253
Homesickness, 265–266, 302
Honor code, 217–218
Housing, off-campus: and choosing
new roommates, 317–319; manag-
ing, 315–317
Hugo, V., 427
Humanities, 156
Huxtable, A. L., 307

I

Immunizations, 381
Independent study, 428–429
Information session, 33
Inoculation record, 103

Insider's Guide to Colleges (Yale Daily
News), 11
Institute of International Education,
384
Interests, defining, 5–9
Internet, 45, 220–221; gaming, 250
iPod, 248
Irving, W., 129
Irwin, D. (mentor), xxxiii–xxxiv
iTunes, 249

J

Jobs, S., 453, 454
Johnson, C. (mentor), xxxiv–xxxv
Joint costs, 134–135
Junior year: abroad, 379–384; academic and career goals for, 368–
371, 408–409; extracurricular
goals, 371–372; financial goals,
374–375; and "junior thesis,"
399–405; physical goals, 373–374;
social goals, 371; spiritual goals,
375–376
Junior Year Abroad Committee, 380,
381

K

Kaplan, Inc. SAT Premier Program, 23
Ketamine, 151
Koegler, C. (mentor), xxvii–xxviii

L

Laca, K., 395
L'Amour, L., 467
Language proficiency, 380
Language requirement, 110–111
Law School, 393–395; application
calendar, 394–395